FINAL CUT PRO

POWER TIPS

FASTER - BETTER - EASIER

LARRY **JORDAN**

Final Cut Pro Power Tips: Faster • Better • Easier
Larry Jordan

Peachpit Press
www.peachpit.com
Copyright © 2023 by Larry Jordan. All Rights Reserved.

Peachpit Press is an imprint of Pearson Education, Inc.
To report errors, please send a note to errata@peachpit.com

Executive Editor: Laura Norman
Development Editor: Robyn G. Thomas
Senior Production Editor: Tracey Croom
Technical Editor: Adam Wilt
Copy Editor: Kim Wimpsett
Compositor: Kim Scott, Bumpy Design
Proofreader: Scout Festa
Indexer: James Minkin
Cover Design: Chuti Prasertsith
Interior Design: Kim Scott, Bumpy Design
Illustrator: Vived Graphics
Cover Photo: BortN66/Shutterstock

ISBN-13: 978-0-13-792879-8
ISBN-10:   0-13-792879-3

To the readers of my Edit Smarter *newsletter,*
whose questions, comments, and tips expanded
my editing education for more than 20 years.

And to Jane.

About the Author

Larry Jordan is a producer, director, editor, author, teacher, and Apple Certified Trainer in Digital Media with more than 50 years of media experience with national broadcast and corporate credits. Based in Boston, he's a member of the Directors Guild of America and the Producers Guild of America. He's been recognized with awards as an "Industry Innovator" and "Top Corporate [Media] Producers in America." An adjunct professor at USC from 2011–2020, he's written 11 books on media and software, written thousands of technical tutorials, and created hundreds of hours of video training. Visit his website at LarryJordan.com.

Other Books by Larry Jordan

- *Dance for Television: A Production Handbook*
- *Adobe CS Production Premium for Final Cut Studio Editors*
- *Adobe Premiere Pro Power Tips*
- *Final Cut Pro HD: A Hands-on Guide*
- *Final Cut Pro 5: A Hands-on Guide*
- *Final Cut Pro Power Skills*
- *Final Cut Pro X: Making the Transition*
- *Editing Truths for Better Living*
- *Edit Well: Final Cut Studio Techniques from the Pros*
- *Techniques of Visual Persuasion*

Special Thanks

Thanks go to Laura Norman, executive editor at Pearson, for her support and encouragement of this book. Robyn G. Thomas for her excellent editorial advice, Kim Scott for her delightful book design, and Adam Wilt, a gifted technical editor who I was honored to have critique my book. (Yes, I made all your changes.)

Almost all the images in this book were ones I've taken on my walks about the world. However, I want to thank Emily Hewitt (EmilyHewittPhotography.com) for her photographs of jewelry designed by Coleman Hewitt. And Norman Hollyn who, 15 years ago, suggested we create a 32-part webisode series teaching students how to make films. From that 2ReelGuys.com was born.

I also want to thank my intrepid team of editorial beta readers, each a full-time Final Cut Pro editor, who provided extremely helpful feedback while reading early drafts of this book: Cindy Burgess, Tom Cherry, Scott Favorite, Scott Newell, Michael Powles, and Jerry Thompson. I'm grateful for their comments and suggestions. You'll find them quoted throughout this book.

Pearson's Commitment to Diversity, Equity, and Inclusion

Pearson is dedicated to creating bias-free content that reflects the diversity of all learners. We embrace the many dimensions of diversity, including but not limited to race, ethnicity, gender, socioeconomic status, ability, age, sexual orientation, and religious or political beliefs.

Education is a powerful force for equity and change in our world. It has the potential to deliver opportunities that improve lives and enable economic mobility. As we work with authors to create content for every product and service, we acknowledge our responsibility to demonstrate inclusivity and incorporate diverse scholarship so that everyone can achieve their potential through learning. As the world's leading learning company, we have a duty to help drive change and live up to our purpose to help more people create a better life for themselves and to create a better world.

Our ambition is to purposefully contribute to a world where:

- Everyone has an equitable and lifelong opportunity to succeed through learning.
- Our educational products and services are inclusive and represent the rich diversity of learners.
- Our educational content accurately reflects the histories and experiences of the learners we serve.
- Our educational content prompts deeper discussions with learners and motivates them to expand their own learning (and worldview).

While we work hard to present unbiased content, we want to hear from you about any concerns or needs with this Pearson product so that we can investigate and address them.

- Please contact us with concerns about any potential bias at https://www.pearson.com/report-bias.html.

Free Additional Chapter—Online

Your purchase of the printed version of this book includes a bonus Chapter 10 that is accessed from your Account page on www.peachpit.com. I couldn't fit everything into the print version. (The digital version includes all ten chapters. No additional download is needed.) This free digital chapter includes tips and advice on:

- The Business of Media
- Clip Speed Changes
- Advanced Export
- 360° Video
- Useful Resources
- Shortcuts

I strongly recommend you download your free copy of this chapter!

You must register your purchase on peachpit.com in order to access the bonus content:

1. Go to **www.peachpit.com/FCPPowerTips**
2. Sign in or create a new account.
3. Click Submit.
4. Answer the question as proof of purchase.
5. Download the Bonus Content from the Registered Products tab on your Account page.

If you purchased a digital product directly from peachpit.com, your product will already be registered, and the bonus Chapter 10 will be included in your digital version.

Credits

Chapter Opener-01: Gajus/Shutterstock

FIG01-01, FIG01-07, FIG01-06, FIG01-11, FIG01-21–FIG01-25, FIG02-01–FIG02-53, FIG02-55–FIG02-72, FIG03-01–FIG03-77, FIG04-01–FIG04-03, FIG04-05–FIG04-41, FIG05-01–FIG05-13–FIG05-30, FIG05-32–FIG05-38, FIG06-01–FIG06-61, FIG07-01–FIG07-61, FIG08-01–FIG08-51, FIG08-53–FIG08-62, FIG08-64, FIG08-65, FIG08-67–FIG08-80, FIG08-83, FIG08-84, FIG08-86–FIG08-102, FIG08-104, FIG08-106–FIG08-111, FIG09-01–FIG09-28, FIG10-01–FIG10-32: Apple, Inc

FIG01-12: Jaromir Chalabala/Shutterstock

Chapter 01, Chapter wrap–Chapter 10, Chapter wrap: tanatat/Shutterstock

Chapter Opener-02: agsandrew/Shutterstock

Chapter Opener-03: Sergey Nivens/Shutterstock

Chapter Opener-04: ESB Professional/Shutterstock

Chapter Opener-05: SimonHS/Shutterstock

FIG05-31: Pradeep Rawat/Pearson India Education Services

Chapter Opener-06: agsandrew/Shutterstock

Chapter Opener-07: Busakorn Pongparnit/123RF

Chapter Opener-08: cobalt88/Shutterstock

Chapter Opener-09: Gunnar Pippel/Shutterstock

Chapter 9, Summary: 495346/Shutterstock

Chapter Opener-10: blackspring/123RF

CONTENTS

INTRODUCTION

Apple Final Cut Pro is a tool we use to tell stories with moving pictures. But owning a tool is not the same as knowing how to *use* that tool. Video editing is the last step in the long process of visual story creation—the last step before sharing that story with an audience. Deadlines are short, budgets are tight, and everyone is stressed. Anything that saves time, simplifies a process, or improves results is a good thing.

That's what this book is about. These 500+ tips, techniques, shortcuts, and hidden gems that will turn you into an editing powerhouse. This book can't teach you how to edit, but it *can* teach you how to edit more effectively.

I've worked in media as an on-camera host, producer, director, and editor for more than 50 years. Over that time, I've learned that one of the worst mistakes an editor can make is to do something "because you can." Technical ability is never a good reason to do anything. Instead, focus your editing on the story you are telling. Then, you'll find yourself doing something "because you should." Because it benefits the story. Because it enables understanding. Because it improves communication.

I have used, studied, taught, and written about Final Cut Pro since 2003; almost 20 years. This book is a collection of the best of what I've learned. During that time, much of our industry has changed, yet much also remains the same. Like all creative arts, editing has styles. Not just styles in genre but styles in clip duration, transitions, titles, effects, color grading...the list is lengthy. Some styles are worth keeping, others not so much.

This book isn't a textbook. I don't cover all the features in Final Cut. This is a book for someone with a specific question who needs an accurate answer right now. I take you deep into the application to tap the hidden power of the program.

The printed version of this book is organized into nine chapters, plus an online chapter, each grouped by subject. (The digital version contains all ten chapters.) Within each chapter, related tips are gathered into sections so you can quickly skim to find the information you need. You can dip into a single tip for a fast answer or read an entire chapter to further your understanding.

One other thing I need to mention. In today's highly monetized, advertising-driven world, no one paid me to mention any products in this book. All my recommendations are tools that I purchased and use every day in my own projects.

I used Apple Final Cut Pro 10.6.3 for all screen shots and tips. If I forgot your favorite or there's a mistake, send me an email and let me know. We will fix it in the next edition. In the meantime, edit well.

Larry Jordan
Andover, MA
July 2022
Larry@LarryJordan.com

CHAPTER 1

VIDEO FUNDAMENTALS

INTRODUCTION

When video editing software is considered a "black box" where clips go in and programs come out, problems arise. Too often, bad decisions made at the beginning of a project cause problems down the line.

Editing video is the hardest thing we can do on a computer. It requires high-performance hardware and high-quality software. But more important, it requires an understanding of video and how computers work along with an ability to tell stories with pictures.

I can't stress enough that the time you spend planning before you start editing saves hours of anguish as the deadline looms. The concepts in this chapter explain "what" and "why." The rest of this book explains "how." These form the foundation upon which Apple Final Cut Pro is built.

- Final Cut Pro Basics
- Video Basics
- Computer Basics
- Storage Basics
- Command Set Basics
- Shortcuts

① The One Overriding Rule of Media

If you remember only one thing, remember this.

*Murphy was
an optimist!*

Murphy's Law rules!

Whatever can go wrong will go wrong and at the worst possible moment.
Plan for it.

FINAL CUT PRO BASICS

These key terms and concepts will get you started using Final Cut Pro.

② Is It Final Cut Pro or Final Cut Pro X?

Apple changed the name.

Final Cut Pro (FCP) was first released in the spring of 1999. Over the years as
major updates were released, we reflected those changes by adding the version
number to the name. This created FCP 1.2, 3, 4, 4.5, 5, 6, and, ultimately, FCP 7.

Final Cut Pro X was released on June 21, 2011, and, in keeping with past practice, we added the version number, in this case the "X," as in FCP X.

Then, in November, 2020, along with the release of Big Sur, Apple dropped
the X and changed the look of the logo (see **FIGURE 1.1**). Big Sur was macOS
version 11, so using the X for Final Cut no longer made sense. This book uses
the current name, Final Cut Pro, or two shortcuts, Final Cut and FCP.

FIGURE 1.1 The latest
Apple Final Cut Pro logo.

③ Basic Final Cut Pro Concepts

These terms define the basic structure of Final Cut.

If you are new to Final Cut Pro, you need to understand these terms to get
started:

- **Library**. This is the Final Cut data file that appears in the Finder. However, it isn't "just a file"; it's a *container* that holds all the elements—or
  links to those elements—used by that library. Libraries can be renamed
  from within Final Cut. However, renaming a library in Final Cut also
  renames it in the Finder.

  There is no limit to the number of libraries you can create and store
  in the Finder. Also, while there is no set limit to the number of libraries you can open in Final Cut, the amount of RAM in your system may
  limit the number of open libraries or the number of clips a library can

contain. (Before you panic, even on 16 GB systems, libraries can contain thousands of clips.)

- **Event**. This is a folder stored inside a Final Cut library. There is no limit to the number of events you can create in Final Cut. However, you cannot store an event in another event. An event appears only in the library, not in the Finder.

- **Project**. This is a timeline into which you edit media. A library can hold multiple projects, and multiple projects can be open at once. However, you can view only one project at a time in the timeline. A project has a maximum duration of 24 hours. Projects can contain thousands of clips, depending upon the amount of RAM in your computer.

- **Media**. These are the clips—audio, video, stills, titles, generators, render files, et al.—that are edited into a project.

- **Managed.** Managed media is stored in the library.

- **External**. External media is stored outside the library.

- **Generated**. Generated media is created by Final Cut from source files. This includes optimized, proxy, and render files. By default, generated media is stored in the library.

④ Why Is It Called a "Library," Not a Project?

Um, this dates back to Ancient Greece.

A project is a thing; a library is a collection of things.

Since the days of ancient Greece, we collect stuff in libraries. That's what a Final Cut library is: a collection of all the different elements used to tell a story using moving pictures. The story itself is created in the project. But those same elements can, and often are, used to tell different stories. These elements are stored in the library.

A project is a thing; a library is a collection of things.

VIDEO BASICS

These key terms and technology explain how digital video works.

⑤ Final Cut Uses Three Types of Video

They are camera source, optimized, and proxy.

Regardless of whether media is stored inside or outside a library, Final Cut supports three types of video media: Camera source, Optimized, and Proxy.

- **Camera source** files (also called *camera native* or *camera masters*). This is the video format shot by the camera. For many cameras, including iPhone and other mobile devices, this video is highly compressed so that it can easily fit on whatever storage the camera uses. But this compression can cause problems when it comes time to edit. (In most cases, audio files are captured in an uncompressed format, because audio files are so much smaller than video.)

Optimized files are camera source media converted into the ProRes 422 codec.

- **Optimized** files. These are camera source files that are converted, generally by Final Cut, into a codec called Apple ProRes 422. Unlike camera source files, ProRes 422 files are specifically designed for high image quality and efficient editing. However, unlike many camera files, ProRes 422 files are quite large. (Not all camera source files need optimization.)

- **Proxy** files. These are smaller, both in frame size and in file size, than either camera source or optimized files. Proxies are highly useful when rough-cutting large-frame-size video, editing on older systems, or doing a multicam edit. The only disadvantage to proxy files is a lower image quality compared to either camera source or optimized media. Proxy files are used for editing; they are rarely, if ever, exported as final output.

6 Why Do We Need to Compress Video?

Because uncompressed files are enormous!

In an ideal world, we would edit and view uncompressed video because the image quality of uncompressed video would be stunning.

The problem is that uncompressed video files are huge. Really huge. Massively *huge*!

A recent blog post[1] from Amazon Web Services (AWS) highlighted typical bandwidth requirements for uncompressed video, illustrated in **TABLE 1.1**.

TABLE 1.1 Bandwidth and storage data for uncompressed video (table statistics provided by Amazon Web Services).		
FRAME SIZE	**DATA RATE**	**TO STORE 1 HOUR**
1280 x 720 pixels	~190 MB/second	~684 GB
1920 x 1080 pixels	~375 MB/second	~1.35 TB
3840 x 2160 pixels	~1,500 MB/second	~5.4 TB

1. https://aws.amazon.com/blogs/media/part-1-back-to-basics-gops-explained/

Clearly, with professional gear, we can move 1.5 GB/second of media files around our computer. But holy smokes, given the amount of media shot on even small productions, that means we're talking dozens of terabytes of data per show. That's a lot! I'd also hate to wait for that much media to download when watching a movie on Netflix.

We compress video simply because uncompressed video files are too big to manage.

This is why we compress media—to make media files manageable during capture, editing, and, ultimately, distribution. And that brings us to codecs.

7 Formats, Codecs...What Are These Things?

These determine everything!

As you'll see in other tips, the word *format* is used in a lot of difference contexts. It's become a catchall for when we can't think of another word to use. A file's "format" determines how that file is stored: its wrapper (see Tip 20, *Media Is Stored in Containers*), the structure of its compressed or uncompressed video and/or audio streams, the video's resolution and aspect ratio, and whether it's interlaced or progressive. If the essence streams (that is, the video or audio) are compressed, the codec (short for "coder/decoder") used to compress the file is part of its format, too. The file format is a key aspect of every digital file. Why? Because the format determines quality, file size, editing efficiency...critical aspects of any digital file.

Some formats and codecs are optimized for recording signals in a camera, others are optimized for media editing, and still others are optimized for distribution. As you probably suspect, there's no one perfect codec or format.

Popular video formats and codecs include:

- MOV (format)
- AVI (format)
- MP4 (format)
- ProRes (codec)
- H.264 (codec)
- HEVC, also called H.265 (codec)
- AVC-Intra (codec)
- XAVC (codec)
- HDCAM (codec)
- DNx (codec)

Popular audio formats and codecs include:

- WAV (format)
- AIFF (format)
- FLAC (codec)
- ALAC (codec)
- MP3 (codec)
- AAC (codec)

Popular still image formats and codecs include:

- TIFF (format)
- PNG (format)
- PDF (codec)
- PSD (format)
- JPG/JPEG (codec)

The results from using a codec can be described using three basic parameters: quality, file size, and editing efficiency. However, as **FIGURE 1.2** illustrates, when you are selecting a codec, you can optimize for only two.

FIGURE 1.2 The three key options when choosing a codec. However, you can optimize for only two.

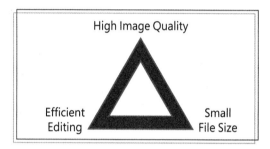

High Image Quality

Efficient Editing

Small File Size

For example, the most efficient editing codecs also create the largest file sizes. These include ProRes, DNx, and GoPro Cineform. Final Cut (and, in fact, all Apple silicon Macs) are optimized for ProRes, which is why I emphasize it in this book.

Codecs determine the digital format into which media is compressed and stored.

In many cases, the codec that a camera records is selected for you by the camera manufacturer. If you are given the option, select the version of that codec that has the highest data (bit) rate. In general, the higher the data rate, the better the image quality.

Here are my recommendations:

- If the camera provides the option, select the codec with the highest data rate.
- If the camera provides the option, shoot progressive video rather than interlaced, unless you are instructed otherwise.
- If you are shooting a compressed format—H.264, AVCHD, HEVC— convert it to ProRes 422 for editing.
- For video created on the computer, for example, Apple Motion or Adobe After Effects, export it using ProRes 4444 with an alpha channel for editing.

- For video you want to distribute, convert the finished, exported project into H.264 in an MPEG-4 wrapper, unless you are told to provide a different codec.
- For audio you plan to edit, use WAV or AIFF formats.
- For audio you plan to distribute, convert the finished, exported project into AAC format.

This is not to say other codecs are "bad," simply that these are good choices to get you started.

8 What's the Best Format for Still Images?

The choice of format makes a big difference in image quality.

Tom Cherry is a professional editor who reviewed an early draft of this book. He commented: "I find it difficult to effectively communicate to clients that their postage-stamp-size letterhead logos are going to look awful when I resize them for video. They will be pixelated and blurry. Sadly, that may be the best version they can find. Instead, I routinely ask them for the largest file size PNG they can find...only to receive a microscopic JPG."

Still image quality is determined by two factors: the codec and the size of the image in pixels. **TABLE 1.2** details the most popular still image formats.

When in doubt, ask for a full-color PNG with the largest pixel dimensions available.

TABLE 1.2 Comparing still image formats.		
FORMAT	**RESULTS**	**NOTES**
TIFF	Usually uncompressed, high quality	Widely supported. Generally used without layers or alpha channels.
PNG	Lossless compression, high quality	Widely supported. Can include an alpha channel.
PSD	A container format with quality that varies based on media stored in the file	Widely supported. Can include layers and alpha channels.
JPEG/JPG	Highly compressed, often of lower quality	Widely supported. Does not include layers or alpha channel.

These guidelines do have exceptions. For example, PNGs can be saved in a limited color format, and JPEGs can actually look good. However, in general, high-quality, full-color PNGs are an excellent still image format for video. Use PSDs if you need layers.

9 Not All Codecs Need Optimization

Many codecs, in addition to ProRes, are already optimized.

Some codecs, like ProRes, are already optimized. *Optimized* is a term that Apple uses to describe codecs that compress entire frames of video (I-frame compression), instead of the changes between frames (Long-GOP compression). See Tip 10, *I-frame vs. Long-GOP: Two Ways to Compress Media*.

Codecs that are already optimized include:

- DV and DVCam
- ProRes
- DNx
- GoPro Cineform
- AVC-Intra
- HDCAM HD
- XDCAM EX
- Apple Animation (though this is only 8-bit)

GOING FURTHER
When in doubt, optimize your media. It pays benefits in editing efficiency and render speed over the long term. If the media is already in an optimized form, FCP won't optimize it again.

However, many popular camera codecs are compressed and benefit from optimization. These include:

- MPEG-2
- H.264
- HEVC (H.265)
- H.266
- AVCHD
- AVCCAM
- AVC-Ultra
- XAVC

Many Intel Macs, and all Apple silicon Macs, support hardware encoding and decoding of H.264 media. In practice, this means you may be able to smoothly edit H.264 media on those systems without dropping frames.

10 I-frame vs. Long-GOP: Two Ways to Compress Media

One emphasizes ease of editing, the other emphasizes small file size.

Uncompressed media files are beyond huge, so all digital media is compressed, even raw files.

I-frame compressed files are easier to edit. Long-GOP-compressed files are smaller.

Each codec determines whether it will use I-frame (Intra-frame) or Long-GOP (Group of Pictures) compression. This choice is hardwired into each codec and can't be changed. Understanding the differences can help you make wiser choices about codecs, especially those used for editing.

Go back into the dim reaches of history, back to a time before cell phones, and you may remember a visual recording technology called *film*. As **FIGURE 1.3** illustrates, film recorded each image complete and intact. In fact, if you held up a piece of film to the light, you could see a series of images extending along the film. Videotape also recorded entire images, though it did so magnetically on tape, rather than photographically.

FIGURE 1.3 Film and videotape record video as a stream of self-contained images (I) called *frames*.

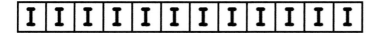

I-frame compression emulates this. Every compressed image is complete and stored in the file. The problem is that, when converted to digital, these individual frames generated huge files. Worse, back in the early days of digital media, storage was slow, small, and expensive. A different option was needed: Long-GOP compression.

The easiest way to picture Long-GOP files is to think of a chess match printed in a book or newspaper. As you read the report of the game, the article doesn't show an image of the chess board after each move. Instead, it details only the *changes* from one move to the next, illustrated in **FIGURE 1.4**. We start with an image of the entire board; then we simply document the specific piece that moves on each play after that. As long as you start at the beginning of the game and track each change sequentially, you can follow the match perfectly.

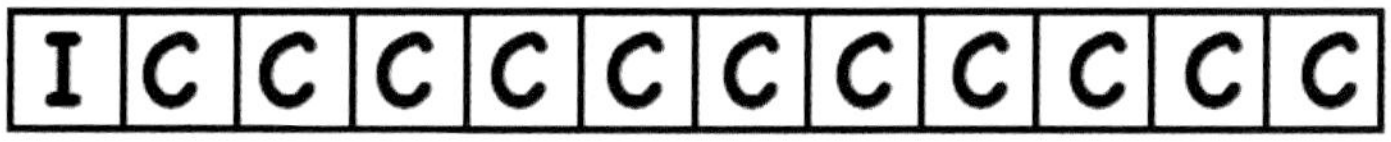

FIGURE 1.4 Long-GOP compression starts by recording the entire image (I), then recording only the changes (C = change) that occur from one frame to the next.

Long-GOP compression builds on this concept. A GOP often consists of 15 video frames, though group lengths can vary by codec down to a single frame. The first image in the group is complete, then the next 14 frames include only the differences between the current frame and frames around it, as **FIGURE 1.5** illustrates.

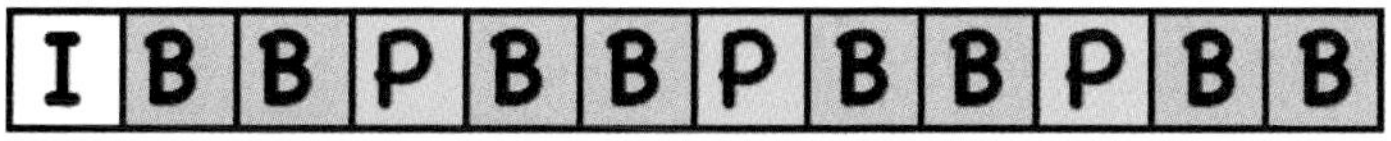

FIGURE 1.5 Every Long-GOP sequence starts with a complete image (I), then stores only the changes between frames (B & P) until the end of the group. The next group then starts with a complete frame and repeats the process.

Because Long-GOP files record only changes, the differences in file size between I-frame and Long-GOP can be dramatic! For example, a 5-second tripod shot of a still life at 30 fps creates 150 images in ProRes, while H.264 would compress that to a single frame with an instruction to repeat it 149 more times.

This is why ProRes files, on average, are six to ten times larger than H.264 files, but they are much easier to edit.

Video codecs, such as H.264, that use Long-GOP "change documents" for compression present a significant challenge for playback. Like the chess match, if you start the video at the beginning, Long-GOP compression is very efficient. The files are small, the changes are applied incrementally and in order, and you can clearly see the moving image as it evolves over time.

However, again like our chess match, if you join a Long-GOP sequence in the middle, say by moving the playhead into the middle of a clip, you can't make any sense of the changes until, behind the scenes, the editing software goes back to the nearest I-frame and reconstructs the changes that occurred from the I-frame until the current position of the playhead. With I-frame video, no reconstruction is necessary, as each I-frame image is complete. Wherever the playhead stops, it can instantly display the complete image.

Long-GOP compression isn't bad, any more than I-frame compression is good. Choosing the right codec depends upon the task.

Matters get more complicated as we place Long-GOP-compressed video on higher layers; cut clips based on content, not I-frame locations; or stack Long-GOP-compressed multicam clips on top of each other. In these instances, the I-frames don't occur at the same time, which means the CPU is constantly going back to find the nearest I-frame, then reconstructing the group from that point for each clip!

Worse, when we edit the middle of a Long-GOP sequence, the entire Long-GOP structure must be rebuilt. A Long-GOP sequence *must* start with an I-frame, because starting with a change frame doesn't provide enough data to reconstruct the entire image.

This is the reason older computers stumble playing H-264 or HEVC video—they can't decode the Long-GOP compression fast enough to make editing feel smooth in real time. There's too much math without enough CPU horsepower.

Long-GOP compression isn't bad, any more than I-frame compression is good. As with most things in video, good or bad depends upon what you are trying to do. Without Long-GOP compression, we couldn't record video using a DSLR camera. Without Long-GOP compression, YouTube videos wouldn't exist. But I-frame video always displays better image quality, edits more smoothly, exports faster, and plays on slower devices.

⓫ Which to Pick: HEVC vs. H.264

Choose H.264, except when compressing HDR media.

In most cases, H.264 is the best choice. Why? Because most modern computers use hardware for H.264 playback and compression, which means your system handles H.264 media more easily. Only the very latest computers (including all Apple silicon systems) accelerate HEVC compression.

H.264 files run on more hardware, so if you are sending files to clients or executives for review, they are more likely to play H.264 than HEVC.

More important, since all social media sites recompress your media, there's no reason to create really small files, because when your project is recompressed, you need extra data for that second compression to discard; otherwise, image quality will suffer.

However, there are two strong reasons for compressing files into HEVC: large frame sizes and High Dynamic Range (HDR) media. (See Tip 26, *What Is HDR?*) H.264 supports frame sizes only up to 4K. HEVC can go larger. Also, 10-bit HEVC supports the full grayscale and color range of HDR media; most H.264 compressors don't. However, only the latest computers support hardware acceleration of 10-bit HEVC. If your system doesn't, expect HEVC compression to take a *long* time.

The short answer is to use H.264, except when compressing HDR media.

⑫ ProRes Was Invented by Apple for Video

Even people who don't like Apple like ProRes.

ProRes is a highly efficient, high-quality video codec invented by Apple and first released in 2007 with Final Cut Studio 2, specifically for video editing. In most situations, the audio accompanying a ProRes video uses an uncompressed format.

As Apple describes in its *Apple ProRes* white paper, "The ProRes family of video codecs has made it both possible and affordable to edit full-frame, 10-bit, 4:2:2 and 4:4:4:4 high-definition (HD), 2K, 4K, 5K, and larger video sources with multi-stream performance in Final Cut Pro.

"Apple ProRes codecs provide an unparalleled combination of multi-stream, real-time editing performance, impressive image quality, and reduced storage rates. ProRes codecs take full advantage of multicore processing and feature fast, reduced-resolution decoding modes. All ProRes codecs support any frame size (including SD, HD, 2K, 4K, 5K, and larger) at full resolution. The data rates vary based on codec type, image content, frame size, and frame rate.

"As a variable bit rate (VBR) codec technology, ProRes uses fewer bits on simple frames that would not benefit from encoding at a higher data rate. ProRes codecs are frame-independent (or "intra-frame") codecs, meaning that each frame is encoded and decoded independently of any other frame. This technique provides the greatest editing performance and flexibility.

"With Final Cut Pro 10.3 or later, you can also export ProRes files inside an MXF metadata wrapper instead of exporting .mov files. This makes the exported video file compatible with a wide range of playback systems that rely on the MXF standard for broadcast and archiving."[2] (See Tip 20, *Media Is Stored in Containers*.)

ProRes is a highly efficient, high-quality video codec invented by Apple specifically for video editing and distribution.

While detailed explanations of these technical terms are more than we need to cover for this book, here are the key takeaways:

- ProRes runs on both Mac and Windows computers.
- ProRes supports any frame size or frame rate.
- ProRes supports Standard Dynamic Range (SDR) and High Dynamic Range (HDR) media. (See Tip 26, *What Is HDR?*)
- Many cameras shoot ProRes directly.
- Other camera media can be easily converted into ProRes.
- ProRes supports a wide variety of compression levels for different editing tasks (mastering, editing, proxies, and so on).
- Final Cut Pro is optimized for ProRes media in a QuickTime wrapper.

13 Meet the ProRes Family

Each version is designed for different media tasks.

NOTE Most of the time, if you are shooting this level of high-end video, you'll be shooting Log files, which I cover in Tip 17: What Is Log Video?

Here are the current members of the ProRes family (with one exception, ProRes RAW, which I'll cover shortly). These descriptions come from the *Apple ProRes* white paper.[2]

- **Apple ProRes 4444 XQ**. The highest-quality version of ProRes for 4:4:4:4 image sources (including alpha channels), with a very high data rate to preserve the detail in high-dynamic-range imagery generated by today's highest-quality digital image sensors. Like standard Apple ProRes 4444, this codec supports up to 12 bits per image channel and up to 16 bits for the alpha channel.

NOTE ProRes 4444 is my favorite high-end format.

- **Apple ProRes 4444**. An extremely high-quality version of ProRes for 4:4:4:4 image sources (including alpha channels). This codec features full-resolution, mastering-quality 4:4:4:4 RGBA color and visual fidelity that is perceptually indistinguishable from the original material. Apple ProRes 4444 is a high-quality solution for storing and exchanging motion graphics and composites, with excellent multigeneration

---

2. *Apple ProRes White Paper*, January, 2020, Apple Inc. www.apple.com/final-cut-pro/docs/Apple_ProRes_White_Paper.pdf

performance. It has 12-bit depth with a mathematically lossless 16-bit alpha channel.

- **Apple ProRes 422 HQ**. A higher-data-rate version of Apple ProRes 422 that preserves visual quality at the same high level as Apple ProRes 4444, but for 4:2:2 image sources. With widespread adoption across the video post-production industry, Apple ProRes 422 HQ offers visually lossless preservation of the highest-quality professional HD video that a single-link HD-SDI signal can carry. This codec supports full-width, 4:2:2 video sources at 10-bit pixel depths, while remaining visually lossless through many generations of decoding and re-encoding.

- **Apple ProRes 422**. A high-quality compressed codec offering nearly all the benefits of Apple ProRes 422 HQ, but at 66 percent of the data rate for even better multistream, real-time editing performance.

  NOTE ProRes 422 is my favorite general-purpose codec.

- **Apple ProRes 422 LT**. A more highly compressed codec than Apple ProRes 422, with roughly 70 percent of the data rate and 30 percent smaller file sizes. This codec is perfect for environments where storage capacity and data rate are at a premium.

- **Apple ProRes 422 Proxy**. An even more highly compressed codec than Apple ProRes 422 LT, intended for use in offline workflows that require low data rates but full-resolution video.

  NOTE ProRes 422 Proxy, at 50% size, is my favorite codec for proxy editing.

14 Which Version of ProRes Should You Use?

The answer depends upon what you want to do.

ProRes is a very capable codec. I recommend its use wholeheartedly, especially for Final Cut Pro editors. But which version should you use? Here's the short answer:

- If you are creating source media using your computer (for example, Apple Motion, Adobe After Effects, Cinema 4D, and so on), export the finished file using Apple ProRes 4444. This creates the largest files, but it also contains the highest-quality color and supports alpha channels (transparency) in the media. It also most closely matches colors created on a computer.

  When in doubt, use ProRes 422 for media shot with a camera.

- If you are working with media shot with a camera, use ProRes 422. This most closely matches the color format shot by most cameras.

- If you are creating proxies, use ProRes Proxy at 50% size. Although H.264 creates smaller files—and there is a value in that—ProRes Proxy is more efficient to edit and has a larger color space (10-bit versus 8-bit).

Can you use other versions? Sure. But these three will get you started in the right direction.

15 What Is Raw Video?

Raw video is camera sensor data, not video.

Raw is data directly recorded from the camera sensor. It isn't video; it's data. It's analogous to an old-fashioned telegraph. Raw media records the beeps. But for us to understand the message, we need to convert those beeps into letters of the alphabet.

RAW isn't video. It's camera data, which needs to be converted into video.

Raw is not an acronym. It means "raw," as in "uncompressed." The key thing about any raw file is that it can be created *only* by the camera. You can't convert existing video into raw later.

Since RED introduced the first on-camera raw format, Canon, Blackmagic Design, and Apple now offer proprietary raw file formats as well. These formats are not compatible with each other.

FIGURE 1.6 illustrates a Bayer pattern. The left image is the data recorded by the sensor. Each square isn't a pixel; it's a "photosite." Each photosite is incomplete, containing only one of the three colors (red, green, or blue) that each pixel requires. This Bayer pattern is stored in the raw file. (Not all cameras use a Bayer pattern; for example, the Blackmagic Design Ursa Mini 12K does not. But all raw data records sensor data in a mosaic pattern.)

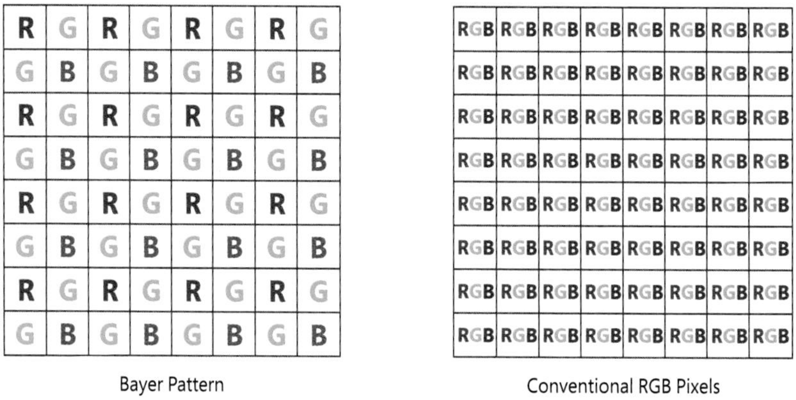

FIGURE 1.6 Raw images start with a mosaic pattern, like the Bayer pattern (left), where each photosite has one color value. Then, de-mosaicing converts the photosites into normal pixels, each containing color values for red, green, and blue.

Bayer Pattern

Conventional RGB Pixels

GOING FURTHER
Don't confuse raw with Log video. Raw is sensor data. Log files are video. However, both require processing and a color grade to look good.

Before a raw file can be edited, it needs conversion, called *de-Bayering* or *de-mosaicing*. This process converts the raw file to video (right image) and determines the frame size and frame rate for the file. Finally, after editing, converted raw files require one final step to process the color, called the *color grade*, to make images look their best.

If your deadlines are tight, shooting raw media is going to slow you down. With sufficient time and the right camera, shooting and editing raw provides great flexibility in how you adjust the look of your images.

⒗ What Is ProRes RAW?

A more efficient RAW format for conversion into video.

"Apple ProRes RAW is based on the same principles and underlying technology as existing ProRes codecs, but is applied to a camera sensor's pristine raw image data rather than conventional image pixels."[3] In other words, ProRes RAW records data directly from the camera sensor—before it is processed into a video image that you can see.

Most single-sensor cameras use a Bayer pattern, or similar color mosaic, to capture color information. What ProRes RAW does that's different from other raw formats is changing *when* it converts that Bayer pattern into video. Apple optimized the timing of this conversion for editing efficiency. Along with the codec, Apple also added the ability to adjust the ISO setting (essentially, video gain) and white point for ProRes RAW media when edited natively.

To access these, select a clip in the timeline (not the Browser); then go to the Info Inspector and switch the menu at the bottom left from Basic to Settings. The red box in **FIGURE 1.7** highlights the new settings available to raw media:

- **Camera ISO.** The ISO setting at which the media was recorded.
- **ISO.** A menu allowing you to change the ISO setting from 50 to 25,600.
- **Exposure Offset.** A slider that provides finer control in adjusting the ISO. The range is one stop lower to one stop higher.
- **Camera Color Temperature.** The white point setting at which the video was recorded.
- **Temperature.** A slider adjusting the white point to any value from 2000K to 15000K. (The availability of this slider is dependent upon the source media format.)

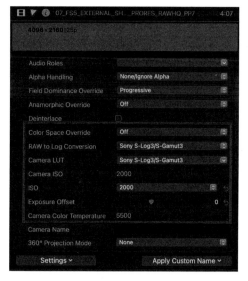

FIGURE 1.7 Specifically for ProRes RAW files, Final Cut supports changing ISO, exposure offset, and camera color temperature (white point).

GOING FURTHER These settings appear only for ProRes RAW media and don't appear when FCP is in proxy mode. The list of cameras supporting this feature is on Apple's website: support.apple.com/HT204203#proresraw.

---

3. *Apple ProRes RAW* white paper, November, 2020, Apple Inc. www.apple.com/final-cut-pro/docs/Apple_ProRes_RAW.pdf

⑰ What Is Log Video?

Log video preserves more of an image's dynamic range.

Log (short for "logarithmic") video records images in a way that captures grayscale values (tones) the same way in shadows—midtones—and highlights. You can use Log, like raw, in both SDR and HDR projects. (See Tip 26, *What Is HDR?*) Log video lets you extract more detail from shadows and highlights during the color grade. All high-end, and many mid-range, cameras can shoot Log format. However, Log files are created in the camera; you can't convert a file to Log format after it's been shot.

Log video preserves more grayscale values in an image.

Rec. 709 encodes brightness (grayscale) values that match how you see scenes, with a contrast optimized for viewing on a monitor. But this results in shadows and highlights that are compressed. Not much "headroom" is available to fiddle with the image's exposure in post: The grayscale relationships are baked in.

Log images are encoded so that the brightness values the camera can capture are given equal weight in the encoding. Log files can be lightened or darkened in post as if the exposure had been adjusted in-camera (within the limits of the captured grayscale range, of course). This allows pulling more values out of the highlights or the shadows than if Rec. 709 encoding were used.

However, Log images will look flat and low-contrast (**FIGURE 1.8**) with elevated midtones and washed-out shadows. They need color grading to look correct.

GOING FURTHER Log files are video; raw files are data. Both raw and Log are ways of recording media with a camera that preserves as much of the grayscale values in an image as possible.

FIGURE 1.8 The source Log file is on the left. It's very gray and not suitable for release. The color-graded version is on the right.

18 What's a LUT?

A lookup table converts numbers into video.

A lookup table (LUT) is a conversion table that tells the computer how to convert the numeric value of each pixel stored on disk into pixels displayed on the screen. Think of a LUT as a translator. The pixel data is stored on the hard disk in Spanish. The LUT translates it into French, English, or...any other language you want. The translation is instant. You can change LUTs at any time, and LUTS can be applied to any media.

- LUTs are nondestructive.
- LUTs change the image instantly.
- LUTs can be changed at any time.
- LUTs can be created by anyone, not just developers.
- LUTs can be used along with other color grading tools.
- LUTs are often used for Log video, but they are also often used to emulate a film stock or a particular creative look.

Final Cut fully supports camera LUTs, which optimize the media shot by a specific camera, and supports custom LUTs that are created to give video a certain look. Final Cut supports LUTs in CUBE or MGA format. CUBE LUTs are also used by DaVinci Resolve.

GOING FURTHER Imported LUTs are stored in [Home Directory] > Library > Application Support > ProApps. Here's an article I wrote that describes how to create a LUT for FCP using Adobe Photoshop: larryjordan.com/articles/create-custom-luts-for-apple-final-cut-pro-x-using-photoshop/.

19 Apple's ProRes White Papers Are a Great Resource

These white papers also detail the storage ProRes requires.

Apple created two excellent white papers describing the ProRes and ProRes RAW family of codecs. More important, Apple provided a table at the end of the ProRes white paper describing the storage bandwidth and capacity requirements for each version of ProRes by frame size and frame rate.

I find myself referring to these tables constantly, not just in writing this book, but in my daily life working with media. You'll find them here:

- *Apple ProRes* white paper: www.apple.com/final-cut-pro/docs/Apple_ProRes_White_Paper.pdf
- *Apple ProRes RAW* white paper: www.apple.com/final-cut-pro/docs/Apple_ProRes_RAW.pdf

Apple created two excellent white papers as references for ProRes and ProRes RAW codecs.

20 Media Is Stored in Containers

Containers hold the different elements of a media file.

OK, we are getting into the weeds a bit here, but this is an important concept. We think of a media clip as being a single "something." But, in fact, it's a collection of somethings held in a single container. (Containers are often called *wrappers* because they "wrap" the different media elements into one place. I also use the term *format*, since the format of the media defines the structure of its container.)

QuickTime, MPEG-4, and MXF are popular media containers.

Containers, like QuickTime or MPEG-4, hold the different elements of a media clip.

If you were to look inside a container (and you generally can't, to prevent ham-fisted miscreants from messing with the file structure), you'd see one or more of the following separate elements collected in the container:

- Video data
- Audio data
- Timecode
- Captions (one for each language)
- Metadata
- And, perhaps, others

Each of these media elements has its own structure and codec, so developers use a container, or wrapper, to bundle these disparate elements together so they can be treated as a single, simple thing. (As editors, we don't need to worry about containers as part of our edit, but it's nice to know why they are there.)

21 Standard Video Frame Sizes

From NTSC to 8K.

Frame size defines the size of an image in pixels. By tradition, the horizontal dimension is listed first. As a note, NTSC and PAL formats use rectangular, rather than square, pixels. Both formats switched between a 4:3 and 16:9 aspect ratio by using the same number of pixels but stretching the width of each pixel horizontally. This allowed a wider image, while using the same number of pixels and bandwidth. This "stretch" drove editors nuts when converting standard definition analog video to digital. Nonsquare pixel formats include:

GOING FURTHER
All video formats are fixed resolution. As an image is displayed on larger monitors, no extra detail is added. The pixels simply get bigger.

- DV
- HDV
- DVCAM
- DVCPRO and DVCPRO 50
- DVCPRO-HD
- HDCAM

TABLE 1.3 lists standard video frame sizes, expressed in pixels.

TABLE 1.3 A list of common video frame sizes from DV through 8K. The horizontal dimension is listed first.

NICKNAME	FRAME SIZE IN PIXELS	PIXEL SHAPE
DV NTSC	720 x 480	Nonsquare
PAL	720 x 576	Nonsquare
DigiBeta NTSC	720 x 486	Nonsquare
720	1280 x 720	Square
1080	1920 x 1080	Square
2K	2048 x 1080	Square
UHD	3840 x 2160	Square
4K	4096 x 2160	Square
5K	5120 x 2880	Square
6K	6144 x 3240	Square
8K	8192 x 4320	Square

22 Standard Video Frame Rates

The range of "normal" frame rates expanded with the move into HD.

Video is a sequence of individual frames (complete pictures) that display fast enough to fool the eye into thinking it sees movement. The rate at which these frames are displayed is called the *frame rate*. It is always defined as *frames per second* (fps).

The early days of TV had only two frame rates: 25 fps and 30 fps. Then, converting film to video began, color was added, HD appeared, and, well, things got out of hand. Here's a list of frame rates currently in use to represent "normal" movement during playback.

- 23.976
- 24
- 25
- 29.97
- 30
- 48
- 50
- 59.94
- 60

The web will accept any frame rate. You don't need to convert frame rates if your video is going to the web.

NOTE A wide range of high-speed frame rates is available to create very smooth slow motion by shooting at an extremely high frame rate. Since these are used only for visual effects and can, in fact, be any frame rate at all, I excluded them from this list.

You don't need to convert frame rates if your video is going to the web.

GOING FURTHER
Converting between frame rates tends to cause jittery playback due to video's use of sequenced still images. However, converting 60 to 30, 59.94 to 29.97, 50 to 25, or 48 to 24 will always yield smooth playback.

In general, to avoid playback problems, always shoot the frame rate you plan to edit and deliver.

23 A Note on "Cinema Quality"

Cinema quality is not determined by frame rate.

Many inexperienced producers feel that to achieve a "cinematic look" for their independent film, they need to shoot or, worse, convert the frame rate they shot to 24 fps. This dubious assertion is based on the fact that film is shot at 24 fps.

For the love of humanity, shoot the frame rate you plan to deliver. Don't convert frame rates.

This belief is wrong and drives me nuts.

While frame rates are *part* of the creative palette, what makes an image look cinematic is the lighting, camera lenses, depth of field, lighting, size of the camera sensor, shutter speed, lighting, shutter angle, color grading, motion blur, and...lighting. Every film you've ever watched on TV was either shown at 29.97 fps (via adding pulldown frames) or sped up to 25 fps if you live outside the United States, not 24 fps.

If you want to shoot 24 fps, please do so. But please don't convert your lovely film from the frame rate you shot to 24 fps simply because you think it will look more "cinematic." It won't. It will look jerky because of the frames that got dropped converting 30 fps, or 25 or 60, to 24 fps.

24 What Is Aspect Ratio?

The relationship between width and height in an image.

Until recently, all video formats were horizontal; they were wider than they were tall. This relationship between width and height is called the *aspect ratio*.

Final Cut supports any frame size, even non-standard ones.

In the beginning, video was 4:3—four units wide by three units high. Why units? Because TV sets back then, like monitors today, were different sizes. This prevented us from describing video in, say, inches. Now that we've moved into the digital era, we can precisely define frame size in pixels but can't define the *size* of each pixel because pixel size varies with monitor size.

Although the web easily supports any frame size or aspect ratio, video is more restrictive. Only four principal aspect ratios are used in video today: 16:9, 4:3, 1:1, and 9:16; see **FIGURE 1.9**. Feature films often use more horizontally extended aspect ratios to give their films a different look, such as 1.85:1 and 2.39:1, but these are special cases. Most video projects use 16:9.

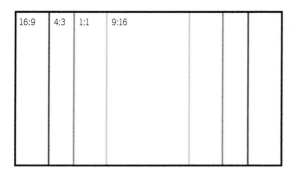

FIGURE 1.9 Four typical video aspect ratios.

16:9 4:3 1:1 9:16

25 What's a Color Space?

Color space defines the range of colors displayed in a video format.

Three color spaces are in use by video today:

- **Rec. 601**. Used by standard-definition (NTSC and PAL) video. This is an older standard and rarely used now. This is similar to Rec. 709, from the perspective of shooting and editing video.
- **Rec. 709**. Used by high-definition (HD) video. It's the most popular color space in use today. It is similar to sRGB.
- **Rec. 2020**. Used by high-dynamic-range (HDR) video.

Color space is independent of frame size or frame rate. **FIGURE 1.10** illustrates the differences in these color spaces. Notice how Rec. 2020 provides a greater range of blue and green shades.

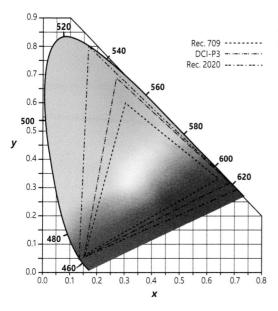

FIGURE 1.10 This chromaticity chart illustrates the differences in color space between Rec. 709, Rec. 2020, and DCI-P3.

Rec. 709 ---------
DCI-P3 ---·---·---·
Rec. 2020 ---·--·---·

GOING FURTHER
DCI-P3, which you hear a lot about when discussing computer monitors, is a midway point between Rec. 709 and Rec. 2020. While DCI-P3 isn't a video color space, it is the color space for digital cinema. So if you're targeting the big screen (or any other distributor requiring a DCP file), you'll want to grade for—and monitor on—a P3 display.

26 What Is HDR?

HDR is a video format, like SDR, that defines colors and brightness.

TV began, all those many years ago, using Standard Dynamic Range to define grayscale values for its images. Then, along came HDR. HDR, like SDR, is a video format. The HDR format is generally defined as media with expanded grayscale values greater than 100 IRE, providing both deeper shadows and brighter highlights, as well as expanded color values that exceed the Rec. 709 color space, mostly in the blues and greens. Although HDR is frequently associated with larger frame sizes, you can easily create HDR media for, say, a 1080p project.

NOTE This is another example of how widely the word *format* is applied to various technical specs.

HDR includes formats such as HLG, PQ, HDR10, and DolbyVision, each of which has specific technical requirements. Not all distributors want or need HDR media. You can create HDR projects from both raw and Log files, but not media shot using the Rec. 709 (SDR) color space. In fact, it's possible to use HDR video in an SDR project, but you won't get the same level of brightness as if it were in an HDR project.

It's possible to convert HDR for an SDR project, the same way it's possible to scale 4K media into a 1080p project.

Although most HDR formats generally require color grading and an HDR-capable video monitor to properly view the images, HLG was designed as a live-broadcast, direct, out-of-camera HDR format, showing a proper HDR image on HLG-compatible displays while still being viewable on an SDR monitor with minimal compromises in appearance. (See Tip 28, *Monitoring HDR*.) Also, in most cases, when you create an HDR color grade, you'll also need to create an SDR color grade for non-HDR viewing.

The benefits of HDR are improved image quality, greater realism (which is a two-edged sword), and future-proofing media. The disadvantages are larger file sizes, time spent color grading, and the extra time and budget required for lighting, lenses, and production value to make the improved image quality worthwhile.

27 Which to Choose: SDR vs. HDR Media?

We are migrating to HDR video, but there's no immediate rush.

The video world is slowly migrating to HDR media. However, while HDR is required for high-end feature films and some streaming services, it is not yet used for broadcast or cable television, social media sites, or anyone requiring media delivery using H.264.

SDR (also called *Rec. 709*) is how we've watched TV since the beginning of HD. (Rec. 601 was used for SD.) HDR expands the range of brightness levels, allows greater color saturation, and even adds more colors in the blue-green range.

The eye-popping difference, though, is in brightness, called *luminance*, which is measured in nits.

- SDR video ranges from 0 to 100 nits (IRE).
- HDR HLG ranges from 0 to 1000 nits.
- HDR10 ranges from 0 to 4,000 nits.
- HDR DolbyVision PQ ranges from 0 to 10,000 nits.

In **FIGURE 1.11**, the size of the Waveform Monitor display (which is how we measure grayscale values; see Tip 281, *The Waveform Monitor*) remains the same, but the brightness values are vastly different. (Just for comparison, a white cloud in a blue sky is about 10,000 nits, the sun at sunset is around 600,000 nits, and the sun at noon is more than 1 billion nits.)

Most projects today use Rec. 709 color and grayscale values, even if they are editing 4K media. Some distributors require HDR, in which case they will specify the format (HDR10, HLG, or PQ), frame size, and frame rate for their system. ProRes 4444 is a good choice for an HDR delivery codec.

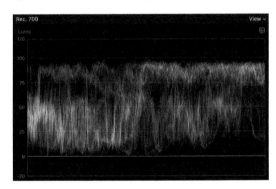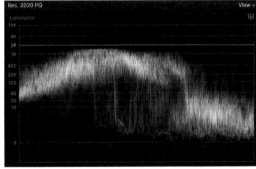

FIGURE 1.11 The Waveform Monitor in Final Cut. Look carefully at the luminance values on the left of each display. Rec. 709 video (left) extends to 100 nits. Rec. 2020 PQ (right) extends to 10,000 nits!

28 Monitoring HDR

Can you watch HDR on a computer monitor?

Maybe. There are two issues here: watching commercially distributed (HDR10) HDR media on your computer and monitoring HDR media during an edit. They are not the same.

NOTE If you are using an
HDR TV as a monitor for
your Mac, go to System
Preferences > Displays
and select High Dynamic
Range. This displays HDR
clips properly on the TV,
provided you are running
macOS 12.x or later.

Regarding commercially released HDR media, Apple writes: "Support for high dynamic range (HDR) video, such as HDR films and TV program from Apple or other providers, requires the latest version of macOS, a compatible Mac model and an HDR10-compatible display, TV or projector."

However, for monitoring HDR media during an edit, the situation is different. In the past, only external HDR video monitors could accurately display HDR media. And they were expensive. Then, Apple released the Pro Display XDR monitor, followed by a variety of M1 MacBook Pros with XDR displays that support "brightness of 1,000 nits (sustained) and 1,600 nits (peak) with a 1,000,000:1 contrast ratio"[4] for HDR content. HDR media is becoming increasingly viewable on computer-grade monitors, but while some monitors can show HDR10, no computer monitor can show the full range of HDR PQ.

To accurately monitor HDR media during an edit, an HDR-capable video monitor is required.

Apple writes: "Final Cut Pro 10.4 or later supports a wide-gamut (Rec. 2020) HDR working space for which log footage is no longer tone-mapped upon conversion. This makes the full dynamic range of the log source footage available to effects in the working space, but it requires the user to reduce the dynamic range of the footage to a specified output range using color-grading controls, custom LUTs, or the HDR Tools effect."

GOING FURTHER Two Apple support documents are relevant to this discussion:

- General HDR media playback: support.apple.com/en-gb/HT210980
- HDR media in Final Cut Pro: www.apple.com/final-cut-pro/docs/HDR_WideColor.pdf

29 What Does Video Bit Depth Determine?

Greater bit depth provides smoother color and grayscale variations.

In video, bit depth determines the number of steps between the minimum and maximum values of a color or grayscale. In audio, the bit depth determines the number of steps between silence and maximum volume. An analogy is a staircase between two floors. Although the vertical position of the floors doesn't change, the bit depth determines the number of steps between them. If the bit depth is small, the distance between steps is huge, making walking upstairs awkward. If the bit depth is larger, the distance between steps is smaller and much easier to manage.

---

4. www.apple.com/macbook-pro-14-and-16/specs/

Although bit depth is written as a single number—such as 8, 10, or 12—it actually represents a power of 2. Here are some examples:

- 8-bit video has 2^8 or 256 grayscale or color values per channel.
- 10-bit video has 2^{10} or 1,024 grayscale or color values per channel.
- 12-bit video has 2^{12}, or 4,096 grayscale or color values per channel.

The greater the bit depth, the smoother the color and grayscale variations in an image.

ProRes files, including ProRes Proxy, are 10-bit, except for ProRes 4444 and 4444 XQ, which are 12-bit. Most AVC and H.264 files are 8-bit. HEVC files can be either 8-bit or 10-bit. Most low-cost cameras shoot only 8-bit images, while higher-end cameras can shoot 10-, 12-, even 14-bit media.

Even if you shoot 8-bit media, all is not lost. When you convert 8-bit media to 10-bit for editing by transcoding into a different codec, the 10-bit file still contains only 8-bit source images. However, converting 8-bit media into 10-bit media has a big advantage. As an analogy, if I dump five gallons of water into a bathtub, the bathtub may be bigger, but there's still only five gallons of water in it. The cool part about the extra space in the bathtub, though, is that if I add more water, perfume, or soap and stir quickly, nothing spills out. The tub has plenty of room for whatever I want to add.

Just so with video. Moving 8-bit video to a 10-bit codec provides plenty of room for effects and color grading. The images may be only 8-bit, but effects and color grading are calculated in 10-bit space. While converting an 8-bit image to 10-bit won't fix any problems in the recording, the larger color space means that fewer artifacts get added during editing and color grading.

In real life if you are shooting a sunset, 8-bit video records only 256 values for each color (red, green, blue). This results in banding (harsh edges) where the gradient lacks enough color values to show a smooth image. (See **FIGURE 1.12**.) Stepping up to 10-bit video expands the colors available by four times, resulting in a more pleasing image.

FIGURE 1.12 This photo illustrates banding. The image on the left was processed in Photoshop to emulate 8-bit video. The image on the right illustrates 10-bit.

30 What's 4:2:0, 4:2:2, and 4:4:4 Color?

"Chroma subsampling," the amount of color in an image.

It should be simple. Color is color is color. But, as you've come to expect, life isn't simple. The reason is that when digital video was first invented, camera processors and storage media were slow and small.

NOTE In analog video, color uses YUV values. Digital video uses YCrCb, but the results are the same. Y equals grayscale, or brightness, and Cr and Cb are color-difference values, which creates the video equivalent of RGB.

The easiest way to decrease file size and minimize processor cycles was to remove color from an image. That's what these numbers represent.

Grayscale (brightness) levels are based either on the green channel or close to the green channel's values because our eyes are most sensitive to green light. That means every pixel has a specific green value. However, while our eyes are very sensitive to brightness, they are less sensitive to color. So to save storage space, colors are averaged across groups of pixels. FIGURE 1.13 illustrates this in a process called *chroma subsampling*.

- **4:4:4** (top). Every pixel in a group of four pixels has a complete YCrCb color value. The 4:4:4 means that, in a group of four pixels, there are four Y values, four Cr values, and four Cb values. However, these 4:4:4 files are big and take time to process and space to store.

- **4:2:2** (middle). Like 4:4:4, this converts pixels to YCrCb colors. But while grayscale values are recorded at full resolution, color-difference values are recorded at half the horizontal resolution. In other words, it takes two pixels to create a complete color value, that is, four Y, two Cr, and two Cb values in every four pixel group. So while the grayscale part of the image has full resolution, the color part of the image has full vertical resolution, but only half of the horizontal resolution.

4:2:0 media will not chroma key or color grade well. 4:2:2 is better, while 4:4:4 is ideal. Most high-end cameras shoot 4:2:2.

- **4:2:0** (bottom). Like 4:2:2, this converts pixels to YCrCb colors. But while grayscale values are recorded at full resolution, color difference resolution is cut in half again, both horizontally and vertically. In other words, it takes four pixels to create a complete color value, that is, four Y, one Cr, and one Cb value in every four-pixel group. So while the grayscale part of the image has full resolution, the color part of the image has half the resolution both horizontally *and* vertically.

If you use a camera to shoot video, any of these color subsampling values will create good-looking images. However, if you are creating green-screen effects, doing extensive color grading, or projecting the image on very large screens, you should record as much color information possible.

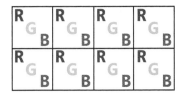 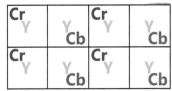 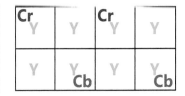

FIGURE 1.13 4:4:4 (left), 4:2:2 (middle), and 4:2:0 (right) chroma-subsampling. 4:4:4 provides the greatest amount of color, while 4:2:0 creates the smallest file.

COMPUTER BASICS

These key terms and technology describe how to optimize our computer for video editing.

31 What's the Best Computer for Video Editing?

This is the one question I am asked more than any other.

We are obsessed with "the best." But when it comes to video editing, chasing the best computer is a waste of time. Why? Because the only possible answer is: It depends.

It depends upon your budget, your schedule, your deadlines, the video formats you edit, how often you change locations…you get the idea. Here's a good analogy: What's the best car, a Tesla Roadster, a Ford F-150 pickup, or a Navistar school bus?

What's the best computer? It depends…

As you can guess, the answer is "It depends." The Roadster is a bad choice for carrying sheets of plywood, the F-150 is a bad choice for carrying 20 school kids, and the bus is a bad choice for a drag race. Yet switch the tasks—the Roadster for speed, the F-150 for carrying stuff, and the school bus for carrying kids—and you have three ideal solutions.

Final Cut Pro runs only on Mac computers, so if you own Microsoft Windows, it won't work. Yes, there are "Hackintosh" Windows systems, which are fine for people with extra time on their hands. However, if you are serious about your editing, get the computer the software was designed for: a Mac.

Every Mac shipped in the last dozen years—every single one—can edit video. The difference between them is how *quickly* they can edit it along with the video frame sizes and frame rates it can comfortably support.

GOING FURTHER It's important to note that technology changes constantly, and gear is quickly outdated. But "outdated" does not mean "nonfunctioning." I know many editors happily making money editing video on gear that's more than a decade old.

⓷ What Stresses Your Computer During Editing?

Editing video challenges your entire computer—especially storage.

Today, as frame sizes expand and more media is shot for each project, the capacity and bandwidth of your storage becomes more important than the speed of your computer. In fact, over time, you'll spend far more for storage than you will for your computer.

Editing video is the most challenging task your computer system can perform. Although some software may push the CPU or GPU harder, video editing stresses *everything*. CPU, GPU, RAM, monitors, storage, bandwidth, protocols, network access, cables...the works.

Editing video is the most challenging task your computer system can perform.

Making editing even harder is that different video formats stress your computer more than others. Here are some tips:

- Larger frame sizes require more from the CPU. You are fine on any computer up to 4K images; beyond that, make sure your computer has enough horsepower to edit.

- Larger frame sizes, lower compression levels, and faster frame rates push storage harder. A 4K/30 fps ProRes 422 video clip requires 78 MB/second for playback. An 8K/30 fps video clip requires 314 MB/second!

- FIGURE 1.14 illustrates how storage bandwidth (the speed your storage transfers data to and from the computer) changes as frame rate increases.

FIGURE 1.14 This chart illustrates the storage bandwidth, in MB/second, required to support different video frame sizes. *(Source:* Apple ProRes white paper.)

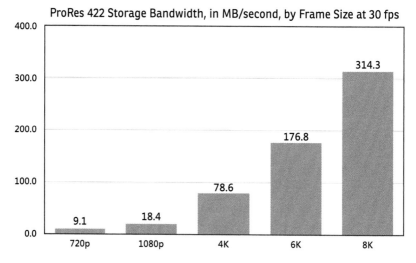

ProRes 422 Storage Bandwidth, in MB/second, by Frame Size at 30 fps

- Highly compressed codecs require more powerful computers to play and edit video smoothly. Older computers may struggle with these formats. (See Tip 7, *Formats, Codecs...What Are These Things?*)
- Multicam editing highly stresses storage because you are playing multiple streams of video simultaneously in real time. (See Tip 42, *Multicam Editing Is a Special Case.*)

33 Optimizing Your Computer for Video Editing

Customization starts when you buy the system, not afterward.

With the exception of the Mac Pro, all Macs are essentially closed systems. This means that you should think carefully about how to configure the hardware before you buy it.

In broad strokes, when it comes to Final Cut Pro, the CPU handles the interface, file handling, and tasks such as scaling and positioning clips. The GPU handles everything that changes the look of a pixel. This includes rendering, color grading, many effects, and export.

If your budget is unlimited, buy whatever computer you want. But if your desire exceeds your budget, here are my suggestions:

- All Macs create the same quality image. The difference is in how *quickly* they create it. Spending more money doesn't buy you better images; it buys you more time by increasing the speed of the computer.
- The Final Cut Pro interface is complex and detailed, with lots of small places to click. I find video editing on a larger screen easier than on a smaller one. For laptops, I prefer the 16" version. For desktops, I prefer a 27" screen or larger.
- For older Intel systems, an i7 or i9 CPU is better than an i3 or i5 and worth spending the extra money to get.
- For newer systems, all Apple silicon chips can edit video. The difference is the speed of render and export.
- For video editing, I recommend at least 16 GB of RAM. I prefer 32 GB. More than 64 GB of RAM won't make a big difference in editing performance.
- The more GPU cores, the faster the system will render and export; however, image quality is the same regardless of the number of GPU cores or how fast they run.
- With Intel systems, the internal Intel GPU is the slowest.

Spending more money doesn't buy you better images; it buys you more time.

- You will always need more storage, so don't waste money buying the largest internal solid-state drive (SSD). Internal SSD drives that are 1 or 2 TB will be fine.

- Budget for external storage. As the saying goes, "You can't be too rich or too thin." When it comes to video editing, there's no such thing as having "too much" storage.

34 Which to Choose: Mouse, Trackball, or Trackpad?

Choose hardware that makes you feel efficient.

When it comes to editing, I'm a serious keyboard junkie. I use keyboard shortcuts for their speed. But when I need to move something, I use the mouse. But there are alternatives: trackpads, trackballs, and others. Scott Newell, an editor and trackball fan, totally disses the mouse and explains why editors need to move to trackballs.

Choose hardware that makes you feel efficient.

As a pointing device, Scott wrote, trackballs provide several advantages in FCP:

- **Support.** Final Cut fully supports trackballs.

- **Ergonomics.** No moving the mouse around the desk: Your hand can remain in the same position, and your fingers do the moving. There's less strain and less fatigue on your hand and wrist.

- **Precision.** A trackball allows precise moves for scrubbing and even more control with a larger ball.

- **Multiple buttons.** Most trackballs contain multiple buttons that you can custom program.

- **Flexibility.** Add an external trackpad such as Apple's Magic Trackpad to make two-finger scrolling lightning-fast. Three-finger swiping makes navigating the timeline super quick, though this does require special setup in Preferences.

GOING FURTHER To reinforce his point, Scott contacted another editor, a "true believer in FCP," to ask what he preferred. That editor replied: "I don't use track balls. I use the Apple mouse and the Contour Design Shuttle Pro for frame-by-frame jogging and customizable buttons." Oops. Scott added: "This just goes to show that you should pick the tool that works best for you."

STORAGE BASICS

Video editing depends upon fast, capable storage. This section describes the relationship between video editing, computers, and storage.

35 What Type of Storage Hardware Do You Need?

Here's how to pick between RAIDs, SSDs, and hard drives.

Basically, larger frame sizes, faster frame rates, or more multicam clips require faster data transfer rates (bandwidth) between the storage system and your computer. The faster the data transfer rate required, the more a storage system will cost.

Three types of storage are big enough and fast enough to support media editing:

- **Hard drive** (HDD or spinning media). This is the storage we are most familiar with. Spinning metallic platters inside the drive store data using long-term magnetic bits. This technology is highly reliable, well-known, and inexpensive. The problem is that a single drive doesn't transfer data very fast.

- **SSD**. This stores data electronically using solid-state chips. The benefit is that SSDs are fast. Earlier SSDs connected via SCSI. The latest SSD technology, called "NVMe," is extraordinarily fast. The problem is that SSDs don't hold as much data as spinning media, and they cost more per terabyte. All currently shipping Macs use NVMe SSDs as their internal drive. They are very fast but don't hold as much as spinning hard drives.

- **Redundant Array of Inexpensive Drives (RAID)**. This is a collection of either spinning hard drives or SSDs. By aggregating these units, RAIDs can provide huge capacity and extremely fast speeds. The problem is that they aren't cheap.

The faster the bandwidth, or the greater the capacity, the more a storage system will cost.

For my editing, I prefer RAIDs. For cost reasons, I populate them with very large spinning hard drives. This works well for all my editing, except multicam. (See Tip 42, *Multicam Editing Is a Special Case*.)

FIGURE 1.15 illustrates typical data transfer rates (bandwidth) between different devices. Since Thunderbolt 4 tops out around 2,800 MB/sec, a RAID containing lots of SSDs can go only as fast as the Thunderbolt protocol. In general, the faster the bandwidth, or the greater the storage capacity, the more the device costs.

GOING FURTHER
As I write this book, I find myself using the term *hard disk* as a generic term for storage. So going forward, when you read *hard disk*, think: "the storage on my computer."

FIGURE 1.15 Selected storage based on data transfer speed. 4 and 8 refer to the number of units in the device.

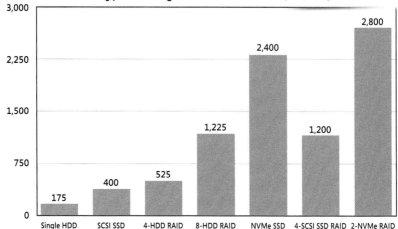

Typical Storage Data Transfer Rates (MB/sec.)

Single HDD	175
SCSI SSD	400
4-HDD RAID	525
8-HDD RAID	1,225
NVMe SSD	2,400
4-SCSI SSD RAID	1,200
2-NVMe RAID	2,800

36 Internal, Direct- and Network-Attached Storage

How to pick what's right for you.

- An **internal SSD** will be the fastest storage, but it also has the smallest capacity and can't be expanded later. A plus, though, to using the internal drive is that it travels with your computer. However, once it fills up, you're stuck. Hands-down, though, internal drives are blazingly fast.

- An **internal Fusion** drive (a spinning disk/SSD combo that Apple used in many iMacs) will be only about as fast as an external single hard drive with the same limitation as an internal SSD: It doesn't hold a lot, and when it's full, the performance of your computer slows dramatically.

- **Direct-attached** storage (that is, storage that's connected directly to your Mac using USB or Thunderbolt) takes two forms: single drives and RAIDs. A single drive is the cheapest, but slowest. A RAID is the best choice when you want the best performance with the greatest storage capacity. Also, unlike an internal SSD, external storage can be expanded almost infinitely at the lowest cost by adding more or larger drives.

- **Network-attached** storage is the best choice to share files within a local workgroup. Although fast enough to support HD media, it will never be as fast as direct-attached storage. It also costs more to set up and maintain than any other storage.

GOING FURTHER RAIDs are configured in RAID levels, balancing performance with data security.

- RAID 0—Fastest performance, but no data redundancy. If a drive dies, all data is lost.
- RAID 4—Best option for SSD RAIDs. Minimizes excessive writes and protects all data if one SSD in the RAID dies.
- RAID 5—Best option for spinning media RAIDs. Excellent performance and protects all data if one spinning hard drive dies.
- RAID 6—Best option for the truly paranoid. Acceptable performance and protects all data if two spinning hard drives die at the same time.

37 What About Storing Media in the Cloud?

Accessing the cloud is too slow for editing media in Final Cut.

One of the intriguing developments in video editing during the recent pandemic was the rise of cloud-based video editing. Rather than storing media locally on your computer, media is stored in the cloud and edited with a web browser.

However, it's important to keep in mind what "the cloud" actually is. Aside from being a brilliant marketing term, the cloud is simply a collection of servers, stored somewhere outside your location, managed by a third party, accessed via the internet, onto which you store data and run server-based applications. In other words, it is a storage device over which you have very limited control.

Cloud-based media editing has many advantages:

- You don't need large amounts of local media storage.
- You don't need a powerful computer to edit.
- You can access both media and projects from any computer.
- Multi-editor collaboration is potentially easier.

However, cloud-based editing also has several disadvantages:

- It takes time and bandwidth to transfer camera source files to a cloud server.
- Media assets and projects are always vulnerable to security breaches and unauthorized access.
- You can lose access to your assets if the cloud company goes out of business.
- Cloud-based editing tends to focus on the enterprise rather than the individual editor.

The biggest reason not to use the cloud for media editing is that Final Cut does not currently support it.

However, the biggest reason not to use the cloud is that Final Cut does not currently support cloud editing because the bandwidth between your computer and the cloud is too slow.

38 Storage Specs to Consider

Here's what the specs mean.

When thinking about storage hardware, consider five elements:

- **How it connects**. Thunderbolt, USB-C, USB...
- **The hardware itself**. RAID, SSD, or hard disk
- **Capacity**. How much it holds
- **Bandwidth** (also called "data rate"). How fast it transfers data
- **Media format**. Codecs, frame size, frame rate, and bit-depth

Storage protocols today are often faster than the storage system itself.

In the past, you could determine storage performance by how it connected (called the *connection protocol*) to the computer, for example, USB-A, FireWire 400, FireWire 800, SCSI. That's because the connection protocol was slower than the storage bandwidth.

Today, protocols are faster than the hardware. So now you need to consider both in tandem. Protocols that are fast enough for video editing include:

- Thunderbolt 2, 3, or 4
- USB-C
- Ethernet 10G

Protocols that may be fast enough include:

- Thunderbolt 1
- USB 3.1 Gen 2
- Ethernet 1G

Protocols that aren't fast enough include:

- USB-A
- Early versions of USB 3.1
- Wi-Fi (in most instances)
- FireWire 400 and 800

39 How Much Storage Capacity Do You Need?

There is never enough storage.

Asking how much storage you need for a project is similar to asking "How long is a piece of string?" The answer, like everything in tech, is "It depends."

Estimating how much storage you'll need is important because you don't want to run out of storage before production is complete. Yes, you can always buy another RAID, but budgeting for more storage is something you want to know before shooting starts, especially if storage costs factor into your budget.

The file size of a media clip is determined by five factors:

- Codec
- Frame size
- Frame rate
- Bit depth
- Duration

When it comes to estimating how much storage you'll need, estimate the number of hours of media shot during production. (I know, I know; which director ever shoots *less* media than they estimate?) Then, multiply those hours by the storage capacity required, in gigabytes, per hour of media. Then, multiply *that* number by 1.5 to account for work files, render files, and the other assorted media you are likely to need for the edit.

The equation is:

$$(\text{hours of media shot}) \times (\text{GB to store 1 hour of media}) \times 1.5 = \text{Approximate storage capacity needed}$$

This number is as good as any to jumpstart your storage planning.

For example, **FIGURE 1.16** illustrates how storage capacity requirements escalate as frame size increases. Many, many projects require terabytes of storage.

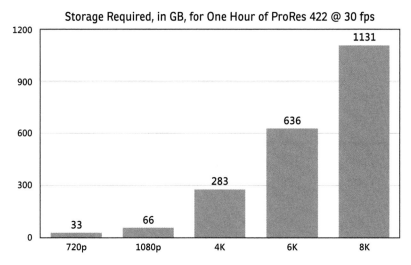

Storage Required, in GB, for One Hour of ProRes 422 @ 30 fps

Frame size	GB
720p	33
1080p	66
4K	283
6K	636
8K	1131

FIGURE 1.16 Storage requirements, in GB/hour, by frame size. *(Source: Apple ProRes white paper.)*

40 How Much Speed Do You Need?

The video format determines storage capacity and bandwidth.

To continue your planning, **TABLE 1.4** lists typical data transfer rates for popular codecs, frame sizes, and frame rates. This is just a sample; there are many variations.

Verify media data rates before determining the speed and capacity needs of your storage.

TABLE 1.4 Storage bandwidth and capacity. 1 GB = 1,024 MB.

CODEC	FRAME SIZE	FRAME RATE (FPS)	STORAGE BANDWIDTH (MB/SECOND)	GB REQUIRED FOR ONE HOUR OF MEDIA
DV NTSC/PAL	480i	30	3.75	13.2
AVCHD	720p	60p	3.0	10.5
AVC–Intra	1080i	30i	12.5	43.9
HDCAM SR	1080p	60	Up to 237	833.2
R3D	1080p	30	38	133.6
XAVC	1080p	30	55	193.4
XAVC	UHD (4K)	30	120	421.9
ProRes Proxy	1080p	30	5.6	20
ProRes Proxy	UHD (4K)	24	18.125	65.0
ProRes 422	1080p	30	18.3	64.3
ProRes 422	UHD (4K)	24	58.8	206.7
ProRes 422	UHD (4K)	30	73.625	265
ProRes 4444	1080p	30	41.25	145.0
ProRes 4444	UHD (4K)	30	165.75	582.7
ProRes 4444	UHD (4K)	60	331.5	1,165.4

41 Why Use Proxies?

Proxies reduce the load on a system, allowing it to edit more easily.

Proxies are smaller versions of your camera source files that are designed to reduce the load on your computer while still allowing informed creative decisions about your content.

Proxy files do not replace camera source media. They simply make it easier to work with media during the rough-cut stage, until it's time to return to the master files for final color grading and output.

Generally, a proxy frame is one-half (50%) the frame size of the original media. So a proxy frame for a Ultra High Definition (UHD) source frame (3840 x 2160 pixels) would be 1920 x 1080 pixels. You can make proxy files even smaller by selecting 25% or 12.5% size, depending upon which is more important: smaller files or seeing more detail in the image. (See Tip 106, *How to Enable Proxies*.)

Reasons to use proxy files (also called *proxies*) include:

NOTE See Tip 492, *Why Proxies Have Lower Image Quality*, for an illustration of the different frame sizes as proxy resolution decreases.

- Vastly simplifying the huge bandwidth needs of multicam editing
- Reducing 6K and 8K frame files to a manageable size during the rough-cut process, where image quality is not the priority
- Simplifying sending files between editors for team projects
- Decreasing the load on the CPU during editing

In short, proxy files are a very useful way to edit video without stressing the computer. While Chapter 3, "Libraries & Media," shows how to *create* proxies, in this tip I want to describe what proxies *are*.

Final Cut Pro can create proxies using either ProRes 422 Proxy or H.264. A quick test showed that starting with a 53 GB ProRes 422 source file, a ProRes 422 Proxy file at 50% was 14% the size of the source file. H.264 at 50% was 3% the size of ProRes 422 file; see **FIGURE 1.17**.

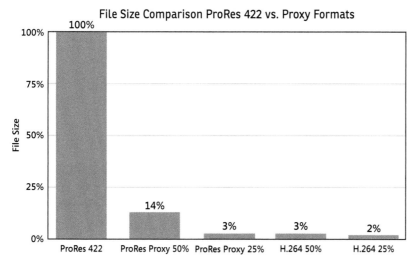

File Size Comparison ProRes 422 vs. Proxy Formats

FIGURE 1.17 This chart shows the difference in file sizes between ProRes 422, ProRes 422 Proxy, and H.264. Although H.264 is smaller, ProRes Proxy is more efficient for editing, especially for multicam work.

My strong recommendation is to use proxy files for multicam edits of more than four cameras. As well, I recommend proxies for frame sizes larger than 4K and using ProRes Proxy, rather than H.264, because it is 10-bit and optimized for editing. However, if saving file space is more important, use H.264.

In both cases, set the frame size to 50% to retain as much image detail as possible.

You should use proxies when creating the rough cut. Then, switch to the camera source files for final effects, color grading, and output. You would never use proxy files for final output. Final Cut switches between source media and proxies with a single mouse click. Even if you forget to switch, Final Cut will warn you if you try to export proxy files, though you can still export them if you wish. (See Tip 491, *Export a Proxy File*.)

> **GOING FURTHER** Chapter 3 shows how to create and edit proxy files. See Tip 106, *How to Enable Proxies*. If you are using H.264 proxies and getting dropped frames, convert your proxies to ProRes 422 Proxy, and this problem should go away.

42 Multicam Editing Is a Special Case

Successful multicam editing requires high-speed hardware.

In a multicam edit you are watching two or more simultaneous video streams and picking between them on the fly.

In a normal video edit, you watch one clip, decide you like it, edit it into the timeline, then move on to the next clip. The edit may contain hundreds of clips, but you watch them one at a time. A multicam edit is one where you are watching two or more simultaneous video streams and picking between them on the fly.

For example, it is not uncommon to record a live performance with 10, 15, or even 20 cameras. That's a lot of media to play at the same time.

FIGURE 1.18 shows how voraciously multicam editing devours bandwidth. Using 4K media, a single hard drive is not sufficient to reliably handle even two streams of data. An older SCSI SSD can't handle more than four. Newer NVMe SSDs and many RAIDs can easily handle 20.

FIGURE 1.18 Multicam editing voraciously devours bandwidth as the number of simultaneous streams increases.

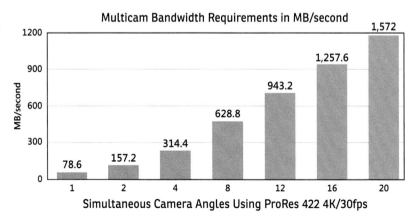

Multicam Bandwidth Requirements in MB/second

Although you can spend a fortune in high-speed data storage, a wiser option for multicam editing is to use proxies. Final Cut makes handling them trivial. (See Tip 41, *Why Use Proxies?*) However, even using proxies, if you plan to do a lot of multicam editing, plan to upgrade your storage to SSDs. The ability of an SSD to easily handle playback of multiple video streams without dropping frames makes the cost worth it.

GOING FURTHER
See the section on multicam editing in Chapter 5, "Advanced Editing."

43 Where to Store Stuff

Where you store the elements for your edit makes a difference.

In general, use the internal drive of your Mac for the operating system, applications, and work files. Although you can use your internal drive for libraries and media, I recommend they be stored on external devices.

Storing these files externally makes moving projects between computers and/or editors a lot easier. Also, as projects grow, adding more external storage doesn't disrupt file linking in Final Cut, which would occur if you moved media from one drive to another. Finally, if you change computers, media and projects won't be affected.

Store libraries and media on your fastest external drive. FCP accesses these files constantly, and speed matters.

Elements such as graphics, photos, Photoshop documents, FCP backups, and audio files can be stored anywhere. They don't take up a lot of space, and they don't need anywhere near the bandwidth that video files require.

> **GOING FURTHER** If you own a late-model computer, your projects are small, and speed is critical, store everything on your internal drive. While the internal drive doesn't provide a lot of capacity to work with large collections of media, nothing currently touches the speed of the internal SSDs of modern Macs.
>
> However, for security and peace of mind, I still recommend using external storage.

44 Final Cut Creates Lots of Files

Here's what they are and where you should store them.

Final Cut creates a lot of files during an edit, most of which are invisible. By default, Final Cut stores libraries in the [Home Library] > Documents folder. You can store libraries wherever you want, provided your storage is fast enough. Chapter 3 explains what these files are, where to store them, and how to configure your system for editing.

GOING FURTHER
Chapter 3 goes into working with media in much more detail.

Although media can be stored in the library, my general recommendation is to store media separately. Motion templates include the titles, transitions, generators, effects, and motion projects that you create for the project. These are small, as no media is generally stored with the template.

TABLE 1.5 lists the various files created by Final Cut and where they should be stored.

TABLE 1.5 Files created or used by Final Cut Pro.				
FILE TYPE	FILE SIZE	WHERE STORED	ACCESS SPEED REQUIRED	UPDATE FREQUENCY
Video files	Large	Outside Library	Fast	Once, to create link
Audio files	Medium	Outside Library	Medium	Once, to create link
Stills and PSDs	Small	Outside Library	Slow	Once, to create link
Library Database	Small	Library	Medium	Constantly
Library Database backups	Small	Outside Library	Slow	Varies, generally every 15 minutes
Render files	Large	Library	Fast	When effect settings change
Video thumbnails	Small	Library	Medium	Once
Audio waveforms	Small	Library	Medium	Once
Analysis files	Medium	Library	Slow	Once
Keywords and Searches	Small	Library	Slow	When changed
Motion templates	Small	Outside Library	Slow	When changed

Although media can be stored in the library, my general recommendation is to store media separately.

45 What's Interlaced vs. Progressive Video?

Interlacing is a mess when viewed on the web.

In the earliest days of television, the technology of picture tubes was such that the entire frame could not be displayed at once without flickering. So engineers solved this by dividing each frame into two fields: the odd-numbered scan lines, then the even; see **FIGURE 1.19**. Some video formats record the odd lines first; others record the even fields first.

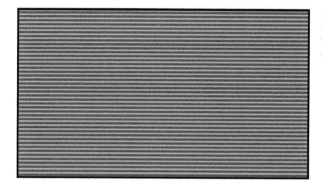

FIGURE 1.19 The red and gray lines represent the two fields of a video frame (odd and even). They are displayed sequentially.

Always record progressive video because it is easy to convert to interlaced without damaging image quality.

Dividing each frame into even and odd fields was called *interlacing*. Each set of lines was stored in a "field." Then, when the image was displayed, the lines were "laced" back together. The problem is that there's a time difference between these two fields. For 30 fps video, the fields were offset by 1/60th of second. This meant that any movement between the two fields created distracting horizontal lines (called *interlace artifacts*) when displayed on a digital device. FIGURE 1.20 compares the difference in image quality between interlaced (left) and progressive (right).

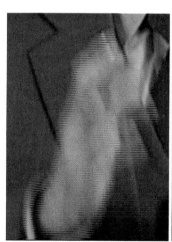

FIGURE 1.20 An interlaced image (left) and the same frame converted to progressive. The interlace lines are gone, but the image is blurrier.

Over the years, TV display technology improved; however, interlacing remained because it decreased the bandwidth that broadcasters needed to transmit a television signal. Even today, many broadcast networks (CBS, NBC, and PBS, to name three) are exclusively interlaced when broadcasting HD signals.

The opposite of interlaced is progressive. This is where the entire frame is captured and displayed at once. Fox, ABC, and ESPN broadcast progressive

NOTE Interlace artifacts are created by the camera when an interlaced image is recorded. They are not created when a previously recorded progressive image is converted to interlaced.

GOING FURTHER
Video formats are often labeled with "i" or "p," indicating whether a video format is interlaced (i) or progressive (p). A common example is 1080i versus 1080p.

images, along with all streaming services and the web. 4K and larger formats are also exclusively progressive.

The solution is to record progressive video wherever possible. It is easy to convert a progressive frame to interlaced without creating interlace artifacts. It is impossible to deinterlace an interlaced image without damaging video quality.

46 Deinterlacing Degrades Video Image Quality

The only way to deinterlace video is to remove pixels.

You can remove interlacing from an image (called *deinterlacing*) in three ways, all of which impact image quality.

GOING FURTHER
An image recorded in progressive format, then converted to interlaced does not display interlace artifacts because there is no time offset between the even and odd field lines.

- Remove one field, then duplicate the remaining lines. This is fast but cuts vertical resolution in half.

- Replace the lines in the second field by blending (that is, dissolving) the line above it in the first field with the line below it, also in the first field. This has a somewhat higher perceived image quality than line duplication. (This is analogous to frame blending for slow motion.)

- Replace the lines in the second field by calculating a new line of video from the line above and below it in the first field. (This is analogous to optical flow.) Hardware optimized for deinterlacing tends to use this option.

47 A Fast Way to Deinterlace a Clip

QuickTime Player is a fast deinterlace tool.

To deinterlace a clip quickly, QuickTime Player is the tool of choice. Here's how:

1. Open an interlaced clip in QuickTime Player.

2. Choose File > Export As > 480p (or the frame size that corresponds to your clip); see **FIGURE 1.21**. It is important not to change the frame size.

3. Give the new file a name and storage location and click Save.

FIGURE 1.21 The Export menu in QuickTime Player.

48 When to Deinterlace Interlaced Video

Interlacing cannot die fast enough for me.

Interlaced video is such a mess. If you are given interlaced video to edit (for example, 480i, 576i, or 1080i) and it is going to broadcast, leave it interlaced, because that is the format the broadcaster needs. If the interlaced footage is going to the web, it is best to deinterlace it. If it is going both to broadcast and the web, you should create two versions: interlaced for broadcast and progressive for the web.

Deinterlacing can be done before the edit by deinterlacing each clip, during the edit by setting FCP to deinterlace automatically, or after the edit by deinterlacing the final exported movie file.

If there are only a few clips, deinterlace them directly in Final Cut:

1. Select the clips in the Browser or timeline.
2. Open the Info Inspector.
3. In the lower left menu, select Settings; see FIGURE 1.22.
4. In the Settings panel, click the Deinterlace button.

FIGURE 1.22 Deinterlace and Field Dominance controls in the Settings panel.

To deinterlace an entire project, either deinterlace media before editing starts or deinterlace the completed project after exporting the finished version. I would generally deinterlace the exported finished movie using Apple Compressor or other software.

Deinterlacing before you start gives you more control over the clips; however, it will take more time and require more storage space.

GOING FURTHER

Enabling the Deinterlace setting in Final Cut causes the frame rate of the selected clips to double. For example, if the frame rate of the original interlaced clips is 29.97 fps, the frame rate of the deinterlaced clips will be 59.94 fps.

Rarely, the field order will be wrong. For standard-definition video, this should be set to Lower First. For HD (and HDV) video, set it to Upper First. Remember, you don't need to use these settings for progressive video. Thank goodness.

COMMAND SET BASICS

This section covers creating, using, and managing keyboard shortcuts and command sets.

49 Understand Keyboard Shortcuts

Here's what I mean when I write a shortcut.

TABLE 1.6 explains how to interpret a written keyboard shortcut in this book.

TABLE 1.6 Defining keyboard shortcut terminology.	
WHEN I WRITE...	**IT MEANS...**
Press	Press a key combination briefly.
S	Press just that single letter, without pressing any other key.
Cmd+1	Press both keys at the same time.
Press and hold Cmd+R	Press both keys at the same time and hold them for the duration specified.
Right-click	To reveal a contextual menu: 1. Click the right mouse button. 2. Press and hold the Control key while clicking. 3. Press two fingers on a track pad. 4. Press two fingers on a Magic Mouse.
Shift+Option+Cmd+R	Using as many fingers as necessary, press all these keys at the same time.

50 Create a Custom Command Set

Command sets contain custom keyboard shortcuts.

Share custom command sets between editors using this menu to export or import them.

Final Cut has a default collection of keyboard shortcuts that Apple calls a *command set*. However, you can create as many custom command sets as you need.

When you create a custom shortcut for the first time, Final Cut requires that you duplicate the default command set. (You can't modify the default set that Apple ships.) Once the command set is duplicated, you can add and revise as many shortcuts as you want.

Click the menu in the top-left corner of the Command Editor (see **FIGURE 1.23**) to create new sets (using Duplicate), import or export sets to share between computers or editors, or delete a command set you no longer need.

51 Create Custom Keyboard Shortcuts

Final Cut has hundreds of shortcuts not assigned to keys.

Final Cut ships with more than 650 shortcuts. (Um, no, I didn't count them. That's what I was told. There's a lot.) However, not all shortcuts are assigned to keys. For example, there's no key assigned to "Close Library," even though that shortcut exists.

FIGURE 1.23 The Command Set menu in the Command Editor.

- To create your own custom keyboard shortcuts, choose Final Cut Pro > Commands > Customize. This opens the Command Editor; see **FIGURE 1.24**. Keys with colors indicate keyboard shortcuts are assigned to that key for the currently selected modifier keys shown at the top. Gray means "available."

- To find an existing shortcut, enter a search term in the top-right Search box.

- To see the shortcuts assigned to a key, select the key and look in the lower-right Key Detail list.

FIGURE 1.24 The Command Editor, where keyboard shortcuts are created.

Create a custom command set to personalize Final Cut. You can even assign multiple key combinations to the same shortcut.

Shortcuts with no key assigned in the Command List (lower center) are available for you to add your own key combination. To connect a key combination with a shortcut:

1. Duplicate the default command set. Apple doesn't allow changes to the default command set. (You need to do this only once.)

2. Search for the shortcut to which you want to add a key, or scroll through the Command list.

3. Click any modifier buttons along the top (blue keys are enabled) to include that modifier with the shortcut.

4. Drag the name of the command on top of the key to which you want to assign it, then let go of the mouse button.

    Or—Select the key you want to assign the command to, then drag the name of the command to a blank line in the Key Detail panel on the right.

Repeat this process if you want to assign more than one key combination to the same shortcut.

To delete a custom shortcut:

1. Click the key to which it is assigned.

2. Locate the shortcut in the Key Detail panel in the lower right.

3. Drag the shortcut you want to remove from the list.

    To see all the shortcuts assigned to a key, select the key, then look in the Key Detail panel in the lower right of the interface. There is no limit to the number of command sets you can create.

4. When you are finished, click Save to record your changes.

NOTE While you can have multiple keys assigned to the same shortcut, you can't have the same key assigned to multiple shortcuts. If you get a message saying a key is assigned elsewhere, if you accept the change, the key will be removed from the older shortcut and assigned to the new one.

GOING FURTHER To switch between command sets, either use the menu in the top-left corner of the Command Editor or choose Final Cut Pro > Commands.

52 A Fast Way to Switch Shortcuts

Final Cut makes it easy to switch between command sets.

You use the Command Editor to create or modify keyboard shortcuts. However, while you can use the menu in the top-left corner of the Command Editor to switch command sets, it isn't necessary to go that deep.

Instead, go to Final Cut Pro > Commands and select the command set you want from the options there; see **FIGURE 1.25**. It's faster.

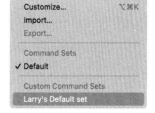

FIGURE 1.25 Switch between command sets using Final Cut Pro > Commands.

53 Find a New Favorite Shortcut

Shortcuts are hidden throughout macOS.

Apple created hundreds of keyboard shortcuts in macOS, then promptly buried them so deeply you'll never find them—unless, that is, you know the secret code...the link to this web page:

support.apple.com/HT201236

CHAPTER 1—VIDEO FUNDAMENTALS SHORTCUTS

CATEGORY	SHORTCUT	WHAT IT DOES
Operating System	Cmd+Tab	Switch between open apps
	Shift+Cmd+A	Open the Application Folder
	Shift+Cmd+U	Open the Utilities Folder
	Shift+Cmd+H	Open the Home directory
	Shift+Cmd+I	Open iCloud Drive
	Cmd+K	Display the Connect to Server window
	Shift+Cmd+K	Display the network volumes in the Finder
Computer Control	Cmd+Delete	Move the selected item to Trash
	Shift+Cmd+Delete	Empty the trash
	Shift+Control+Eject/Power	Turn off the display
	Control+Cmd+Q	Instantly lock the screen
	Control+Eject/Power	Display the Sleep dialog
	Option+Cmd+Eject/Power	Instantly put computer to sleep
	Control+Cmd+Eject/Power	Instantly restart
Finder Operations	Spacebar	Display contents of selected file
	Cmd+spacebar	Open/Close Spotlight
	Control+Cmd+spacebar	Display emoji character viewer
	Fn [on laptops]	Display emoji character viewer
	Cmd+double-click	Open folder in separate window
	Control+Cmd+O	Enable/Disable Stacks
	Shift+Cmd+D	Toggle the Dock open or closed

 ## CHAPTER WRAP

This chapter took us deep into computers, storage, and media. Optimizing hardware and planning your next project may seem a slow way to start, especially when what you really want to do is edit. But I assure you, the time you spend getting your gear ready and planning the edit pays dividends in a smoothly running system with far less stress during the edit itself.

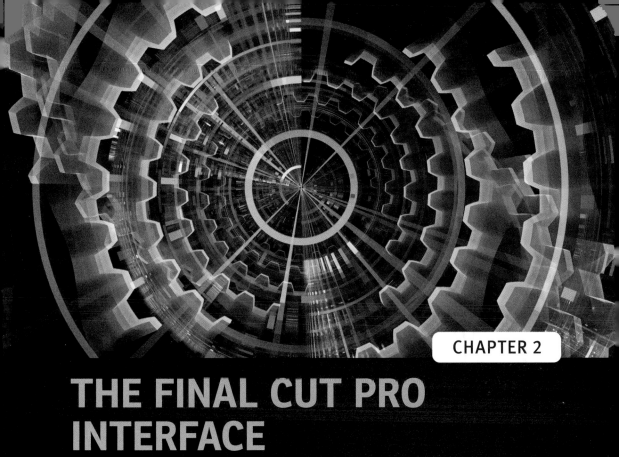

CHAPTER 2

THE FINAL CUT PRO INTERFACE

INTRODUCTION

This chapter introduces the Final Cut Pro interface and explains its general operation. Chapters are divided into sections that group similar tips together. Near the end is a section on troubleshooting, in the event bad things happen. (All screen shots are from Final Cut Pro 10.6.3.)

- The Interface
- Optimize Preferences
- The Browser
- The Timeline
- The Viewer
- Hidden Views
- Troubleshooting
- Shortcuts

54 Download the Final Cut Pro User Guide

Help files exist as online files and as a download.

The complete Final Cut Pro User Guide is available online or as a download.

Download the complete Final Cut Pro User Guide to your computer. This reference can be viewed, searched, and annotated. As well, all links referenced in it are clickable.

The downloaded book file is stored in Applications > Books. The PDF can be stored wherever you want. Apple updates it with every new version. To get your free copy:

1. Open Final Cut.

2. Choose Help > Final Cut Pro Help.

3. At the bottom of the Help page, click a link to download a PDF version or a version for Apple Books.

NOTE I prefer the PDF version because it is easy to search and annotate, and it can be stored anywhere.

THE FINAL CUT PRO INTERFACE

This section explains how to use what you see on the screen.

Get to Know the Interface

The main areas of the Final Cut Pro user interface, shown in **FIGURE 2.1**, include:

- **Library List** (shortcut: Cmd+`). Located in the top-left corner, this sidebar displays all open libraries and associated events.

- **Browser** (shortcut: Cmd+1 to select). Located next to the Library List, this displays all currently open media. Press Control+Cmd+1 to show/hide this.

- **Timeline** (shortcut: Cmd+2 to select). Located at the bottom of the interface, this displays the clips you are editing into a project.

- **Viewer** (shortcut: Cmd+3 to select). Located in the upper center of the interface this displays whatever clip is active in the Browser or Timeline.

- **Inspector** (shortcut: Cmd+4). This panel is where you make changes to whatever is selected; just about everything in Final Cut can be selected.

- **Effects browser** (shortcut: Cmd+5). This contains audio and video effects that can be applied to clips in the timeline. However, many effects are located outside of the Effects browser.

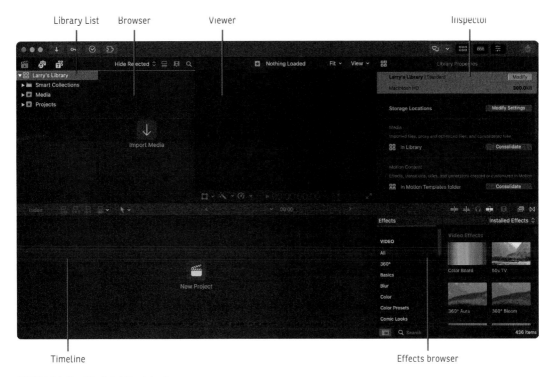

Library List   Browser   Viewer   Inspector

Timeline   Effects browser

FIGURE 2.1 The Final Cut Pro interface.

- **Playhead.** Visible only in a clip or timeline, this vertical line moves during playback. By definition, this displays exactly one frame—the frame under the vertical line.
- **Skimmer** (shortcut: S). Visible only in a clip or timeline, this is a high-speed way to review clips. This is useful to review clips in the Browser, Media Import window, or timeline.

When the skimmer is active, the playhead is ignored. To use the playhead, turn the skimmer off (S).

GOING FURTHER The Inspector has ten variations, depending upon which element is selected. Each variation has its own icon; see Tip 64, *There Is One Inspector—with Multiple Faces*.

55 Modify the Final Cut Interface

The interface is designed for a single screen but can be modified.

The Final Cut interface is fully assembled, meaning that although you can't separate interface elements, like the Browser, you can make small changes such as sizing panels or the entire screen.

As the arrows in **FIGURE 2.2** illustrate, drag a vertical or horizontal edge to resize a panel. Most panels can be resized.

You can enable or disable portions of the interface by clicking a button; see **FIGURE 2.3**. For example, click one of the three icons in the top-left corner to:

- Toggle the Library List (red arrow) open or closed.
- Toggle the Photos, Music, Apple TV, or Sound Effects browsers.
- Toggle the Titles or Generator browser.

FIGURE 2.3 These three horizontal buttons toggle different browsers. Blue indicates the active browser.

FIGURE 2.2 Resize a panel by dragging a horizontal or vertical edge.

The buttons in the top right of the interface allow you to select which portions of the interface to display, as shown by the labels in **FIGURE 2.4**:

1 Display the selected interface on a second connected computer monitor (see Tip 60, *Expand the Interface with Two Computer Monitors*). This icon is hidden if a second monitor is not connected.

2 Toggle the Browser open or closed (shortcut: Control+Cmd+1).

3 Toggle the timeline open or closed (shortcut: Control+Cmd+2).

4 Toggle the Inspector open or closed (shortcut: Cmd+4).

5 Share (export) a project (shortcut: Cmd+E).

GOING FURTHER
If you are connecting a video monitor via an A/V connection to display full-screen video, the second computer monitor button is ignored.

FIGURE 2.4 These buttons reveal or hide different interface elements. The menu determines what's displayed on a second monitor.

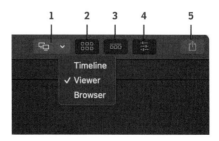

56 Workspaces—Hidden Enablers of Productivity

Use the workspaces Apple built or create your own.

Apple ships with four prebuilt interfaces (called *workspaces*) that are optimized for specific tasks. You can find them in Window > Workspaces. Although you can create these workspaces yourself (see Tip 55, *Modify the Final Cut Interface*), using the Workspace menu (or its keyboard shortcut) gets you there faster.

- **Default** (shortcut: Cmd+0). This is the standard Final Cut Pro interface that you see when you open the application.
- **Organize** (shortcut: Control+Shift+1). This turns off the timeline and enlarges both the Browser and Inspector. It is optimized for organizing media and adding metadata and keywords.
- **Color & Effects** (shortcut: Control+Shift+2). This turns off the Browser and opens the video scopes, Inspector, and Effects browser (**FIGURE 2.5**).
- **Dual Displays** (shortcut: Control+Shift+3). This assumes a second computer monitor is attached to your computer displaying whatever interface element is selected in the Dual Monitor menu (see Tip 60, *Expand the Interface with Two Computer Monitors*).

FIGURE 2.5 The Color & Effects workspace showing, clockwise from top left: video scopes, Viewer, Inspector with color wheels, Effects browser, and timeline.

57 What Can You Put in a Workspace?

Quite a lot, actually, and much of it is turned off by default.

Final Cut supports multiple displays with a somewhat customizable interface.

Final Cut supports multiple displays: the main computer monitor, a second computer monitor, and a dedicated video monitor. All are somewhat customizable; see **FIGURE 2.6.** We will cover these options in separate tips.

FIGURE 2.6 Display options in Window > Show in Workspace (left) and Window > Show in Secondary Display (right).

> **GOING FURTHER** For the record, while I edit using two monitors, I tend to run Final Cut on one large monitor with other apps open in the second.

58 Create Your Own Custom Workspace

FCP supports an unlimited number of custom workspaces.

Once you've dragged, pushed, hidden, or displayed interface elements to attain interface nirvana, it's time to save it as a custom workspace.

1. Choose Window > Workspaces > Save Workspace; see **FIGURE 2.7.**
2. Give the file a name and click Save.

FIGURE 2.7 The Save Custom Workspace dialog.

Your new custom workspace shows up at the top of the Workspace list. Although there's no technical limit to the number of custom workspaces, practically it doesn't make sense to wade through dozens of them.

> **GOING FURTHER** Not all interface elements appear in a workspace. Only those listed in the Show in Workspace menu, along with the two floating timecode windows, will be saved and displayed the next time you open a custom workspace.

59 Create a Custom Workspace Keyboard Shortcut

This also can create shortcuts for any application.

FCP doesn't provide keyboard shortcuts for user-modified/saved workspaces. However, you can create them in System Preferences > Keyboard > Shortcuts; see **FIGURE** 2.8.

1. Open System Preferences > Keyboard (top red arrow).
2. Click Shortcuts (middle red arrow).
3. Click App Shortcuts (bottom red arrow).
4. Click the plus icon.
5. In the dialog, choose Final Cut Pro from the Application menu.
6. Enter the menu name precisely as it appears in the menu, dots and all.
7. Enter the key combination you want to use as a shortcut in the Keyboard Shortcut field.
8. Click Add to close the dialog; then quit System Preferences.

Create custom shortcuts for any app using System Preferences > Keyboard > Shortcuts.

Every app I use on a daily basis uses at least one of these custom shortcuts. They are invaluable.

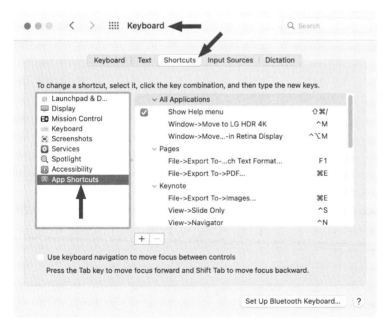

FIGURE 2.8 Create custom keyboard shortcuts in System Preferences > Keyboard > Shortcuts.

60 Expand the Interface with Two Computer Monitors

This menu controls what's shown on a second monitor.

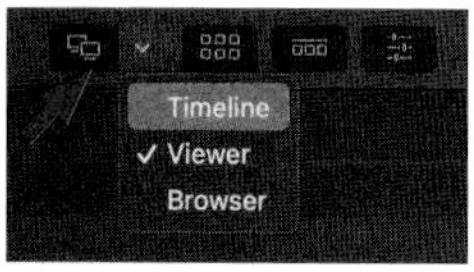

FIGURE 2.9 This icon enables a second computer monitor and what it will display.

Final Cut supports spreading its interface across two computer monitors. When you connect a second monitor, the icon shown in **FIGURE 2.9** appears (red arrow).

1. Click the white chevron next to the two-monitor icon to choose what to display on the second monitor:
   - Timeline (with video scopes)
   - Viewer (full screen with playback controls)
   - Browser (with Library List)

2. Click the two-monitor icon (red arrow) to switch Final Cut from using a single to dual display. Click this icon again to turn off the second display. It turns blue when a second monitor is active.

61 Play Video on a Calibrated Video Monitor

Final Cut supports video playback to a separate monitor.

NOTE There's a difference between a computer monitor and a video monitor. Final Cut supports both.

There are computer monitors and video monitors. Video monitors are optimized and calibrated for video playback and generally connected via HDMI or SDI. Calibrated video monitors are strongly encouraged for color-critical SDR and HDR editing.

If you connect a video monitor, Final Cut can play the timeline directly to it full screen. This includes the Apple Pro Display XDR. Playing the Viewer to a computer monitor does not provide the same color accuracy; see Tip 60, *Expand the Interface with Two Computer Monitors*.

GOING FURTHER
You can also use this video output to feed external test equipment, such as quality control (QC) measurement gear.

1. Connect the device, then choose it from the menu at the bottom of Final Cut Pro > Preferences > Playback; see Figure 2.21.

2. Choose Window > AV Output and make sure the correct device is checked.

62 The Background Tasks Window

Here's how to control Final Cut's background activity.

One of the reasons Final Cut Pro is so fast is that it pushes a lot of its work to the background. This means while you concentrate on playing and editing clips, FCP waits. Then, when you pause to think, FCP jumps into action. "In the background" means that the computer is working behind the scenes without disturbing what you are doing. If the computer is busy in the foreground, background activity stops. This allows the full resources of the computer to concentrate on you.

Watch and control this activity using the Background Tasks window. Using this isn't required, but it's there if you are curious. To open this window, click the icon indicated by the red arrow in **FIGURE 2.10** or press Cmd+9.

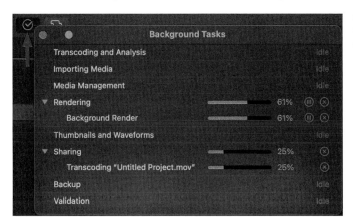

FIGURE 2.10 The Background Tasks window.

Running tasks display a small triangle to the left of the process name.

- To see more details, click the triangle next to the name.
- To pause a task, click the Pause (two parallel lines) button on the right.
- To cancel a task, click the "x" in a circle, also on the right.

63 Interface Icon Colors Are Significant

Blue means active.

Final Cut uses a variety of interface colors to indicate status; see **FIGURE 2.11**.

- **Blue** means something is active.
- **Gray** means it is inactive.
- **White** means the text is for information or labeling.
- **Yellow** means a clip, or clip range, is selected or that the Range tool is active.

FIGURE 2.11 Blue icons indicate active elements; gray are inactive and white are labels.

64 There Is One Inspector—with Multiple Faces

The icon and contents of the Inspector change based on selection.

To open or close the Inspector panel, press Cmd+4.

The Inspector is where you make changes—to just about everything. There's exactly one Inspector, located in the top right of the interface. However, the Inspector assumes a different name, icon, and function depending upon what is selected. For example, the Video Inspector is active when a video clip is selected. The Inspector can take ten different forms; see **FIGURE 2.12**.

FIGURE 2.12 A Photoshop composite of the ten Inspector icons: (left to right) Library, Generator, Transition, Text Animation, Text Formatting, Video, Color, Audio, Info, and Share Metadata. The Library and Transition Inspectors are shown as active (blue). In real life, only one Inspector icon is active (blue) at a time.

The active Inspector displays a blue icon at the top of the Inspector. Switch between different Inspectors by clicking its icon.

65 Change the Height of the Inspector

Double-click the Inspector title bar to change its height.

Here are three tips to change the Inspector display:

- To open or close the Inspector, click the Inspector icon (top red arrow in **FIGURE 2.13**), or press Cmd+4.

- To enlarge the Inspector so it fills the screen vertically, double-click the title bar (middle red arrow). Double-click again to shrink it back to half-height (shortcut: Control+Cmd+4).

- To hide or reveal a parameter group, move the cursor to the right of the group name. Click Show to show details for that parameter, and click Hide to hide them (lower red arrow).

FIGURE 2.13 Double-click the title bar to enlarge/shrink the Inspector. Click Hide or Show to reveal individual parameter groups.

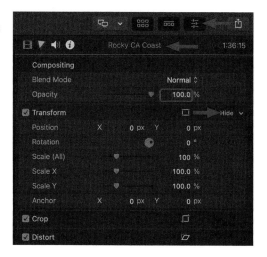

66 A Shortcut to Sharing

This shortcut speeds exports.

Apple calls exporting *sharing*. This is true, I guess, but it strikes me as unnecessarily cute. The most obvious way to export a project is to use File > Share. But a faster way is to use the Share icon; see **FIGURE 2.14**.

The Share icon lists current export destinations. Change these using Final Cut Pro > Preferences > Destinations; see Tip 75, *Optimize Destination Preferences*.

1. Open the project you want to share into the timeline.
2. Make sure the timeline is active.
3. Choose your export option from this menu.

For details on how to configure this menu, see Tip 483, *The Share Icon*.

FIGURE 2.14 The Share icon lists current destination options.

67 The Hidden Extensions Icon

This icon appears only when you install at least one extension.

A hidden feature in Final Cut Pro is workflow extensions. These are software tools from third-party developers that connect into and extend the features of Final Cut Pro. You are using a third-party app *inside* FCP. Workflow extensions are available from:

- ADD (Audio Design Desk)
- APM Music
- CatDV
- EVO ShareBrowser
- Frame.io
- KeyFlow Pro
- Primestream

- Postlab Merge
- Ripple Training
- Shutterstock
- Simon Says
- Universal Production Music
- FontAudition-X

FIGURE 2.15 The Workflow Extension icon and installed extensions menu.

Once you install at least one extension, you'll see the icon in the top-left corner of the FCP interface (shown by the red arrow in **FIGURE 2.15**). If you install more than one, you'll also see the menu.

GOING FURTHER Apple's website lists all third-party tools that work with Final Cut Pro: apple.com/final-cut-pro/resources/ecosystem/.

OPTIMIZE PREFERENCES

Preferences customize Final Cut Pro to the way you want to work.

68 Optimize General Preference Settings

Not all preferences are created equal. Here are some to change.

To display preference settings, choose Final Cut Pro > Preferences. There are five preference panels. Over the next several tips, I'll show you how I optimize mine. When it comes to the General preferences panel, see **FIGURE 2.16**; there are two settings to consider:

- **Dialog Warnings**. When FCP displays a warning, there's often a button that says "Don't show this again." If you click one of these by mistake, click Reset All to reset the warnings.
- **Color Correction**. This defaults to the Color Board. I will confess, it took me about six years to make my peace with the Color Board. I can now use it successfully, but I prefer to use the Color Wheels. Changing this setting means that whenever you create a new color correction, Final Cut defaults to whatever you select.

Change any of these preferences at any time; however, changing a preference setting does not affect any existing media or projects.

FIGURE 2.16 The General preferences panel.

69 A Quick Note on Measurements

Final Cut offers two different measurement systems.

At the bottom of the General preferences window (**FIGURE 2.17**) is Inspector Units with two measurement options: Pixels and Percentages.

When Percentages is chosen (see the red arrow in **FIGURE 2.18**), some settings are expressed as a percentage. Although percentages are helpful, I prefer pixels.

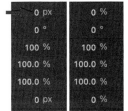

FIGURE 2.18 Note the difference in the top line when the Units preference setting is changed.

FIGURE 2.17 The General preferences window showing the two measurement options.

70 Optimize Editing Preferences

I recommend changing three of these settings.

The next preferences panel is Editing; see **FIGURE 2.19**. Most of these settings are fine, though you should be aware of what they do.

- **Show detailed trimming feedback**. This displays the Trim Edit window when trimming clips; see Tip 227, *The Trim Edit Window*. I recommend you select this.

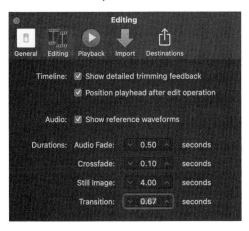

FIGURE 2.19 The Editing preferences panel.

- **Position playhead after edit operation**. When selected and you edit a clip to the timeline, the playhead jumps to the end of the newly edited clip. If unselected, the playhead remains in its current position. I recommend you select this.

- **Show reference waveforms**; see FIGURE 2.20. This is handy when editing audio clips with low levels. When selected, Final Cut displays ghost images of audio waveforms in the timeline as though that audio were at full level. These "ghosts" help you make more accurate audio edits. This is a display-only function; nothing about the audio is changed. If audio editing is new to you, select this.

FIGURE 2.20 Look carefully and you'll see ghosted waveforms that show what the levels would look like at full volume.

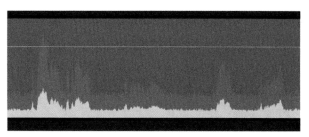

- **Durations** timing. The default transition can be applied using keyboard shortcuts. These settings determine duration defaults. Changing these settings does not change any transitions already applied to timeline clips. Still Image sets the default import duration of stills, Photoshop files, and still frames. The only duration I suggest you change is Transition. I find the default duration of one second is too long. So I shorten it to 0.67.

GOING FURTHER Reference waveforms don't appear in clips when there is at least one spike of audio near 0 dB. They appear only if the audio of the entire clip is universally low.

71 Optimize Playback Preferences

These defaults are fine—with one change.

The Playback preferences panel, as shown in FIGURE 2.21, has excellent defaults, except I recommend selecting all the options, including *If a frame drops, stop playback and warn*. Dropped frames are always serious. It is important to know what caused them, then fix it before things get worse.

Rendering means Final Cut is calculating new media. It stops automatically whenever you play, edit, or trim a clip. Most of the time, the default render settings are fine. However, if you have an older system and rendering interferes with your work, change *Start After* to 5 seconds. If that doesn't help, unselect Background render and render a project as necessary from the Modify menu.

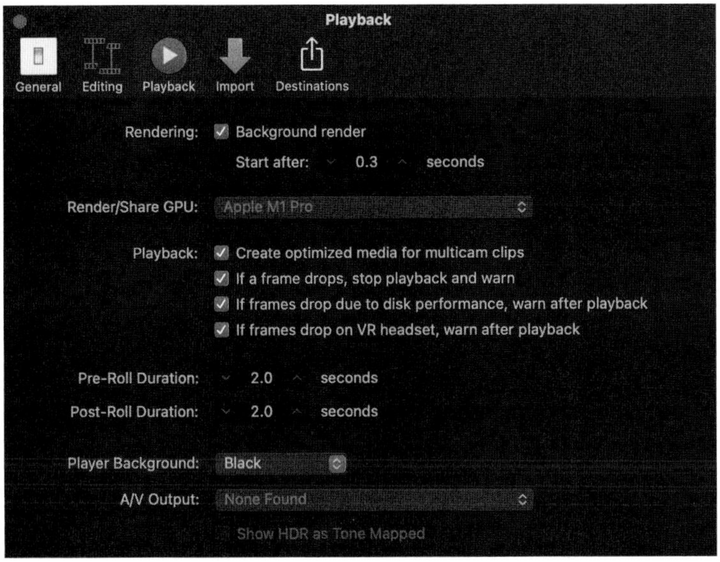

FIGURE 2.21 The Playback preferences panel.

GOING FURTHER The black background of the Viewer can be changed to white or checkerboard. I change this to checkerboard, for example, when working with multiple images and want to see what's transparent versus solid. All backgrounds export as black, unless the export format allows transparency (such as ProRes 4444, ProRes 4444 HQ, PNG, or TIFF), in which case the background will be transparent.

72 What Do Dropped Frame Errors Mean?

Dropped frame warnings are never good.

A dropped frame warning in Final Cut means that, for some reason, one or more frames of media were not able to play successfully in real time. Dropped frame warnings should never be ignored or turned off, as they can impact the quality of the final, exported project.

There are five main causes of dropped frames:

- A stock footage clip has problems (this is the most typical).
- The storage system is too slow to play the media you are editing, for example, if you are playing ProRes 422 files off a USB-A thumb drive.
- The CPU is not fast enough to play the media you are editing, for example, editing H.264 media on an older computer system.
- The effects applied to a clip are too complex to play without rendering.
- A multicam clip is too large or complex to play in real time.

Dropped frame warnings should never be ignored or turned off.

The solutions are fairly simple:

- Convert the stock footage clip to ProRes 422 or replace it.
- Move your media to faster storage.
- Optimize the camera source media to the default format of ProRes 422.
- Render effects before playing them (Modify > Render All).
- Use proxies, rather than camera source, for editing multicam clips.

In all cases, never ignore dropped frame errors.

73 Use a High-Quality Audio Monitor

Macs include good speakers. Monitor speakers are better.

Just as you can connect an external high-quality video monitor to precisely display your video, you can also connect high-quality audio monitor speakers. Currently, I'm using a pair of Yamaha HS5 monitor speakers connected to a Focusrite Scarlet 2i2, which then connects to my computer via USB-A. The sound is stunning.

To enable this, select System Preferences > Sound, as shown in **FIGURE 2.22**, and check the audio interface you are using for your system. Final Cut uses the system audio settings for recording and playback.

FIGURE 2.22 System Preferences > Sound, with the Scarlet 2i2 audio interface selected for output.

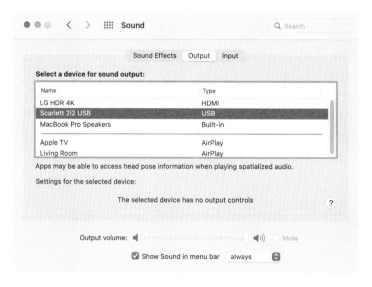

74 Optimize Import Preferences

The default settings will get in your way.

The Import preferences panel, as shown in **FIGURE 2.23**, determines how the media you import using the Media Import window, *and* media that you drag into FCP, are handled.

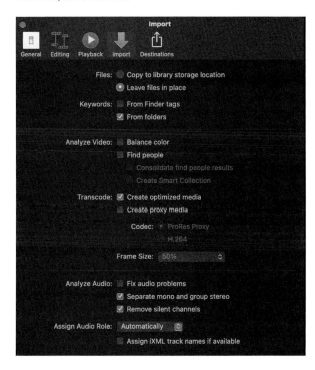

FIGURE 2.23 The Import preferences panel. This is discussed more fully in Chapter 3.

Import preferences also change whenever you change settings in the Media Import window.

I'll explain these in more detail in Chapter 3, "Libraries & Media," but I want to include them here with the rest of Final Cut's preferences. Figure 2.23 shows the settings I use.

GOING FURTHER
I find that automatically balancing color on import is not worth the time. Better color tools are available once you edit clips into the timeline. Find People takes a long time, generates large analysis files, and isn't that useful. AI still can't beat logging your clips.

75 Optimize Destination Preferences

Every editor's needs are different, but I prefer simplicity.

The Destination preferences window, as shown in **FIGURE 2.24**, determines the default options when you choose File > Share. Every editor is different, and I'm grateful that Apple provided a wide range of options here. However, all my projects are exported as a high-quality ProRes 422 or 4444 file, suitable for any conceivable need, as well as archiving.

Then, from that exported project file, I create as many compressed versions as are necessary—though I use other software for that. There's no sense tying up Final Cut—even though exporting happens in the background—for a task that can be batch processed and better controlled using other software tools.

- To set a destination as default (shortcut: Cmd+E), right-click and choose Make Default from the menu.

- To add a destination, drag it from the right pane to the left.

- To adjust the default settings for a destination, select the destination on the left, then adjust them on the right. These settings become the defaults the next time you choose that destination.

- To remove a destination, right-click the icon and choose Delete from the menu.

- The stacking order in the left panel determines the display order in File > Share and the Share icon in the interface. To change the stacking order, drag titles up or down.

GOING FURTHER
Once a default destination is set, send a project to it by pressing Cmd+E.

THE BROWSER

The Browser is where you organize and review project elements before and during editing. It can be displayed in the main interface or on a separate computer monitor.

76 The Browser Settings Menu

This menu controls the display and operation of the Browser.

The Browser is where you view all the elements you can access for editing. Its display is controlled by the Browser settings menu in the top-right corner; see **FIGURE 2.25**:

- The top slider adjusts the size of thumbnails in the Browser.
- The second slider adjusts whether you see a single thumbnail (All) or a film strip with thumbnails at time increments set by this slider.
- Grouping and sorting are different ways of organizing clips in the Browser.
- Waveforms displays or hides audio waveforms for clips with audio in the Browser. They are off by default.

Continuous Playback is a time-saving feature, but it's off by default.

FIGURE 2.25 The Browser settings icon (red arrow) and the pane itself.

That brings us to the Continuous Playback option. When this is selected, when you play a clip in the Browser and the playhead reaches the end of the clip, it automatically starts playing the next clip. This continuous playback occurs whether you are playing at normal speed or fast-forward (see Tip 192: *Playback Shortcuts*).

Continuous playback is a great way to review and log a series of clips without touching the keyboard or mouse.

NOTE View > Playback > Loop Playback must be turned off for continuous playback to work.

77 Eight Ways to Sort Browser Clips

By default, clips are sorted by the date they were created.

Final Cut seems to obsess about when clips were created. It's the default sort option in the Browser, as if everything we shoot is in chronological order.

NOTE Sort By can be changed only in Filmstrip mode, not List mode. In List mode, click a column heading to sort by it; click again to reverse the sort order.

If this drives you as crazy as it does me, click the small Browser settings menu icon at the top of the interface, as shown in **FIGURE 2.26**, and choose a sorting option that works better for you. I use file names. They can be sorted in ascending or descending order.

FIGURE 2.26 Click the Browser settings menu icon, then choose from the Sort By menu (left) or Group By menu (right).

78 Group Clips in the Browser

Don't like sorting? Try grouping!

Instead of sorting the clips within the Browser, you may want to group clips based on similar characteristics. Again, the Browser settings menu comes to the rescue. Click the small icon indicated by the red arrow in Figure 2.26 to display the Browser settings menu. There are nine different ways to group and display clips in the Browser.

GOING FURTHER
Don't get confused by the label. You can put any data in these user-defined fields (Reel, Scene, Camera Name, and Angle), then sort them.

These four fields use data supplied by you:

- Reel
- Scene
- Camera name
- Camera angle

These are simple text fields. Enter any data that helps you sort clips; the data doesn't actually need to relate to the field name.

79 Display Audio Waveforms in the Browser

Audio waveforms display the volume of the audio in a clip.

Enabling audio waveforms in the Browser, as shown in **FIGURE 2.27**, makes it easy to quickly set an In or Out by looking at the waveform without playing the clip over and over (see Tip 194, *Marking a Clip Sets the In and Out*). However, this display setting is off by default in the Browser to avoid cluttering the Browser.

Waveforms are displayed, as shown in **FIGURE 2.28**, under all Browser clips that contain audio. If you edit music, the waveform also makes it easy to see the beats.

FIGURE 2.28 The audio waveform displayed in a clip.

FIGURE 2.27 In the Browser settings menu (top arrow) select Waveforms to display audio waveforms for clips in the Browser.

GOING FURTHER
Reference waveforms, if enabled in Preferences > Editing, don't appear in Browser clips.

80 The Hidden Meaning of Clip Color Lines

Browser clip colors highlight clip status.

Ever wonder what those color bars displayed in Browser clips mean? **FIGURE 2.29** illustrates:

- **Blue**. A clip with at least one keyword applied.
- **Red**. A rejected clip.
- **Orange:** A clip used in the currently active project in the timeline.
- **Yellow box**: A clip marked with an In and Out.
- **Green**: A favorite clip.
- **Purple**. A clip that has analysis keyframes applied.

GOING FURTHER
To see rejected clips, change the menu at the top of the Browser (red arrow in Figure 2.29) from Hide Rejected Clips to All Clips.

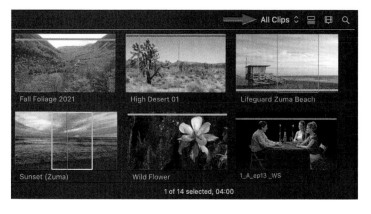

FIGURE 2.29 The different color bars in the Browser, which can also apply to regions within a clip, indicate a clip's status.

81 Turn Off Those Color Lines in the Browser

Here's how to hide those red, green, blue, and orange lines.

If the horizontal color lines in the Browser are bothering you, as shown in Figure 2.29, turn most of them off using View > Browser > Marked Ranges. (Unselecting turns them off.) The orange Used Clip indicator is disabled/enabled using View > Browser > Used Media Ranges.

82 Deleted Browser Clips Are Not Actually Deleted

They are simply hidden.

Press Delete to hide a clip. Press Cmd+Delete to actually delete it from the library, but not from your hard disk.

When you select a clip in the Browser and press the Delete key, the clip disappears from the Browser. Except...it isn't actually deleted. It's hidden. As Figure 2.29 illustrates, when you delete a clip, it's flagged as "Rejected." Normally, it also disappears.

However, when you change the Browser settings menu to All Clips, those rejected clips now appear with a red bar at the top. If you want to resurrect the clip, select it and press U. That "un-rejects" it.

To actually delete a clip, select it and press Cmd+Delete. That removes it from Final Cut but *not* from your hard disk.

83 Browser Badges—Explained

These badges indicate special kinds of clips.

When you add, import, or drag a clip into the Browser, most of the time it just sits there. But sometimes, a small badge appears, most of the time in the top-left corner. **FIGURE 2.30** shows what those badges mean.

FIGURE 2.30 1. No badge, selected range; 2. Compound clip; 3. Audition clip; 4. Compound clip; 5. Multicam clip; 6. High-frame rate clip; 7. Synced clip; and 8. Clip still stored on camera.

84 Even Browser Clip Edges Share Secrets

Look more closely at the edges of clips in the Browser.

If your clips are longer than a few seconds, slide the second slider in the Browser settings menu, as shown in Figure 2.30, to the right to increase the number of thumbnails shown per clip. Then, if you look closely at clips in the Browser, you'll notice something different about the edges; see **FIGURE 2.31**.

- A torn edge on the right of a thumbnail in the Browser indicates a Browser clip that continues to the line below.

- A torn edge on the left of a thumbnail in the Browser indicates a Browser clip that continues from the line above.

- A clean edge of a thumbnail in the Browser indicates the start or end of a Browser clip.

FIGURE 2.31 From top to bottom: a clip continued on the next line, a clip continued from the line above, and the end of a clip.

85 The Skimmer: A Tool I Love to Hate

The skimmer is useless — except when I really, really need it.

I have this love/hate relationship with the skimmer. I love using it in the Browser and Media Import window. It makes reviewing clips fast and easy. But when I move the skimmer down to the timeline, it makes editing almost impossible. It jumps all over, and I end up putting clips or cuts in the wrong place.

Toggle the skimmer on or off by pressing S. This shortcut is great, because I turn it on in the Browser and turn it off in the timeline.

But there's another secret that's really useful: Skimmer Info, illustrated in **FIGURE 2.32**. To turn it on, press Control+Y. When enabled, this displays the name of the currently skimmed clip in the Browser, along with the timecode location of the playhead or skimmer, whichever is active. This is useful for logging or when a client sends a paper edit with timecode locations written on it.

FIGURE 2.32 Skimmer info, the info bubble above the clip, includes the file name and the timecode of the position of the skimmer or playhead. It is visible only in the Browser.

This display is a great way to make sure you are setting Browser clip Ins and Outs in the right place.

Press S to toggle the skimmer on or off.

GOING FURTHER Scott Newell, an editor who reviewed an early version of the book, says, "Not sure why you hate the skimmer in the timeline. I use it in the timeline as well as the Browser with no problems whatsoever. I love it. I also use a trackball and trackpad for navigating (I much prefer it to a mouse); it makes a huge difference in editing. Huge."

86 Top-Secret Hidden Browser Clip Menu

Create new projects faster.

Right-click any clip in the Browser to reveal this hidden clip menu; see **FIGURE 2.33**. Each of these options also appears in the menu bar at the top of the application.

FIGURE 2.33 Right-click any Browser clip to reveal this contextual menu filled with common media management options.

NOTE OK, all this menu is, really, is another contextual menu. But isn't it much more exciting to think of this as a special, top-secret, hidden menu that only you and I know about? Of course it is.

However, there's one big benefit to using New Project from this menu. If you create a new project using this option, Final Cut creates a new project that matches the specs of the selected clip, opens that project, and edits that clip into the project as the first clip.

This is a fast way to create a project with the specs you need without knowing the details about those specs in the first place.

87 A Hidden Project Menu

Manage projects faster from inside the Browser.

Right-click a project in the Browser, and you'll see the menu shown in **FIGURE 2.34**.

- **Play.** Opens a project into the timeline and plays it.
- **Open Project**. Opens a project into the timeline, but doesn't play it. This is the same as double-clicking the project icon in the Browser.
- **Share Project**. This is a fast way to export the project to one of your current destinations.
- **Move to Trash**. Removes the project from the library. I tend to use the keyboard shortcut: Cmd+Delete.

Tip 142, *Don't Duplicate a Project—Create a Snapshot*, describes why snapshots are the best option for backing up a project. Avoid using Duplicate.

FIGURE 2.34 Right-click a project name or icon in the Browser to reveal this menu. Avoid using both versions of Duplicate Project.

88 View Clip Labels (Metadata) in Browser

A wealth of information is only one click away.

Normally, you view clips in the Browser using thumbnails. However, if you click the icon indicated by the top red arrow in **FIGURE 2.35**, the display switches to list view.

- Each column can be sorted by clicking the column header to select it. Click the header again to reverse the sort order.
- Change column widths, similar to Microsoft Excel or Numbers, by dragging the small vertical dividers in the column headers.
- Change the position of columns by dragging the column header to a new position.

FIGURE 2.35 The Browser metadata list.

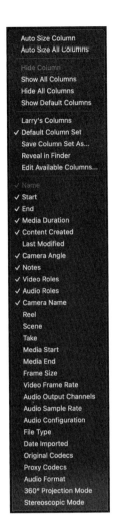

89 Hidden Browser Metadata Fields

Only a small portion of available metadata is displayed.

Although the Browser displays a lot of metadata in list view, it is only a fraction of the data that Final Cut tracks for each clip. To see more options, right-click any column header; see **FIGURE 2.36.**

This reveals almost 30 potential display columns. If an item is selected, it's displayed in the Browser. To change the display, select or unselect the fields you want.

The choices at the top of this menu help you manage the columns. In fact, rearrange the columns as you see fit, then save the arrangement as a custom column set. I use a custom column set when reviewing media prior to editing.

By the way, enabling Last Modified is a great way to find out the last time you changed a project.

NOTE The only disadvantage to all this data is that it is hard to see it in the normal FCP interface. Instead, display the Browser using a second computer monitor (see Tip 60: *Expand the Interface with Two Computer Monitors*.)

GOING FURTHER All the data in these columns and more can be found in the Info Inspector. Fields that are automatically filled by Final Cut, such as Codec, Frame Size, or Frame Rate, can't be changed.

FIGURE 2.36 This lists the different data that can be displayed in Browser list view. (Checked means currently displayed.)

90 Different Ways to View the Browser

All gathered together in one place.

There are lots of ways to configure the Browser so it shows what you need. We've already looked at the Browser settings menu. However, you will also find these options in the View > Browser menu; see **FIGURE 2.37.**

Although some of these options are the same as the Browser settings menu, for example, for grouping and sorting, many are unique to this menu.

FIGURE 2.37 The View > Browser menu.

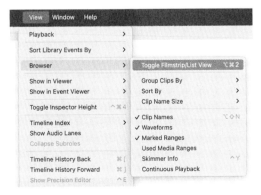

91 The Photos, Music, Apple TV & Audio Sidebars

These sidebars may, or may not, be useful for you.

When FCP was first released, these, um, things were called *browsers*. Along the way they got renamed to *sidebars*. Whatever you call them, you can find them by clicking the middle icon at the top left of the interface; see FIGURE 2.38. (It's the icon in blue.)

- **Photos.** This displays all shared images in the Photos application. However, I find it easier to use Photos for my personal images and to store images for a project in a separate folder.

FIGURE 2.38 The list of browsers in the Photos, Music, Apple TV, and Audio sidebars.

- **Music.** This displays the contents of your Music library, which could then be added to the timeline. The problem is that you almost certainly don't own the rights to the music inside it, which will get you in legal trouble. Sharing a library with another editor does not transfer any files in the Music folder. Worse, you can't archive Music files easily when you archive your library. Instead, store the music you need for your project in a separate folder outside the Music application. This makes accessing, sharing, and backing up the music for your project much easier.

NOTE To clarify: Photos is in a sidebar. The images are displayed in a browser.

NOTE The Music folder also displays any audio projects shared from either GarageBand (use Share > Song to Music) or Logic Pro (use File > Share > Song to Music).

- **Apple TV.** This displays all non-copy-protected files in your Apple TV library. As with Photos, I don't use Apple TV for any media that will be used in Final Cut. I always store media files outside any Apple applications.

The Sound Effects sidebar is very cool, and I'll discuss it in the next tip.

92 The Sound Effects Sidebar

Hundreds of royalty-free sound effects are ready for your project.

The Sound Effects sidebar is *really* cool; see FIGURE 2.39. First, download the extra media from Apple. (See Tip 123, *But Wait...There's More!*) Apple provides these free sound effects for use in any video project, royalty-free.

Once they're installed, click the middle sidebar icon in the top left of the interface, then click Sound Effects. Scroll through the list of files—or search for something using the Search box in the top-right corner of the panel—to find something you like.

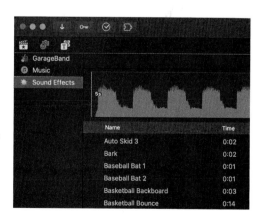

FIGURE 2.39 The Sound Effects browser, with a small sample of its hundreds of sound effects. All are royalty free.

GOING FURTHER
Jerry Thompson, an editor who reviewed an early draft of this book, added, "Here's how to easily add third-party sound effects to this browser. Drag the *folder* containing new sound effects into Macintosh HD > Library > Audio > Apple Loops > Final Cut Pro Sound Effects and they will show up in the Sound Effects browser."

Play or skim the waveform to hear what it sounds like.

If you like it, drag the waveform into the timeline. The clip will be colored green, as are all audio clips, and placed where audio clips are displayed—below the Primary Storyline. This extensive library of effects can, when used in moderation, ahem, improve almost every project.

THE TIMELINE

The timeline is the heart of every edit. It's where you turn a collection of diverse clips into a story.

93 Why Doesn't the Timeline Scroll?

It's one of the great mysteries of life.

Why doesn't the Final Cut timeline scroll? I don't know. It's a mystery. I've asked Apple this exact question—for ten years now—so far with no answer. It's the number-one requested feature for Final Cut.

CommandPost is an essential, and free, utility for Final Cut Pro.

But there's a great workaround: CommandPost (www.commandpost.io). CommandPost is a free and open source native macOS application that acts as a bridge between control surfaces and software that doesn't natively support control surfaces, such as Apple's Final Cut Pro and Adobe After Effects.

As well, CommandPost supports scrolling the timeline, exporting the contents of the Timeline Index, and providing a wide variety of customizable automation tools. I've used it for years.

94 Manage Projects with This Hidden Menu

However, don't use Duplicate Project!

Click the name of your project at the top center of the timeline to reveal five more options for managing a project; see **FIGURE 2.40**. However, I *strongly* recommend you never use the first one, Duplicate Project. (See Tip 142, *Don't Duplicate a Project—Create a Snapshot*.)

FIGURE 2.40 Click the project name to reveal this menu. The only option I recommend you not use is Duplicate Project.

Most of these options are self-evident. However, the two Close options require an explanation. Even though only one project is visible in the timeline, once you open a project from the Browser into the timeline, FCP loads it into memory and doesn't remove it, even if you switch to another project. The benefit is the speed with which FCP can display an open project back into the timeline.

For projects that are small, say less than a few hundred clips, these open projects aren't a problem. But if you are editing several massive projects, closing any projects that you are not editing will free RAM for other uses.

Project files are stored in the Library, and the Library is always saving your changes. So when you close a project, you are simply releasing RAM. The project is not removed from the Library, nor deleted from your storage.

Never duplicate a project; always use project snapshots.

95 Switch Projects Faster Using Timeline History Chevrons

The Timeline History remembers all open projects.

Once you open a project in the timeline, it stays open, even if you open another project into the timeline. (Most of the time, this is a good thing. See Tip 94, *Manage Projects with This Hidden Menu*.) One benefit is that switching between projects—once you know how—is almost instantaneous.

The timeline history chevrons are the secret to the switch; see **FIGURE 2.41.** Think of these as selecting projects on a slider, where the first project you opened is on the left, and the most recent project you opened is on the right. Click the arrows to instantly navigate to an earlier project (left chevron) or a later one (right chevron). Click and hold a chevron to see the open projects in that direction. The two arrows contain different lists, so be sure to check both.

This is easier to use than to explain. I use these—and their keyboard shortcuts—a lot.

FIGURE 2.41 The timeline history arrows indicated, yup, by the red arrows.

GOING FURTHER

- Cmd+[to go back one project in the timeline history.
- Cmd+] to go forward one project in the timeline history.

96 Timeline Control Icons

These icons customize the timeline.

The icons in the top left of the timeline control editing. (Chapter 4, "Basic Editing," covers these in detail.) The icons in the top right, as shown in **FIGURE 2.42**, determine what controls are active in the timeline. The following is a key to the numbers in the figure.

All of these are covered in more detail in other tips.

1 Enables/disables skimming (shortcut: S).

2 Enables/disables audio skimming (shortcut: Shift+S).

3 Solos selected timeline clips (shortcut: Option+S).

4 Enables/disables Snapping (shortcut: N).

5 Opens the Timeline Display control panel.

6 Opens the Effects browser (shortcut: Cmd+5).

7 Opens the Transitions browser (shortcut: Control+Cmd+5).

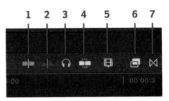

FIGURE 2.42 Timeline icons.

97 Timecode Displays Location

Timecode is the foundation of video editing.

Timecode is a label that uniquely identifies each frame of video in a clip or project.

Timecode is a label that uniquely identifies each frame of video in a clip or project. Although most audio doesn't use timecode, timecode is essential for video. Final Cut uses timecode to determine where each clip starts and ends, how long it runs, and where it fits in the project. Timecode is what makes edits frame-accurate. Without timecode, you could still edit by counting frames, but it wouldn't be as fast or convenient.

Timecode is displayed as four pairs of numbers: HH:MM:SS:FF, which stands for HOURS:MINUTES:SECONDS:FRAMES. Although timecode can represent real time, most often it does not.

FIGURE 2.43 shows the three timecode displays in Final Cut:

- **Playhead (skimmer) location**. Large white numbers (36:23) centered under the Viewer.
- **Project duration**. Smaller white numbers (1:00:00) to the right of the project name.
- **Selected clip or range duration**. Yellow numbers (4:19) that appear only when something is selected in the timeline.

FIGURE 2.43 The three timecode displays in Final Cut.

98 The Timecode Display Holds Secrets

The timecode display can take you places.

The timecode display at the bottom center of the Viewer shows the current location of the playhead (skimmer).

Hidden in the timecode display at the bottom of the Viewer is a powerful navigational tool; see FIGURE 2.44. Normally, the timecode displays white numbers that show the current position of the playhead.

FIGURE 2.44 The three states of the timecode display, from top to bottom: current position, ready for data entry, and the jump location.

However, if you click the white numbers, the timecode field empties and switches to data-entry mode (shortcut: Cmd+D). Enter the timecode location you want to jump to, then press Return. Assuming your project contains media that extends to that location, the playhead will instantly jump there.

99 Two Floating Timecode Windows

These floating timecode windows serve as location maps.

Final Cut has two floating timecode windows: one for the project and the other for source media. You can move these wherever you want. In most cases, I drag them to my second monitor. Grab a corner to resize either of them.

- Choose Window > Project Timecode to open the Project Timecode window; see FIGURE 2.45. This displays the current location of the playhead in the timeline. Right-click the numbers to copy the timecode to the clipboard.

- Choose Window > Source Timecode to open the Source Timecode window; see FIGURE 2.46. This displays the location of all source media in the timeline under the playhead. (I find this window to be the most useful.)

FIGURE 2.45 The floating Project Timecode window. Right-click to copy the timecode to the clipboard.

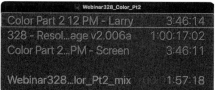

FIGURE 2.46 The floating Source Timecode window.

Right-click in the Source Timecode window to:

- Copy only the timecode of the selected clip in this window to the clipboard.
- Copy the file name and the timecode of the selected clip in this window to the clipboard.
- Copy the file name and the timecode of clips in this window to the clipboard.

I don't use the Project Timecode window often because it is easy to see the current timecode display under the Viewer. However, I regularly use the Source Timecode window to check the sync between clips.

GOING FURTHER
Open Final Cut
Pro > Commands >
Customize, search for
timecode, then assign
keyboard shortcuts to:

- Toggle the Project
  Timecode window
  open or closed.

- Copy the project
  timecode.

- Paste the project
  timecode.

💯 Moving Around the Timeline

Final Cut does the math, while you avoid using punctuation.

Imagine your playhead is somewhere in the timeline, but you want to get it somewhere else, fast. *Of course* you could drag it. How boring. The keyboard is faster.

- To move the playhead to a specific timecode location, press Control+P, enter the new timecode location, and press Return.
- To move a specific distance, press the plus (+) key to jump forward or the minus (–) key to jump back, then type the amount of time you want to jump. (For example, type **+512** to jump 5 seconds and 12 frames forward. Or type **–2306** to jump back 23 seconds and 6 frames.)

In either case, you don't need to click in the timecode field or add punctation.

> **GOING FURTHER** Final Cut even does the math. Assuming you are in a 30 fps project, type +60 to jump forward two seconds. Or type –123 to jump back four seconds and three frames. (As a European example, if you edit a 25 fps project, entering +75 will jump the playhead 3 seconds forward.)

THE VIEWER

The Viewer is a dynamic window where you view clips under the playhead, or skimmer, in the Browser or timeline. It can be displayed in the main interface or on a separate computer monitor.

101 Even the Viewer Has a View Menu

This is not the same as the View menu in the menu bar.

In the top-right corner of the Viewer is the View menu; see **FIGURE 2.47**. Click the word *View* to reveal an array of ways to modify the Viewer. Many of these are explained in their own tip. Here, I'll just show how to access the menu.

Although you can't set preferences for these options, I did assign keyboard shortcuts to several. For example, in the Command Editor, I searched for *Show Title* and found the Show Title/Action Safe Zones command. I assigned this the apostrophe key ('). Now, whenever I need to see Action Safe or Title Safe, I press an apostrophe. I also created a shortcut for Show Custom Overlays.

102 Enlarge the Viewer Full Screen

Here's how to toggle the Viewer to full screen and back.

Assuming you don't own a dedicated video monitor—and you'd know if you did because you spent the money for it—here's a way to toggle the Viewer full screen.

In the lower-right corner of the Viewer are two diagonal arrows; see **FIGURE 2.48**. Click the arrows to enlarge the Viewer full screen (shortcut: Shift+Cmd+F). Press Esc to reduce its size to normal.

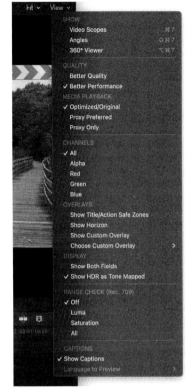

FIGURE 2.47 The View menu in the Viewer. This is not the same as the View menu in the menu bar.

FIGURE 2.48 Click the diagonal arrows to expand the Viewer to full screen. Press Esc to bring it back.

GOING FURTHER If you connect a second computer monitor, click the Two Monitor icon at the top right of the Viewer to move the Viewer full screen to the second monitor. See Tip 60, *Expand the Interface with Two Computer Monitors*.

103 Display Action Safe and Title Safe Zones

These safe zones help assure proper framing for titles and effects.

In the old days of TV, when picture tubes ruled the world, the image shown on a TV in the home was cropped compared to the original image at the broadcast network. This was caused by how television picture tubes worked. This cropping varied by picture tube and age.

As a media creator, you have no control over how your final project is viewed.

So decades ago, television engineers created two "safe zones"—Action Safe and Title Safe—so that the production folks creating a show could frame shots so that even a badly misaligned TV set in the home still displayed the essential elements of the picture.

These standards are still followed today because of one simple fact: As a media creator, you have no control over how the final image will be seen by the viewer. It is not unusual for edges of an image to be cropped due to a misaligned projector, a bad monitor, poorly designed HTML code, or...anything, actually. You have no control.

Final Cut indicates these safe zones using thin gold rectangles; see **FIGURE 2.49**. Here are the rules:

- **Full frame**. The entire image must fill the frame, with no blank edges.
- **Action Safe**. Keep all essential action, actors, and other key visual elements inside Action Safe.

NOTE Safe zone rectangles display in the Viewer but don't export.

- **Title Safe**. Keep all essential titles, logos and other important graphics inside Title Safe.

These framing rules apply for all projects *except* those for the web. The web uses a slightly looser rule: Because you don't know how people will view your projects, keep all essential elements *and text* inside Action Safe (that's the outer rectangle) while still filling the entire frame with an image.

FIGURE 2.49 Action Safe is 5% in from all edges. Title Safe is 10% in. These boundaries are still followed in professional media today for framing titles and effects. Action Safe should be used for framing web projects.

GOING FURTHER Because I use safe zones for all my edits, I've assigned it a custom keyboard shortcut: apostrophe ('). This makes it easy to toggle on and off.

104 Better Quality vs. Better Performance

The View menu does not alter image quality during editing or final export.

One of the more confusing options in the View menu is the choice between Better Quality and Better Performance. I mean, do I really need to choose?

No. Not at all. This controls a display feature of the timeline.

As shown in **FIGURE 2.50**, these two options determine how the CPU prioritizes its time. When you select Better Quality, the CPU prioritizes image quality. When you select Better Performance, the CPU prioritizes real-time playback. The real difference is whether you want to save time rendering while you edit. Personally, I set this to Better Performance. The slight dip in image quality is more than offset by time savings in not waiting for rendering to complete.

This setting doesn't affect the final export. FCP *always* renders and exports everything at best quality.

FIGURE 2.50 Both of these options affect timeline playback only, not export.

GOING FURTHER
While it is true that exports always render at the highest quality, if you are viewing proxies, exports will use proxy media, not the camera source or optimized clips, as their source.

105 Custom Viewer Overlays

Like the safe zones, these display in the Viewer but don't export.

There's an option in the Viewer > View menu that I find myself using every week: Overlays. Overlays appear in the Viewer, like the watermark overlay in **FIGURE 2.51**, but don't export. I use the Overlays option to make sure text in the project doesn't conflict with a watermark or to protect an image shot in 16:9 within a 4:3 frame.

FIGURE 2.51 This custom overlay appears in the Viewer but doesn't export.

Create an overlay using any image editing program, then save it as a PNG or TIFF file with a transparent background. (I recommend PNG.) Create any image you want—keep in mind this will be visible in the Viewer, so try to keep the overlay elements minimal so they don't block the video below it.

To choose an overlay, go to the View menu in the Viewer (not the menu bar) and choose Custom Overlay (red arrow in **FIGURE 2.52**). If you added an overlay already, it will appear in the list. Otherwise, choose Add Custom Overlay and select it in the Finder.

To enable or disable the overlay display, choose View > Show Custom Overlay. (Unselecting an option turns it off.) Or select the opacity you want for the overlay image; see **FIGURE 2.53**.

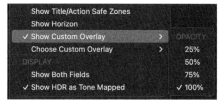

FIGURE 2.52 This View menu adds new overlays or selects one you've already used.

FIGURE 2.53 Turn overlays on or off, as well as adjust their opacity, in this menu.

As another example, I created an overlay that I use to reframe 16:9 shots into 4:3 or 9:16 (vertical) images; see **FIGURE 2.54.**

FIGURE 2.54 This is a custom overlay that I use for reframing 16:9 shots into 4:3 or 9:16.

GOING FURTHER Custom overlays are stored in [Home Directory] > Library > Application Support > ProApps. When creating custom overlays, you'll get the best results by creating them at the same size as the project frame size.

106 How to Enable Proxies

Proxies provide efficiency and speed for large frame size and multicam projects.

Chapter 1, "Video Fundamentals," discussed the benefits of creating proxy media for projects with large frame sizes, multicam editing, or running Final Cut on slower systems. What I didn't mention was how to enable proxies: Go to the View menu in the top-right corner of the Viewer, as shown in **FIGURE 2.55**, and look at the options in the Media Playback section of the menu.

In the past, we could choose only between viewing the source/optimized file or the proxy file. Recently Apple added a much more useful choice: Proxy Preferred.

- **Optimized/Original.** This default setting plays the highest quality version of the media.
- **Proxy Preferred.** This plays proxy files, if they exist, and source files if they don't.
- **Proxy Only.** This plays proxy files if they exist and displays a giant red flag in the Viewer if they don't.

If you want the best performance, choose Proxy Preferred, then make sure you create proxy files. If you want the highest image quality, choose Optimized/Original. If you are editing proxy files and try to export them, Final Cut will warn you; see **FIGURE 2.56**.

NOTE Tip 162, *Create Proxies After Importing Media,* explains how to create proxies.

Proxies provide efficiency and speed for large frame size and multicam projects.

FIGURE 2.55 The proxy options in the Viewer > View menu.

FIGURE 2.56 Final Cut warns you before exporting a proxy file by accident (left).

107 How to View Transparency

Transparency, for clips or projects, is stored in the alpha channel.

The default display setting for clips is 100% full screen and 100% opaque; see **FIGURE 2.57**. That's fine for most edits; we want to see the image.

But once we move into effects, we often want to combine multiple images in the frame or add titles. These require transparency. The "alpha channel" stores which pixels in a clip or project are opaque, which are translucent, and which are transparent. (All title clips, for example, are transparent except for the text itself.)

To view transparency, go to Viewer > View and choose Channels > Alpha; see **FIGURE 2.58**. Normally, the screen will be solid white, which means the entire image is opaque.

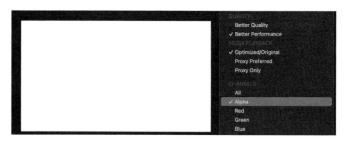

However, if we scale a clip to 50%, meaning that the image fills only half the frame, as shown in **FIGURE 2.59**, there are large black edges around the clip.

When you view the alpha channel for that scaled clip, as shown in FIGURE 2.60, you see that the clip displays white (opaque), while the background displays black (transparent). Shades of gray indicate translucency.

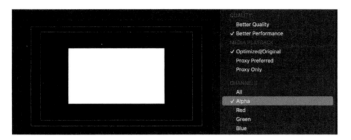

FIGURE 2.60 When Alpha is selected, white indicates opaque areas, black indicates transparent areas, and gray (not shown) indicates translucency.

108 Make the Viewer Background Transparent

Use a checkerboard background when you need to see transparency.

In addition to viewing the alpha channel, the Viewer has another trick to help you see transparency: the Viewer background. By changing Final Cut Pro > Preferences > Playback, as shown in FIGURE 2.61, you can make the Viewer background display black, white, or a checkerboard.

Change this setting to make the Viewer background display a checkerboard. Similar to Photoshop, this makes it easier to see transparency in the frame.

FIGURE 2.61 Changing these backgrounds won't affect export. All backgrounds export as black.

NOTE If you export using a codec that supports alpha channels, such as ProRes 4444, the background will be black, but the alpha channel will also be included so that transparency data is retained with the clip.

109 The Little Red Box in the Viewer

This icon indicates you are zoomed in to the Viewer too far.

Zooming in to the Viewer is useful to see fine details in an image to place an effect. But accidentally hiding a portion of the image can drive you nuts during editing. When this little red box appears in the Viewer, as shown in FIGURE 2.62, it means that you are zoomed in to the image in the Viewer so closely that the Viewer cannot display the entire image. The red box acts as both a warning and a navigation tool.

Zooming in to the Viewer does not change the image size in the timeline.

- To navigate inside the Viewer, drag the red box.
- To remove the red box, press Shift+Z. (Or change the percent menu in the top-right corner of the Viewer to Fit.) The entire image now displays inside the Viewer.

FIGURE 2.62 This red box appears when the entire image is too big to fit in the Viewer. Drag the red box to navigate.

HIDDEN VIEWERS

Two special-purpose displays can make editing and color grading easier. But they are off by default and not easy to find.

110 The Event Viewer

The Event Viewer previews whatever clip is selected in the Browser.

A hidden viewer in Final Cut is the Event Viewer; see **FIGURE 2.63**. One of the benefits of the Viewer is that it displays whatever clip is active in the Browser or timeline. However, it is often helpful to have two onscreen windows: one to show the Browser clip and the other to show the timeline. The Event Viewer is often referred to as a *preview monitor*.

FIGURE 2.63 The Event Viewer displays and plays Browser clips.

To open it, choose Window > Show in Workspace > Event Viewer (shortcut: Control+Cmd+3). This display may be a bit cramped on a smaller monitor. The Event Viewer provides preview and playback of Browser clips.

Once opened, skim or play any Browser clip in the Event Viewer. The key benefit is that a larger image helps match action between shots, or carefully evaluate the image for unwanted elements—such as mic booms—before editing it into the timeline.

If you need it, it's there. If you don't, it remains hidden so it doesn't take up screen space.

GOING FURTHER
The Event Viewer has the same controls for size and view as the Viewer's View menu. You can display the Event Viewer or Comparison View, but not both at the same time.

111 The Comparison View

This displays still frames to compare differences between shots.

The Comparison View is designed to assist with matching shots during color grading. However, it is stored in an unusual place: Window > Show in Workspace > Comparison View (shortcut: Control+Cmd+6). Unlike the Event Viewer, the Comparison View shows only still frames.

This displays a window, as shown in **FIGURE 2.64,** to the left of the Viewer. By default, it shows the Out of the preceding clip on the left, along with the frame under the timeline playhead on the right. Click Next Edit to view the In of the next clip. This makes it easy to compare successive shots to determine whether colors and actions transition smoothly.

But there's a second option: Comparing still frames from key scenes in a project. Click the Saved button at the top, then click Save Frame at the bottom. This captures a still image of the frame under the playhead. In the Saved screen, click Frame Browser. This displays the comparison stills, as shown in **FIGURE 2.65,** taken for this project. Final Cut stores up to 30 stills.

FIGURE 2.64 The Comparison View shows still frames to compare shots.

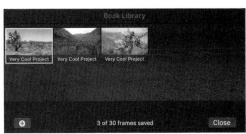

FIGURE 2.65 The Frame Browser in the Comparison View. Click a still frame to display it.

Click a still frame to display it in the Comparison View. Now, move the playhead around the timeline to compare the frame under the playhead with the selected frame to help maintain color consistency.

GOING FURTHER You can't display the Event Viewer and Comparison View at the same time. The Comparison View has the same display options as the Viewer. Open the View menu at the top of the Comparison View to see the options.

TROUBLESHOOTING

Here are a variety of tips to help you fix problems before you get an ulcer.

112 Four Troubleshooting Techniques

Here's what to do first when your Mac acts flakey.

Macs are solid, reliable, high-performance machines. However, every so often, one decides to take leave of its senses. Here are four things to try before you contact Apple Support:

- **Quit Final Cut and restart your computer**. It surprises me how many times a simple restart gets everything working properly again.

Trashing Final Cut Pro preferences does not delete any libraries, projects, or media.

- **Re-render your project**. Most Final Cut problems are caused by bad render files or bad media.

   To delete render files:

   1. Select your project in the Browser.
   2. Choose File > Delete Generated Project Files.
   3. Select Delete Render Files.

      Final Cut will then rebuild any necessary render files when you next open the project into the timeline.

- **Trash FCP preference files**. Preference files control every aspect of Final Cut, far more than just the preference files you can set manually. Trashing them resets Final Cut to Apple's defaults and cleans up a lot of weirdness that creeps in over time.

   To trash preferences:

   1. Quit Final Cut.
   2. Press and hold both the Option and Cmd keys while restarting FCP from the Dock.

3. Click the blue Delete Preferences button, as shown in FIGURE 2.66.

Trashing preferences resets customized preference settings, but not keyboard shortcuts, to their default settings. This means you'll need to re-customize preferences after trashing.

As a caution, resetting preferences also empties the Recent Library list displayed when you choose File > Open Library. *Don't panic!* This did not delete your libraries or media; it simply removed the file names from this list. Go to the Finder and double-click the Library file to open it. Once you open it, the library will return, again, to this list.

FIGURE 2.66 Click the blue Delete Preferences button to reset Final Cut to Apple's default settings.

- **Boot into Recovery Mode** and run First Aid on both internal hard drives. Hidden inside your Mac is a special volume called the *Recovery volume*. This holds a limited version of macOS along with several repair utilities.

   1. Use one of the following methods to start up into Recovery:
      ▲ For Intel Macs, restart your Mac while pressing and holding Cmd+R. Keep holding this until the thermometer scrolls halfway across the screen. Wait until the main window appears.
      ▲ For Apple silicon Macs, press and hold the power button until you see "Loading Startup Options."

      After a bit—the process is not instantaneous—a window appears asking what you want to do.

   2. Click Run Disk Utility. Click the Options icon, then click Continue.

      On the left side of Disk Utility, one or two "Macintosh HD" drives appear, depending upon which version of the macOS you are running. Each of these is a separate volume.

   3. Select each volume in turn, then click the First Aid button. This runs a series of repair utilities on your internal drives. This process can take several minutes, so be patient. If other drives are listed, ignore them. When you've repaired one or both Macintosh HD drives, restart your system without touching the keyboard.

Ideally, one of these steps returns your system to normal. If not, it's time to call Apple Support. Assisting you is what they are there for.

GOING FURTHER When you trash preferences, the operating system creates a special diagnostic file named VideoAppDiagnostics...tar.gz. This compressed System Report contains logs and settings that describe the current state of your computer, but no personally identifiable information. In the event of a system crash, this report is automatically sent to Apple to troubleshoot the problem. However, although this file is also created when you trash preferences, it is not sent to Apple. You can trash it.

113 When Final Cut Pro Unexpectedly Quits

Yes, this happens to me too

Here I am, happily writing a book about Final Cut, when the application crashes, displaying the screen you see in **FIGURE 2.67**.

FIGURE 2.67 This report appears when Final Cut crashes. It is automatically sent to Apple after a crash.

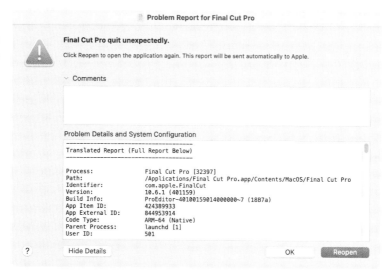

Although this is frustrating, there's actually good news here. First, because of the speed with which FCP saves your work, everything you were doing up until the moment of the crash is most likely safely saved. (I've experienced this personally, and it is very reassuring.)

Next, Final Cut creates a system report that describes in deep technical detail the type of crash, what you were doing when it crashed, and the state of your system at the time. It also creates this report when you delete FCP preferences. (None of this, by the way, contains any personally identifiable information. It is anonymous.) This crash report is then sent automatically to Apple so it can research this issue further.

Finally, if you want to resume your work with Final Cut, click Reopen, and FCP reopens and loads whichever libraries were open at the time of the crash.

My recommendation, though, is that when Final Cut crashes, restart your computer. Yes, this takes a bit more time, but it resets your system to a known-good state allowing Final Cut Pro to run more smoothly.

> **GOING FURTHER** Here's a link that explains in more detail what technical information is sent to Apple after a crash or when you report a problem: support.apple.com/guide/mac-help/mh27990/mac.

114 How to Trash Third-Party Plug-ins

Third-party plug-ins are generally stored in one of three places.

You can't trash the plug-ins that Apple ships with Final Cut. But you can trash plug-ins created by other developers. They are generally stored in one of three places, depending upon where the developer decided to store their files.

- [Home Directory] > Movies > Motion Templates
- Macintosh HD > Library > Plug-ins > FXPlug
- Macintosh HD > Library > Application Support > ProApps > Plugins

If the plug-in is stored in a folder, delete the entire folder. If the plug-in you want to delete isn't there, contact the developer for instructions.

115 Fix a Yellow Alert

Sometimes, the FCP database doesn't update fast enough.

If you see a yellow "missing media" alert in Final Cut, you may not be missing media. This may be a database problem where Final Cut did not make an update fast enough. This may happen when using external files, such as Photoshop documents or Motion projects.

If this happens to you, try this:

1. Select everything on the timeline (shortcut: Cmd+A).
2. Copy it to the clipboard (shortcut: Cmd+C).
3. Click anywhere in the timeline to deselect everything.

    The yellow alert should disappear.

116 Does Zapping PRAM Still Work?

Um, no.

On older computers and operating systems, a troubleshooting technique used to be "zapping the PRAM." On older systems, this sometimes helped. On newer systems, not so much. In fact, this doesn't work at all for Apple silicon Macs.

Apple support writes: "NVRAM (nonvolatile random-access memory) is a small amount of memory that your Mac uses to store certain settings and access them quickly. PRAM (Parameter RAM) stores similar information, and the steps for resetting NVRAM and PRAM are the same.

Zapping PRAM works only on older Intel-based Macs.

NOTE Resetting PRAM
does not work for Apple
silicon Macs.

"Settings that can be stored in NVRAM include sound volume, display resolution, startup-disk selection, time zone, and recent kernel panic information. The settings stored in NVRAM depend on your Mac and the devices that
you're using with your Mac."

To reset both NVRAM and PRAM:

GOING FURTHER
Here's a link to Apple's
website that describes
what PRAM does in
more detail: support.
apple.com/HT204063.

1. Shut down your Mac.

2. Restart it and immediately press and hold Option+Cmd+P+R.

3. Keep pressing those keys for about 20 seconds, or until you hear a
   second restart chime. (Not all systems play the chime.)

   This resets those stored settings. You will probably need to reselect
   your default printer after doing this.

117 Saving Is Automatic—So Are Backups

Final Cut saves instantly and creates backups automatically.

I've had Final Cut crash a fraction of second after I changed something in
the timeline. Every time that's happened, whatever I did was already safely
saved to disk. So, yup, Final Cut saves your latest changes the instant you
make them.

For that, I'm very grateful.

*Final Cut saves
and backs up
library files—
automatically.*

It also automatically backs up the library database every 15 minutes, unless
no changes were made during that time. By default, these backups are stored
in [Home Directory] > Movies > Final Cut Backups.

It is important to note that the library database does not include any media.
Media should be backed up separately, outside of Final Cut. The library database *does* include the names and contents of all events, the names and locations of all clips and associated metadata, and the contents of every project.
In other words, it includes everything needed to go back to an earlier version
and start editing—except the media itself.

118 Restoring from a Backup

Restoring isn't hard, but you should know your options.

Your worst nightmare just occurred—the project you are editing just became
trash. Now what? Restore from a backup.

Backups are always made of the library, not projects. So when you restore,
you are switching to an earlier version of your current library. This older
library includes an earlier version of the project you are currently editing.

You can restore a library in two ways:

- **If the trashed project is open**, choose File > Open Library > From Backup. This displays a list of all the backups that exist for the current library. Pick a version of the library that you know is good.

- **If the trashed project won't open**, backup files are stored in [Home Directory] > Movies > Final Cut Backups. Inside it are folders for each library that has backups. These are simply copies of normal libraries that are time-stamped and stored in a specific place. There's nothing unusual about them.

  In either case, double-click the backup library you want to open and start editing.

GOING FURTHER Backups are created only when you make changes to a library. If nothing changes, no backups are made. Changing backup locations does not move existing backups.

Backups are simply copies of normal libraries that are time-stamped and stored in a specific place.

119 How to Change Where Final Cut Stores Backups

Final Cut stores library backups in the Movies folder.

By default, Final Cut always makes backups of the library file and stores them in [Home Directory] > Movies > FCP Backups. However, you can change this to a different location or turn off backups for that library altogether.

To do so:

1. Select the Library you want to adjust in the Library sidebar (to the left of the Browser).

2. The Library inspector displays information about the library similar to that shown in **FIGURE 2.68**.

FIGURE 2.68 The Inspector > Library Properties window.

- Choose Storage Locations > Modify Settings to open the dialog shown in **FIGURE 2.69**.

NOTE While turning off backups saves storage space, the risk of losing all your work does not make this option attractive.

- Select Choose from the Backups menu and pick a different storage location. Or choose Do Not Save to turn off backups entirely for that Library.

FIGURE 2.69 The Library Storage Locations window. Change backup locations using the Backups menu.

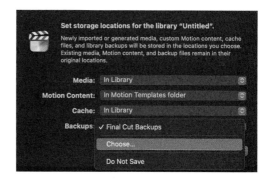

GOING FURTHER My recommendation is to store Final Cut backups on a separate drive from the one holding your libraries. That way, if something happens to the original library or the drive holding it, the backup, which is stored on a separate drive, should be safe.

120 Monitor Your Mac Using Activity Monitor

This essential utility lets you see what's happening under the hood.

Without question, Activity Monitor is my favorite Mac utility; see **FIGURE 2.70**. You'll find this in Applications > Utilities. This essential tool displays stats for CPU activity, energy (battery), memory, local storage, and network activity.

Once you open it, choose Window > Activity Monitor to display the main window. The top portion of the window displays the processes (think "software") currently running on your system. *Leave this top section alone!* (There is no problem scrolling through the list at the top to see what's running, but don't click any of the buttons at the top or attempt to stop any of these processes, unless you *really* enjoy watching things blow up!)

- Click CPU (at the top) to monitor CPU activity between different applications. (Maximum CPU % = the number of cores times 100%.)
- Click Memory to monitor how RAM is allocated between applications.
- Click Energy to monitor battery use, charge, and application energy use (applies only to laptops).
- Click Disk to monitor the speed of file transfers on locally attached storage.
- Click Network to monitor network traffic bandwidth and which applications are currently accessing the network.

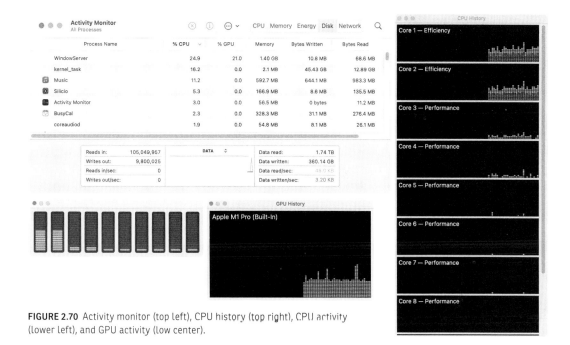

FIGURE 2.70 Activity monitor (top left), CPU history (top right), CPU activity (lower left), and GPU activity (low center).

When monitoring Disk or Network activity, look in the lower-right corner. Data received indicates the speed of data coming *into* your computer (reads). Data sent indicates the speed of data *leaving* your computer (writes).

Go to the Window menu, at the top, to display real-time graphs showing:

- CPU Activity
- CPU History
- GPU History

I use this utility daily—I'm endlessly fascinated by what the computer is doing behind the scenes.

NOTE Recently, it was discovered that Activity Monitor does not accurately report how work is shared between the CPU cores, especially on Apple silicon systems. Nor does it report work done using hardware acceleration for media. I'm sure this will be updated, but Apple is not in a hurry about it.

121 Archive Active Versions of Final Cut

This potentially provides future access to older programs.

Before I share these steps, let me say that archiving is a fraught mess. There's no good, reliable way to guarantee that the projects you sweated over will open two years from now. They may. But not always. (See Tip 493, *Export an XML File*.) FCP, the macOS, and plug-ins all change. The tech industry never looks back.

NOTE Before you revert to an earlier version, archive or delete the version of Final Cut Pro currently stored in your Applications folder. Also, if you revert to an earlier version of Final Cut Pro, it may also require an earlier version of the macOS, so keep a note of which version of Final Cut Pro uses which version of the macOS. You can have only one version of Final Cut installed at a time.

For projects you expect to work on again in the future, you may want to archive the version of Final Cut that created it. According to an Apple KnowledgeBase article, to back up the currently installed Final Cut Pro application:

1. Create a new folder in the Applications folder, and name it after the application (for example, "Final Cut Pro 10.6.3"). To check your version of Final Cut Pro, open the application and choose About Final Cut Pro from the Final Cut Pro menu.

2. Select the Final Cut Pro application in the Applications folder. Choose File > Compress "Final Cut Pro." It will take a few minutes to compress.

3. Move the resulting Final Cut Pro.zip file into the folder you created in step 1.

4. Move the folder containing the ZIP file to a backup drive.

   These ZIP files can be stored anywhere.

GOING FURTHER The best archive option is to keep an older computer running an older compatible version of macOS along with the version of FCP you used to edit the project. This way, hardware, operating system and software all work together and can be used to restore an older library. Oh! Remember, also, to create an XML backup (see Tip 493, *Export an XML File*).

122 The Dock Holds Secrets

Open Libraries faster from the Dock.

The Dock looks innocent, just sitting there on your screen. But if you right-click it, options appear; see **FIGURE 2.71**.

Use the Dock to open a specific library, launch Final Cut when you log in to your computer, or other options. The Dock gets you started faster.

FIGURE 2.71 Any recent library can be launched from the Dock.

123 Bul Wail...There's More!

Here's how to get free sound effects for Final Cut Pro!

Hidden in plain sight in Final Cut is a special download that contains royalty-free sound effects, music, and other stuff.

To access it, go to Final Cut Pro > Download Additional Content.

This opens System Preferences > Software Update; see **FIGURE 2.72**. If new content is available, a link displays. Otherwise, this panel will be empty.

The downloaded content is located in the Sound Effects browser.

FIGURE 2.72 The Software Update panel is empty. Sigh...

CHAPTER 2—INTERFACE SHORTCUTS

CATEGORY	SHORTCUT	WHAT IT DOES
Interface	Cmd+Tab	Fast switching between apps
	Cmd+H	Hide Final Cut Pro
	Control+Cmd+F	Display interface full screen
	Shift+Cmd+F	Display Viewer full screen
	Shift+Z	Fit image into Viewer or fit project into timeline
	Cmd+[plus] / [minus]	Zoom into or out of Viewer or timeline
	Cmd+[- or - Cmd+]	Timeline History go back—or—go forward
	S	Enable/disable the Skimmer
	Cmd+1	Make the Browser active
	Cmd+2	Make the timeline active
	Cmd+3	Make the Viewer active
	Cmd+4	Toggle the Inspector open/closed
	Cmd+5	Toggle the Effects browser open/closed
	Cmd+6	Go to Color Inspector
	Cmd+7	Show/hide the video scopes
	Cmd+9	Open Background Tasks window
	Control+P	Jump playhead to specific timecode location
	Control+Cmd+1	Toggle display of the Library List and Browser on or off
	Shift+Cmd+2	Toggle Timeline Index open/closed

CHAPTER WRAP

Far too often, we click buttons or choose from menus without understanding why. When you treat editing software like it's a magic box, bad things happen. Worse, when something goes wrong, you don't know how to fix it.

Experience teaching thousands of students convinces me that when you take the time to understand how and why an application works the way it does, you become much more successful in creating effective projects.

LIBRARIES & MEDIA

INTRODUCTION

The beating heart of Final Cut Pro is a database that lives in the library. So it's with the library that we need to start. In this chapter, we create libraries, import media, and get organized for editing.

You may think of editing as combining clips to create a story. Although storytelling is the reason we edit, I think a larger part of editing is deciding what to leave out. Either way, the first step is to create a container, fill it with media, and organize it. Projects evolve during editing. Getting organized early helps you surmount the chaos that surrounds every production.

- Libraries, Events & Projects
- Import Media
- Organize Media
- Customize the Timeline
- Shortcuts

124 Library Strategy

Let's think about media and libraries for a minute.

When I compare Final Cut to Avid Media Composer, Adobe Premiere Pro, or even DaVinci Resolve, what strikes me is Final Cut's flexibility, especially when it comes to importing and organizing media. There are many different ways to get organized for a new project. Here are some thoughts:

- Store libraries on your fastest drive.
- You can move libraries between drives with no problems at any time, provided the drive is fast enough to support playback and large enough to hold it.
- You cannot store Final Cut libraries on servers, though there are a few exceptions, such as the Jellyfish. You *can* store media on servers.
- Where possible, organize media before importing it and store it on a fast drive with a large capacity.
- When storing media and related files outside the library, create a primary Project Media folder with as many folders inside it as you need. Organizing media by projects in subfolders contained inside a single primary folder simplifies backups, transfers, and archiving. macOS easily supports thousands of folders inside a single folder.
- Inside that primary media folder in the Finder, I create separate folders for music, graphics, stock media, Photoshop projects, and camera media. In other words, I create as many subfolders as needed for that project.
- Copying media into a library is fine, provided you are the only one using that media, you don't need to share it with other libraries, and you have sufficient storage capacity to hold both the original media and the copies.
- If you plan to share the media between multiple libraries, storing it outside the library is much more efficient.
- If you are sharing media between software, for example, Final Cut and Resolve, you must store media outside the library.
- If you are sharing media between editors, storing media outside the library is more flexible, but storing it inside the library may make transferring the library and media easier.

Every project is different. The key is to get organized before you start.

Personally, I store my media outside the library. Although there is no perfect project organizational structure, the key is to be organized *before* you start editing. Editing is hard enough; it becomes impossible when you can't find the clip you need when you need it.

LIBRARIES, EVENTS & PROJECTS

Everything you create in Final Cut, every story you tell, is built using a combination of libraries, events, and projects.

125 Create, Rename, and Close a Library

Libraries are the foundation of Final Cut Pro.

At its core, Final Cut Pro is a database designed for editing media. That database is stored in the library. Therefore, before starting any editing project, the first thing you *must* create is a library. The good news is that the first time you open Final Cut, it automatically creates a new Untitled library for you. This is a perfectly good place to start any project...once you rename it.

To rename a library:

1. Select its name in the Library List.
2. Press Return; see **FIGURE 3.1**. (You can also click the name, but Return is faster.)
3. Enter the new name.

Renaming a library in Final Cut also renames it in the Finder. So don't use punctuation in the library name, except for parentheses, commas, hyphens, or underscores.

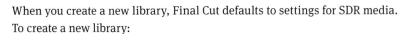

FIGURE 3.1 Select the library name in the Library List; then press Return to rename it.

When you create a new library, Final Cut defaults to settings for SDR media. To create a new library:

1. Choose File > New > Library.
2. In the Save dialog that appears (see **FIGURE 3.2**), give the library a name and storage location.

FIGURE 3.2 This dialog names and saves a new library.

NOTE The Library List is contained in this left-side sidebar. You'll see several other browsers use this as well.

By default, libraries are stored in the Documents folder. I chose, instead, to save mine in Movies. You can save libraries wherever you want, provided the storage is fast enough.

To close a library without deleting it:

1. Select the library name in the Library List.

NOTE Never delete a library in the Finder if it is open in Final Cut Pro.

2. Choose File > Close Library.

   Or—right-click the library name and choose Close Library; see **FIGURE 3.3.**

FIGURE 3.3 Open this contextual menu by right-clicking the library name in the Library List.

You can't delete a library from within Final Cut. Instead, quit Final Cut, then delete the library in the Finder.

> **GOING FURTHER** A library is not a file, even though it looks like it. Instead, it's a special file container called a *package*. Hidden inside that container is the library database along with folders containing the different media elements for that library.
>
> Take a look inside the library by right-clicking the library icon in the Finder and choosing Show Package Contents. However, don't move, or rename, anything stored inside this package. Moving or renaming library elements in the Finder is likely to break the library. That would be bad.

126 The Library List Menu

Use this menu to better manage your libraries.

Right-click any item in the Library List (the sidebar on the far left) to reveal the menu shown in **FIGURE 3.4.**

As a keyboard junkie, I tend to use keyboard shortcuts for most of these options, but if you don't know them, this menu is helpful. The one feature I use the most is Close Library, which has no assigned keyboard shortcut (although you can create one; see Tip 51, *Create Custom Keyboard Shortcuts*).

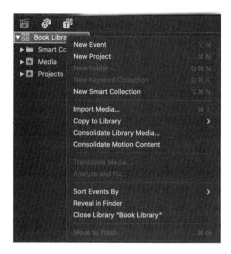

FIGURE 3.4 Right-click a library name in the Library List to reveal this menu.

127 Create a New Library from an Event

Transferring files does not affect the current project.

This feature creates a new library from an existing event, transferring copies of the existing media to the new library. Perhaps you want to create a library containing all drone clips or interviews from March. Whatever. You can do it.

1. Right-click the name of the event in the Library List.
2. Choose Copy Event to Library > New Library; see **FIGURE 3.5**.

Done. All contents are copied while the source library is untouched.

FIGURE 3.5 Copying event media into a new library.

GOING FURTHER
This technique also works to move media or projects to a new library.

128 Change Library Storage Locations

By default, most elements are stored in the library.

When Final Cut creates a new library, it also creates default locations to store library elements. Although you can't change the defaults, you can change these locations after the library is created. Again, by default, most everything associated with a library is stored in the library. This prevents one of the banes of video editing—broken links—but it also means that the library itself can get big. *Very* big.

To help manage what is stored in the library:

1. Select the library name in the Library List.

   The Library Inspector opens displaying the library properties; see **FIGURE 3.6**.

2. Click Modify Settings.

   The dialog shown in **FIGURE 3.7** appears. The settings can be different for each library.

   - **Media**. This setting can be overridden when importing media using the Media Import window. Media dragged into a library is stored in the library unless you change this setting.

   - **Motion Content**. This affects only custom Motion templates that you create. Templates from Apple or third-party developers are stored elsewhere on your system.

   - **Cache**. These work files include render and analysis files. Although you can store them externally, I recommend leaving them in the library. This is why the library needs to be stored on fast storage.

   - **Backups**. By default, these are stored in a folder named after the library inside [Home Directory] > Movies > Final Cut Backups. You should store these on a different drive from the library files.

GOING FURTHER
You'll also see this Modify Settings dialog when copying media between libraries. It has the same purpose there.

FIGURE 3.6 Library settings are displayed in the Library Inspector.

FIGURE 3.7 The Library Storage Locations dialog determines what is stored where in each library.

129 Final Cut Pro Statistics

Just the facts, ma'am.

As you start creating libraries and projects, here are some statistics to keep in mind:

- A Final Cut library supports an unlimited number of clips, subject to available RAM.
- A Final Cut project supports an unlimited number of clips, subject to available RAM.
- A Final Cut project can be up to 24 hours long.
- A Final Cut project supports an unlimited number of layers.
- A Final Cut multicam clip supports up to 64 angles, although codec, frame size, frame rate, storage speed and capacity, and CPU speed may limit the number of active angles.

The phrase "subject to available RAM" is kind of squishy, as it is influenced by RAM, codec, frame rate, and frame size. In general, libraries and projects should easily support thousands of clips with 32 GB of RAM.

130 How Big Is Your Library?

Here's a fast way to find out.

Select a library in the Library List and look at the Library Inspector. At the top, it displays where your library is stored and how big it is; see **FIGURE 3.8**.

In this case, I'm storing this library on my internal drive because I use it only to create examples for this book. Notice that it takes 122.7 GB in storage.

GOING FURTHER
If you delete generated media to recover storage space, Final Cut doesn't update this file size estimate until you quit the app and restart it.

FIGURE 3.8 Library Properties, in the Library Inspector, displays the storage location and library file size (red arrow).

131 Consolidate Library Media

Consolidate gathers all library media into one place.

Right-click the library name in the Library List and choose Consolidate Library Media. The window shown in **FIGURE 3.9** appears. (Or select the library in the Library List; then choose Consolidate Media from the Info Inspector.)

FIGURE 3.9 The Consolidate
Library Media dialog.

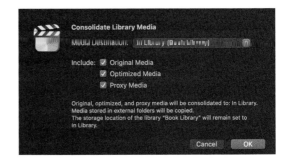

Let's say you have media stored across several folders on one drive or multiple drives attached to your system. Now, you want to collect those files and transfer them to a new storage location, gather them into a single library, or archive them. This menu option collects your media into a location you specify so you don't have to worry about finding every last clip manually.

Change the Media Destination setting to reflect where you want to store the gathered media. This could be in the library or in a folder on external storage. Then, use the checkboxes to tell Final Cut what media, specifically, you want to consolidate.

GOING FURTHER
This does not trim media; that is, it doesn't remove any media you are not using in a project. It simply gathers existing media from multiple locations and stores it in one place.

To prevent broken links in other libraries, Final Cut follows these rules:

- When you consolidate files stored *outside* of a library into a folder also stored outside the library, they are moved.
- When you consolidate files *into* a library from an external folder, they are copied.

132 Final Cut Library Manager

A great Final Cut Pro tool from Arctic Whiteness.

An essential utility to maintain libraries is Final Cut Library Manager. This:

- Displays all libraries on all disks in one window.

Final Cut Library Manager is an essential utility for Final Cut editors.

- Simplifies and automates removing generated media.
- Searches for library, event, project, and clip names, as well as notes, comments, and keywords.
- Indicates if files are disconnected.
- Builds Final Cut libraries from templates.
- Duplicates, moves, and deletes libraries.

I'm a huge fan. I've used Final Cut Library Manager for years.

GOING FURTHER The Final Cut Library Manager is available at arcticwhiteness.com/finalcutlibrarymanager/.

133 Create, Rename, and Modify an Event

Remember, an event is just a folder with a fancy name.

When you create a new library, Final Cut also creates one new event. Why? Because every library *must* contain at least one event. That's the rule. After that, create as many events as you like.

To create a new event, do one of the following:

- Choose File > New > Event.
- Press Option+N.
- Right-click anywhere in the Library List and choose New Event; see **FIGURE 3.10**.

FIGURE 3.10 Right-click anywhere in the Library List to display this menu.

Once you create a new event, the dialog in **FIGURE 3.11** appears. The key decision, after giving the event a name, is whether you want to create a project for it at the same time. Although this is a time-saving step, which I cover in Tip 141, *Create a New Project for SDR Media*, most of the time I create projects separately because I want to control where they are stored.

FIGURE 3.11 You can use the New Event dialog to also create a new project that will be stored in that event.

To rename an event:

1. Select the event name in the Library List.
2. Press Return to rename it.

To delete an event:

1. Select it and press Cmd+Delete.

   Or—right-click the event name and select Move Event to Trash; see **FIGURE 3.12**.
2. Confirm you want to delete the event; see **FIGURE 3.13**.

Deleting an event also deletes any media stored *inside* the Final Cut library. However, it does not delete any media stored *outside* the library.

FIGURE 3.12 This is the bottom portion of the contextual Library List.

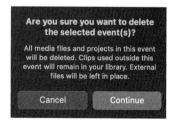

FIGURE 3.13 Final Cut wants to make sure you don't delete an event or media by accident.

*An event is just
a folder with a
fancy name.*

GOING FURTHER
- By default, new events are given the name of today's date.
- Although there is no limit on the number of events you can create, keep the number reasonable.
- You cannot create two events with the same name.
- You cannot store or reference the same clip in different events. However, as Tip 137, *Store the Same Media in Multiple Events*, explains, there is a work-around.
- You cannot store one event inside another event.

134 Create as Many Events as You Need

Events organize the library in FCP, like folders organize the Finder.

Every library and project is different, but **FIGURE 3.14** shows two typical event layouts that I use a lot.

- For simple projects, like my tutorial demos, I create a library with two events: Media and Projects. (For some reason, having an event with today's date drives me nuts.)

GOING FURTHER
One of the benefits to using Final Cut Library Manager is creating library templates for library formats you use frequently.

- For more complex projects, like editing my weekly webinars, I use more events. You are welcome to use whatever combination of events you want.

FIGURE 3.14 An event list for a simple project (left) and a more complex one (right).

135 Copy Events Between Libraries

Easily copy events and their contents.

Copying events is a great way to consolidate frequently used elements such as company logos, theme music, and graphics from multiple projects into one library. It's also helps when you want to copy an event or project between libraries so a second editor can work on a derivative project, like a promo for a show.

To copy an event, make sure both the new and existing libraries are open in Final Cut.

1. Select the event name.

2. Drag the event name from its current position to the name of the library where you want to copy it.

   Or—choose File > Copy Event to Library > [Library Name].

3. In the dialog that appears (see **FIGURE 3.15**), indicate which generated media you want to copy in addition to the source media files.

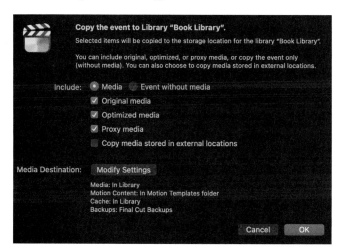

FIGURE 3.15 This dialog determines which media gets copied from one library to the next.

If you are copying the media to send to a second editor, refer to Tip 138, *An Empty Library Simplifies Collaboration*. In general, if you plan to edit the media you are copying, move the media and all generated media. If you are copying assets for archiving, save storage space and move only the original media.

GOING FURTHER If you store media outside the source library, only the links to the source media are copied. This does not increase the file storage.

If you store media inside the source library, the media files will be copied from one library to the next. Although copying assures that no links break, it also doubles the storage used by this media because the source clips are now stored in two different libraries. Any generated media associated with the source media in that event—optimized or proxies—is also copied from the old location to the new.

136 Move Events Between Libraries

Easily move events and their contents.

Moving events makes sense when you want to split a library or reduce library size in general. It is easy to move an event and its contents from one library to another, regardless of where your media is stored.

To move an event, make sure both the new and existing libraries are open in Final Cut.

1. Select the event name.
2. Press the Cmd key and drag the event name from its current library on top of the name of the new library in the Library List.

    Or—choose File > Move Event to Library > [Library Name].
3. In the dialog that appears (see **FIGURE 3.16**) indicate which generated media you want to move, in addition to the source media files.

FIGURE 3.16 The move event dialog box. Source files are always moved; moving generated files is optional.

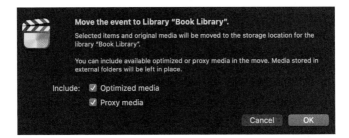

The event and its files move from one library to the next. Moving files does not increase storage.

> **GOING FURTHER** If you store media outside the source library, only the links to the source media are moved.
>
> If you store media inside the source library, the media files will be moved from one library to the next.
>
> You can choose whether to move generated media associated with the source media in that event from the old location to the new.

137 Store the Same Media in Multiple Events

To do this, create independent media clips.

Normally, a clip can be stored in only one event. This technique creates independent copies of the same media without requiring more storage space. This requires importing media using Leave Files in Place (see Tip 156, *Choose the Right Media Import Settings—Part 1*).

Normally, dragging a clip from one event to another moves the media file.

However, to create independent clips, select a clip (or group of clips) and start to drag it into a different event. Then, *while dragging*, press and hold the Option key until you drop it into a new event. This copies the clips into the new event as independent clips.

Each clip copied this way can be independently renamed, edited into the timeline with different In/Out points, or have different effects applied to either version of the clip without changing any other copies. This process does not duplicate media; it copies only the link to the media, which means that you are not using extra storage to make a copy. Also, these copies are not clones; whatever you do to one clip does not affect the other. You can create as many copies as you need.

138 An Empty Library Simplifies Collaboration

Empty libraries and empty events are designed for collaboration.

The big problem with collaboration is the huge size of media files. Proxy files can help but have lower resolution. Proxies are fine for a rough cut, but not for final effects, color grading, or output. You could transfer files to the cloud, but depending upon the speed of your internet connection, transferring several terabytes of media could take a day or two, assuming the connection doesn't break and force you to start over again.

Final Cut has a better solution: create an empty library or event. Well, not "empty" as such, but close. An "empty" library (see **FIGURE 3.17**) includes links to all events, media, edited projects, keywords, metadata…everything— except the media itself. These "empty" libraries are very small and easy to email or share via iCloud or Dropbox.

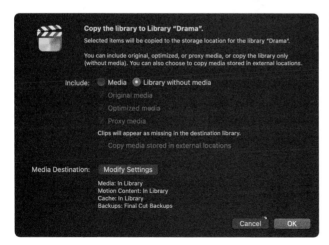

FIGURE 3.17 When creating a library for collaboration, select Library without media.

For this to work, you need to clone your existing media drive and send it to the second editor or store the media on a server if you are both on the same network. It is important that the name and structure of the cloned drive are the same as yours.

When the new editor gets the library, they simply relink to the first missing clip. Because the volumes, folders, and media of the two drives are the same, once the first file links, Final Cut automatically finds the rest.

To create an empty library:

1. Start by cloning, meaning "perfectly copy," the source files to a second drive and physically send that drive to the other editor. This bypasses all the delays in uploading files to and from the cloud.

2. Create a new "empty" library of an existing library or an "empty" event of an event containing the current project in an existing library.

An "empty" event is a normal event containing the project you are currently editing, but copied without including media. If you add media to an existing library, copy that media into a separate event, then copy that event into a new library without including the media. Send that library to the second editor; see **FIGURE 3.18**.

When the second editor receives it, they simply open it and keep editing. If both editors are on the same network, it is important to note that while two editors can work in the same *library* at the same time using this system, they can't work in the same *project* at the same time. Final Cut does not have the ability to reconcile changes between two different versions of the same project. Best practice is for each editor to have their own project file in the shared library.

GOING FURTHER
Carbon Copy Cloner, from Bombich Software, is an excellent tool for cloning drives. It is available from bombich.com.

To complete the collaboration process, the second editor sends a new empty library back to the first, who copies only the project files back to their system to integrate the latest changes.

139 Another Collaboration Option: Proxy Libraries

This is the best option when an additional editor doesn't have media.

Creating a proxy library is a good option when sending a second editor a copy of your library to work on but they don't have media. Here's how:

1. Right-click an existing library that you want to share in the Library List to the left of the Browser.

2. Choose Copy to Library > New Library.

3. Name the new library and click Save.

4. In the next window, check the Proxy media checkbox; see **FIGURE 3.19.**

This copies all library databases, events, and projects into a new library. It duplicates any existing proxy files and vastly reduces the size of the new library, making it much easier to send via the web to another editor.

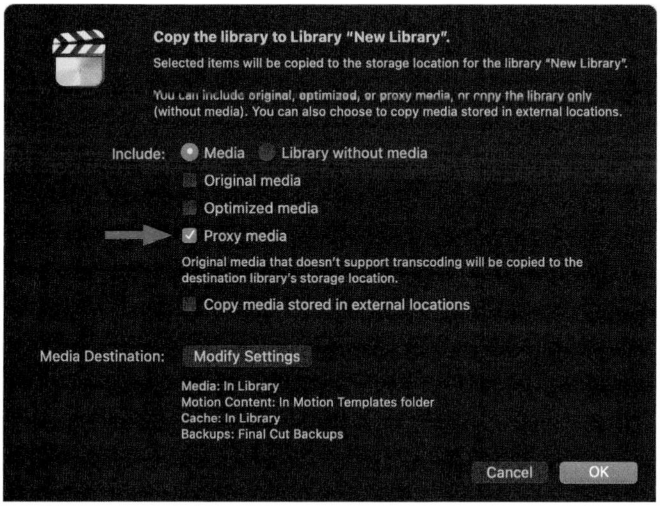

NOTE When you choose to copy proxies and some or all proxies do not exist, FCP pops up a dialog that offers to generate them. If you select Transcode, the proxies will be generated; if you click Cancel, the library copy is terminated.

FIGURE 3.19 Use this option to create a smaller library to send to a second editor.

GOING FURTHER
The checkbox "Copy media stored in external locations," when selected, copies audio, alpha channel video, and still images along with the media proxy files.

140 Consolidate Motion Templates

Move Motion templates into a library before transferring the library.

Most of the time, storing Motion templates outside the library makes a lot of sense because it simplifies organization and reuse. However, if you plan to share your library with another editor, they won't have access to any custom templates you created unless you store them in the library itself. To do this:

1. Select the library in the Library List.

2. In the Library inspector, choose Storage Locations > Modify Settings.

3. Change Motion Content to In Library; see **FIGURE 3.20**.

4. Click OK.

5. Choose Motion Content > Consolidate. This copies (not moves) custom Motion templates used by that library into the library.

FIGURE 3.20 The Library Storage Locations dialog.

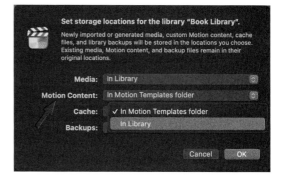

GOING FURTHER
Motion templates created by Apple or third-party developers are stored separately and not affected by this consolidation.

141 Create a New Project for SDR Media

Final Cut Pro defaults to editing Standard Dynamic Range media.

When you create a new project, Final Cut defaults to using Standard Dynamic Range (SDR) media. (For the alternative, see Tip 145, *Create an HDR Project*.)

To create a new project, do one of the following:

- Choose File > New > Project.
- Press Cmd+N.
- Right-click in the Library List and select New Project from the contextual menu.

This displays the Automatic Project dialog; see **FIGURE 3.21**. The benefit to using Automatic is that the technical settings for a project are set based upon the first clip edited into it. As long as you have a clip with the settings you need, this is fast and easy: Give the project a name, pick an event to store it in, click OK, and you're done.

FIGURE 3.21 The automatic new project dialog.

If your first clip does not have the size and format you need for this project, drag a clip that has the necessary format to set the project then edit your starting clip. Once the parameters are set and at least one clip is in the timeline, the settings won't be changed by adding more clips. Once there are at least two clips in a project, that first placeholder clip can be deleted.

However, with some projects, either the clips don't match the specs you need or you need specific specs for that project. In that case, click the Use Custom Settings button. This displays the Custom New Project dialog; see **FIGURE 3.22.**

FIGURE 3.22 The Custom New Project dialog. Every technical setting for a project can be adjusted here.

An SDR project can be any frame size. You can work with these defaults or create a custom size for a special use. The Video drop-down menu is also helpful in creating vertical and square projects. Apple's Help files provide further descriptions for these options. To switch between Automatic and Custom, click the Use ... Settings button in the lower-left corner.

GOING FURTHER I always create an event specifically to store projects. Yes, there's a Smart Collection that does that, but I developed this habit long before Apple released that Smart Collection feature.

Once you edit one clip into the project, the frame rate cannot be changed. All other settings can be changed at any time. Changing the render file format causes all files to rerender.

Final Cut can edit video at any frame size. In the Advanced Settings dialog, select Custom from the Video menu, then enter the frame size you want to edit.

142 Don't Duplicate a Project—Create a Snapshot

Snapshots are independent files; duplicates are not.

Whether you use the timeline menu (see Tip 94, *Manage Projects with This Hidden Menu*) or the contextual menu in the Browser (see **FIGURE 3.23**), you are given the option of duplicating a project. While creating backups is a great idea—and one I strongly recommend—duplicating a project is not the correct choice. Instead, use Snapshot Project.

FIGURE 3.23 Duplicating a project does not create an independent project. Snapshots do. To access this menu, right-click the project icon in the Browser.

GOING FURTHER
Multiple editors have stressed to me how important this tip is. While duplicating a project may work most of the time, snapshots work *all* the time. This is important. Please use snapshots.

The reason is that when you duplicate a project, any multicam or compound clips in the first project are linked, not duplicated, into the new project. This means that if you change the multicam or compound clip in either the source project or any duplicate, it changes everywhere!

This dynamic linking by default is inexcusable.

Instead, make a project snapshot (shortcut: Shift+Cmd+D). Here, every element is independent. Any changes you make to any element in one project won't reflect back to the source. To access this menu in the Browser, right-click the project icon you want to copy.

143 The Fastest Way to Format a New Project

Drag and drop your clip into the timeline.

Setting up a new project—and getting the settings right—is a major pain. Here is a faster way; see **FIGURE 3.24**:

1. Choose File > New > Project (shortcut: Cmd+N).
2. Give the project a name.
3. Pick a storage location.
4. Make sure the words "Use Custom Settings" are visible; if not, click Use Automatic Settings located in the lower-left corner (see the red arrow in Figure 3.24).

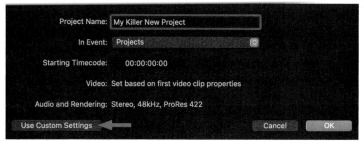

FIGURE 3.24 The Automatic Settings, displayed here, mean that the project will match the technical settings of the first clip you drag into it in the timeline.

5. Click OK.

6. Open the project in the timeline.

Now, when you drag the first clip into the timeline, it will automatically configure the project to match the technical settings of that clip.

Ta-dah! Done.

GOING FURTHER
If your first clip does not have the size and format you need for this project, drag a clip with the right format to set the project, then edit your first clip after it. Once the parameters are set and at least two clips are in the timeline, delete the first clip.

⑭ Modify an Existing Project

Everything but the frame rate can be changed after editing starts.

To modify a project, select it in the Browser and do one of the following:

- Choose File > Project Properties.
- Press Cmd+J.

The Project Properties panel opens in the Inspector; see **FIGURE 3.25**.

Click the blue Modify button to see the Custom Project Settings dialog shown in Figure 3.25.

FIGURE 3.25 The Project Properties panel in the Inspector.

To rename a project:

1. Select it in the Browser and press Return.
2. Type in the new name.

To delete a project, select it in the Browser then do one of the following:

- Choose File > Move to Trash.
- Right-click the Project and choose Move to Trash; see **FIGURE 3.26**.
- Press Cmd+Delete.

FIGURE 3.26. Right-click the project name to reveal the project contextual menu.

Final Cut does not allow changing project frame rates once one or more clips are edited into a timeline.

To make a backup of a project:

1. Right-click the project name in the Browser.

2. Choose Snapshot (shortcut: Shift+Cmd+D).

   The snapshot is timestamped and named for the original project. There is no limit to the number of snapshots you can create; however, you can't create a snapshot of an empty timeline. This menu option is also shown in Figure 3.26.

145 Create an HDR Project

Setting up an HDR project is almost the same as SDR, but not quite.

By default, Final Cut creates SDR libraries and projects. However, switching to HDR is easy. Even better, editing HDR media in Final Cut is the same as editing SDR, provided that before you start, you change a library setting and use an external, HDR video monitor to display media.

1. Select the library in the Library List.

   The Inspector automatically displays the Library Properties dialog.

2. Click the blue Modify button; see **FIGURE 3.27**.

FIGURE 3.27 This is a composite image of two dialogs. Standard should be used for SDR. Use Wide Gamut HDR for HDR.

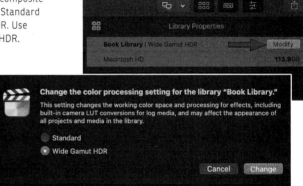

3. In the dialog that appears, change the setting to Wide Gamut HDR.

4. Create a new project (shortcut: Cmd+N).

5. In the Project Settings, click Use Custom Project (see **FIGURE 3.28**), and select the appropriate settings.

   • **Video**. An HDR project can be any frame size; however, most of the time it will be 4K or larger. Figure 3.28 illustrates the various frame size presets in Final Cut.

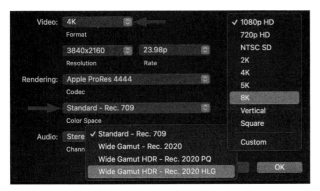

FIGURE 3.28 A composite image showing the color space options and video frame size menu for an HDR project.

- **Rendering**. Rendering in ProRes 422 is faster, creates smaller render files, and looks good. Rendering in ProRes 4444 is more color accurate. My suggestion is to use ProRes 422 for editing, then switch to ProRes 4444 for the final color grade and output.

- **Color space**. HDR requires some version of Rec. 2020. However, don't use Rec. 2020 itself; that is a discontinued option. Instead, use one of the two current HDR formats: Rec. 2020 PQ or 2020 HLG. Your distributor will tell you the format they need.

GOING FURTHER With the exception of Apple's Pro Display XDR, computer monitors can't display accurate HDR. Although you can view and edit HDR clips in an SDR timeline, if you want to view HDR as HDR, an HDR video monitor is required. HDR monitors are not cheap, but they are getting cheaper. Don't attempt to color grade HDR as HDR on a computer monitor.

146 Be Careful Changing File Names

File names are tricky beasts.

Following these rules will minimize the chances of breaking the links between Final Cut and the media in your library:

- Because files are linked to Final Cut using their path name, be careful changing any file or folder name in the Finder.

- When storing media inside the Library, never change the names of anything stored inside the Library package using the Finder.

- When storing media outside the Library, the path name that Final Cut uses to link to files includes the name of the storage volume (your hard disk), the names of all folders between the top level (root) and the folder that contains the media, and the file name itself.

Never change the name of any volume, folder, or file that contains media after you've imported that media into Final Cut.

- Never change the name of any volume, folder, or file that contains media after you've imported that media into Final Cut.
- Never change the name of files that were copied from a camera card.
- It is okay to change the name of any folder at any time that doesn't contain files imported into Final Cut.
- It is okay to change the name of any stand-alone file before you import it into Final Cut, provided it was not first stored as part of the files in a camera card.

IMPORT MEDIA

Now that the structure for the edit is built, the fun part starts: importing and reviewing media.

147 Before You Import Media

This is a really important point.

Always copy the entire contents of a media card to its own folder on your storage before importing.

Before you import media, always copy it to permanent storage. Why? Because it simplifies importing. The reason is that many compressed formats (for example, AVCHD) store media elements across multiple folders in the camera card. If you copy only some of the files or some of the folders, essential metadata could get lost.

So if you are copying media from a camera card, copy the entire contents of the card into its own folder on your storage. One folder per card. Don't just copy some of the files in the card; all too often this breaks longer files. However, you can, and I often do, store media card folders inside other folders to keep them organized on my hard disk.

Also, when you copy media from camera cards, never rename any files contained in the card. This too could break the links that connect the different media elements together. Rename only the *folders* that contain the contents of the media card.

NOTE When importing files directly from a camera card, Final Cut always stores them in the library.

Although it is possible, and Final Cut supports it, never import files directly from the camera card. Why? Because Final Cut remembers the card as the source of the media, rather than a hard disk location. If Final Cut ever loses the media, it will ask you to re-insert the card. Since that card was erased a long time ago, you are in for a very frustrating experience. Besides, copying media to your storage system means that it is now included with your standard backup routine. (You do have a backup routine, right?)

148 Drag Clips into Final Cut Pro

Dragging clips from the Finder is fast, is simple, and works.

One easy way to add a clip from the Finder is to drag it into the Browser or timeline. When you do, the current Preferences > Import settings apply.

- If you drag a clip into Final Cut from the Finder, it is stored in the Library.
- If you drag a clip into the Browser, it is sorted according to the current Browser sort settings.
- If you drag a clip into the timeline, it is added to the lowest layer available at the position of the playhead. It is also added to the Browser in the same event that holds the project.
- If you drag multiple clips, they are added in the order they were selected.

The only downside to dragging is a lack of control over the import. But dragging works.

GOING FURTHER
You can also use copy/paste to move files from the Finder into the timeline, but not the Browser. Copy/paste is fast, but using the Media Import window provides more control.

149 Import Media Using the Media Import Window

Dragging media is fast; this provides far more control.

Most of the time, I import media before I create a new project. Importing media is how you make Final Cut aware of the shots you want to use. There's nothing wrong with dragging one or more clips into the Browser or timeline. It is fast and simple; see Tip 148, *Drag Clips into Final Cut Pro*.

However, you have more control when you use the Media Import window. To open it, do one of the following:

- Press Cmd+I.
- Choose File > Import Media.
- Click the small down arrow in the top-left corner of the interface, next to the key.

The Media Import window (see **FIGURE 3.29**) has four areas:

- Source list, such as cameras, tape drives, and digital storage
- Viewer
- Thumbnails or file list
- Import options (see Tip 74, *Optimize Import Preferences*)

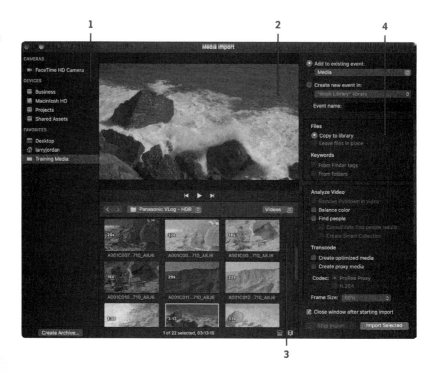

Just as with the Browser, thumbnails in the Media Import window can be
played, skimmed, or stepped through using the skimmer, trackpad, J-K-L
keys, or left/right arrows.

Importing clips does not increase the library size, as long as you are storing
media outside the library. In that case, all you are importing is the path name
to the media. This is a tiny text string, not the media itself. If you are copying
files into the library, then, yes, that will copy those clips and double the storage taken by the duplicated clips.

150 Multiple Ways to Play a Clip

You can use a trackpad, mouse, or keyboard.

These tips apply to any window where you can play a clip or thumbnail.

- To play a clip forward, click the right-pointing arrow under the Viewer.
- To play a clip forward, press the spacebar.
- To play a clip in reverse, press Shift+spacebar.
- To skim a clip, enable the skimmer (press S), then drag across the clip
  or thumbnail.
- To play a clip one frame at a time, press the left/right arrow keys.

- To play a clip using the keyboard, use the J-K-L keys.

  - J plays backward.

  - K stops.

  - L plays forward.

  - Press J twice to play backward at double-speed.

  - Press J multiple times to go even faster, up to about 10X.

  - Press L twice to play forward at double-speed.

  - Press L multiple times to go even faster, up to about 10X.

  - Press and hold J and K to play in slow-motion reverse.

  - Press and hold K and L to play in slow-motion forward.

You can play a clip using a trackpad, mouse, or keyboard.

151 Import Photoshop Files with Layers

Final Cut imports each layer individually.

When Final Cut imports a Photoshop document, it imports each layer separately, though still as part of the Photoshop clip. This means you can adjust each layer—even disable it—without affecting any other layers.

To see the different layers, double-click the image in either the Browser or timeline. This opens it in the timeline; see **FIGURE 3.30**. The top image is the multilayer Photoshop document in the Viewer. The bottom portion shows the layers.

Any changes you make to the Photoshop image opened in the timeline are saved with the image in the Browser and travel with it when you edit the clip in the timeline. To close a Photoshop clip opened into the timeline, open any other project.

Here's what you can do with a Photoshop document:

- Hide a layer by selecting it in the timeline and pressing V.

- Animate a layer, for example, to have it slide into the frame.

- Change the timing of when a layer appears by trimming an edge.

- Add transitions to a layer, for example, to have a layer fade in at a specific time.

- Delete a layer by selecting it and pressing Delete.

- Scale a layer.

- Reposition a layer.

FIGURE 3.30 A Photoshop file in the Viewer, with its layers revealed in the timeline.

I often create layered Photoshop files without positioning the elements, as shown in Figure 3.30. This provides more flexibility when animating the elements in Final Cut. You add effects to Photoshop layers the same as any other clip.

152 Import PDF Files

Scale PDF images before bringing them into Final Cut Pro.

When you import a PDF file into Final Cut, it gets converted into a PNG. This causes problems when you scale the image because PDF files, generally, retain image quality when they are scaled. PNGs do not.

FIGURE 3.31 Exporting a file from Preview as a PNG. Note the resolution setting.

Essentially, Final Cut creates the PNG at 100% of the size of the PDF page after it is scaled to fit within the frame size of your project, not the original size of the PDF itself. This conversion means that we can't zoom in to a portion of the PNG image without seriously losing image quality.

To import a PDF and retain image quality (see **FIGURE 3.31**):

1. Open the PDF in Preview.
2. Choose File > Export and set the export format to PNG.
3. Set Resolution to 400.

This exports the PDF as a PNG at a high enough resolution that you can frame this as you see fit. (An 8.5 x 11 inch PDF page creates an image that's 3400 x 4400 pixels.) You should export each page of a PDF as a separate file. If you need a larger image from the PDF, increase the resolution.

> **GOING FURTHER** There are two types of PDFs: those that originated as bitmaps and those that originated as vectors. Photos, scans, and Photoshop documents do not scale very well, if at all. Text, Illustrator files, or images created using musical notation software should scale perfectly.

153 Import Media Display Options

These icons enable several useful options.

At the bottom of the Media Import window are two icons; see **FIGURE 3.32**. The left icon toggles between List and Thumbnail view. The right icon, though, does a lot more:

- The top slider, similar to the Browser settings menu, changes the height of thumbnails.

- The lower slider, similar to the Browser settings menu, determines how often a new poster frame is displayed. All shows one poster frame for the clip. Sliding this to the right determines how often to display a new poster frame. This ranges from one every 30 minutes of media to one every 1/2 second.

- Waveforms, when selected, display audio waveforms under all clips that have audio.

- Hide Imported Clips hides any clips from this source or folder that are already imported.

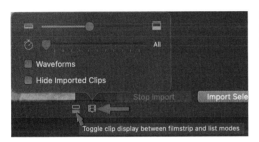

FIGURE 3.32 Clip controls at the bottom of the Media Import window.

154 How to View Timecode During Import

Normally, the Media Import window doesn't show timecode.

Here is the problem: The producer just handed you a sheet of paper with a list of all the clips they want you to import, arranged by source clip timecode. Except how do you see timecode during import?

Easy.

When the Media Import window is open, press Control+Y (see **FIGURE 3.33**) to display skimmer info. As you skim over a clip, the source timecode and clip name are displayed.

FIGURE 3.33 Press Control+Y to display the file name and timecode while skimming a clip in the Media Import window.

GOING FURTHER
To enable or disable the skimmer, press S.

155 Create Favorite Import Locations

This is my favorite import shortcut.

I have most of my media stored on either a local workgroup server or an attached RAID. In both cases, the media is often buried multiple folders deep. It is a pain in the posterior to keep navigating to the same location in the Media Import window.

Fortunately, Final Cut lets us create favorite locations for importing media. To do so, in the Media Import window, navigate to the folder you want make a favorite, then drag the folder name on top of the word "Favorites." It is instantly added to the Favorites list; see **FIGURE 3.34**.

To remove a location from the Favorites list, right-click the name and select Remove from Sidebar; see **FIGURE 3.35**.

FIGURE 3.34 Create a favorite location by dragging a folder name on top of the word "Favorites."

FIGURE 3.35 Right-click the name to remove a favorite location from the list.

MANAGE MEDIA

Once imported, it's time to review and organize media. Final Cut offers lots of ways to do just that.

156 Choose the Right Media Import Settings—Part 1

The options are both impressive and intimidating. Here's what to pick.

The Media Import panel lists all the various import options for your media. There are so many, in fact, that choosing becomes intimidating...what happens if you choose wrong?

Well, um, nothing, really. You may waste some storage space, create files you don't need, or store something in the wrong place. But nothing you choose is going to permanently damage or destroy anything. That is a relief. Still, it saves time and storage space to make the right choices the first time.

So here goes. We'll do this in four parts; see **FIGURE 3.36**.

The first choice is easy. Everything you import or create in Final Cut must be stored in an event. The two radio buttons at the top allow you to select which event you want to use or create a new one.

Selecting where to store files, though, is the most significant decision you make during import.

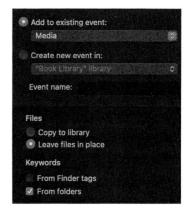

FIGURE 3.36 The top third of the Media Import settings column.

- **Copy to library**. This is the safest option. This copies, not moves, the media from wherever it is into the library. This option is required if you are transferring media from a camera, MicroSD or SD card, or other removable device. This option prevents losing media or breaking links. However, it also doubles your storage needs and prevents sharing that media between different libraries, unless both libraries are open in Final Cut at the same time.

    This last point is important. Neither the Media Import window nor other applications can see media stored in a library.

    However, there are three good reasons for copying files into your Library:

    - The files are stored within the Library, thus preventing broken links.
    - It's easier to back up files stored in a single FCP library file.
    - It's easier to transfer or archive the library and its media when both are stored inside a single library. If you are a new user of Final Cut, I recommend you use this option as you learn the program.

- **Leave files in place**. This is the most flexible option, provided you copied all media to your hard disk before importing it. This option means that Final Cut imports only a link to that media, not the actual files. This decreases storage requirements, supports media sharing between libraries, and simplifies media management because you can see the actual files on your storage using the Finder.

    The only downside, and it's a big one, is that if you move those files, rename them, or rename a folder that contains them, you break all the path names, called *links*, to those files stored in Final Cut. Relinking is possible, but it takes time and can be tricky.

Deciding where to store files is the most significant import decision you need to make.

157 Choose the Right Media Import Settings—Part 2

Keywords make finding media a whole lot easier.

Keywords, which we'll cover later in this chapter, are a great way to organize and find the clips you need quickly. During import, Final Cut can create them automatically; see **FIGURE 3.37**.

GOING FURTHER
You can search for Finder tags using Spotlight if you enter Tag: [tag name] in the search box. For example, you can enter Tag: Wide-shot.

- **Finder tags** are assigned to a file, not just a media clip, by right-clicking the file name in the Finder and selecting Tags. The Finder tags menu (see **FIGURE 3.38**) appears. Here you can assign colors and labels to a clip. Final Cut will turn those into keywords during import. Your experience may be different, but I never found Finder tags worth the work, so I don't use them.

- **Folder names**, however, are useful. Although it's generally a bad idea to rename media clips in the Finder, I often rename the folders that hold those clips. When the Folder names option is selected, those folder names are turned into keywords during import. This is a feature I use a lot.

FIGURE 3.37 The Keywords section in the Media Import settings (above).

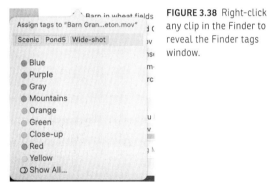

FIGURE 3.38 Right-click any clip in the Finder to reveal the Finder tags window.

158 Choose the Right Media Import Settings—Part 3

Continuing our discussion.

FIGURE 3.39 shows the next group of settings. Again, one of these decisions is easy, while the other is significant.

- **Analyze Video.** For the details, read Apple's Help files. I've never found these settings useful. "Remove Pulldown in video" refers to film transfers. "Balance color" doesn't work. "Find people" takes too long, and even when it works, you will get better results logging clips manually. So in short, leave these unchecked.

- **Transcode**. This is the important decision. I recommend always selecting "Create optimized media." This converts source media into ProRes 422, for improved editing performance. If a media format doesn't need optimization, this choice is grayed out.

Many times, you won't need proxy files. But for frame sizes larger than 4K or multicam editing, proxies are helpful. If editing performance is more important, select ProRes Proxy at 50%. If small files are more important, select H.264 at 25%. Keep in mind, however, that older systems may have problems playing H.264 files without dropping frames. Also, the smaller the frame size percentage, the lower the image quality.

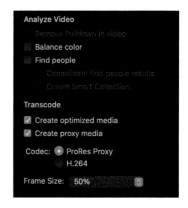

FIGURE 3.39 The middle section of Media Import settings.

GOING FURTHER By default, if you don't optimize media, Final Cut matches the project settings to the format of the camera source media. The default export setting is ProRes 422.

(159) Choose the Right Media Import Settings—Part 4

Wrapping up our discussion.

The last section of these Media Import settings is fairly easy to summarize; see **FIGURE 3.40**. My preferences are already selected in the image.

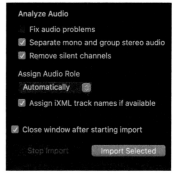

FIGURE 3.40 The lower third of the Media Import settings.

- **Fix audio problems**. This dials in audio enhancements to improve the sound of your audio. I don't use this. My feeling is that audio cleanup should be done during the mixing process, rather than messing with clips on import. You can add these audio enhancements later, during editing, if needed. (See Tip 331, *Adjust Automatic Audio Enhancements*.)

- **Separate mono and group stereo audio**. This is a big plus. Most of what we record is not stereo, but dual-channel mono where different actors are on different tracks or the interviewer is on one track while the guest is on another. This option separates those two tracks into dual mono files to simplify editing. I use this all the time.

- **Remove silent channels**. This applies only if you are importing audio files with more than two channels. Some cameras and audio recorders can record 16 tracks, or more, of audio. If any of them are empty and this option is selected, Final Cut removes the empty channels so as not to clutter up the timeline with empty tracks. If you are importing only two channel files, this setting doesn't apply.

- **Assign Audio Role**. Automatic is a good choice. This, too, is a feature I use every week. (See Tip 334, *Understanding Roles*.)

- **Assign iXML data**. This applies only to audio files using the Broadcast WAV format with labels applied to tracks during recording. If an audio track is labeled, Final Cut creates and assigns an audio subrole to match the label. Leave this selected; it does no harm.

- **Close window**. If you are importing from only one folder into one event, select this. If you are importing from multiple folders or sending files into multiple events, deselect this so the Media Import window doesn't close every time you click Import Selected.

GOING FURTHER Apple's Help files state: "When you import a clip with the 'Analyze and fix audio problems' import option selected, only severe audio problems are corrected. If the clip contains moderate problems, these appear in yellow next to Audio Analysis in the Audio Enhancements section of the Audio inspector after the clip is imported. To correct these problems, you need to automatically enhance audio in the Audio inspector." Audio enhancement is covered in Chapter 6, "Audio."

160 Assign Custom Audio Roles During Import

Roles are especially useful for audio mixing and export.

Roles are unique to Final Cut and highly useful in organizing projects and mixing audio. When you import a clip, Final Cut automatically assigns it to one of five default roles:

- Titles
- Video
- Dialogue
- Effects
- Music

FIGURE 3.41 Assign custom roles using the Assign Audio Role menu.

Most of the time, because we are importing source clips, those five choices are fine. But you may want to assign custom roles to, say, Photoshop graphics, Motion projects, or final audio mixes. That's where Assign Audio Roles comes in; see **FIGURE 3.41**.

Once you create a custom role, which is discussed Tip 334, *Understanding Roles*, it appears in this menu. For example, here I'm importing the final audio mix for a project. This menu assigns a custom role to the imported audio clips, which I can then enable for the final export of my project.

161 Record the FaceTime Camera

Provided you enable security settings to allow it.

When the Media Import window is open, you can record your FaceTime camera directly into Final Cut, provided you change security settings to allow it.

To enable Final Cut to record the camera:

1. Choose System Preferences > Security & Privacy > Camera and select the checkbox for Final Cut Pro; see **FIGURE 3.42**.

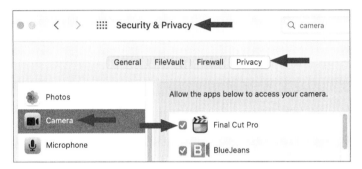

FIGURE 3.42 Select the blue box for Final Cut to record your FaceTime camera.

2. Open the Media Import window and select FaceTime HD Camera in the left sidebar to record the camera; see **FIGURE 3.43**.
3. Click the blue Import button in the lower-right corner to start recording.
4. Click Stop Import to stop recording.

   The file name of this new clip is timestamped and stored in the event you selected in the Media Import window.

GOING FURTHER Recording your camera is useful for recording temp tracks or creating a placeholder for a scene still to come.

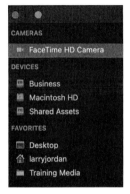

FIGURE 3.43 Select the camera you want to record. Then, click the Import button to start recording.

162 Create Proxies After Importing Media

Proxies are a vital part of editing multicam or large frame size media.

Proxies are smaller files that are optimized for highly efficient editing. They are designed to simplify rough cuts and multicam editing. By design, they do not have as high an image quality as optimized or camera source media.

You can create proxies during import; see Tip 158, *Choose the Right Media Import Settings—Part 3*. This is the best option when creating a multicam project—because using proxies means you can play and edit more cameras simultaneously—or when editing video with large frame sizes.

NOTE Audio in proxy files is the same as the source or optimized media, generally, high-quality and uncompressed.

Using proxies reduces storage bandwidth and simplifies complex edits.

However, you can also create proxies after the fact. To do so:

1. Select the event or clips you want to create proxies for.

2. Choose File > Transcode Media; see **FIGURE 3.44**.

FIGURE 3.44 To create prox- ies, check the appropriate radio button. Reducing the frame size reduces file size.

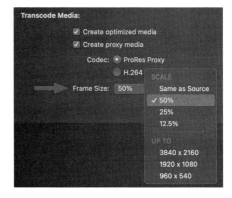

GOING FURTHER
You use this same pro- cess to create optimized media after importing. Optimizing always creates media using the ProRes 422 codec with uncompressed audio.

My recommendation is to use ProRes Proxy as the codec and 50% as the frame size. Decreasing the frame size reduces the media file size, but it also reduces image quality.

H.264 is a good option when you expect to transfer files to another col- laborating editor. The files are about 10% the size of ProRes Proxy media. However, H.264 requires a more modern computer, made, say, after 2017, for smooth editing. H.264, however, is not a good codec for multicam work.

163 A Fast Media Check

Here's a fast way to see what media exists for any clip.

It is easy to lose track of which media exists for a clip. To find out:

1. Select the clip you are curious about in either the Browser or timeline.

2. Go to the Info Inspector and scroll down to the bottom; see **FIGURE 3.45**.

    A green light means that file format exists. A red light means it doesn't.

FIGURE 3.45 The top screen shows both optimized and proxy media are missing for this clip. The Transcode Media button simplifies creating missing media. The bottom screen shows that all formats exist, while the Transcode Media button is hidden.

There's no harm in creating, or not creating, optimized or proxy media, aside from the storage space it takes. These indicators simply let you know what exists and what doesn't.

GOING FURTHER
You can create opti-mized or proxy media directly from the Info Inspector by clicking the Transcode Media button. It displays the same screen shown in Tip 162, *Create Proxies After Importing Media*.

164 What a File with a Broken Link Looks Like

Final Cut tries its darnedest to keep track of all your files.

Over the years, Final Cut has gotten more robust in tracking file name changes so that clips don't unlink. In fact, if Final Cut is running and you accidentally change a file name in the Finder, more times than not, Final Cut will track the change and update its database.

But every so often, it loses track. (A file that Final Cut can't find is called *offline*.) An offline file displays the red and yellow icon shown in **FIGURE 3.46**. You need to relink media to get it reconnected; see Tip 165, *Relink Missing Media*. To find missing media, see Tip 181, *Find Missing Media*.

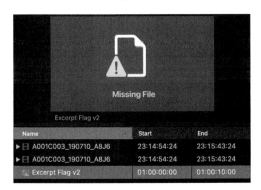

FIGURE 3.46 The icon indicates a missing file. The file name in the Browser list is also flagged with a yellow warning alert.

165 Relink Missing Media

Final Cut makes relinking or replacing media fast and easy.

Oops! You opened your project in FCP, and those red missing file icons appear. Or you need to replace temporary media with the finished files. Don't panic! As long as you know roughly where the original files are located and you didn't rename them in the Finder, relinking your media should be straightforward.

Previously, Final Cut Pro made you pinpoint exactly where the missing media file was stored to relink it. Now, simply select a folder containing the missing file (or a folder that contains the folder with the missing file), and FCP will automatically search within that location to find the file.

To relink a media file:

1. Select the missing file(s) in the Browser.

   Or—select an event.

   Or—select the library.

2. Choose File > Relink Files.

   A relink dialog (see **FIGURE 3.47**) pops up. You can choose to relink all missing files or replace all selected files.

FIGURE 3.47 The Relink Media dialog box.

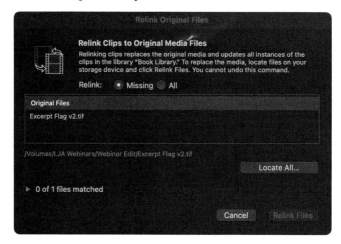

3. Click the Locate All button and choose the drive or folder holding the missing file(s).

NOTE The speed of this file search will depend upon how close you are to the missing file. Searching a hard disk filled with thousands of files will take longer than if you select the folder containing the missing file.

4. Choose Relink Files.

   The missing files are relinked.

   If files are stored in multiple folders, once you find the first missing file, FCP will quickly find all the rest—provided you haven't moved files into different folders in the Finder. If you have, simply continue locating missing files. You don't need to find all files to reconnect the ones you found.

GOING FURTHER You can use this same relink dialog to replace all existing media in an event or library provided the new files have the same name. For example, if you were emailed proxy files from the set to begin editing, then a day or two later the full-resolution files arrived on a hard disk, select the files you want to replace in Final Cut, then using this dialog, select Relink > All. Click Locate All and navigate to the requested file. FCP will switch to the new files while retaining all edit points, transitions, and effects.

166 Create Render Files

Render files are created automatically by FCP as it needs them.

If you never apply a transition, scale a clip, or apply an effect, you'll never need to render files. However, if you change the source media in any way in the timeline, Final Cut creates render files, which are simply new media calculated from the old to apply a setting or effect. Render files are also created anytime Final Cut can't play a clip in real time.

Computers today are so powerful that we can often play clips with effects applied in real time, without waiting for FCP to render. However, for more complex effects or for the best image quality, waiting for FCP to render will make a difference. You'll know this is necessary if FCP starts reporting dropped frames.

To render a file means to calculate new media based on the settings applied to the source media in the timeline.

Final Cut alerts you when it needs to render by displaying white dots at the top of the timeline (see **FIGURE 3.48**). When these appear, rendering automatically starts the next time you pause playback—unless you change the render timing settings in Preferences > Playback (see Tip 71, *Optimize Playback Preferences*), as shown in **FIGURE 3.49**.

FIGURE 3.48 The white dots at the top of the timeline indicate sections needing to render.

FIGURE 3.49 Preferences > Playback determines how quickly rendering starts after playback—or moving the cursor—stops. Rendering can also be disabled, which may benefit older computer systems.

167 Delete Generated Media

Delete render files you don't need to recover storage space.

Render files accumulate. There is only one render frame for each frame of a video clip. This means that if you keep rendering the same file over and over, earlier render files are deleted and replaced. However, if you trim a clip, render files from the portion no longer showing in the timeline are *not* erased. This means you can continue trimming without always re-rendering. Also, if you delete a clip, its render files are not deleted, just in case you decide to add the clip back into the timeline in the future.

To save space, delete unused render files.

For this reason, it's a good practice to delete unused render files every few days during heavy editing. We can delete all generated media—optimized, proxy, and render files—from clips, projects, and libraries. However, you can choose to delete unused media only from events (**FIGURE 3.50**).

My preference is to delete render files from events and not worry about projects or libraries.

1. Select the library/event/project from which you want to delete files.

2. Choose File > Delete generated [*selected object*] media.

3. In the screen that appears, select Delete Render Files. After a few seconds of processing, the render files are gone.

FIGURE 3.50 This dialog appears when you want to delete render files.

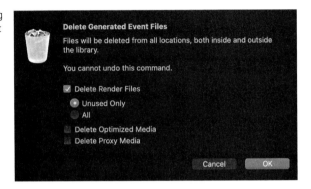

Delete Generated Event Files

Files will be deleted from all locations, both inside and outside the library.

You cannot undo this command.

☑ Delete Render Files
    ● Unused Only
    ○ All
☐ Delete Optimized Media
☐ Delete Proxy Media

Cancel   OK

Oops...!

But what if you delete render files that you still need? Not to panic. Final Cut automatically re-creates any missing render files the next time it needs them. This means that deleting render files simply to save space won't help. All missing render files are instantly rebuilt. No space saved.

Deleting *unused* render files, though, saves storage space. Also, deleting render files when a project is done is a good practice as it reclaims storage space for files that were needed only for editing. If you reopen the project in the future, any missing render files are re-created.

GOING FURTHER When deleting generated media files, especially from libraries, I've found that Final Cut doesn't actually recover that storage space until you quit Final Cut and relaunch it.

ORGANIZE MEDIA

How well you organize media after import determines how likely you are to find the shot later when you need when you need it.

168 Quick Specs Check

This is a fast way to check frame size and frame rate.

The three most important technical specs for a clip or project are codec, frame size, and frame rate. By the time a project is created and media is imported, you've pretty much handled the codec aspect. So here is a fast way to check the frame size and frame rate of projects or clips:

1. Select it.
2. Look at the top of the Info Inspector; see **FIGURE 3.51**.

There you'll see listed the clip or project name, frame size, frame rate, audio configuration, and duration.

FIGURE 3.51 (Top to bottom) 4K HDR project, 360° video project, and individual clip.

169 Use Favorites to Flag Shots You Like

Two keyboard shortcuts can help quickly organize clips.

You found a clip you like, or maybe just a portion of a clip. Make it a Favorite. Favorite clips, or ranges, display a green bar at the top of the Browser; see **FIGURE 3.52**. Favorites are a very fast way to build a "selects" reel of clips you want to use in your project.

- Select a clip, or range inside a clip in the Browser.
- Press F to flag (or indicate) the selected range is a Favorite.

FIGURE 3.52 Green bars indicate Favorites; red bars indicate Rejected; gold boxes indicate selections.

- If you find a clip, or range, you don't like, press Delete to flag it as Rejected. Rejected clips display a red bar at the top.
- To unflag a clip, select the portion you want to restore and press U. Unflagged clips contain no bar.

The default display setting for the Browser is Hide Rejected Clips. Rejected clips instantly disappear from the Browser, but they are not deleted, merely hidden. Change the menu at the top of the Browser to All Clips (see **FIGURE 3.53**) to re-display any rejected clips or ranges.

GOING FURTHER
This tip is a big time-saver for flagging clips you like. As a fast follow-on tip, click the green or blue line at the top of a Browser clip to set an In and Out specifically matching that range.

To actually delete a clip from Final Cut, press Cmd+Delete. This does not delete it from storage, unless it is stored inside the library and it is not in use on a timeline.

FIGURE 3.53 This menu at the top of the Browser determines the clip display options for the Browser.

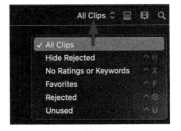

170 Find Unused Media

This is a fast way to find out what's available.

Final Cut also tracks both unused and duplicate media; see Tip 214, *Find Duplicated Media*. To see which media is used in the current project, that is, the project currently open in the timeline:

1. Select the Browser.
2. Choose View > Browser > Used Media Ranges.

   The orange bar indicates currently used media; see **FIGURE 3.54**.

To view only unused media, select Unused from the Browser menu.

FIGURE 3.54 The orange bar indicates media edited into the current timeline. Select Unused from the Browser menu to see only unused media.

GOING FURTHER
You can also use the Search Filter dialog to find unused media; see Tip 180, *More Search Options*.

171 Add Notes to One or More Clips

Adding notes in the Inspector is more reliable than the Browser.

You can add notes to any clip in the Browser, using the Notes field. But I've found adding notes in the Browser awkward and not always available. A more reliable alternative is to use the Info Inspector; see **FIGURE 3.55.**

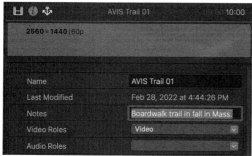

FIGURE 3.55 The clip Notes field in the Info Inspector.

GOING FURTHER
Apply the same note to multiple clips by selecting them in either the Browser or the timeline. Then, enter the note in the Notes field of the Info Inspector. This applies the note to all selected clips. The contents of all notes are searched when you do a Find operation (see Tip 172, *The Highly Efficient Search Box*).

Select the clip, or clips, in the Browser or timeline to which you want to add a note. Open the Info Inspector (shortcut: Cmd+4) and enter the information you want.

You can view notes in the List View of the Browser and the Info Inspector.

172 The Highly Efficient Search Box

The Browser search box searches across multiple metadata fields.

At the top right of the Browser is a small magnifying glass. Click it and the search box opens; see **FIGURE 3.56.**

FIGURE 3.56 Click the magnifying glass icon to open the Browser's search box.

This is a text search field. Using the text you enter, Final Cut searches all file names, notes, markers, and customizable text fields displayed in the General settings menu of the Info Inspector; see **FIGURE 3.57**. The search results are displayed in the Browser.

To limit a search, say to only text in a Notes field, click the chevron next to the magnifying glass (see **FIGURE 3.58**), and choose the text fields you want to search.

FIGURE 3.57 Enter custom data for one or more selected clips in the Browser using the General menu (bottom arrow) in the Info Inspector.

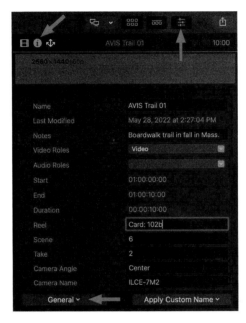

FIGURE 3.58 Click the chevron next to the magnifying glass to limit which text fields are searched.

FIGURE 3.59 Each entry is a panel containing dozens of metadata fields, many of which are customizable (left).

173 Metadata Goldmine

Final Cut tracks hundreds of metadata entries per clip.

At the bottom left of the Info Inspector is the Basic metadata button. Click it to reveal several more metadata menus; see **FIGURE 3.59**. Of these, General is the most useful. Each of these menus displays dozens of customizable metadata fields in the Info Inspector to organize your media. Choose Edit Metadata View to create your own custom metadata panel.

174 Edit Metadata Fields

The Info Inspector is the easiest place to add custom metadata.

Although you can enter text in the Notes field in the Browser, the Info Inspector provides a wealth of additional fields you can use to label, categorize, and find clips. You've already seen how the General menu provides custom data fields. However, choosing Edit Metadata View (see **FIGURE 3.60**) displays the Metadata Views window with hundreds of custom metadata fields that can be enable for every clip.

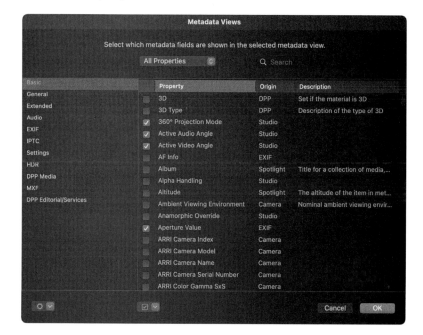

FIGURE 3.60 Use the Edit Metadata window to create custom metadata fields that can be saved and shared between libraries.

FIGURE 3.61 The General panel (lower red arrow) in the Info Inspector (top-left arrow) offers dozens of customizable text fields.

GOING FURTHER
Apple's Help files provide more information on what these fields are, how to organize them, and how to create custom menus (see **FIGURE 3.61**).

175 Keywords Allow More Flexible Organization

Assign one or more keywords to clips or clip ranges.

Custom metadata fields are useful, but they are also time-consuming to enter and require editors to think like librarians. Keywords offer more granular ways to organize your media than creating Favorites and provide many different ways to search for them. Plus you can add them far faster and easier than custom metadata.

To apply a keyword:

1. Select a clip range, a clip, or a group of clips in the Browser; then either click the small key icon at the top left of the FCP interface or press Cmd+K.

    The Keywords for Selection dialog opens; see **FIGURE 3.62**.

2. Enter a word or short phrase that categorizes the selected clips.

    In this screen shot, I've selected two clip ranges with flower images and applied the "Flower" keyword to both selected clips.

3. Press Return to apply the keyword to the clips.

Keywords are case agnostic and may not contain commas. One- or two-word keywords are best.

FIGURE 3.62 The Keywords for Selection dialog, located below the Browser.

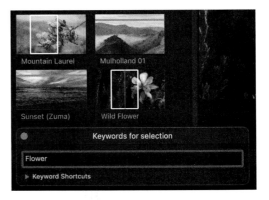

176 A Faster Way to Add Keywords

Add keywords via keyboard shortcuts.

In Tip 175, *Keywords Allow More Flexible Organization*, you learned how to apply keywords. Here's how to do it faster. Click the small arrow next to Keyword Shortcuts in the floating Keywords window. This reveals the Keyword Shortcuts panel; see **FIGURE 3.63**.

The first nine keywords you created are stored in this panel.

- To apply a keyword to a selected clip, clip range, or group of clips, either type the shortcut or click the numbered shortcut button.
- To change the text entry for one of the nine, delete the word that's there and type a new one. This change doesn't change any existing keywords.
- To remove all these presets, press Control+0 or click the button next to Remove All Shortcuts.

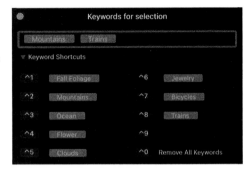

FIGURE 3.63 The Keyword Shortcuts panel.

Although the number of keyword shortcuts you can add is unlimited, Final Cut stores only nine.

177 Keywords Create Keyword Collections

Collections are dynamic and even faster than using Find.

As you add keywords to clips, they are also added to the Library List as a keyword collection. (Click the triangle next to the event name to reveal them.) Keyword collections are dynamic. As soon as you add a keyword to a clip, the collection is automatically updated.

- Click a collection, and only those clips assigned that keyword are displayed; see **FIGURE 3.64**. This quick search is virtually instant.
- Cmd-click (or Shift-click) more than one collection name, and only those clips that contain at least one of the selected keywords are displayed. (Logicians call this a *Boolean OR*.)
- To remove a collection, along with that keyword assigned to individual clips, right-click a collection and choose Delete Keyword Collection at the bottom of the menu (shortcut: Cmd+Delete).

I use keyword collections a lot.

GOING FURTHER
The first time you add a keyword to a clip or clip range, a blue bar appears at the top of a clip. That's a visual indicator showing that at least one keyword was applied and to which part of the clip.

Keyword collections make searches virtually instant.

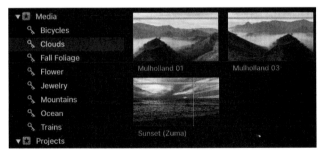

FIGURE 3.64 Click a keyword collection, like Clouds, and only those clips assigned that keyword are displayed.

178 Two Keyword Speed Tips

Apply and modify keywords faster.

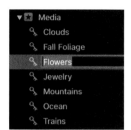

FIGURE 3.65 Changing the spelling of the keyword collection changes that keyword in all clips.

Keyword collections also make applying keywords to clips or ranges faster. Select all the clips to which you want to apply an existing keyword, then drag the clips on top of the appropriate keyword collection. Ta-dah! Keyword added.

If you suddenly realize that a keyword is misspelled, don't worry. Select it in the keyword collection (see **FIGURE 3.65**), and change the spelling. This changes the keyword for every clip or range to which it is applied.

GOING FURTHER If you delete a keyword collection, you also delete that keyword applied to all clips.

179 Keywords Enable a Very Powerful Search

Keyword collection searches are fast.
Search filters are fast and more flexible.

Now we get into some really exciting stuff—an extremely fast and powerful search. If you want to search an entire library, select the library in the Library List. If you want to search only a single event, select the event in the Library List. You can't search a selected group of events.

1. Click the magnifying glass at the top of the Browser.

2. Click the small rectangular icon to the right of the search box (lower red arrow); it's supposed to look like a clapper slate (see **FIGURE 3.66**).

   This opens the full Search Filter panel; see **FIGURE 3.67** (shortcut: Cmd+F). Click the plus icon and select keywords from the menu. This displays all the keywords assigned to all the clips in that which you selected—a single event or the entire library.

FIGURE 3.66 To reveal search filters, click the magnifying glass, then the clapper icon (above).

FIGURE 3.67 The Search Filter panel showing a list of the metadata that can be searched (right).

3. Select the keywords you want to search for; see **FIGURE 3.68**.

4. (Here is the powerful part.) From the "Include Any" menu, choose:

- **Include Any**. To include all clips that contain *any* of these keywords.

- **Include All**. To include only those clips that contain *all* of these keywords.

- **Does Not Include Any**. To exclude all clips that contain *any* of these keywords.

- **Does Not Include All.** To exclude all clips that each contain all of these keywords.

NOTE Include Any generally finds the largest number of clips, while Include All finds the fewest.

FIGURE 3.68 Select only those keywords you want to search for; then, from this menu, determine how inclusive the search should be.

⑱⓪ More Search Options

Almost unlimited search possibilities.

In the Search Filter dialog, go back to the plus icon, where you'll find 12 different criteria; see **FIGURE 3.69**. This composite screen shot illustrates menus to search for media you've used or not yet used, as well as specific frame sizes, media types, or media formats. And more.

Although this is way overkill for smaller projects, it's a life-saver for projects with thousands of clips.

FIGURE 3.69 A composite of some of the additional search criteria available in the Search Filter dialog.

181 Find Missing Media

Find any type of media missing in an event or library.

Missing media is the big downside to storing media outside the library. Worse, even in smaller projects, it can be hard to figure out what's missing. The Search Filter dialog can help.

1. Click the plus icon (see **FIGURE 3.70**) and select Media Representation.
2. Repeat two more times. (If you aren't using optimized or proxy media, you can omit this step.)
3. From the menus, select the types of missing media you want to find; see **FIGURE 3.71**.

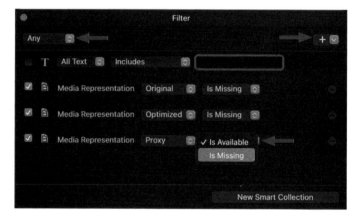

FIGURE 3.70 Select search criteria, such as Media Representation, from the plus icon menu.

FIGURE 3.71 Use the Search Filter dialog to find all missing files. Note Any is selected and Text is unchecked.

GOING FURTHER
As shown here, you can apply the same search criteria more than once to fine-tune the range of a search.

4. From the top menu, change All to Any to find all media meeting any of these conditions.
5. Deselect Text, to avoid searching text fields.
6. Click New Smart Collection to save these settings and begin the search.

182 Secret Search Icons

Here's how to tell if there's an active search.

When you look at the search box in the Browser, it will tip you off if there's an active search—but it uses a secret icon code; see **FIGURE 3.72**.

For example, in Figure 3.72, these small icons indicate, from top to bottom:

- An active text search
- An active keyword search
- An active used media search
- An active media type search
- A search on multiple criteria: media type, roles, and keywords
- Click the X in a circle to cancel the search and empty the search box.

FIGURE 3.72 These search box icons indicate if there is an active search.

🔘 183 Smart Collections

Smart Collections are dynamic saved searches.

At the bottom of the Search Filter dialog is the New Smart Collection button; see Figure 3.71. When you click it, Final Cut saves those search criteria into a Smart Collection; see **FIGURE 3.73**. In addition to saving your search settings, a Smart Collection is dynamic. As you modify clips, for example, adding keywords or adding them in the timeline, they appear or disappear in the Smart Collection as they meet or don't meet the search criteria.

- Click a Smart Collection to display the clips that meet its criteria. In Figure 3.73, I'm searching for unused cloud or flower clips.
- Rename the Smart Collection as you would an event or project.
- Double-click the name of a Smart Collection to reopen it so you can change its search criteria; then save it again inside the Search Filter dialog.
- Right-click a Smart Collection to delete it (or press Cmd+Delete). Deleting a Smart Collection does not delete any clips or keywords.

Smart Collections are dynamic, modifiable saved searches.

FIGURE 3.73 A renamed Smart Collection. Note the icon.

184 It's OK to Rename Clips...in Final Cut

Nothing breaks as long as you rename in Final Cut.

Any clip imported into Final Cut can be renamed—in Final Cut.

Sometimes, it really, really helps to rename a clip, which you can do—as long as you know where. Any clip imported into Final Cut can be renamed in Final Cut using any name that works for you. Renaming a clip in the Browser does not affect its name in the Finder or break any links to that file in any other library.

However, once you import a clip, don't rename it in the Finder.

185 Rename Clips in Batches

Batch renaming speeds standardizing clip names.

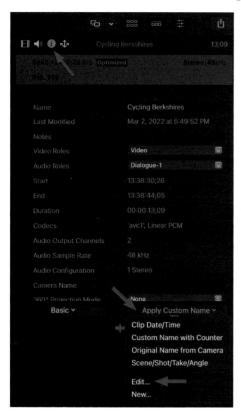

FIGURE 3.74 Select Apply Custom Name to rename a batch of clips. Click Edit for additional naming options.

This is a summary from an Apple KnowledgeBase article.

When you import media into Final Cut Pro, the clips often contain meaningless names, such as those assigned by the camera. Although you can rename clips individually, you can also rename a selection of clips as a batch in the browser, after the media has been imported. Final Cut Pro provides customizable naming presets that make renaming large numbers of clips efficient and easy.

To rename a batch of clips, using a naming preset:

1. In the Final Cut Pro Browser, select the clips you want to rename.

2. If the Inspector isn't visible, choose Window > Show in Workspace > Inspector (shortcut: Cmd+4).

3. Click the Info Inspector button at the top of the Inspector; see **FIGURE 3.74**.

4. In the Info Inspector, click the Apply Custom Name pop-up menu and choose a naming preset.

The clips selected in the Browser are renamed.

GOING FURTHER An extensive clip renaming capability is built into Final Cut. Click the Edit button in the Apply Custom Name menu; then read Apple's Help pages for instructions.

CUSTOMIZE THE TIMELINE

These tips illustrate how to customize the timeline to the way you want to work.

186 Customize the Timeline

This affects only display, not export.

Final Cut offers several ways to customize the look of the timeline. Over in the top-right corner of the timeline, click the icon that looks like a film strip; it's blue in **FIGURE 3.75**. This is the Clip Appearance button.

FIGURE 3.75 Timeline customization options. Click the blue icon at the top-right of the timeline to display this pane.

- The top slider zooms in to or out of the timeline. (For me, it is faster to use keyboard shortcuts: Cmd+[plus], Cmd+[minus], and Cmd+Z.)

- The six icons on the second row determine the ratio of displaying the audio waveform to the image. The far-left icon displays the audio waveform only; the second from the right displays the image only. The far-right icon reduces the height of all tracks to thinner lines so you can see the overall organization of your project.

- The slider on the third row determines the height of timeline clips.

- The five checkboxes at the bottom enable the display of the following:
  - **Clip names**.
  - **Angles**. Multicam camera angle names.
  - **Clip Roles**. See Tip 238, *Timeline Index—Roles*.
  - **Lane Headers**. These apply only when you are displaying roles.
  - **Duplicate Ranges**. This shows duplicate media in the timeline; see Tip 214, *Find Duplicated Media*.

187 A Super-Fast Way to Zoom In to the Timeline

Press Z, then drag in the timeline to zoom in to an area.

You can use keyboard shortcuts to zoom in to the timeline, but this is even faster. Press Z while dragging the mouse over the part of the timeline you want to zoom in to; see **FIGURE 3.76**.

Let go of the mouse and, Ta-dah!, you're there.

GOING FURTHER
To reset the timeline so the entire edit fits into the visible timeline, press Shift+Z.

FIGURE 3.76 Press Z while dragging to zoom in to that section of the timeline.

188 Hide the Sidebar

This is a quick way to make room to see more clips.

The sidebar, in the top left of the interface, displays libraries along with categories for music, sound effects, titles, and generators; see **FIGURE 3.77**.

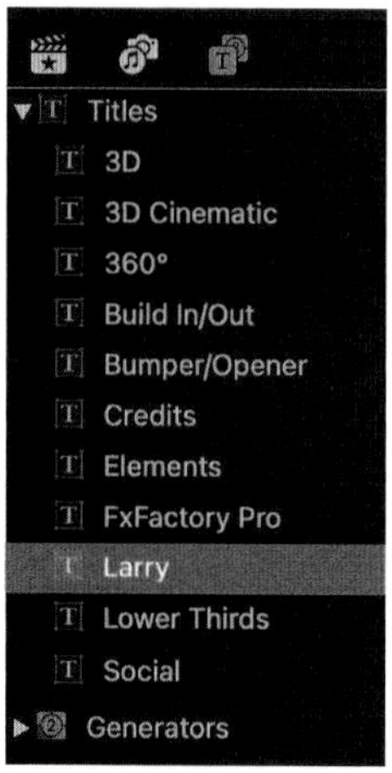

To hide the sidebar, click any of the three icons that are blue. To turn it back on, click the same icon again.

> GOING FURTHER The keyboard shortcut for toggling the sidebar is Cmd+~ (tilde).

FIGURE 3.77 Enable or disable the sidebar by clicking one of the three blue icons. Click it again to make it reappear.

▼ T Titles
  T 3D
  T 3D Cinematic
  T 360°
  T Build In/Out
  T Bumper/Opener
  T Credits
  T Elements
  T FxFactory Pro
  T Larry
  T Lower Thirds
  T Social
▶   Generators

189 What If Frame Rates Don't Match

There is only one frame rate in a project.

In an ideal world, which I'm told exists though I haven't worked in it, the frame rate you shoot matches the project frame rate you edit, which matches the frame rate you deliver to the client.

Then, there's the real world, where frame rates propagate like rabbits. What happens then?

There is only one project frame rate, just as there is only one project codec. Although you can mix and match source clip codecs and frame rates into the project, those different clips get converted into the project codec and frame rate during render and export.

The project frame rate *always* wins. Final Cut converts non-project-standard frame rates to match the project—either on the fly, when it renders, or when it exports.

For smoothest results, frame rates that are multiples of each other convert the best. Faster frame rates generally convert down okay. Slower frame rates tend to stutter a bit when converted up. Most of the time, you'll notice the stutter only during a smooth pan, a smooth tilt, or on-screen action.

There is only one frame rate per project. The project frame rate. Period.

The basic rule is to shoot the frame rate you need to deliver. If you can't, then shoot double the frame rate. If frame rate conversion is critical, take a look at the clip first in Final Cut. If it looks good, great. If not, you'll need to convert the frame rate of the clip using other software before bringing it into Final Cut for editing.

190 How to Change the Frame Rate of a Project

Normally, you use project settings. Sometimes, that doesn't work.

By default, Final Cut sets the frame rate of a project based upon the frame rate of the first clip edited into it. Most of the time, this works great. However, what if you don't have a clip with the right properties? Well, you could create a custom project, or you could use this work-around.

When you know the frame rate and frame size you want, edit any full-screen generator into an empty project. This displays the pop-up window shown in **FIGURE 3.78**.

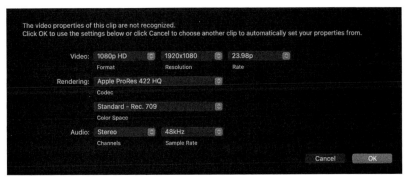

FIGURE 3.78 This project setting dialog appears only when you edit a title, graphic, or generator into an empty timeline.

Use the menus to create the settings you need. When you click OK, the generator edits into the timeline.

Now, go ahead and edit a couple of other clips. At this point, you can remove the generator. Once at least one clip is edited into a project, the frame rate settings are locked.

GOING FURTHER These days editing Zoom videos is common. Many Zoom videos are 25 fps and designed for posting to the web. In this case, edit the video at 25 fps. Don't convert the frame rate. The web easily handles any frame rate, so edit the frame rate in which the video was shot. The editing process is the same, regardless of frame rate.

191 Correct the Aspect Ratio of a Clip

This tip doesn't reframe; it merely resizes.

Most of the time, Final Cut accurately senses the aspect ratio of a clip. However, sometimes, especially with older SD clips using nonstandard aspect ratios, it doesn't. Here's how to fix this problem:

1. Select the clip, or clips, that you want to correct in either the Browser or the timeline.

2. Open the Info Inspector.

3. In the lower-left corner of the Inspector, change the pop-up menu from Basic to Settings.

4. To change the selected clips to a 16:9 ratio, in the Settings window, change the Anamorphic Override from None Set to Widescreen; see **FIGURE 3.79**.

5. To change the selected clips to a 4:3 aspect ratio, in the Settings window, change Anamorphic Override to Standard.

This doesn't reframe clips. It simply converts the aspect ratio.

GOING FURTHER
Anamorphic Override appears only for 4x3-native standard-definition clips; it's not there on 16x9-native clips, nor on 1440x1080p clips. So this is something you may see for only a few specific types of media.

FIGURE 3.79 Standard converts the aspect ratio to 4:3. Widescreen converts it to 16:9.

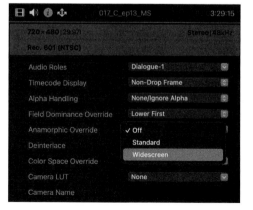

CHAPTER 3—LIBRARIES & MEDIA SHORTCUTS

CATEGORY	SHORTCUT	WHAT IT DOES
Import	Cmd+I	Open Media Import window
	Control+Y	Display skimmer info
Organizing	F	Flag a clip, or range, as a Favorite
	Delete	Flag a clip, or range, as Rejected
	U	Reset a clip, or range, to Unflagged
	Cmd+K	Open Keywords dialog
	Shift+Cmd+K	Create new keyword collection
	Control 1 - 9	Apply keyword tag (nine choices)
	Cmd+F	Open Search Filter dialog
	Option+Cmd+N	Create a new Smart Collection
Operation	Shift+Cmd+R	Reveal selected item in Finder

CHAPTER WRAP

The story is clear in our mind or in the script. Our gear is ready. Libraries and projects are created. Media is imported and organized. Now, the fun part starts: editing.

CHAPTER 4

BASIC EDITING

INTRODUCTION

Editing is where the spark of creativity first lights. Editing decides which portion of each clip to show and where it goes in the timeline. Trimming adjusts where two clips touch, called the *edit point*. Trimming is critically important to storytelling because it adjusts how smoothly one shot flows into the next. Often, you'll spend more time trimming than editing, even for simple projects.

In this chapter, we—finally!—move into actual editing. There's so much to cover that we'll divide editing and trimming into two parts: basic techniques in this chapter and advanced techniques in the next.

- Mark Clips
- Edit Clips
- Editing Tools
- Trim Clips
- Timeline Index
- Shortcuts

DEFINITIONS FOR THIS CHAPTER

- **Editing**. Editing decides what clips to use, their order, and duration.
- **Trimming**. Trimming adjusts where two clips touch.
- **Through edit**. This is a cut (edit) in a clip where nothing was removed on either side.
- **Camera**. The camera represents the eye of the audience. Every time you change the shot, you move the audience to a new place. Treat the audience gently, and be careful not to disorient them.
- **Primary Storyline** (aka magnetic timeline). This is the black bar in the middle of the timeline. Designed for speed and to minimize errors, it's where you put the principal clip for each scene.
- **Layer**. Other NLEs call these *tracks*. Apple prefers the term layers. Layers are horizonal levels that hold clips above or below the Primary Storyline. There is no limit to the number of layers in Final Cut.
- **Connected clip**. This is a clip on a higher (or lower) layer that "connects to" a clip on the Primary Storyline. Connected video clips go above the Primary Storyline, while connected audio clips go below it. Connected clips are always rendered to match the project settings.
- **Storyline**. This is a group of connected clips on a higher (or lower) layer that are treated as a single clip. It can hold audio or video but can't contain clips on multiple layers.
- **B-roll**. This is an old film term describing video clips placed on a higher layer to illustrate what the clip in the Primary Storyline is discussing.
- **Downstream** (**upstream**): Timelines are often described as water flowing from the beginning (left) to the end (right). *Downstream* refers to all clips from the playhead (skimmer) to the right. *Upstream* refers to all clips from the playhead (skimmer) to the left.
- **Snapping**. When enabled, this option snaps the playhead (or skimmer) to edit points and markers. When snapped to an edit point, the playhead (skimmer) is always parked on the In.
- **In**. This is where the playback of a clip starts, which is most often not the start of the clip.
- **Out**. This is where the playback of a clip ends, which is most often not the end of the clip.
- **Range**. This is the part of a clip, or timeline, defined by an In and an Out.
- **Handles**. This is extra audio and video before the In and/or after the Out used for trimming and transitions.

Editing decides clip order and duration. Trimming adjusts where two clips touch.

- **Edit point**. This is where two clips touch in the timeline. An edit point has three "sides" or edges: the In, the Out, and both the In and the Out.
- **Ripple trim**. This adjusts one side of an edit point, the In or the Out. Ripple trims always alter the duration of a project.
- **Roll trim**. This adjusts both sides of an edit point at the same time. Roll trims never alter the duration of a project.
- **Timeline element**. This is shorthand for things in the timeline: clips, titles, generators.

MARK CLIPS

Marking clips begins the editing process. This determines the start and end of each clip when edited into the timeline.

(192) Playback Shortcuts

There are a variety of ways to play clips.

The easiest way to play any clip is to press the spacebar.

- **Shift-spacebar**. Plays a clip in reverse.
- **J**. Plays a clip in reverse.
- **J-J**. Plays a clip in reverse at double-speed.
- **J-J-J**. Plays a clip in reverse at 4X speed.
- **L**. Plays a clip forward.
- **L-L**. Plays a clip forward at double-speed.
- **L-L-L**. Plays a clip forward at 4X speed.
- **J-K**. Plays a clip in reverse in slow motion.
- **L-K**. Plays a clip forward in slow motion.

Here are more playback shortcuts that work in the timeline:

- **/**. Plays the selection.
- **Shift+?**. Using the durations set in Preferences > Playback, shifts the playhead from its current location back to the pre-roll duration, plays through the edit, then stops at the end of the post-roll duration. It then returns the playhead to its original position. This is often used to review continuity through an edit point.
- **Shift+Option+I**. Plays from the beginning of the Browser clip or timeline to the end.

Skim clips with the mouse, trackpad, or trackball, as well as play clips using the keyboard.

- **Shift+Option+O**. Plays from the current playhead (skimmer) position to the end of the selected region or timeline.
- **Shift+Cmd+F**. Displays and plays the timeline full screen. (Press Esc to exit.)
- **Cmd+L**. Toggles playback looping on or off. When enabled, this jumps the playhead from the end of a clip or selected range back to the beginning. You won't see the effect of this shortcut until playback resumes.

193 Snapping—the Secret to Precision

This "snaps" the playhead (skimmer) to an In or a marker.

Snapping works even if the Position tool is active.

You enable snapping (shortcut: N), which is off by default, by clicking the Snapping icon in the top-right corner of the timeline (see 4 in **FIGURE 4.1**). When enabled, it "snaps" the playhead, or skimmer, to the In at any edit point, the In or Out of any marked range, or the location of any marker.

Snapping works in both the Browser and the timeline. It ensures that the playhead is correctly positioned at the In of a timeline clip when doing an insert or overwrite edit.

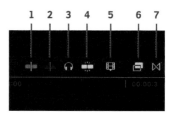

FIGURE 4.1 Click the Snapping icon (4) in the top-right corner of the timeline to enable snapping. (See Tip 96, *Timeline Control Icons*, for definitions of the rest of these controls.)

194 Marking a Clip Sets the In and Out

Marking reduces the time you spend trimming.

NOTE Make selections "on the fly" while playing Browser clips by pressing I or O at the desired point during playback.

To mark a clip means to set an In and/or an Out. This marked area is called a *range*. Clips are marked in the Browser. Move the playhead, or skimmer, where you want the clip playback to start, and press I. Then, move the playhead (skimmer) where you want playback to end, and press O. If no In is set, FCP defaults to the start of the clip. If no Out is set, FCP defaults to the end of the clip.

Final Cut indicates this area, called a *range*, in the Browser by surrounding it with a gold box; see **FIGURE 4.2**. That gold box does not indicate the image you are editing; rather, it indicates the duration of the clip you are editing into the timeline.

You can also select a range in a Browser clip by dragging across the clip with the Select (arrow) or Range tools. If the clip extends to a second row, either drag across the break or extend it by Shift-clicking. Option-drag to replace an existing range with a new range.

Here are some other useful shortcuts:

- **X**. Select the entire clip.
- **Option+X**. Remove the marked range.
- **Shift+I**. Jump the playhead to the In.
- **Shift+O**. Jump the playhead to the Out.
- Click-drag one of the yellow vertical lines to adjust the In or Out.

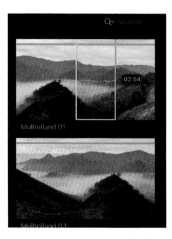

FIGURE 4.2 A selected range (top) for a Browser clip. The numbers in the box indicate its duration.

GOING FURTHER When you mark a range using a keyword (see Tip 175: *Keywords Allow More Flexible Organization*) or a Favorite (see Tip 169, *Use Favorites to Flag Shots You Like*), the Browser clip containing it displays a blue (keyword) or green (Favorite) bar at the top of the clip thumbnail. Click the bar and, Ta-dah!, the range is instantly marked with an In and an Out.

195 Select Multiple Ranges in One Clip

You don't need to create just one range at a time.

A range is that part of a clip with an In and/or an Out. Although it is normal to use multiple ranges from the same clip, Final Cut has a unique feature: You can select more than one range in a clip *at the same time*, provided the ranges don't overlap.

FIGURE 4.3 (top) Multiple selected ranges in a single clip. The lower clip has no ranges in it.

- To create a single range, drag the playhead, or skimmer, across a Browser clip.
- To create multiple ranges, create the first range either using the Range tool or entering an In and Out. Then Cmd-drag to select additional ranges in the same clip; see **FIGURE 4.3**.
- To select a single range, click a range.
- To select multiple ranges in one clip or across several clips, Cmd-click.
- To deselect a selected range, Cmd-click it.
- To delete a selected range, Option-click it.

GOING FURTHER You can edit multiple sections of the same clip into the timeline simply by editing each one individually. What makes this tip special is the ability to select multiple ranges in the same clip at the same time; then edit them as a group into the timeline.

196 Browser Clip Icons

Here's what these strange clip icons mean.

Once you mark a clip, new icons appear in the corners of clips; see
FIGURE 4.4. These frame markers are visible in the Browser and Viewer
when the playhead (skimmer) lands on the appropriate frame. None of these
icons export.

Here's what they mean.

FIGURE 4.4 The playhead is parked on the In (top) or Out (bottom) of a Browser clip.

The playhead is parked on the In (top) or Out (bottom) of a timeline clip.

The playhead is parked on the first frame of the timeline (top), the last frame of the timeline (middle), or past the end of the timeline (bottom).

EDIT CLIPS

Once clips are marked, editing determines their order in the timeline.

197 The Magnetic Timeline Is Not Evil!

It's incredibly helpful—once you learn what it does.

The magnetic timeline is designed to prevent problems and speed editing.

Nothing has been so vilified in Final Cut Pro as the magnetic timeline.
But once you understand it, it becomes an amazing tool. Prior to Final Cut
Pro (X), a big problem in all video editing systems was very quick flashes of
black caused by one to two frame gaps in the timeline. These were impossible
to see unless you were zoomed way in to the timeline. These were so bother-
some that Final Cut Pro 7 even added a special shortcut to find and remove
these gaps.

Final Cut Pro (X) fixed that. When clips were edited into the Primary Story-line, which is the black channel in the middle of the timeline, they would automatically shift position so that edit points always touched. This made editing faster because you no longer needed to perfectly position the play-head or skimmer before making the edit.

Clips edited to higher layers (Apple prefers not to call these *tracks*) always connect to clips in the Primary Storyline. This speeds editing because if you move, say, a talking head clip in the Primary Storyline, all the B-roll and sound effects clips connected to it move in sync with it.

These two operational changes make editing a lot faster and more secure than on any other NLE. However, as you'll learn in this chapter, there are many techniques that temporarily suspend this magnetic behavior to create exactly the edits you have in mind.

⓳⑧ Final Cut Pro Supports Four Edit Options

Append, insert, overwrite, and connected.

Final Cut supports four types of edits: append, insert, overwrite, and connected. These four edits determine how and where clips are edited from the Browser into the timeline.

- **Append** (shortcut: E). This places the selected Browser clip, or clips, into the Primary Storyline at the end of all existing clips in the timeline. It ignores the position of the playhead or skimmer. Append edits do not alter, move, or replace any existing clips.

- **Insert** (shortcut: W). This inserts the selected Browser clip, or clips, into the Primary Storyline at the position of the playhead (skimmer) and pushes all clips to the right of the edit point downstream for the duration of the inserted clip. Insert edits do not alter or replace any existing clips.

- **Overwrite** (shortcut: D). This edits the selected Browser clip, or clips, into the Primary Storyline at the position of the playhead (skimmer) and replaces whatever clips are currently in the Primary Storyline for the duration of the incoming clip. Overwrite edits do not move any existing clips.

- **Connected** (shortcut: Q). This places the selected Browser clip, or clips, onto the next highest layer above (for video) or below (for audio) the Primary Storyline such that no existing clips are replaced, over-written, or moved.

The four edit options in Final Cut Pro are append, insert, overwrite, and connected.

199 Editing Icons, Tools, and Shortcuts

Yes, you can drag a clip, but these shortcuts are faster!

When it comes time to move a shot from the Browser into the timeline, you have three choices:

- Drag it.
- Use an editing icon/button.
- Use a keyboard shortcut.

Dragging a clip is easy. Keyboard shortcuts are much faster.

Dragging works. It's easy, but it isn't very precise, and it isn't very fast.

FIGURE 4.5 illustrates the five editing icons (yup, one is hidden). The numbers for the icons correspond with the callout numbers in Figure 4.5:

1. Connected edit

2. Insert edit

3. Append edit

4. Overwrite edit

5. Chevron menu to select between editing audio only, video only, or both

The chevron menu remains set until you change it. It doesn't automatically reset.

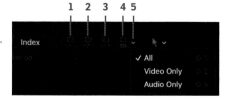

FIGURE 4.5 Editing icons: 1. Connected, 2. Insert, 3. Append, 4. Overwrite, 5. Menu.

Although these editing icons are helpful to editors who are new to the program, my preference is shortcuts. I'm a keyboard junkie. These shortcuts mean I can keep one hand on the mouse and the other on the keyboard while editing.

- **E.** Append edit.
- **W.** Insert edit.
- **D.** Overwrite edit.
- **Q.** Connected edit.
- **Shift+1.** Edit clip audio and video.
- **Shift+2.** Edit clip audio only.
- **Shift+3.** Edit clip video only.

200 What's a Connected Clip?

A connected clip is any clip not in the Primary Storyline.

Either a clip is in the Primary Storyline or it is connected to it. These connections are visible as light blue dots on top of the Primary Storyline clip representing the In of the connected clip. There is no limit to the number of clips connected to a Primary Storyline clip, nor the number of layers in a project.

A clip either is in the Primary Storyline or is connected to it.

The big advantage to connected clips is that they always stay in sync with the Primary Storyline clip. This means that if you have B-roll, sound effects, or even a music cue connected to a Primary Storyline clip, then decide that the Primary Storyline clip would work better elsewhere in the project, simply move the Primary Storyline clip. All the clips connected to it tag along without losing sync.

> **GOING FURTHER** Captions, titles and video clips, along with clips containing both audio and video, are located above the Primary Storyline. Audio-only clips are located below the Primary Storyline.

201 What's a Clip Connection?

All clips are connected vertically, but you can move the connection.

All clips not on the Primary Storyline are connected to the Primary Storyline clip; see **FIGURE 4.6**. These clips are called, not surprisingly, *connected clips*. This connection means that if the Primary Storyline clip moves, all clips attached to it move as well.

Those connections are indicated by light blue dots at the top of the Primary Storyline clip unless the connected clip is selected, in which case you see a faint blue line. By default, connections are set to the In of the connected clip.

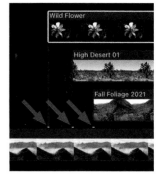

FIGURE 4.6 Clips on layers always connect to the clip on the Primary Storyline.

Most of the time, this connection location is fine. Sometimes, though, you need to move the connection to a different Primary Storyline clip. To do so, press and hold Option+Command then click anywhere inside the connected clip. The connection moves to wherever you click.

202 What's a Storyline?

A storyline is a collection of connected clips and transitions.

Apple has evolved the storyline function since FCP was first released. Now, a storyline is a collection of clips and transitions that are treated as a single entity; see **FIGURE 4.7**. A storyline can contain audio or video clips.

FIGURE 4.7 Two separate connected clips (left) and a connected storyline (right). The connected storyline has only one connection and a gray bar on top. The separate clips each have a timeline connection and no bar on top.

A connected storyline treats a group of clips as though they were on the Primary Storyline:

- Clip edges touch.
- Spaces between clips are not allowed, unless inserted as a gap clip.
- Dragging one clip shuffles other clips.
- Transitions are supported.

The most common use of storylines is when transitions are added; see Chapter 7, "Transitions & Titles." However, a connected storyline is used whenever you want to group one or more clips. Storylines can group clips only on the same layer. (To group clips on multiple layers, use a Compound clip. See Tip 245, *What's a Compound Clip?*)

- To create a storyline, select the clips you want to group and choose Clip > Create Storyline (shortcut: Cmd+G). If there's a gap between clips, Final Cut adds a gap clip between them.
- To break apart an existing storyline, choose Clip > Break apart clip items (shortcut: Shift+Cmd+G).
- To move a storyline, drag it by the top bar.
- To rearrange or trim a clip inside a storyline, select it and drag the clip, just like a clip in the Primary Storyline.
- To delete a clip from inside a storyline, select it and press Delete.

You'll find yourself using storylines the most when adding transitions.

203 Move Primary Storyline Clips

Move the clip; leave the connections. This is a grave decision.

Usually, if you delete a Primary Storyline clip, all the clips connected to it are deleted as well. (They aren't actually deleted, but they are removed from the timeline.) However, if you have a clip connected to a Primary Storyline clip, it's possible to move or delete the Primary Storyline clip *without* changing the position of the connected clip around it.

The trick is to press and hold the grave (`) accent key on your keyboard before you do anything. (This is the same key as tilde [~], just below Esc on U.S. keyboards.) You'll see an odd little orange globe icon next to the cursor; see **FIGURE 4.8**. You can now move or remove the Primary Storyline clip from under the connected clip without the connected clips moving! All the clips to the right then move left to fill the gap.

FIGURE 4.8 Pressing the grave (`) key while dragging moves a Primary Storyline clip without moving the clips attached to it.

GOING FURTHER The location of the grave/tilde key varies by keyboard language. It is located near the Shift key on some international keyboards.

204 Constrain Clip Movement

Press and hold Shift while dragging a clip.

Moving clips by dragging them sideways in the timeline adjusts the timing of your story. However, when you drag a clip vertically from one layer to another, the one thing you don't want is for the clip to change its horizontal position, because that changes its timing.

So here's the secret: Press and hold the Shift key while dragging a clip up or down in the timeline to prevent it from *shifting* from side to side. (See, a pun!)

205 Change Clip Durations

If you know what you need, this is faster than dragging.

Most of the time, we change the duration of a clip by dragging an edge; this is called *trimming*. However, there is a faster way, provided you know the duration you need. Good uses for this are changing the duration of a transition, title, or still image. You can also use this to change the duration of several selected timeline clips. Here's how:

1. Select the elements you want to change.

2. Press Control+D. This switches the Timecode field under the Viewer to Duration mode.

3. Enter the duration you want—without using punctuation—then press Return.

This shortcut can change multiple selected clips at once, with each clip having the same duration. If a clip lacks sufficient duration, Final Cut extends the Out to the end of the clip but doesn't change clip speed or invent new media.

Final Cut automatically calculates the correct duration based upon the frame rate of the project and adjusts the duration of the element accordingly. I use this technique frequently in every project I edit, especially for transitions.

> **GOING FURTHER** Final Cut adds punctuation and does the math for you. For example, based on a 30 fps project:
> - You type 30 and Final Cut enters 1:00.
> - You type 120 and Final Cut enters 4:00.
> - You type 45 and Final Cut enters 1:15.
> - You type 123456 and Final Cut enters 12:36:08.

206 Use Three-Point Edits for Greater Precision

These edits are designed for speed and precision.

A three-point edit precisely controls where an edited clip starts and ends without changing the duration of the project.

There are two general philosophies about how to edit a clip into the timeline:

- Drag the clip to the timeline, then figure out what to do with it.
- Figure out what to do with the clip, then edit it to the timeline.

Ultimately, they probably take the same amount of time; it just depends upon where you want to do your thinking. This tip falls into the second philosophical camp.

A three-point edit is when the duration of a range in the Timeline determines where an edited clip from the Browser will begin and end. These are used in an already edited project where you need to insert a shot, without changing the duration of the overall sequence. These edits provide both precision and speed. Here's how it works:

1. Set an In for a clip in the Browser.

2. Use the Range tool to set an In and Out in the timeline. (You can't just select a clip.)

3. Press D to perform an overwrite edit.

   This edits the Browser clip into the selected range in the timeline, matching the In of the Browser clip to the In of the timeline range, then replacing the remainder of the timeline range with the Browser clip.

4. Press Q to perform the same edit, but place the new clip on a higher layer.

The benefit to a three-point edit is precision. You can precisely control where an edited clip starts and ends without changing the duration of the project.

GOING FURTHER
This edit will fail if the Browser clip is not long enough to fill the timeline duration. Also, there's no need to create an edit using four points. If there's an In and an Out in the timeline, Final Cut ignores any Out in the Browser.

207 Create a Back-Time Edit

Back-time edits emphasize the end of a clip.

Back-time edits are a variation of the three-point edit. They are used when you care more about where a clip ends than where it starts. Sports is the classic example. You want to see the runner crossing the finish line more than where they started.

In technical terms, a back-time edit is one where the Out of the clip in the Browser is matched to the Out of a range in the timeline. Then Final Cut automatically calculates where to place the In. It doesn't play the clip backward; it simply determines the edit from the Out, rather than the In. Here's how:

- Set an Out in a clip in the Browser.
- Set an Out in the timeline, or use the Range tool to set both the In and Out.
- Press Shift+D to back-time edit the clip into the timeline.

  Or—press Shift+Q to back-time edit the clip to a higher layer.

GOING FURTHER
Whenever you set an Out in the timeline, you always set a range. When the edit is performed, the duration of the timeline range determines the duration of the Browser clip. The Browser In is ignored. This edit will fail if the Browser clip is not long enough to fill the range in the timeline. In that case, shorten the duration of the timeline range.

208 Replace Edits Replace a Timeline Clip

Final Cut supports three variations of replace edits.

Yesterday, you edited a clip into the timeline. Today, you realize it's the right duration but the wrong clip. Replace edit to the rescue. A replace edit always replaces a clip in the timeline with a clip from the Browser. You can't replace a timeline clip with another timeline clip.

To create a replace edit, you don't need to select the timeline clip. Mark (set an In and Out) in the Browser clip, then drag it on top of the timeline clip you want to replace. A menu pops up (see **FIGURE 4.9**), displaying the Replace options.

FIGURE 4.9 The five options for a replace edit. Drag a Browser clip on top of a timeline clip to display this list.

- **Replace**. This replaces the timeline clip with the Browser clip and uses the duration of the Browser clip (shortcut: Shift+R).
- **Replace from Start**. This replaces the timeline clip with the Browser clip and uses the duration of the timeline clip (shortcut: Option+R).
- **Replace from End.** This replaces the timeline clip with the Browser clip by editing the Out of the Browser clip to the Out of the timeline clip, then using the duration of the timeline clip to set the In of the Browser clip. This is basically a back-time edit, except it replaces the timeline clip. (A shortcut is available, but not assigned to a key.)
- **Replace with Retime to Fit**. This is discussed in Tip 210, *When to Use Replace with Retime to Fit*.
- **Replace and Add to Audition**. This is discussed in Chapter 5, "Advanced Editing." See Tip 244, *Create Auditions in the Timeline*.

209 Use a Replace Edit to Replace Audio

Find and fix missing audio in less than a second.

You edited a clip into your project yesterday only to realize that you accidentally deleted the audio. Suddenly you really, really need that audio today. In this case, Undo won't work. The mistake happened too long ago. Replace edit to the rescue.

A replace edit is a blindingly fast way to replace accidentally deleted audio.

Here's a fast way to fix the missing audio problem:

1. Put the playhead (skimmer) anywhere in the timeline clip you want to fix. Don't even select the clip.
2. Press Shift+F.

   This creates a match frame of the timeline clip in the Browser.
3. Press Shift+1.

   This makes sure you are editing both audio and video into the timeline.

   Once you press Shift+1, you don't need to press it again. Final Cut leaves this setting unchanged from one edit to the next.
4. Press Option+R.

   This replaces the timeline clip with the clip in the Browser, but matches the duration of the Timeline clip.

You can replace missing audio in less than half a second!

210 When to Use Replace with Retime to Fit

Fit-to-fill edits always change the speed of the incoming clip.

A variation on the replace edit is the Replace with Retime to Fit option, also called a *fit-to-fill* edit. This is used to create a speed effect or if the B-roll clip is too short to fill the timeline clip. This is similar to the Replace from Start option, but it requires a duration for the Browser clip. Unlike the three replace edits discussed in Tip 208, *Replace Edits Replace a Timeline Clip*, this changes the speed of the Browser clip so that the duration of the new clip matches the duration of the original timeline clip.

FIGURE 4.10 Drag a Browser clip on top of a timeline clip to reveal this menu.

1. Set an In and Out for the Browser clip you want to use. The duration is important.

2. Drag the Browser clip on top of the timeline clip you want to replace; see **FIGURE 4.10**. (A shortcut is available, but not assigned to any key.)

3. In the menu, select Replace with Retime to Fit.

Final Cut changes the speed of the Browser clip to precisely match the duration of the timeline clip. The Retime to Fit option always changes the new clip's speed.

GOING FURTHER
The orange or blue bar that appears in the timeline over the new clip is called the *Retime Editor*. See Tip 504, *The Retime Editor*. Press Cmd+R to make the bar disappear.

211 Markers

Markers are the yellow sticky notes of video editing.

I love markers; see **FIGURE 4.11**. These cheerful little flags scattered throughout a project serve as navigational beacons, a list of tasks to do or that are done, even chapter markers for QuickTime movies and DVDs. Whether you create markers in the timeline or Browser, the process is the same.

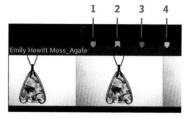

FIGURE 4.11 The four marker types: 1. Marker, 2. Chapter, 3. To-do, 4. Completed to-do. (Jewelry image ©2022 EmilyHewittPhotography.com)

- To create a marker, put the playhead (skimmer) where you want it, and press M.

- To modify a marker, double-click the marker icon to open the Marker dialog.

- To move a marker, right-click it and choose Edit > Cut. Move the playhead (skimmer) to the new location, and choose Edit > Paste.

  Or—place the playhead (skimmer) on the marker and press Control+, [comma] or . [period] to move the marker left or right one frame at a time.

- To jump the playhead to a marker, press Control+; [semicolon] or Control+' [apostrophe].
- To delete a marker, either double-click it and click the Delete button in the Marker dialog or right-click it and select Delete from the menu.

When you modify a marker, the Marker dialog appears; see **FIGURE 4.12**.

FIGURE 4.12 The Marker dialog. The top buttons create a: 1. Marker, 2. To-do marker, and 3. Chapter marker. (Jewelry image ©2022 EmilyHewitt Photography.com)

212 Create Chapter Markers

Chapter markers are great for QuickTime navigation, not just DVDs.

I use chapter markers in many of my QuickTime and MP4 movies; see Figure 4.12. They create little navigational thumbnails used in QuickTime Player, and other video players, to jump to a specific scene in a movie. You don't need to create DVDs to use chapter markers.

1. If a marker already exists, double-click it to open the Marker dialog box.

   Otherwise, put the playhead (skimmer) where you want it, and press M.

2. Press M a second time to open the Marker dialog box.

3. Click the far-right icon (3 in Figure 4.12) to create a chapter marker.

Chapter markers generally display a poster frame in the video player. That round orange dot (see **FIGURE 4.13**) selects the frame used for the poster frame. It is located 16 frames after the marker to avoid displaying the middle of a dissolve as the poster frame. To choose a different frame, drag the round dot to the frame you want to use, which need not be in the same clip.

FIGURE 4.13 The orange marker is a chapter marker. The round orange dot selects the poster frame for that marker. Drag the dot to change the frame. (Jewelry image ©2022 EmilyHewittPhotography.com)

213 Gaps and Timeline Placeholders

Gaps and placeholders have a variety of uses.

A *gap* is a clip that is opaque and solid black, with a default duration of two seconds, though the duration can vary as much as you want. I use gaps to separate scenes, to add a short pause, or simply as an indicator that something is missing. To add a gap, choose Edit > Insert Generator > Gap (shortcut: Option+W). This inserts a two-second gap clip at the position of the playhead (skimmer). You can adjust the duration of a gap the same as any other clip.

Placeholders are similar to gaps in that they are variable duration clips edited into the timeline but used to simulate missing shots. The content of the placeholder is adjusted in the Inspector.

GOING FURTHER
These placeholders aren't true storyboard tools. For example, you can't move the people inside them. But they are useful in visually thinking through missing shots and basic composition.

- To add a new placeholder, choose Edit > Insert Generator > Placeholder (shortcut: Option+Cmd+W).

- To modify an existing timeline placeholder, select the clip in the timeline. Click the Generator icon (red arrow) at the top of the Inspector; see **FIGURE 4.14**. In the panel that appears, select the objects you want to appear in the placeholder.

FIGURE 4.14 Placeholder content options in the Generator Inspector.

214 Find Duplicated Media

This is a fast way to find shots used more than once.

Apple recently added a feature that quickly finds duplicated media in a project. Apple calls these *duplicated ranges*. This feature is off by default. To display media used more than once in a project:

1. Open the Clip Appearance button in the top-right corner of the timeline (see **FIGURE 4.15**), and select the Duplicate Ranges checkbox.

   Clips that use the same media are flagged in the timeline with hash marks at the top of the clip; see **FIGURE 4.16**.

FIGURE 4.15 Display duplicated media using the Clip Appearance menu.

2. Open the Timeline Index, click the chevron (red arrow), and choose Show Clips with Duplicated Ranges; see **FIGURE 4.17**.

Selecting a clip in the Timeline Index selects it in the timeline and moves the playhead to the In of that clip.

FIGURE 4.16 Clips that share the same media are indicated with hash marks (above).

FIGURE 4.17 The Timeline Index shows clips that share media. When you select a clip, other clips sharing its media are highlighted in blue (right).

EDITING TOOLS

Editing tools are used to select, modify, trim, or move timeline clips.

215 The Tools Palette

These are the tools you'll need for editing and trimming.

FIGURE 4.18 Click the chevron to reveal the timeline Tools palette.

This toolset, like most, is hidden. Click the arrow icon with the chevron at the top of the timeline to reveal it; see **FIGURE 4.18**.

- **Select** (shortcut: A). (We often call this the *Arrow* tool.) A general-purpose tool for moving and selecting stuff.
- **Trim** (shortcut: T). Used for roll and slip trimming.
- **Position** (shortcut: P). Turns off the magnetic timeline to move clips independently.
- **Range Selection** (shortcut: R). Sets an In and/or Out range in the timeline or Browser. This is a specialized form of the Select tool.
- **Blade** (shortcut: B). Cuts clips.
- **Zoom** (shortcut: Z). Zooms in to or out of the timeline.
- **Hand** (shortcut: H). Moves the timeline without moving any clips.

216 The Power of the Position Tool

The Position tool disables the magnetic timeline.

The Position tool (shortcut: P), see **FIGURE 4.19**, moves any clip anywhere, even leaving gaps, by disabling the magnetic properties of the timeline. Essentially, when the Position tool is active, Final Cut edits like every other nonlinear editor.

- When you drag a clip, the clip doesn't spring back. Instead, a clip of black video, called a *gap*, is inserted between the end of the previous clip and the one you are moving.
- When you trim clips, it leaves a gap.
- When you drag one clip on top of another, the edge of the new clip overwrites the old clip.
- When you move a clip, any open space created is filled with a gap.

The Position tool provides a choice on how our clips behave when we move them; enabling the magnetic timeline or turning it off.

FIGURE 4.19 The Position tool overrides the magnetic timeline.

GOING FURTHER
To temporarily switch to the Position tool, press and hold P. When you let go, Final Cut reverts to the previous tool.

217 The Range Tool Doesn't Select Anything

The Range tool sets an In and Out in the timeline or Browser.

The Range tool (shortcut: R), see **FIGURE 4.20**, is a specialized form of the Select tool. All it does is set an In and Out in the timeline or Browser. Select the Range tool from the Tools palette.

The Range tool is used in the Browser but, more commonly, in the timeline. (The timeline allows only one In and Out at a time.) While you can use I and O to set the In and Out, the Range tool is simpler—you just drag.

An In and Out is not the same as a selection. Timeline ranges are as small as a few frames in the middle of a clip or span multiple clips. Ranges generally don't end at the edges of a clip, though they can; see **FIGURE 4.21**. Ranges are used for the following:

FIGURE 4.20 The Range tool sets Ins and Outs.

- Exporting a portion of the timeline
- Adjusting audio levels within the range
- Adjusting keyframes within the range
- Creating three-point and back-time edits
- Deleting portions of a clip, or a section of the timeline that doesn't include entire clips

To remove a range selection, click outside the yellow range bounding box with the Arrow tool.

FIGURE 4.21 A timeline range spanning two clips. Note the adjustment handles on the In and Out.

218 Cut Clips with the Blade Tool

Both the Blade tool and shortcuts work, but they work differently.

The Blade tool (shortcut: B), see **FIGURE 4.22**, cuts clips. So does Cmd+B. But they cut clips differently.

Select the Blade tool from the Tools palette. The Blade tool cuts single clips anywhere, whether the clip is selected or not. If you press Shift, the Blade tool cuts *all* clips—including captions—where you click.

Cmd+B cuts one or more clips but only at the position of the playhead (skimmer).

FIGURE 4.22 The Blade tool cuts clips.

- If no clips are selected, Cmd+B cuts the Primary Storyline clip.
- If some or all clips are selected, it cuts only selected clips.
- If a selected clip is disabled (V), it cuts the clip anyway.

The Blade tool is more flexible in terms of where it cuts. Cmd+B is more efficient and selective by cutting only selected clips at the position of the playhead (skimmer).

219 The Zoom Tool

This is a faster way to change the scale of the timeline.

The Zoom tool (shortcut: Z), see **FIGURE 4.23**, changes the scale of the timeline, without affecting any clips.

- To zoom in, select the Zoom tool and click in the timeline.
- To zoom in to a specific section of the timeline, drag the Zoom tool over the area you want to view.
- To zoom out, Option-click the Zoom tool in the timeline.
- With another tool selected, press and hold Z, then click or drag to resize the timeline. Final Cut zooms in; then, when you let go of Z, it selects the previous tool.

FIGURE 4.23 The Zoom tool scales the timeline.

GOING FURTHER These three zoom shortcuts work in both the timeline and the Viewer:

- Press Cmd++ [plus] to zoom in.
- Press Cmd+- [minus] to zoom out.
- Press Shift+Z to fit the timeline, or Viewer, into the window.

220 The Hand Tool

The Hand tool is a mover.

The Hand tool (shortcut: H), see **FIGURE 4.24,** moves the timeline without moving anything *in* the timeline. It's the only tool that can't select or modify a clip in some way.

1. Select the Hand tool from the Tools palette.
2. Drag it in the timeline.

   The timeline moves, but the clips don't.

Even faster:

1. Press and hold H.
2. Drag to where you want to go, then let go.

   Final Cut switches back to the previous tool.

FIGURE 4.24 The Hand tool moves the timeline without moving clips.

GOING FURTHER Another way to move left or right in the timeline is to drag the small slider at the very bottom of the timeline. I find the Hand tool much easier to use.

221 The (Hidden) Delete Key

This is especially helpful for laptop keyboards.

Full-size keyboards have two delete keys: the big one labeled Delete and the small one labeled Del. The big one deletes text to the left; the small one deletes text to the right.

But what if you are using a laptop? The Del key doesn't exist. That's where the hidden Delete key comes in; see **FIGURE 4.25.**

- Press the Delete key to delete text to the *left*, as always.
- Press Fn+Delete to delete text to the *right*.

I use this all the time.

FIGURE 4.25 The dual-purpose Delete key on a laptop keyboard.

GOING FURTHER Pressing Delete removes the selected clip from the timeline. Fn+Delete replaces the selected clip(s) with a gap of the same duration.

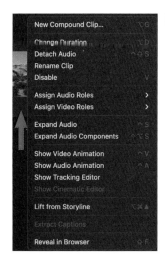

FIGURE 4.26 Right-click any timeline clip to reveal this contextual menu.

222 The Timeline Clip Menu

Just like the Browser and Viewer, the Timeline has a hidden menu.

Right-click any timeline clip to reveal its hidden (contextual) menu; see FIGURE 4.26. Most of these options involve editing or trimming. We'll cover them in other tips.

TRIM CLIPS

Trimming adjusts where two clips touch. Editing builds the story. Trimming makes it perfect. You'll spend far more time trimming than editing; it's that important.

223 Trimming Basics

Here's how to trim an edit point.

An edit point is where two clips touch. It has three sides: the Out of the outgoing clip, the In of the incoming clip, and both the In and the Out.

To trim an edit point, do one of the following:

- Select the Arrow (Select) tool (shortcut: A) and drag either the Out or the In; see FIGURE 4.27. This is a *ripple trim*; because it adjusts one side of the edit, its effect ripples through the rest of the timeline.

- Select the Trim tool (shortcut: T) and drag both the Out and In at the edit point. This is called a *roll trim*; because it adjusts both sides of the edit, it rolls the edit point to a new location.

FIGURE 4.27 Trim the Out of the outgoing clip by dragging with the Arrow tool.

As you drag, the numbers above the edit point indicate current timecode (left) and the amount the selected frame or edit point moves during the trim. In addition to dragging, there are several keyboard shortcuts you can use to trim. Put the playhead (skimmer) at the edit point you want to adjust and do the following:

- Press left square bracket to select the Out.
- Press right square bracket to select the In.
- Press backslash [\] to select both the In and the Out.
- Press comma [,] to move the selected edit point one frame left.
- Press period [.] to move the selected edit point one frame right.
- Press Shift+, to move the selected edit point ten frames left.
- Press Shift+. to move the selected edit point ten frames right.

With an edit point selected in the timeline:

1. Press + [plus] to switch the timecode display into data-entry mode and tell FCP you intend to move the selection to the right.

   Or—press – [minus] to switch the timecode display into data-entry mode and tell FCP you intend to move the selection to the left.

2. Enter the number of seconds and/or frames you want the selected object to move.

3. Press Return to apply the shift.

As long as a selected edit point has sufficient handles and is not blocked by another nonselected clip, it will instantly move. For example:

- Type +16 then press Return to move the selection 16 frames to the right.
- Type −8 then press Return to move the selection 8 frames to the left.

GOING FURTHER
If one or more clips are selected in the timeline, these shortcuts will also move the clips, as long as they aren't blocked by another clip.

(224) Handles Are Essential for Trimming

Handles are extra video at the ends of a clip.

Handles are extra media before the In or after the Out. They are essential for trimming and transitions, because if you need to move the In earlier or the Out later, you need extra media to do so.

Final Cut alerts you whether the end of a clip (either In or Out) has handles; see **FIGURE 4.28**. If the selected end of a clip is yellow, there are additional frames beyond the edit point. If the edge is red, that is the end of the clip.

GOING FURTHER However, the yellow bracket does not indicate how much handle there is. It might be only one frame. When there is no handle, you can trim a clip shorter, but not longer.

FIGURE 4.28 A red bracket means no handles. A yellow bracket indicates handles.

225 Trim the Top and Tail of a Clip

Sometimes you just need something quick and dirty.

If the deadline were any closer, it would be sitting in your lap. All you need is to trim the beginning and end of a timeline clip and export it. There's no time to drag anything. For greatest speed, use the skimmer to hover over the trim point. Don't click anything.

The whole process takes mere seconds from trim to export with exporting happening in the background. **TABLE 4.1** lists these shortcuts.

TABLE 4.1 Top and tail trimming shortcuts

SHORTCUT	WHAT IT DOES
Option+[	Trim the start of a clip to the playhead (skimmer).
Option+]	Trim the end of a clip to the playhead (skimmer).
Option+\	Trim the clip to the selected range. (This requires using the Range tool to set a range.)
Cmd+E	Export the clip to the default destination.

226 The Hidden Precision Editor

The Precision Editor is an incredible teaching tool.

If editing and trimming are new to you, the Precision Editor is an interactive way to learn and develop your trimming skills. To open it, double-click any edit point; see **FIGURE 4.29**. The edit point opens with the outgoing clip on top.

- To adjust the Out, drag the top edit point (top arrow). This creates a ripple trim.
- To adjust the In, drag the bottom edit point (bottom arrow). This, too, creates a ripple trim.
- To adjust both the In and the Out, drag the gray box control between the layers (middle arrow). This creates a roll edit.
- The darker areas at the end of each clip indicate the amount of handles, or extra video, before the In or after the Out.
- A selected clip edge that's yellow means the clip has handles. A red edge means no handles.
- To exit the Precision Editor, press Esc, or double-click the middle roll trim icon (middle arrow).

This is a great teaching tool to learn what happens during a trim and the importance of handles for effective trimming.

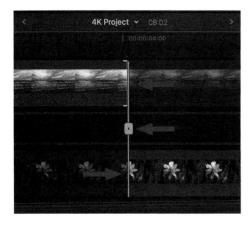

FIGURE 4.29 The Precision Editor. The Out is selected in the top layer.

GOING FURTHER
The limitation to the Precision Editor—and it's a big one—is that it does not allow trimming audio separately from video. So I use this as a teaching tool, but not for actual editing.

227 The Trim Edit Window

Provides feedback on what you are doing in the timeline.

The Trim Edit window appears only if you enable Preferences > Editing > Show detailed trimming feedback; see FIGURE 4.30.

When you grab the edge of a clip with either the Select (Arrow) or Trim tool and drag, the Trim Edit window appears; see FIGURE 4.31.

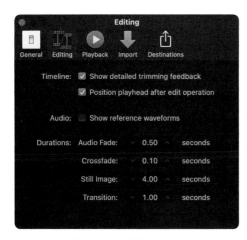

FIGURE 4.31 The Trim Edit window. The Out is on the left; the In is on the right.

FIGURE 4.30 Preferences > Playback.

The left side of the window shows the Out at the edit point. The right window shows the In at the edit point. As you drag the selected portion of the edit point, this window shows what's changing.

If "Show detailed trimming feedback" is not selected in Editing > Preferences, Final Cut displays only the frame you are adjusting. I prefer seeing both windows, which is why I turn this preference on. It is much easier to trim using the Trim Edit window. (See Tip 70, *Optimize Editing Preferences*.)

228 A Super-Fast Trimming Shortcut

This keyboard shortcut is a high-speed trimming tool.

Shift+X is the fastest way to move a selected edit point.

Sometimes, you just want to move the selected edit point somewhere else. Quickly.

1. Select the side of the edit point you want to move.
2. Position the playhead (skimmer) where you want it to go.
3. Press Shift+X.

This technique is called an *extend edit*. The selected edit point jumps to the playhead, provided there are sufficient handles on the clip you are trimming and that the move is not blocked by another clip. I use this all the time for adjusting title durations, roll trims, and adjustment layers.

229 Split Edits: The Workhorse of Editing

Split edit: When audio and video edit points occur at different times.

Without question, to me, the most important trim is a split edit; see **FIGURE 4.32**. This is where the audio and video edit points occur at different times. Split edits are generally created in the Primary Storyline.

Tip 305, *Split Trims Edit Audio Separately*, shows how to do this in detail. I mention it here because it is relevant to editing and trimming.

FIGURE 4.32 A split edit with the audio edit rolled to the right of the video edit.

230 Enable Clip Skimming

Clip skimming is a fast way to review a timeline clip.

Turn skimming off (S). Put the cursor inside a timeline clip, and drag. Nothing happens.

Press Option+Cmd+S. Now drag the cursor inside a timeline clip. See how quickly you can see the contents of that timeline clip in the Viewer?

Why would you do this? Imagine you have multiple clips stacked vertically with an effect that blocks most of those clips (a very typical effect, by the way). Clip skimming displays a clip even if it is blocked by another clip on a higher layer.

There's no need to use this technique if you have only one layer of timeline clips.

GOING FURTHER
The only other way to view a lower-layer clip that is blocked by a higher-layer clip is to select all the upper clips and press V to turn off their visibility. To make these clips visible, select them and press V again.

231 How to Use Audio Clip Skimming

Clip skimming enables audio review in high speed.

You first met skimming in Chapter 2, "The Final Cut Pro Interface." Audio clip skimming is a special form of clip skimming. It's a fast way to review a single audio clip, without hearing any other audio clips above or below it. It lets you zero in on the sound from a specific clip.

1. Choose View > Clip Skimming.

   Or—press Shift+S.

2. Drag the cursor across the clip in the timeline you want to hear.

Repeat the same keystrokes to turn clip skimming off.

GOING FURTHER
Final Cut shifts the pitch of skimmed audio so it sounds fast but not squeaky.

232 A Slip Trim Optimizes B-Roll

Slip trim: Adjust content without changing location or duration.

Another hidden trimming tool that I can't live without is the Slip tool. This tool adjusts the content of a shot, moving it earlier or later, without altering the clip location in the timeline or the clip duration. It's like a window in a wall. You can't change the size or position of the window, but by shifting your position, you can change the view.

Slip trims adjust clip content without changing its location or duration.

1. Select the Trim tool (shortcut: T).

2. Click in the *middle* of the clip you want to adjust.

3. Drag left or right.

   The Trim Edit window opens up and displays the In of the slipping clip on the left and the Out on the right.

I use this constantly to find the best piece of B-roll that fits a precise duration and location.

I set the timing of a clip during the edit. I adjust the content once it's in the timeline using a slip trim until I find the content that works best for my story.

THE TIMELINE INDEX

The Timeline Index is unique to Final Cut. It tracks and organizes all elements in the timeline in searchable lists.

233 The Timeline Index

This is a powerful tool for navigation and organization.

The Timeline Index is unique to Final Cut and a highly powerful tool to organize all the elements in the timeline. Apple describes it as a list-based view of the timeline. I use it constantly to view clips, markers, keywords, titles, and roles, as well as select clips and navigate the timeline. As you play a project, the playhead in the timeline and the horizontal playhead in the Index move in sync.

To open the Index (see **FIGURE 4.33**), do either of the following:

- Click the Index button in the upper left of the timeline.
- Press Shift+Cmd+2.

Here's what you can do in the Timeline Index:

- View a list of all clips in the currently open project, sorted chronologically.
- Click any clip name, or other element, to jump the playhead to it and display it in the Viewer.
- Select one or more clips or other elements in the timeline.
- Rename a clip—select it, enter a new name, and press Return.
- Search for a clip, title, marker, or other timeline element—by name or a portion of its name.
- Delete an element to delete it in the timeline.
- View and add notes. (However, I find it easier to select the clip, then add the note in the Info Inspector; see Tip 171, *Add Notes to One or More Clips.*)
- View active multicam angles.
- View, reassign, and edit roles.

FIGURE 4.33 The Timeline Index. Click the word "Index" to open.

234 Timeline Index: Customization

Modify columns in the Timeline Index like the Browser.

The Timeline Index organizes all the elements in the timeline into a list, just like a spreadsheet.

- To change column widths, drag the dividing lines between column headers.
- To move columns, drag and rearrange column headers.
- To reveal more columns, right-click a column; see **FIGURE 4.34**.

  This feature is not available for the Roles tab, which doesn't use columns.

FIGURE 4.34 Right-click a column header to reveal hidden Timeline Index columns.

235 Timeline Index: Navigation

The Timeline Index is faster than scrolling through the timeline.

The Timeline Index is built for speed and organization. It is a fast way to find a clip—audio, video or title—for example, to check spelling or apply an effect.

In **FIGURE 4.35**, if you look closely along the left edge, you'll see a faint playhead (the red arrow points to it). This echoes the movement of the timeline playhead, because the Timeline Index is simply the timeline itself, recast as a list.

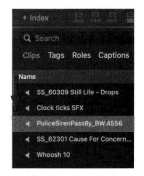

- To locate an element, enter text in the search box.
- To jump to and select a clip, click any line of text.
- To select a range of clips, Shift-click more than one line of text.
- To select any clips you click, Cmd-click more than one line of text.
- To delete clips, select a line, or a group of lines, and press Delete.

Once something is selected, it is easy to add an effect, move the group, or delete it.

FIGURE 4.35 Click any line of text to move the playhead to that element and select it.

236 Timeline Index: Clips

Find, sort, rename, and navigate clips.

1. Open the Timeline Index and click Clips; see **FIGURE 4.36**.
2. At the bottom, choose to view all clips or filter them into Video, Audio, or Titles.

GOING FURTHER
Changing the text of
a title in the Timeline
Index changes only its
name; it doesn't change
the content in the title
itself. That requires
selecting and changing
the text clip itself. Also,
you can't spell-check
titles using the Time-
line Index.

I find the Titles option very helpful at the end of a project. I can quickly jump from one title to the next to verify format and spelling. This high-speed review is far faster than scrolling through the timeline and hoping that I spot them all.

FIGURE 4.36 The Clips panel in the Timeline Index with audio clips selected.

237 Timeline Index: Tags

This is the most useful section of the Timeline Index.

The Tags portion of the Timeline Index (see **FIGURE 4.37**) is the most useful to me. (Roles are second.) This displays all markers and keywords. The following numbered list corresponds to the number callouts in Figure 4.37:

1. All tags
2. All standard (blue) markers
3. All keywords
4. All keywords created though analysis (for example, Find People)

5. To-do markers
6. Completed To-do markers
7. Chapter markers

All my videos include chapter markers for navigation. Similar to titles, I use this panel to find and review each marker before final export. Also, in Tip 240, *Timeline Index: Markers*, I'll show how to use to-do markers to create an editing checklist for your project.

FIGURE 4.37 1. All tags, 2. Blue markers, 3. Keywords, 4. Analysis keywords, 5. To-do markers, 6. Completed mark- ers, and 7. Chapter markers.

238 Timeline Index: Roles

Roles are incredibly useful for audio, but they are not easy to understand.

When Apple introduced roles to Final Cut, I found them intimidating and alien. But in the years since, I spent time learning how to use them, and now, they are part of almost all my projects. The Timeline Index simplifies using roles; see **FIGURE 4.38**. Chapter 6, "Audio," provides details on how to use roles.

As an example, I use roles every week when editing my webinars. I do the edit in Final Cut, then send the audio to Adobe Audition for audio cleanup and sweetening. That mixed audio is exported as a stereo pair and imported back into Final Cut with a Final Mix role assigned to it. Using this section of the Timeline Index, I can disable all dialogue and effects clips and enable the final mix with one mouse click. No messing with layers or individual clips. Works great.

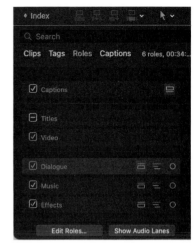

FIGURE 4.38 The Roles panel in the Timeline Index.

239 Timeline Index: Captions

Use the Timeline Index to find and edit captions.

The Timeline Index is extremely useful when finding and reviewing every caption in a project; see **FIGURE 4.39**. In operation, it works the same as the Clips panel.

What I really like about this panel, though, is the ability to double-click a caption to open it for editing in the timeline. This is something you can't do for titles, though you can do it for markers. However, you can't use the Timeline Index to change the timing of a caption. Caption durations are changed only in the timeline.

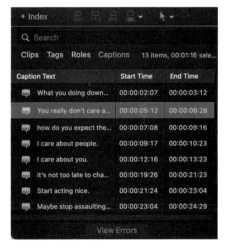

FIGURE 4.39 The Caption panel in the Timeline Index.

240 Timeline Index: Markers

Here are some additional tricks you can do with markers.

Although you can't copy and paste markers from the Timeline Index (see **FIGURE 4.40**), here are some things you can do:

- Select one or more markers and delete them.
- Display markers by category: Chapter, Standard, To-do, and Completed.
- Double-click a marker to open it for editing.
- Add a note to a marker, which is different from its text.

You can even build an editing checklist in the timeline, then display it in the Timeline Index; see **FIGURE 4.41**. To see To-dos, click the icon indicated by the left red arrow. Click the icon to the right of it to see all completed To-dos.

Click the icon to the left of a To-Do marker in the Timeline Index to mark it as completed.

FIGURE 4.40 Four different markers and their icons (top to bottom): Chapter, Standard, To-Do, and Completed To-Do. Note the horizontal playhead below Scene 2.

FIGURE 4.41 Use the Timeline Index to build a To-do List. Select between To-do (left arrow) or completed To-do items (right arrow).

GOING FURTHER To see a specific marker type, click one of the buttons at the bottom of this panel, see Tip 237, *Timeline Index: Tags.*

CHAPTER 4—BASIC EDITING SHORTCUTS

CATEGORY	SHORTCUT	WHAT IT DOES
Marking	I	Set an In at the playhead (skimmer)
	Shift+I	Jump playhead to the In
	Option+I	Delete the In
	O	Set an Out at the playhead (skimmer)
	Shift+O	Jump playhead to the Out
	Option+O	Delete the Out
	X	Set In and Out for entire clip
	Option+X	Delete both In and Out
Editing	E	Append selected clip to end of timeline
	W	Insert selected clip at playhead (skimmer)
	D	Overwrite selected clip at playhead (skimmer)
	Q	Edit selected clip at playhead (skimmer) on higher layer
	Cmd+V	Paste clip into Primary Storyline at playhead (skimmer)
	Option+V	Paste clip into layer above Primary Storyline at playhead (skimmer)
	Option+Cmd+Up arrow	Lift the selected clip in the Primary Storyline to a higher layer
	Option+Cmd+Down arrow	Overwrite selected connected clip into Primary Storyline
	Cmd+G	Consolidate upper layer clips into a connected storyline
	Shift+R	Replace timeline clip with Browser clip, use Browser clip duration
	Option+R	Replace timeline clip with Browser clip, use timeline clip duration
	Option+W	Insert gap at playhead
	Cmd+B	Cut selected clip(s) at playhead (skimmer), does not cut captions unless they are selected
	M	Add marker
	Option+M	Add marker and open marker dialog
	Control+[Comma/Period]	Move marker under playhead (skimmer) left/right one frame
Trimming	Shift+X	Extend Edit to position of playhead
	[-] - \	Select left, right, or both edit points for trimming
	[Comma/Period]	Move selected edit point or clip left/right one frame
	Shift+[Comma/Period]	Move selected edit point or clip left/right ten frames
	Shift+drag	Constrain the movement, when dragging a timeline clip, to up or down only
	Shift+Blade tool	Cut all timeline clips, including captions, at the position you click
Selection & Navigation	S	Toggle skimming on/off
	N	Toggle snapping on/off
	V	Toggle clip visibility on/off
	Shift+Cmd+2	Display/Hide Timeline Index
	Control+; / '	Jump playhead to previous/next marker
	Cmd+Up arrow	Select clip on next higher layer in timeline
	Cmd+Down arrow	Select clip on next lower layer in timeline

CHAPTER WRAP

Well, that was intense. This chapter covered the basics of editing and trimming. In the next chapter, we'll head into weeds looking at advanced editing and trimming techniques in Final Cut Pro.

ADVANCED EDITING

INTRODUCTION

This chapter looks at a variety of advanced techniques that supplement
traditional editing and trimming, including several that are unique to
Final Cut. You may not need these very often, but it is helpful to know
what they are and how they work. Why? Because they can save time,
simplify editing, and make your projects look better.

- Definitions
- Ingenious Techniques
- Compound Clips
- Multicam Editing
- Closed Captions
- Color Basics
- Video Scopes
- Shortcuts

- **Angle**. One layer (track) within a multicam clip. Angles can hold multiple clips.

- **Audition**. A group of clips that you preview to select only one clip for the timeline. Auditions are designed for previewing in the timeline but are created or viewed in the timeline or Browser.

- **Lower-third**. Text that appears at the bottom of the frame and is permanently displayed as part of the image. Permanent titles have the greatest amount of formatting flexibility.

- **Closed captions**. Text that can be turned on or off. Formatting is limited, but the number of supported languages is not. Final Cut can create, time, format, and output captions as separate files or burn one of them into video.

You won't need all of these, but each can save you time.

- **Compound clip**. A "mini-project." An organizational tool grouping clips located on one or more layers of the timeline into a single "nest." You can store compound clips inside other compound clips. Compound clip settings do not need to match the project settings.

- **Multicam clip**. A set of two or more video clips connected using a common sync point and grouped into a single clip. Multicam is most often used for editing performances. FCP supports up to 64 camera angles in a multicam clip, but only one angle is visible at a time. Most commonly combined with a finished audio mix, multicam clips can contain clips of different frame sizes, frame rates, and codecs.

- **Grayscale**. The shades of gray in an image. This ranges from pure black to pure white. Every pixel has its own grayscale value.

- **Video scopes**. Analytical tools that display real-time technical grayscale and color values of each frame during playback. FCP has three scopes: Waveform Monitor, Vectorscope, and Histogram. (It also provides an RGB Parade, which is a variation of the Waveform Monitor.)

INGENIOUS TECHNIQUES

This collection highlights specialized techniques, such as modifying source clips, smart conform, and Auditions, that solve tricky editing problems.

241 Modify a Source Clip

Add effects to a clip before editing it into the timeline.

Often, adjusting a clip before you edit it can save a lot of time. For example, let's say you plan to use a variety of segments from the same clip and you don't want to waste time color grading individual clips later. Easy.

Select the clip in the Browser and choose Clip > Open Clip.

Open Clip is a fast way to modify a clip before editing starts.

This opens the clip in the timeline, just as though you edited it there, but it isn't in any project—yet. Add whatever effects you want, for example, color correction. To close the clip when you are done, open any project into the timeline. Those changes are now saved into the Browser clip and will travel with it when it is edited into the timeline.

> **GOING FURTHER** If you need to modify a timeline clip, which had an effect previously applied in the Browser, select the timeline clip and choose Clip > Open Clip. There you can remove/reset the effect. Changes made to either the Browser source clip, or any timeline iteration of it, won't affect other iterations of that clip already edited into the timeline.

242 Reframe Clips Using Smart Conform

Smart Conform converts the aspect ratios of selected clips.

Smart Conform takes an existing clip, or a group of clips, and intelligently crops it to fit into a different aspect ratio—for example, converting media shot at 16:9 into 1:1 for Instagram or 9:16 for vertical advertising. Here's how this works:

1. After editing a project in the correct aspect ratio, for example 16:9, create a new project with the aspect ratio you need, for instance, Vertical (which uses 9:16). It is important that the frame size of the new project *not* match the existing project.
2. From the existing project, copy the clips you want to convert.
   Copying leaves the original project untouched.
3. Paste them into the new project.
4. Select those clips in the new project, and choose Modify > Smart Conform.

Final Cut applies Spatial Conform and selectively crops each clip to contain what it feels is key content. To see an overlay of the original clip (see **FIGURE 5.1**), enable the Transform on-screen controls (lower-left red arrow), then click the Dual Boxes icon in the top-right corner of the Viewer (upper red arrow). This shows the current framing, plus a grayed-back view of the entire image so you can easily adjust framing if necessary.

GOING FURTHER
Smart Conform is fast
and generally makes
good decisions but
often requires key-
framing to fine-tune
the horizontal position.

Choose Transform > Position settings in the Video Inspector to adjust the
horizontal (X) position. Or, more often, add keyframes to shift the horizontal
position during playback.

FIGURE 5.1 A 16x9 image in a
vertical project, with Smart
Conform enabled.

243 Auditions Preview Possibilities

Auditions group clips for preview and comparison prior to editing.

Auditions organize clips into sets, which are easily reviewed in the timeline,
to select which one to use in an edit. Auditions:

- Can contain different clips to compare different takes
- Can include the same clip multiple times, each with a different effect,
  to see which effect works the best
- Can include audio, video, or both
- Can include clips with different durations

*Auditions are a
fast and flexible
way to preview
multiple clips.*

Here's an easy way to create an Audition in the Browser:

1. If you want to use only a portion of a clip, mark the range in the
   Browser.
2. Cmd-click to select the Browser ranges you want to add to an Audition.
3. Choose Clip > Audition > Create (shortcut: Cmd+Y).

   A new Audition clip appears in the Browser with a spotlight icon in the
   top-left corner.
4. Edit the new Audition clip into the timeline.

To switch between clips:

1. Select the Audition in the timeline and press Y.

   The Pick window appears; see **FIGURE 5.2**.

2. Play the timeline, and the clip in the Pick window plays.

3. Click the clip on either side of the center image, and play the timeline again.

   The new clip now plays. The timeline duration changes to reflect the new clip, as well.

   Auditions preserve alternate edits without affecting the other clips in the timeline. When you're not reviewing the clips in an audition, the audition functions like an individual clip. You can trim an Audition, apply transitions between Auditions and other clips, and even add keywords and markers.

FIGURE 5.2 The Audition pick window above an Audition clip in the timeline. Click grayed images on either side to switch the preview.

4. Review the clips in the Audition and decide which one works best in your project.

5. Click Done.

   This hides the unwanted clips and keeps the selected clip in the timeline. It also retains the duration, plus any keywords, markers, or effects applied to the Audition.

(244) Create Auditions in the Timeline

Here's a fast way to create an Audition in the timeline.

Let's say you have clips edited into a project, except one doesn't feel quite right. Hmm...which clip to replace it with? Auditions can help you choose.

To create an Audition directly in the timeline, drag one or more Browser clips on top of a timeline clip; see **FIGURE 5.3**.

FIGURE 5.3 Drop a Browser clip on top of a timeline clip to reveal this menu.

- **Add to Audition.** This creates an Audition containing both the timeline and the Browser clips without changing the image displayed in the timeline.

- **Replace and Add to Audition.** This replaces the timeline clip with the first clip you selected in the Browser then builds an Audition.

- Press Y to open the Audition for editing.

- To break apart an Audition in the timeline, select it, then choose Clip > Break Apart Clip Items (shortcut: Shift+Cmd+G).

COMPOUND CLIPS

Compound clips are mini-projects that do things regular projects can't. They are a useful tool in timeline organization, repeating elements, and visual effects.

245 What's a Compound Clip?

A collection of clips, grouped and treated as a single clip.

FIGURE 5.4 Compound clip icons: (Top) Browser. (Bottom) Timeline. (Jewelry image ©2022 EmilyHewittPhotography .com)

A compound clip (see **FIGURE 5.4**) is, essentially, a project with its own settings and properties that can be placed inside other projects. It groups multiple clips into a single entity and can hold audio, video, still images, even other compound clips, placed on one or more layers. It can be created in either the Browser or the timeline but is most commonly created in the timeline.

It is amazingly powerful, flexible, and deep. You can edit them into a project, trim them, change their speed, and add effects and transitions. They are dynamic; change the contents of any compound clip and *all* iterations of that compound clip change as well. Once created, you work with them the same as any clip.

You can use a compound clip to:

- Simplify a complex section of the timeline or an entire project by consolidating all clips into a single compound clip.
- Combine a video clip with one or more audio clips to avoid moving elements out of sync.
- Group multiple Browser clips into a single compound clip.
- Create a section of a project with different settings than the project itself.
- Create special effects that aren't easily created in the timeline alone.

To create a compound clip, select the clips you want to group in the Browser or timeline and choose File > New > Compound Clip (shortcut: Option+G). If you are creating a compound clip in the timeline, the clips can be on different layers.

When you create a new compound clip, you can select in which event it will be stored. I prefer creating a specific event for compound clips—which makes them easier to find—and storing them there.

GOING FURTHER
Compound clips can have different image sizes, frame rates, audio tracks, and render settings than your project. They don't *need* to be different, but the key point is that they *can* be different.

When a compound clip is edited into the timeline, the compound clip is rendered automatically to match the project settings.

246 Use Compound Clips to Organize Clips

Compound clips are great at organizing complex timelines.

A common use for a compound clip is to organize the timeline. **FIGURE 5.5** illustrates a complex, multilayer timeline section.

1. Select the clips you want to group.

2. Choose File > New > Compound clip (shortcut: Option+G).

3. Give the compound clip a name, pick the event to store it in, and click OK.

4. Double-click a compound clip to edit its contents.

   - To modify the settings of a compound clip, select it in the Browser, go to the Info Inspector, and click Modify. Compound clip settings are similar to those used to create projects.

   - To close a compound clip, open another project into the timeline, or use the Timeline History arrows.

   - To disassemble a compound clip, choose Clip > Break Apart Clip Items (shortcut: Shift+Cmd+G).

NOTE The duration of a compound clip is set in the timeline. You can't adjust the In or Out of a compound clip from inside the compound clip.

The clips are coalesced into a single clip and displayed in the timeline. During playback, a compound clip will play back exactly as the clips did before the compound clip was created.

FIGURE 5.5 (Top) Timeline clips selected for a compound clip. (Bottom) The compound clip. Note the compound clip icon in top-left corner of the lower clip (red arrow).

GOING FURTHER Compound clips are stored in the library and available to all projects in that library. But they are not automatically shared between libraries.

247 Compound Clips Are Dynamic

Change any compound clip and all its iterations also change.

In addition to its organizational skills, compound clips have a secret power: They are dynamic. This makes them different from projects, because we can't put one project inside another project. But we *can* add compound clips into one or more projects.

Compound clips are dynamic. Change one, and they all change.

For example, let's say you created a transitional bumper to separate different sections of your project. Convert that bumper into a compound clip, then edit it into your project as many times as you need. Oops, the audio was wrong, and there's a typo in the title.

Double-click a compound clip in the Browser or timeline to open it in the timeline. Make your changes. As soon as you close the compound clip, all its iterations in the timeline are instantly updated.

248 Make a Compound Clip Independent

Independent compound clips do not change each other.

By default, all compound clips are dynamic. Change one, and all its iterations change. Most of the time, this is what you want. However, sometimes, you may want to use the video in a compound clip but change the text each time it is used.

Normally, you can't—until you know this secret.

Edit a second iteration of the compound clip into the timeline. Then, make this compound clip independent:

Make compound clips independent to prevent unexpected changes.

1. Select the compound clip in the timeline.

2. Choose Clip > Reference New Parent Clip.

   Two things happen: A copy of the compound clip appears in the Browser (with the same name, with "copy" added at the end), and the compound clip in the timeline is replaced with this independent copy.

   Now, when you make changes to the independent copy—which you can rename—the original compound clip and any other iterations in the timeline do not change.

249 Caution: Compound Clip Audio

Be careful when using mono audio in a compound clip.

Compound clips cannot output mono audio, only stereo or 5.1 surround. If the audio in a compound clip is stereo or surround, everything is good.

However, if the compound clip contains a mono audio clip, adding that compound clip to a stereo project will cause the audio levels to drop −6 dB.

This may seem weird, but it's normal due to how mono audio is treated in a stereo mix. The easiest way to prevent this is make sure the number of audio channels in your compound clip match the number of audio channels in your project.

GOING FURTHER
This audio level change is called the *pan law* or *pan rule*. You can look it up on Google. Audio is discussed further in Chapter 6, "Audio."

250 Caution: Compound Clips Hide Markers

Markers inside a compound clip are not visible in the timeline.

If you add markers of any type (general, to-do, or chapter) to one or more clips inside a compound clip, when you close that compound clip and edit it into the timeline, those markers and their notes are not visible.

The simplest work-around is to open the compound clip into the timeline then use Timeline Index > Tags (see **FIGURE 5.6**) to note the position of each marker. Finally, add them manually to the compound clip in the timeline or Browser.

FIGURE 5.6 Use the Timeline Index to determine marker location.

However, this works only when the compound clip timecode of the compound clip matches the project timecode.

When the timecodes don't match, here's the workaround:

1. Copy the clips inside the compound clip.

2. Step outside the compound clip and temporarily paste them *above* the compound clip in the timeline (shortcut: Option+V).

3. With the compound clip selected and snapping turned on, move the playhead to each marker in the individual clips above it.

4. Right-click the marker and choose Copy.

5. Select the compound clip in the timeline and press Command+V to paste the marker.

6. When all markers are copied, delete the top-line clips.

251 Create a Transition Between Compound Clips

Unlike normal clips, you can make compound clips longer!

When you create a compound clip, Final Cut ignores any media outside the compound clip and locks the duration. This means that, by definition, the In and Out of a compound clip are also the start and end of the media. In other words, compound clips have no handles.

Although we can always trim a compound clip shorter to create handles, sometimes we don't need it shorter—we need it longer. When we double-click a compound clip to open it in the timeline for editing (see **FIGURE 5.7**), the white lines at each end define the duration of the compound clip. The problem is we can't drag these white lines to extend the clip.

FIGURE 5.7 The two white lines define the duration of a compound clip.

Here's the workaround (the Out is easy, the In is not). To change the Out:

NOTE I should mention that the easiest solution, if you expect to use transitions with compound clips, is to make the compound clip longer than you need when you create it, so you have handles when you need them.

1. Double-click the compound clip to open it for editing.
2. Drag the clip at the *end* of the Primary Storyline to the right to extend video past the Out. Now, when you drag the Out of the compound clip in the timeline, you'll have extra handles.

   The key is to extend the clip in the Primary Storyline of the compound clip, not a clip above it on a higher layer.

However, the position of the In can't be moved earlier. Instead:

1. Trim the In of the compound clip in the timeline to create the handle you need.
2. Open the compound clip and, using the Trim tool, slip the contents of the first clip to display the images you need. (See Tip 232, *A Slip Trim Optimizes B-Roll*.)

GOING FURTHER When you create a compound clip, you are creating a master clip. Every time you edit that compound clip into the timeline, you are editing a *linked* copy of that master clip. Whatever changes you make to the original compound clip are reflected in all iterations of it in the timeline.

252 Create Oversized Compound Clips

Interesting effects are possible when compound clips are larger than the project.

A compound clip is a "mini-project." Unlike connected storylines, compound clips don't need to match the project settings. This provides an opportunity for interesting effects. For example, create a very large compound clip, then have it slowly travel through the frame of the project—like text scrolling horizontally displaying the name of a movie.

NOTE I cover effects in more detail in Chapter 8, "Visual Effects."

The secret is to create an extra-large compound clip. Here's how:

A compound clip is a mini-project.

1. Make sure nothing is selected in the Browser.
2. Choose File > New > Compound clip (shortcut: Option+G).
3. Give it a name.
4. Click the Use Custom Settings in the lower left. (Custom settings don't need to match any specific aspect ratio.)
5. Set the Video menu to Custom; see **FIGURE** 5.8.
6. Enter a large horizontal dimension, for example, 10,000 in Figure 5.8.
7. Make sure the frame rate matches the project frame rate.
8. Set any other parameters you need.
9. Click OK.

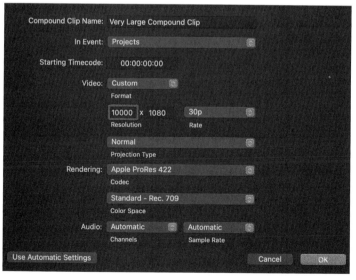

FIGURE 5.8 These custom Compound Clip settings are available only when creating an empty compound clip.

Compound clips can contain text, clips, generators, effects, even audio.

Double-click the compound clip to open it in the timeline and add whatever elements you want it to contain. In my example, to get text to fly across the screen, you would also keyframe the horizontal (X) Position setting of the compound clip.

> GOING FURTHER   By default, compound clips inherit the frame size and frame rate of any selected clips when the compound clip is created. That's why you need to create an empty compound clip to change the frame size.

253 Apply Effects to Compound Clips
Effects are applied inside or outside a compound clip.

FIGURE 5.9 illustrates a very wide compound clip (10,000x1080 pixels) with text in it, edited into a layer in a 1080p project over an image of the desert in the Primary Storyline. (Text and titles are covered in Chapter 7, "Transitions & Titles.")

The text inside the compound clip has a blend mode (Stencil Alpha) applied to insert a gradient color into the text. Then, the compound clip itself has an Effects > Stylize > Drop Shadow added to make the text stand out from the background.

I show this effect here simply to expand your thinking about what's possible with compound clips.

FIGURE 5.9 A split-screen showing the contents of a compound clip (left) and the final effect applied in the timeline (right).

> GOING FURTHER   Creating a compound clip of the entire project makes it easy to apply global adjustments, such as Broadcast Safe (see Tip 480, *Apply the Broadcast Safe Effect*) or adjusting master audio levels. Another way to accomplish a global change is to use an adjustment layer (see Tip 456, *Create an Adjustment Layer*).

MULTICAM EDITING

As cameras become cheaper, shooting productions with multiple cameras becomes more popular. Final Cut Pro provides tools for editing multicam projects that are both powerful and easy to use.

254 Multicam Clips Are for Editing

Multicam is like directing a live show, not for creating effects or audio mixes.

Multicam is the editing equivalent of directing a live production, where you get to pick which camera the audience will see at any one time. Many editors think that multicam is used to create projects where multiple images appear on-screen at the same time. It isn't.

NOTE Multicam is not used for switching a live event. All video needs to be recorded before it can be edited.

- Multicam editing displays multiple cameras that recorded the same scene at the same time from different angles so you can decide which one of them you want to view in the timeline at any given instant.

- Multicam editing does not create split screens, multiple images, or similar effects. It is simply a way of choosing between different shots.

- Multicam editing does not create audio mixes. You can hear the audio from only one angle at a time. In fact, most multicam editing is done after the audio is mixed.

- Multicam is not used for editing scenes shot using multiple takes in front of one camera; such as traditional single-camera film production.

- If you are editing a longer performance, it helps to break one long multicam clip into smaller chunks, such as a song or scene, to keep the editing process manageable.

- Don't use multicam to display multiple images at the same time in the timeline. Instead, stack the different clips vertically, then adjust image size to see more than one image at once.

Multicam editing is more similar to editing a live production than a film shoot. (Except it isn't live.)

The best way to think of multicam editing is editing a live show from a variety of simultaneous video inputs with the audio coming from an audio mixing board. The benefit to multicam, though, is the ability to view all angles simultaneously, decide which one you like, edit it, then change your mind until you are happy with the results.

GOING FURTHER Editor Scott Newell wrote: "Multicam is near and dear to my heart. I can't emphasize enough how important it is to use proxies for editing multicam. So, too, is adding color correction prior to editing."

⟨255⟩ Multicam Clips Require Lots of Bandwidth

The more clips in the multicam clip, the faster the storage required.

GOING FURTHER
While spinning hard disks can transfer data quickly, the issue of how long it takes the heads inside a spinning hard disk to jump from one clip to another (called *seek time* or *latency*) limits multicam playback. As the number of cameras in the multicam clip increases, you may need to move the media files to a large-capacity high-speed SSD for smooth playback during editing.

A multicam clip plays multiple video clips simultaneously. Although the video streams playing in the Angle Viewer are optimized for smooth playback and are not using the full bandwidth of the original clips, still multicam clips require high-speed storage with a fast connection to the computer. Although the display of the clips is handled by the CPU, actual playback performance depends upon the speed of your storage. A system that happily edits 4K single-camera video may choke editing 4K multicam.

TABLE 5.1 compares the bandwidth requirements for editing different frame sizes of ProRes 422/30. Keep in mind that the Angle Viewer relies on a combination of CPU, GPU, and the media engine streaming multicam clips for editing. It doesn't use the full bandwidth. Other codecs will require different bandwidth, but you get the idea: Storage bandwidth matters. This rapid increase in bandwidth is the key reason I recommend editing multicam clips using proxy files.

TABLE 5.1 Bandwidth requirements for multicam editing			
MULTICAM STREAMS	**1080P PRORES PROXY**	**1080P PRORES 422**	**UHD* PRORES 422**
2	11.25 MB/s	36.75 MB/s	147.25 MB/s
4	22.5 MB/s	73.5 MB/s	294.5 MB/s
8	45 MB/s	147 MB/s	589 MB/s
12	67.5 MB/s	220.5 MB/s	883.5 MB/s

*UHD is considered a 4K image: 3840 x 2160 pixels. True 4K is 4096 x 2160 pixels.
Source: *Apple ProRes* white paper (January 2020)

⟨256⟩ Prep Multicam Clips Before You Start

Label camera clips to keep things organized during an edit.

NOTE Once a multicam clip is created, camera angle names can be changed only in the Angle Editor, not in the Inspector.

You don't need to label multicam clips, but it helps keep things organized if you do. Often, clip names are cryptic, so adding more readable text helps during the actual edit. In the Browser, select each multicam clip, then go to the Info Inspector and add the camera angle and name; see **FIGURE 5.10**.

Camera angle names are automatically displayed in the Angle Editor and Angle Viewer; see **FIGURE 5.11**. These names can use any text—whatever helps keep the different cameras straight in your mind during an edit.

FIGURE 5.10 Add an optional camera name and angle to a video clip in the Info Inspector.

FIGURE 5.11 Camera angle names are displayed automatically in the Angle Viewer.

GOING FORWARD You can also select clips in the multicam Angle Editor then add names in the Info Inspector. In this screen shot, in addition to the names, I also positioned angles based on where the talent is looking, rather than clip or angle name (see Tip 260, *Change the Display Order of Multicam Clips*).

257 Sync Multicam Clips the Easy Way

Syncing a multicam clip isn't hard, provided you have audio.

Although there are a variety of sync options when you create a multicam clip, here is an easy way to do it. However, it requires that you record essentially the same audio on every camera. To create a multicam clip automatically:

Syncing multicam clips using audio is easy, but it assumes every camera recorded the same audio at the same time during production.

1. Select the clips you want to group into a multicam clip in the Browser.
2. Choose File > New > Multicam Clip.
3. In the dialog shown in **FIGURE 5.12**, fill out the usual name and event fields.
4. Click OK.

   As long as every camera records the same audio—either from an audio mixing board or from camera mics—when you click OK, Final Cut will sync all angles by aligning the audio in each clip.

FIGURE 5.12 The Automatic Settings panel for a multicam clip.

Depending upon the number and length of each clip, syncing could take a few seconds to a few minutes, so be patient. Notice, also, that the multicam settings are based on the file format of the clips inside it.

However, this system breaks down if one or more cameras does not contain audio, if the cameras contain different video formats, or if the camera format does not match the project settings. In that case, you need to use the Advanced Settings, covered in the next tip.

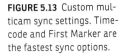 Advanced Multicam Syncing

Here's what to do if the automatic multicam settings don't work.

The benefit to using audio for syncing multicam clips is that it is easy. But reality often interferes.

- Deselect "Use audio for synchronization" to disable automatic syncing.

For more complex situations, click the Custom Settings button, see Figure 5.12, to reveal the Custom Settings; see **FIGURE 5.13**.

FIGURE 5.13 Custom multicam sync settings. Timecode and First Marker are the fastest sync options.

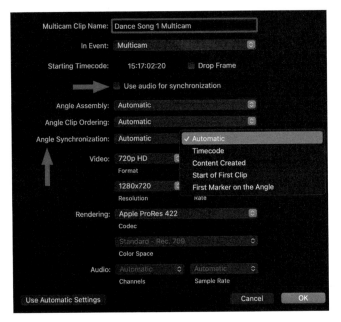

In Angle Synchronization:

- **Automatic**. Syncs using audio. Use this only if all cameras have the same audio recorded on it.

- **Timecode.** This is the fastest and most precise way to sync multicam clips. However, it requires that all cameras record the same timecode; plus you would need a timecode generator, timecode distribution system, and cameras capable of recording external timecode on set during production.

- **Content Created.** This syncs based upon the content creation date and time of a clip. It's accurate only to ± one second. Don't use it.

- **Start of the first clip.** This assumes that all cameras start at the same time. They never do. Don't use this either.

- **First Marker on [Each] Angle.** This is also an extremely fast way to sync clips and, for my low-budget productions, is the best and simplest choice.

Rather than invest in timecode gear that costs a lot, I invest in a slate (see **FIGURE 5.14**), which is cheap. Position a production assistant so that all cameras can see the slate, start recording, and clap the slate. On larger productions, you can use a camera flash, provided you don't shine it in the lens of a camera. In the worst case, record someone clapping their hands in a highly visible fashion. Anything to provide a clear sync point for all cameras.

Then, before you create the multicam clip, in the Browser set the first marker in each clip where the clapper comes down. You can then verify the sync point and, if necessary, adjust it in the Angle Editor. (See Tip 259, *The Multicam Angle Editor*.)

GOING FURTHER
The Angle Assembly menu determines the clip order when a multicam clip is built. If you number either the camera angle or the camera name in the Info Inspector, selecting the appropriate choice in Angle Assembly will organize the multicam angles in that order.

FIGURE 5.14 A typical film slate. Set markers in each multicam clip at the clap.

259 The Multicam Angle Editor

The Angle Editor is where you adjust multicam clips.

Once clips are synced, double-click the multicam clip to open it in the Angle Editor; see **FIGURE 5.15**. This is where you can tweak (adjust) the contents of a multicam clip before editing starts. (An "angle" acts like a layer in the timeline.)

- If you use markers to indicate the In and Out, there's a chance they may be off a frame or two. Select the clip in the angle, then press , [comma] or . [period] to shift the clip one frame left or right. Press Shift+, [comma]/. [period] to shift in ten-frame increments. I frequently need to tweak alignment to get the most accurate sync.

- Click the Video Monitor icon (1) to select the video clip you want to see in the Viewer before editing starts. This is called the *monitoring angle*. You can monitor only one video clip at a time. The video monitor has no impact on the edit. Blue means active.

- Click the Audio Monitor (2) to determine which audio clips you hear before editing starts. While this can monitor audio from multiple clips, during and after editing you can hear only one audio clip at a time. Audio monitoring has no impact on the edit. Blue means active.

- Click the down chevron (3) to reveal the multicam contextual menu with more options.

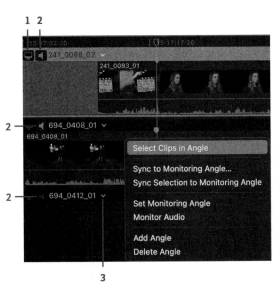

FIGURE 5.15 The Multicam Angle Editor: 1. Video monitor button, 2. Audio monitor button, and 3. chevron. The contents of the menu are displayed on the right.

260 Change the Display Order of Multicam Clips

Clips display in the order they are stacked in the Angle Editor.

Notice in Figure 5.11, the two close-ups are next to each other on the top row. This makes it easier to cut their dialogue. However, that was not how the multicam clip was first constructed.

Clips always display in the Angle Viewer in the order they are stacked in the Angle Editor. To change the stacking order, drag the thumb (red arrows) of an angle up or down; see **FIGURE 5.16**. I regularly change the grouping of shots to place related shots next to each other during an edit.

> **GOING FURTHER** You can change the stacking order at any time during an edit without messing up anything.

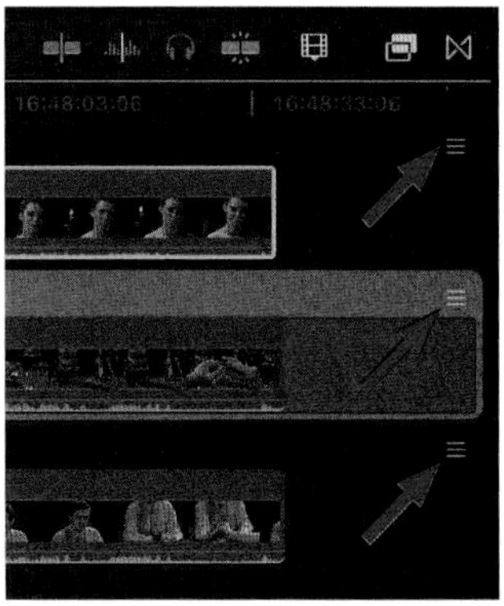

261 Set a Multicam Clip for Editing

Editing is simple—the setup is tricky.

Editing a multicam clip is easy, but setting it up in the Angle Viewer (see **FIGURE 5.17**) is often confusing. Trim the multicam clip in the Browser, the same as any other clip, then edit it into the timeline. (You can, of course, also trim it in the Timeline.) For all the details on multi-cam editing, please refer to the Final Cut Pro Help files. Here are the key steps to get you started:

FIGURE 5.16 Drag a thumb (red arrow) to change the stacking order of clips in the Angle Editor.

1. Press Shift+Cmd+7 (or choose View > Show in Viewer > Angles) to display the multicam Angle Viewer.

2. When the Angle Viewer opens, it shows the first four clips in your multicam clip. To see more clips, if they exist, click the "bank switcher" (lower red arrow in Figure 5.17).

3. When preparing to edit a multicam clip, click the waveform button (top red arrow in Figure 5.17) to select it, then click the angle image that has the audio you want to use. FCP draws a green box around it.

FIGURE 5.17 By default, the multicam Angle Viewer displays the first four images in a multicam clip.

The three icons in the top left choose (from left to right): editing audio and video, just video or just audio.

NOTE If you need to switch both audio and video during the edit, click the left button at the top left (red arrow in Figure 5.17). This cuts both audio and video, with the active angle surrounded by a yellow box.

4. Click the middle edit only video icon and select the first video clip you want to use in the edit. Final Cut draws a blue box around it. As long as the middle icon remains active, you can edit video as much as you want, without editing the audio.

The reason this is important is that multicam clips do not create audio mixes. Instead, most multicam editing is done to a fully mixed audio track stored in one audio clip. Select and set the audio clip *before* setting the video clip to assure that multicam edits affect only the video.

262 Change the Multicam Viewer Display

The default is four angles; the maximum is 16.

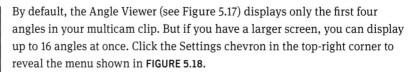

By default, the Angle Viewer (see Figure 5.17) displays only the first four angles in your multicam clip. But if you have a larger screen, you can display up to 16 angles at once. Click the Settings chevron in the top-right corner to reveal the menu shown in **FIGURE 5.18**.

You can also use this menu to display clip timecode overlaid on the image, as well as the camera angle or clip name. These are entered in the Info Inspector; see Tip 256, *Prep Multicam Clips Before You Start*.

If you have two monitors on your system, switch the Viewer to the second monitor (see Tip 60, *Expand the Interface with Two Computer Monitors*). This displays both the Viewer and the Angle Viewer on a second monitor. By moving these to a second display, the individual clips in the multicam are larger and easier to see.

FIGURE 5.18 The Angle Viewer Settings menu, part of a multicam edit.

263 Editing a Multicam Clip

Editing is as easy as point-and-click.

Click a multicam angle to cut and change the shot. Option-click to change the shot without cutting.

With the Angle Viewer open, begin playback of the multicam clip. When you see a shot you like, click its image in the Angle Viewer. This cuts the multicam clip in the timeline and changes the downstream shot to the one you clicked; see **FIGURE 5.19**.

However, you don't need to decide in real time. Put the playhead where you want to make a change and click the angle you want to use. FCP cuts the multicam clip and changes the angle.

Hmm...except, in reviewing a shot later, you decide that another angle is better. Put the playhead in the timeline shot you want to change and Option-click the new angle. This switches the shot, without cutting it. (Essentially, this does a replace edit without the folderol.)

FIGURE 5.19 Click an image to cut between multicam angles. Option-click to switch shots without cutting.

GOING FURTHER For true speed, use the keyboard to edit. Press a number on the keyboard to select and cut to that angle. (For example, press 2 to cut to angle 2.) Press Option+[a number] to switch to a different angle without cutting. (For example, pressing Option+3 switches the current shot to angle 3.)

264 Trim a Multicam Edit Point

Only roll trims are supported.

Multicam edits can be trimmed, like any other clip in the timeline. Using the Arrow (Select) tool, select the edit point then drag, or use the keyboard, to adjust the position of the edit.

However, see **FIGURE 5.20**, notice that only a roll trim is supported—both the In and Out are selected. That's because if you trimmed just one side (a ripple trim), it would knock the multicam clip out of sync. To prevent that, Final Cut allows only roll trims.

FIGURE 5.20 Any multicam edit point can be trimmed using a roll trim to adjust timing while protecting the audio and video sync. Ripple trims are not allowed.

265 Don't Flatten a Multicam Clip

Final Cut has a better way.

One of the differences between multicam clips in Final Cut versus Adobe Premiere Pro is that, in Premiere, multicam clips can be flattened when editing is complete. *Flattening* disconnects all the unused clip segments, so only the segment in the timeline plays. Flattening significantly reduces storage bandwidth when you are done editing the multicam clip.

Final Cut doesn't offer that option. Instead, FCP flattens automatically.

Final Cut flattens multicam clips automatically.

- If the Angle Viewer is visible and you are editing a multicam, all angles stream.
- If the Angle Viewer is closed and you are playing a multicam clip in the timeline, only the visible angle is streamed.

This means that once editing is complete, Final Cut treats multicam clips as though they were flattened. However, if you ever need to re-edit a multicam clip, simply open the Angle Editor, and all clips in the multicam clip are linked, online, and ready to edit.

256 Put Multiple Clips in One Multicam Angle

This is another way to create a montage.

It is easy to think of a multicam clip as one clip per angle. However, that's not true. As **FIGURE 5.21** illustrates, you can checkerboard multiple clips, alternating clips between angles. Then edit the multicam clip, changing shots as needed. Finally, after editing is complete, select the edited multicam clip in the timeline and press Cmd+T.

Ta-dah! Dissolves instantly appear between all segments.

Another use for this might be adding B-roll shots above an interview, but, frankly, B-roll and cutaways are easier to edit directly in the timeline.

FIGURE 5.21 One multicam angle (track) can hold multiple clips.

GOING FURTHER There's no limit to the number of clips stored in one multicam angle. You can add up to 64 angles in one multicam clip, though your storage may not support the required bandwidth.

267 Modify a Multicam Clip After It's Built

Multicam clips can be changed, even after they are edited.

There's a quick and easy way to modify a multicam clip, even after editing is complete. In the timeline, not the Browser, double-click the multicam clip. This opens it in the Angle Editor (see Tip 259, *The Multicam Angle Editor*).

A hidden feature of the Angle Editor is that you can delete an existing clip from the multicam clip, replace it with a different clip, or add an angle so you can add a forgotten clip to the multicam, for example, to add a shot that you missed when the multicam clip was first assembled.

To do so:

1. Click the down chevron; see Figure 5.15.
2. Select Add Angle.

   This creates a new angle.
3. From the Browser, drag the clip you want to add and sync it manually.

   You can also use this procedure to add audio clips or graphics.

Multicam clips can always be modified, even after editing.

GOING FURTHER
Any clips added or deleted to a multicam clip are also added or deleted from the edited multicam clip in the timeline plus in any other projects that use the same multicam clip. Switch back into multicam editing mode to add them to the timeline edit.

268 Add Effects to a Multicam Clip

The most popular use for this tip is color correction.

You can add effects to individual clips inside a multicam clip before you start editing, or after it, for that matter. The most common reason to do so is color correction; see **FIGURE 5.22**. Color correct the source clip in the multicam clip, and all the shots derived from it in the timeline are instantly color graded. This saves a ton of time.

1. Double-click the multicam clip to open it in the Angle Editor.
2. Select the clip in the camera angle you want to color correct/grade.
3. Press Control+Cmd+1 to hide the Browser.
4. Press Cmd+7 to display the video scopes.
5. Open the Color Inspector and adjust the color of the clip until you are happy.

To add effects to a clip, other than color grading, open the Effects Browser and drag the effect you want on the clip inside the Angle Editor. (Chapter 8 covers effects in detail.)

NOTE The Comparison View can help match shots when grading a multicam clip; see Tip 111, *The Comparison View*.

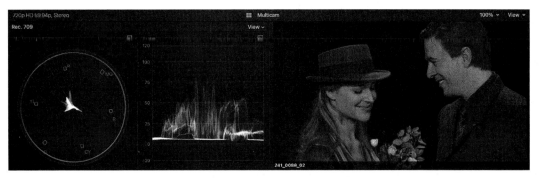

FIGURE 5.22 Vectorscope (left), Waveform monitor, and the image they are analyzing (right).

> **GOING FURTHER** Scott Newell edits a lot of multicam clips. In a note he added: "Multiple cameras rarely match and bad color matching ruins any believability of a multicam scene. It screams 'shot with more than one camera' and takes your mind away from what's going on in the scene. (At least for me it does)."
>
> I explain more about color grading in Chapter 8.

269 Access Audio Channels Inside a Multicam Clip

You can't mix audio in a multicam clip, but you can access channels.

Although you can't mix audio from different clips in a multicam clip, you can access individual audio channels within the currently active clip.

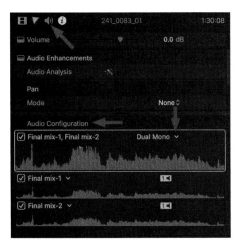

1. Double-click the multicam clip to open it in the timeline.

2. Select the clip that contains the audio channels you want to access.

3. In the Audio Inspector (see **FIGURE 5.23**), change Audio Configuration from Stereo (the default) to Dual Mono. This displays all the individual audio channels in the clip.

4. Close the multicam clip and go back to the timeline.

5. Select the multicam clip segment you want to access.

FIGURE 5.23 Audio Inspector icon (top red arrow). To reveal individual audio channels, change Stereo to Dual Mono (lower-right red arrow).

6. Choose Clip > Expand Audio Components (shortcut: Control+Option+S). Each audio channel is displayed separately under the video clip; see **FIGURE 5.24**. You can trim, silence, or adjust levels on each individual channel in the timeline.

7. To close the expanded clip, choose Clip > Collapse Audio Components.

You can adjust these audio channels at any time during your edit.

FIGURE 5.24 Individual audio channels for the active clip can be trimmed and adjusted. However, you can't hear audio from more than one clip.

GOING FURTHER
It will make your editing life a lot easier if you edit a multicam clip to a completed audio mix. Multicam is great for video, but even though it would be great to do an audio mix from a multicam clip, you can't. You can hear audio only from the currently active clip in the timeline.

CLOSED CAPTIONS

Captions are already required for many productions and helpful for all others. However, captions are not titles. This section explains what you need to know to use them well.

270 Not All Captions Are Alike

Caption formats vary widely, but none look as good as a title.

Captions are "timed text," visible text on-screen that appears and disappears in sync with audio or video. They are used for subtitles (language translations) and closed captions (text for the hearing impaired). Captions can be turned on or off under the viewer's control. The viewer can select between languages, assuming captions for more than one language are supplied. Captions appear above all other elements on the screen.

Final Cut supports three different caption formats: SCC, SRT, and iTT. All three are designed for readability. Only one caption (language) can be visible at once and captions can be turned on or off at any time. The U.S. Federal Communications Commission's rules about closed captioning include details about caption accuracy, placement, and synchronicity. They don't say anything about formatting. In fact, captions are not designed for styling.

- **CEA-608** (also called *SCC* and *EIS-608*). This was the original caption format. They are embedded in the video stream. It's the only caption format that can be embedded. They are stored in hexadecimal format

GOING FURTHER
Editor Jerry Thompson commented: "I always create a CEA-608 version, an iTT version, and an SRT version for all deliverables. I typically create my CEA-608 first, select all the captions in the timeline, right-click, and choose 'Duplicate Captions To New Format.' Then just skim through and make any adjustments if needed. Now you are ready for most all deliverables."

that permits only 32 characters per line, and up to four lines per frame. There is very limited support for formatting or position adjustment. An embedded SCC file supports only one language.

When in doubt, create SRT captions and treat them as plain text.

- **SRT** (SubRip Text). This is probably the most popular caption format, supported by most online services and broadcasters. It is always exported as a "side-car file," which is a file separate from the video file. As such, SRT supports multiple languages, one language per side-car file. SRT supports basic formatting changes including font, color, placement, and text formatting. However, there is no clear standard for these style changes. Even if you apply them to your captions, there is no guarantee that the software playing your movie will know how to interpret them. It is best not to format SRT captions.

- **ITT** (iTunes Timed Text). According to Apple's Help, "The iTT standard features formatting, color, and placement options, including a wider range of alphabets, making it the best choice for languages with non-Roman characters. iTT captions are imported or exported as separate files, but they can't be embedded in an output media file the way CEA-608 captions can." This caption format supports the greatest amount of formatting, but is supported by the fewest platforms.

When in doubt, create SRT captions and think of them as plain text.

> **GOING FURTHER** Final Cut Help files provide more information on captions. As well, here are two links for editors creating captions in the United Kingdom:
> - bbc.github.io/subtitle-guidelines/
> - www.capitalcaptions.com/services/closed-captioning-services/closed-captions-legal-obligations/

⟨271⟩ Two Ways to Import Captions

The easiest way to create captions is to import them.

The easiest way to create captions is to create them outside of Final Cut, then import them.

Although you can create captions individually inside Final Cut, it is far more likely that captions are created by the service that transcribes the audio from your program into text. Then, all you need to do is import the captions and make sure the timings are correct.

One of the questions the transcription service will ask is what caption format you need. Captions are not easily converted between formats, so make sure the format you are ordering is the format required by your distributor.

To import a caption file, choose File > Import Captions.

You could also export and import captions using an XML file. However, an XML file contains the entire project, including captions, media, and timeline. When importing a caption file, you are just importing the captions themselves and placing them on the timeline.

272 Enable Captions Using the Timeline Index

Enable or disable languages with a single mouse click.

You can display only one caption track (called a *language subrole*) at a time. Displayed captions are called *active*. However, you can edit or modify any caption whether the caption track is active or not.

Captions are controlled from the Roles section of the Timeline Index; see **FIGURE 5.25**.

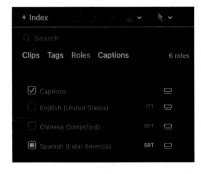

FIGURE 5.25 Captions are enabled, or disabled, using the Timeline Index.

- To enable/disable displaying all captions, click the Captions checkbox at the top left.

- To display a caption subrole, select the box to the left of the name (Spanish in Figure 5.25).

- To select that language subrole, click the language name. You can select a caption track without displaying it.

You can display only one caption track at a time.

- To show or hide that caption subrole in the timeline, click the small monitor box on the right. You can hide extra languages without removing them from the project.

273 Start with the Right Role

Captions require roles.

Before you create your first caption, create the right role for it. Choose Modify > Assign Caption Roles > Edit Roles; see **FIGURE 5.26**. From this menu, select the caption format you need.

FIGURE 5.26 Create a role using Modify > Assign Caption Roles > Edit Roles before creating individual captions. Roles determine the caption format.

Once the Caption role is created, click the small plus icon to select the language; see **FIGURE 5.27**. It defaults to the language you set for your computer in System Preferences > Language & Region. Languages are set by the Caption role, not the individual caption.

GOING FURTHER
Once a caption is created, you cannot convert it to a different caption format. You can, however, copy and paste text between captions.

When you add a new caption, you also assign it to the appropriate Caption role.

FIGURE 5.27 Click the Caption Role button to create a new role. Click the Language button to select the language for that caption track.

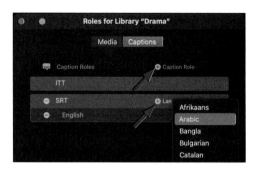

274 Modify Captions

Most of the time, treat captions like clips.

Once you create (Edit > Captions > Add Caption) or import a caption file, you can add, modify, trim, or delete individual captions. The only difference between clips and captions is that captions using the same language can't overlap, be too short, or be too near each other. Fortunately, FCP warns you if there's a problem by changing the color of the offending caption clip to red.

- To add a caption, put the playhead where you want the caption to appear and choose Edit > Captions > Add Caption.
- To edit the contents of a caption, double-click the caption clip; see **FIGURE 5.28**.

FIGURE 5.28 Double-click a caption to modify the text.

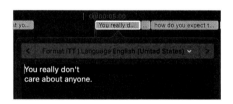

GOING FURTHER
Different caption formats have different limits on characters, position, duration, and where a caption can end. Final Cut will warn you if a caption is out of spec.

- To assign a caption to a different language, click the chevron next to the name at the top of the caption.
- To adjust the timing of when a caption appears, drag it horizontally in the timeline.
- To adjust its duration, trim the edge.
- To delete a caption, select it so it is surrounded by a gold box, then press Delete.

275 Easily Edit SRT Captions

SRT captions are easily edited outside of Final Cut.

SRT captions are stored in a simple text file; see **FIGURE 5.29.** You can open these in any text editing program. I use Applications > Utilities > Text Edit. You could also use BBEdit.

The format of the data is very specific:

- **Caption number.** This unique, sequential number is placed on the first line of a caption.
- **Timecode.** This indicates the start and end of the caption, with the last set of numbers set off by a comma and representing milliseconds, not frames.
- **Caption text.** This is one or two lines of text. Notice that this text file does not contain any text formatting.

NOTE If you format the SRT caption, you'll see formatting instructions included using HTML-style formatting. In general, the more you avoid formatting, the more compatible the caption.

```
●●●        Internet to Mars - Dialog.srt
1
00:00:07,770 --> 00:00:11,610
In another role that I have
at the Jet Propulsion Laboratory

2
00:00:11,610 --> 00:00:15,390
we've been working for the last six years
or so on the design of an interplanetary

3
00:00:15,390 --> 00:00:20,010
extension of the Internet. And what
we're saying is that we want to standardize

4
00:00:20,010 --> 00:00:24,630
the communication standards, the protocols,
that are used in space because

5
00:00:24,660 --> 00:00:29,080
if we do that, each time we launch a
new mission to go to Saturn or Jupiter
```

FIGURE 5.29 This is a typical SRT caption file. Note the simple, rigid formatting, including the weird arrows.

As long as the text lines don't run too long, you can easily correct spelling, fix punctuation errors, or move words between captions directly in this text file.

GOING FURTHER Although you can correct timing in this file, it is easier to correct timing using the tools in Final Cut to make sure that you aren't violating any caption timing rules.

276 Caption Translation Tip

SRT captions are also easy to translate.

This tip was first provided by Carsten Ress and posted to my website.

Carsten was looking for a way to export subtitles (in a closed captions format) from FCP as text, send it to translation, then import it back again as subtitles. Here's what he did:

1. Export the subtitles from Final Cut as an SRT file. (Although the extension is .SRT, you can open the file in any text editor.)

   The translator replaced the text with the translation, leaving caption numbers and timecode untouched.

2. Import the translated SRT file into a new language role.

   The subtitles can be translated while retaining the original timing.

Be careful with the TXT document, as small changes in the format (for example, adding additional text) can result in error messages during the reimport of the subtitles.

Also, Spherico.com makes a series of caption plugins that can import, export, and convert captions. These can also help if you want to burn the subtitles into the video file with more formatting options.

> **GOING FURTHER** Carsten adds: "This workaround is delicate. In my last project, the translator used double quotation marks (" ") which are not supported in SRT files. This led to an error message during import. Make sure there are no 'illegal' characters, to avoid error messages while importing the SRT into Final Cut. Using the wrong quotes prevented all captions from importing."

COLOR BASICS & VIDEO SCOPES

Understanding color and the video scopes will make a huge impact on the quality of your visuals. This section covers color and the video scopes. Chapter 8 shows how to put these tools to work.

277 Grayscale, Even More Than Color, Drives Emotions

SDR grayscale values are defined by regions.

Brightness levels in an image, called *grayscale values*, define how light or dark each pixel is. These levels are displayed by the Waveform Monitor and loosely categorized into seven regions; see **FIGURE 5.30**. For SDR video, these levels are:

1. **Super-white**. Values greater than 100 IRE.
2. **White**. Values equal to 100 IRE.
3. **Highlights**. Values between 66–100 IRE.
4. **Mid-tones** (also called *Mid-gray*, or just *Mids*). Values between 33–66 IRE.
5. **Shadows**. Values between 0–33 IRE.
6. **Black**. Values exactly equal to 0 IRE.
7. **Super-black**. Values below 0 IRE.

Both super-white and super-black are illegal levels. Although you can post media containing these levels to the web, they are not allowed in media destined for broadcast, cable, digital cinema, DVD, or commercial streaming media. Adjusting these levels is part of the color correction/grading process. It's a good habit to practice controlling these levels regardless of distribution.

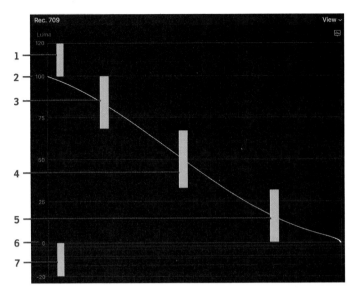

FIGURE 5.30 SDR (Rec. 709) grayscale values are displayed in the Waveform Monitor and grouped into seven regions. While this displays IRE values, the concept is the same for millivolts.

We will use these terms constantly when describing an image and color. (HDR has similar ranges, but not the same values.)

GOING FURTHER Here's an easy way to think of the grayscale values in an image:

- Shadows give an image its richness.
- Highlights provide energy.
- Midtones set the emotional tone and suggest time of day.

278 Color Is Like a Grapefruit

Hue, saturation & luminance are easiest to imagine in 3D.

Grayscale is two-dimensional. Color is 3D. When our eye sees a color, it says, "Ah...blue!" But with video, we need more precision than that. All digital images and video define color using RGB (red, green, and blue) values, each with three components:

- **Hue**. The shade of a color—red, cyan, purple, and so on.
- **Saturation**. The amount of a color, where gray is unsaturated and bright red is fully saturated.
- **Luminance** (also called *luma* or *brightness*). How light or dark a pixel is. These were the grayscale values discussed in Tip 277, *Grayscale, Even More Than Color, Drives Emotions*.

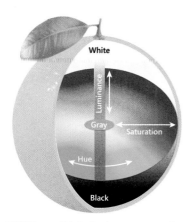

FIGURE 5.31 Think of colors as a grapefruit containing three axes: hue (angle around grapefruit), saturation (distance from center), and luminance (distance north or south).

The easiest way to visualize how these color are organized is to imagine a grapefruit; see FIGURE 5.31. Connect a line from the north pole to the south. Then, along that line, sort every shade of gray starting with pure white at the north and smoothly flowing to pure black at the south. Now, every shade of gray, its luminance value, is defined by where it's located on that vertical line.

Saturation radiates out from that center line. Saturation, the amount of a color, increases as distance from the center line increases.

Finally, hue is defined as an angle. In the grapefruit illustration, red is in the upper left; blue is on the right; while green is in the lower left. Each of these three primary colors is 120 degrees apart, which also matches how colors are displayed in the Vectorscope.

We can now precisely describe each color using three numbers:

1. Its angle around the grapefruit (hue)
2. Its distance from the center (saturation)
3. Its height from north to south (luminance)

We refer to these as HSL for hue, saturation, and luminance.

279 Colors, Like Grayscale, Are Defined Using Regions

Colors are grouped by primary and secondary colors.

If we cut the grapefruit, introduced in Tip 278, *Color Is Like a Grapefruit*, at its equator and look inside, we would see the color range shown in FIGURE 5.32.

FIGURE 5.32 Primary colors (P) and secondary colors (S). See how this emulates the interior of the grapefruit? We will see this color organization again when we look at the Vectorscope.

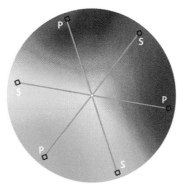

Luminance (brightness) is perpendicular to the page, so every shade of gray is a single dot in the center of the circle. Saturation increases as distance from the center increases. And hue varies by angle.

There are three primary (P) colors: red, green, and blue. There are also three secondary (S) colors: cyan, magenta, and yellow. Secondary colors are the exact opposite of their primary.

> **GOING FURTHER** Here are two color rules to keep in mind for the future:
> - Digital colors are additive. Equal amounts of red, green, and blue combine to equal white. This is what a camera does when it white balances; it equalizes the red, green, and blue values of a white card.
> - To remove a color, add its opposite color. You'll learn how to apply these rules in Chapter 8.

280 Intro to Video Scopes

Of the three scopes in Final Cut, two are really important.

Final Cut has three principal video scopes; see **FIGURE 5.33**. Each of these analyzes and displays the value of every pixel in the current frame displayed in the Viewer.

- **Waveform Monitor.** In Luma mode, the Waveform Monitor displays grayscale values.
  - **RGB Parade.** This is a variation of the Waveform Monitor, though it is often described as though it was a separate video scope. It displays color values separated into the three primary color channels of red, green, and blue.

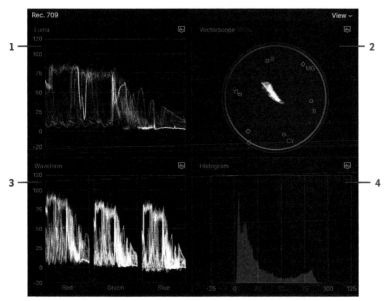

FIGURE 5.33 FCP video scopes: 1. Waveform Monitor, 2. Vectorscope, 3. RGB Parade, and 4. Histogram.

NOTE The RGB Parade is the default display for the Waveform Monitor. But changing the Waveform Monitor to Luma is *much more helpful*. See Tip 285, *Video Scope Icon*.

- **Vectorscope**. In YUV mode, this displays color hue and saturation values.

- **Histogram**. This, like the Histogram in Photoshop, displays the gray-scale range from dark (left) to light (right).

Choose View > Show in Viewer > Video Scopes (shortcut: Cmd+7) to display or hide the scopes. The brightness of each scope is adjustable in the View menu in the top-right corner of the scope display. (See Tip 284, *The Video Scope View Menu*.)

281 The Waveform Monitor

The Waveform Monitor displays the grayscale values of an image.

The Waveform Monitor is one of the two most important video scopes. It displays the grayscale value of every pixel in the frame displayed in the Viewer, but nothing about color.

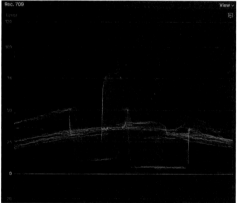

However, by default, the Waveform Monitor displays an RGB Parade which is not very helpful. Instead, using the Video Scope Icon, change this to Luma. (See Tip 285, *Video Scope Icon*.)

When looking at the Waveform Monitor, unlike any other scope, we can use terms like "on the left of the image" or "in the center." We can refer to an image from left to right. But we can't use up or down since these define brightness levels in the scope.

Darker pixels are toward the bottom; brighter pixels are toward the top. Looking at the screen shot in **FIGURE 5.34**, we can say:

- The center of the image is brighter than the two sides.

- The left side has something brighter than the right side.

- No values exceed 100 IRE.

- No values go below 0 IRE.

- The blue bar on the right is darker than the red bar on the left.

FIGURE 5.34 The Waveform Monitor (top) displays the grayscale values of every pixel in this balloon image (bottom).

What we can't say, though, is what the image is. The Waveform Monitor describes an image by its brightness, not its content.

282 The Vectorscope

The Vectorscope displays the colors values of an image.

The Vectorscope is equal to, but opposite of, the Waveform Monitor. The Waveform Monitor displays grayscale values. The Vectorscope displays the color values of every pixel displayed in the Viewer. This is the technical equivalent of looking at the equator of the grapefruit we first saw in Tip 278, *Color Is Like a Grapefruit*; see **FIGURE 5.35**.

Gray is in the center. Saturation increases from the center to the edge. Hue varies by angle around the Vectorscope, with red at 11:30 (near the top). However, the Vectorscope tells us nothing about grayscale values. That's why we use the Vectorscope in tandem with the Waveform Monitor.

In this image, the Vectorscope shows the colors from the balloon image. The lower red arrow points to the single dot for grayscale values running perpendicular to the scope. The upper red arrow displays the skin tone line, which is the color of red blood under skin. (We'll talk more about the use of that in Chapter 8.) As you look at the scope, saturation increases as you extend out from the center, and hue changes with the angle.

Looking at the Vectorscope, we can say:

- There's a clump of red in the image.
- There are two clumps of blue in the image, one small and one big.
  That big blue clump is generally where blue sky appears and is a different color blue from the small blue clump.
- There's also a lot of yellow there, but almost no magenta, green, or cyan.

FIGURE 5.35 The Vectorscope displays the color values of every pixel in this balloon image. The yellow lines were added by me to indicate color saturation limits between targets.

However, like the Waveform Monitor, we can't use the Vectorscope to describe content, even though our eyes tell us we are looking at balloons when we see the image itself.

Also, notice the small boxes. Those are called *color targets*. (The small letters label the colors, from the top clockwise, red, magenta, blue, cyan, green, and yellow.) They represent maximum saturation values for each of the three primary and secondary colors. It is good practice to make sure that saturation levels never exceed those lines. (Those pale yellow lines are not actually displayed in the scope; I added them to illustrate saturation limits between targets.)

283 Display Video Scopes on a Second Monitor

Scopes are displayed along with the Viewer on a second monitor.

One of the benefits to using a second monitor to edit video is displaying both the Viewer and video scopes (they travel together) on a larger screen. This provides greater detail to see what's inside the frame, or scope, more clearly.

To do so:

1. Press Cmd+7 to display the scopes.

2. From the chevron drop-down menu displayed in **FIGURE 5.36**, select Viewer.

3. Click the Dual Monitor icon indicated by the red arrow.

   The Viewer and video scopes now appear on a second monitor.

4. Switch the scopes to vertical using the View menu.

5. To consolidate the interface back to a single monitor, click the Dual Monitor button again.

FIGURE 5.36 Click the Dual Monitor button to display a portion of the interface on a second monitor.

> **GOING FURTHER** The Dual Monitor button appears only if you have a second computer monitor attached to your computer and turned on. With a 5K monitor, you can display a 4K image at 100% and still have room for the scopes.

284 The Video Scope View Menu

You can display from one to four scopes—horizontally or vertically.

The View menu, in the top-right corner of the video scopes panel, determines how many scopes will be displayed and how they are arranged; see **FIGURE 5.37**. My preference is the side-by-side option in the top-right corner. I like seeing both the Vectorscope and Waveform Monitor at the same time.

- **Vertical Layout**. This puts the scopes under the Viewer. Although this is really cramped for a single monitor, it is often the preferred choice when using two monitors and displaying the Viewer on the second monitor.

- **Show Guides**. This displays a thin, white, horizontal line on the Waveform Monitor and Histogram that measures and displays gray scale values. Hover over the scope to quickly read a value. Or click to fix the line in place, then drag the line up or down. Drag the line off the top or bottom of the scope to make it float with the cursor again.

- **Monochrome**. This converts the colors displayed in the scopes to grayscale, though it does not alter media or the timeline.

- The **slider**, at the bottom, determines the brightness of the display trace in the video scope display.

(285) Video Scope Icon

Select and customize the video scope display.

The small icon just below the View menu determines which scope is selected and how it's configured; see **FIGURE 5.38**.

FIGURE 5.37 The Video Scope View menu determines how many scopes are displayed, how they are arranged, and the look of the display.

My recommendations are:

- Set Waveform Monitor to Luma. This provides the most accurate grayscale display.

- Most US editors are comfortable using IRE for all SDR video. European editors may be more comfortable using millivolts. You get to pick.

- Set Histogram to either Luma or RGB Parade.

- Set Vectorscope to 100%, Vector, and Show the Skin Tone Indicator. (That indicator is very important, as you'll learn in Chapter 8.)

FIGURE 5.38 The video scope selection and configuration menus: (l-r) Waveform Monitor, Vectorscope, and Histogram.

CHAPTER 5—ADVANCED EDITING SHORTCUTS

CATEGORY	SHORTCUT	WHAT IT DOES
Trimming	Cmd+G	Group clips on the same layer into a storyline
	Cmd+Y	Create an Audition from selected clips
	Y	Open an Audition for selection
	Shift+F	Reveal match frame in Browser
	Option+F	Edit match frame into timeline
Compound Clips	Option+G	Create a compound clip
	Shift+Cmd+G	Break apart a compound clip
Multicam	Shift+Cmd+7	Display the Angle Viewer
	1–9	Cut and switch to one of the first nine angles in a multicam clip
	Option+1–9	Switch, without cutting, to one of the first nine angles in a multicam clip
	Shift+V	Set the angle for the Video Monitor
	Shift+A	Set the angle for the Audio Monitor
	Control+Option+S	Expand audio or compound clip components
Captions	Option+C	Add a caption
	Control+Shift+C	Edit the selected caption
	Control+Option+Cmd+C	Split the selected caption
	Shift+Cmd+2	Open the Timeline Index
Video Scopes	Cmd+7	Display the video scopes
	Control+Cmd+W	Display the Waveform Monitor
	Control+Cmd+V	Display the Vectorscope
	Control+Cmd+H	Display the Histogram

CHAPTER WRAP

Many of these tools are unique to Final Cut Pro, which means that learning them gives you a competitive advantage. You may not need all the tools we've covered, however, they are fun to play with and simplify editing complex projects. Plus, understanding color and the video scopes will make all your projects look better.

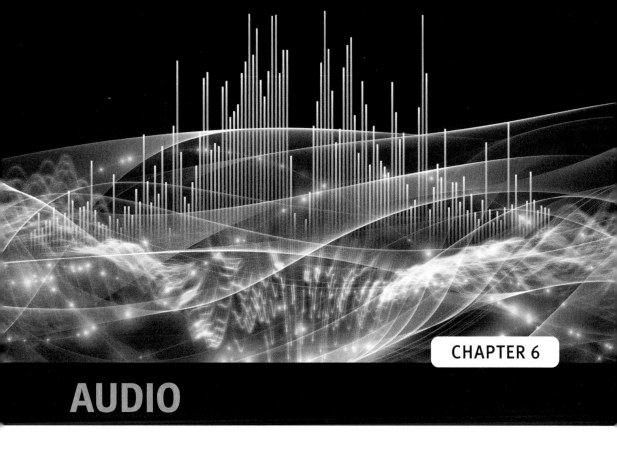

CHAPTER 6

AUDIO

INTRODUCTION

It is said—and I agree—that the best way to improve the quality of a film is to improve the quality of its sound. Yet audio scares many editors—mostly because they don't understand it. This is a shame, because audio can do so much for video, much more cheaply and easily.

Keep in mind that the most valuable piece of audio mixing equipment is between your ears. When mixing, we need to do more than watch the meters. We need to carefully *listen* to the audio in our projects to make sure the sound and picture are working together to enhance the story.

In this chapter, we look at the full range of Final Cut audio tools—from edit to final mix.

- Audio Prep
- Edit Audio
- Levels & Pan
- Audio Inspector

- Roles
- Audio Mixing & Effects
- Shortcuts

- **Audio clip**. A media clip containing one or more channels of audio. It may, or may not, be linked to a video clip. Audio clips use different codecs from video. Also, except for BWF files (Broadcast WAV), audio clips don't contain timecode. AIF and WAV are the two most popular uncompressed, high-quality audio formats.

- **Channel**. This contains the recording of one mic, or the sound destined for one speaker. An audio clip can contain multiple channels.

- **Component**. Apple's name for an audio channel.

- **dB** (deciBel). The technical measure of audio volume on an instant-by-instant basis. One dB is equal to the minimum change in audio level that is perceivable by an 18-year-old person with normal human hearing. However, don't assume that 0 dB is dead quiet. In most cases, it means "full volume." Yup, audio is measured in negative numbers.

- **Loudness**. The technical measure of audio volume over time, which is more representative of how our ears hear sound. Loudness is measured in Loudness Unit Full Scale (LUFS) or Loudness K-weighted Full Scale (LKFS). These two measures are identical, just with different labels. 1 LU equals 1 dB.

- **Waveform**. The visual representation of the amplitude (or volume) of an audio clip over time.

- **Mono**. An audio clip containing exactly one channel.

- **Stereo**. An audio clip containing two discrete channels, played simultaneously, with channel 1 providing the sound for the left speaker and channel 2 feeding the right speaker.

- **Dual-Channel Mono**. An audio clip containing two or more discrete mono channels, where there is no sense of "left and right." Typical examples are an interviewer (channel 1) and guest (channel 2). Or dialogue between four actors where each actor wears their own mic and is recorded to their own channel. This is the most common audio format used in video production and editing.

- **Surround**. A distribution format (for example, after an audio mix) where five (plus subwoofer) or seven (plus subwoofer) audio channels are combined into one audio clip.

- **Double-system**. This records video on a camera, while recording audio on a separate digital recorder. The big benefit to this is high-quality audio without constraining the movement of the camera. The disadvantage is that these clips require syncing during the editing process.

- **Sync** (or synced).
  - A linked clip containing audio and video.
  - The process of linking audio to a video clip.
  - Coordinating and monitoring the timing of multiple clips (that is, multicam).
- **Level** (also gain and volume). The measure of the loudness of a sound, measured in decibels (dB). Although these terms are technically different—gain refers to input, and volume refers to output—for this chapter we'll use them interchangeably; and we'll mostly use level.
- **Pan**. In a stereo or surround mix, pan determines where a sound is placed in space between two or more speakers.
- **Crossfade**. The audio equivalent of a dissolve, where one clip fades out as the other clip fades in.
- **Absolute** level. This measures exactly how loud a sound is. Audio meters display the absolute levels of an audio clip.
- **Relative** level. This measures how much a sound level is changed compared to the level at which it was recorded. Audio mixing deals with relative levels.
- **Distortion**. Audio that was recorded, or exported, at such a loud level that the audio sounds awful. Distorted audio, in general, can't be repaired. It is bad.
- **Room Tone**. The sound a room or set makes when no one is talking; for example, air conditioning, traffic noise, birds chirping, that sort of thing. Room tone is recorded during production to fill audio gaps created during editing.
- **Mix**. The process of blending the sounds from project audio clips such that the blend sounds pleasing. The audio mix is one of the last steps in the editing process.
- **Stem**. A component of a finished mix. There are three principal stems: dialogue, sound effects, and music.
- **Keyframe**. Keyframes are used to automate a parameter change during playback, such as levels or pan. We always use keyframes in pairs.

The best way to improve the quality of a video is to improve the quality of its audio.

AUDIO PREP

These basic audio concepts and hardware support what we can do with audio in Final Cut Pro. They also apply to any other audio or video application.

286 Human Hearing and Sample Rate

Sample rate determines frequency response.

Normal human hearing is a range from 20 Hz to 20,000 Hz. (*Normal* is defined as the hearing of an 18-year-old.) As we get older, we lose the ability to hear high-frequency sounds. *Everything* we hear is pitched somewhere along this range. There isn't a set of frequencies for noise with another set of frequencies for speech. All sounds are contained within this single frequency range.

As a general guide, record audio for video at a 48,000 (48K) sample rate and 16-bit depth. Mix audio at 32-bit depth.

- Human speech is, roughly, 100–6,500 Hz for men and 200–8,000 Hz for women (roughly five octaves).
- Vowels are low-frequency sounds.
- Consonants are higher-frequency sounds.
- The deepest note on a piano is 27.5 Hz. The highest note is 4,186 Hz.
- When the frequency doubles, the tone goes up an octave. (The opposite is also true.)
- When the audio level increases by 6 dB, the volume doubles. (The opposite is also true.)

Sample rate determines the frequency response. Most audio for video is recorded at 48,000 samples per second. The Nyquist theorem (yes, there will be a test) states that to calculate the maximum frequency of an audio recording, divide the sample rate in half. So 48,000 samples per second equals a maximum frequency of 24,000 Hz, which exceeds human hearing. (Another common sample rate, used by CD audio to reduce file size, is 44,100 samples per second.)

287 What Does Audio Bit Depth Determine?

It's a volume thing.

Just as digital video uses bit depth (to define color and grayscale ranges), so does audio. Audio bit depth determines the signal-to-noise ratio (SNR) and the dynamic range (the difference between the softest and loudest passages) of an audio clip. Bit depth applies only to Linear PCM (uncompressed) audio, such as WAV and AIFF. Compressed formats, such as AAC, AC3, or MP3, don't use bit depth. Audio bit depths range from 8–32 bit.

In general, record audio using 16-bit depth. Mix audio at 32-bit depth. I would not recommend doing any audio work at less than 16-bit depth.

288 Which to Pick: Speakers or Headphones

Monitor speakers are best, but headphones can work in a pinch.

It's the age-old question: Should I mix on speakers or headphones? Based on conversations with every audio engineer I've asked, the answer is unanimous: use monitor speakers for the final mix. Headphones are so precise that you spend hours correcting problems that no one else will hear. However, once the mix is done, it's good practice to listen to it on a variety of devices... just in case there's a problem.

However, note the term *monitor speakers*. These are speakers designed to provide a flat frequency response from below 100 Hz to over 16,000 Hz. *Flat* is the key word. When you are mixing, you want to hear what's actually in your audio, not artifacts (such as bass boost) introduced by cheap consumer speakers.

Headphones are fine for editing, but for the final mix, use monitor speakers.

Personally, I'm a big fan of Yamaha HS5 and HS8 monitor speakers. I'm listening to a pair of HS5s as I write this. They have clean sound, rich bass, and a clarity that makes it easy to hear what's in my audio and what I need to fix. There are many other good choices for monitor speakers.

In general, don't mix with subwoofers, unless you know the project will play on a system with subwoofers. Also, do a final listening pass using cheap speakers to replicate small TV speakers, or mobile devices, just to make sure the essential audio can still be heard.

Headphones are fine for editing, but for the final mix, use monitor speakers.

289 What's a Waveform?

The visual representation of audio volume over time.

In the "olden days" audio editors would edit audio using magnetic tape, slowly dragging the tape across the playhead of the audio tape recorder to determine where to make an edit. We'd mark that spot with a grease pencil (hence the term *marked*). It was slow, painstaking, and until you developed the skill, remarkably error-prone. I know, I started my career editing audio tape.

Waveforms make editing audio so much easier! A waveform is shown in **FIGURE 6.1**. Where the blue "waves" are tall, the audio is loud. Where they are short, the audio is soft. Where there's a gap (left red arrow), the actor is pausing for breath between sentences. Between sentences is always a good place to make an edit.

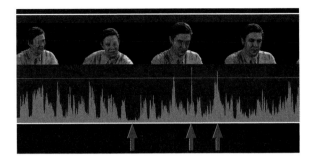

FIGURE 6.1 The waveform displays a visual representation of the volume (amplitude) of an audio clip. Valleys (left arrow) are good places to make edits.

In this waveform, the levels are consistently good—not too soft and, except for two places (the two right arrows), not too loud. (The middle arrow points to a waveform with a red top, which probably indicates a cough or laugh or other overly loud sound that is most likely distorted.)

The thin horizontal line is the audio level control. We'll cover that later in this chapter.

Where the waveform is tall (right red arrow), the audio is loud, but not dangerously so. Audio close to the maximum level (center red arrow) is called *peaking*. Those levels require watching during the mix.

So to read a waveform, look at its overall height throughout the clip to see how consistent the. audio levels are, watch for valleys as places to make an edit, and check peaks to make sure the audio isn't distorted.

290 Supported Audio Formats

Be careful editing or mixing MP3 audio.

Final Cut Pro supports a wide range of audio formats:

- AAC
- AIFF
- BWF
- CAF
- MP3
- MP4
- RF64
- WAV

The default audio format for Final Cut is WAV. This, like AIF, is uncompressed and provides the highest-possible quality. BWF is the only format that can include timecode.

NOTE Apple's website for technical details on each of these formats: support.apple.com/guide/final-cut-pro/supported-media-formats-ver2833f855/mac

291 Audio Import Settings

Better audio starts at import.

Improving audio quality starts when it is recorded, but that requires a separate book. In terms of editing, pay attention during import. In the lower-right side of the Media Import window are several audio options; see **FIGURE 6.2**.

- **Fix audio problems**. Final Cut includes a suite of tools to fix common audio problems, including raising low audio levels, reducing background noise, and removing hum. Since problem clips in the timeline can be analyzed and fixed later (see Tip 331, *Automatic Audio Enhancements*), I don't recommend using this option during import. You can remove these fixes later, but it takes time.

- **Separate mono and group stereo**. Final Cut analyzes and marks the channel assignment for audio clips as mono, stereo, dual-channel mono, and surround.

- **Remove silent channels**. Many cameras record more than two audio channels. If an audio clip has more than two audio channels and one or more of them are empty, Final Cut removes the channel and flags the clip as "Autoselected."

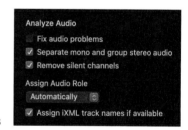

FIGURE 6.2 These are my recommended audio import options.

- **Assign Audio Role**. Final Cut analyzes the audio clip and assigns a role automatically based upon whether FCP thinks the clip is dialogue, sound effects, or music. The default role is Dialogue. Roles are easily changed later. I leave this set to Automatically except when I want an audio clip assigned a specific, custom role.

- **Assign iXML track names if available**. Some high-end audio recording devices allow naming audio channels on the digital recorder used on set. Those names are saved in iXML format. FCP can read these labels and assign them as subroles to specific audio components (channels) in the clip. Leaving this on does no harm, even if you don't need it.

My preferences are shown in Figure 6.2.

292 Timeline Settings Affect Audio Display

The timeline minimizes audio waveforms. Here's how to change it.

When you first drag a synced clip to the timeline, the audio waveforms are pretty hard to see. That's because Final Cut thinks that what you *really* want to see is the picture. Sigh...how foolish. Go to the top-right corner of the timeline and click the icon shown by the red arrow in **FIGURE 6.3**.

When you click one of these six icons, the display height of the waveform changes; see **FIGURE 6.4**. These don't affect audio levels, just how the clips look in the timeline. My display preference is the blue icon in Figure 6.3.

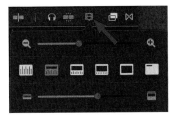

FIGURE 6.3 The Timeline Settings dialog. These icons determine the height of the video and waveform display. The lower slider determines the height of the clip.

FIGURE 6.4 The range of display options matching the icons in Timeline Settings.

GOING FURTHER

- Control+Option+Up/Down arrows switches between clip appearance icons.
- Shift+Cmd+[plus]/[minus] increases/decreases clip height in the timeline.

293 What an iXML File Looks Like

I was curious, so I tracked one down.

iXML files are created on the set by a dedicated audio technician using professional audio recorders that allow the tech to assign each input source a name. These names are imported as subroles by Final Cut. After import, the editor can change the name as needed.

FIGURE 6.5 shows what an iXML file looks like. Each of the channels in the clip is labeled based on the source of the audio.

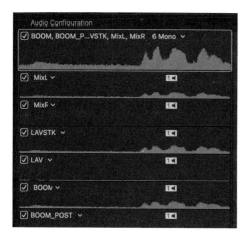

FIGURE 6.5 Typical channel and subrole labeling for an iXML audio file.

294 Sync Double System Audio Automatically

Syncing connects two separate clips into one.

Final Cut can automatically sync audio and video clips. A typical example is double-system sound where one video clip is synced to one or more audio clips.

Sync audio clips using audio content, timecode, date/time created, start of first clip, or first marker.

Similar to multicam syncing, audio clips are synced using audio content, timecode, date/time created, start of first clip, or first marker. If both the camera and audio clip contain similar audio, the easiest way to sync is for Final Cut to match the audio automatically. Depending upon the lengths of the clips, this could take from a few seconds to a few minutes.

To automatically sync clips:

1. Select the clips you want to sync in the Browser. Remember, while you can sync an unlimited number of audio clips, you can include only one video clip.

2. Choose Clip > Synchronize Clips (shortcut: Option+Cmd+G)

   Or—right-click one of the selected clips and choose Synchronize Clips.

   Here are the key choices in the dialog that appears; see **FIGURE 6.6**.

   NOTE If you need to sync more than one video clip, use a multicam clip.

   • Leave "Use audio for synchronization" selected so that Final Cut syncs on the audio in the clips.

   • Leave "Disable audio components on AV clips" selected if you don't want to hear the audio from the video clip. Most of the time, you don't.

3. Click OK.

   The synced clip appears in the Browser, ready to edit.

FIGURE 6.6 The automatic
synchronize clips dialog.

GOING FURTHER *Similar audio* means the same audio, but not necessarily the same quality. For example, the camera records temp audio using the camera mic, while the external audio recorder records high-quality audio directly from the mics on talent.

295 Sync Double System Sound Manually

Manual syncing provides more options to determine sync points.

Although multicam editing syncs multiple video clips with multiple audio clips (see Chapter 5, "Advanced Editing"), a typical audio example is syncing one video clip to one or more audio clips recorded using a separate audio recorder. Similar to multicam syncing, clips are synced using audio content, timecode, date/time created, start of first clip, or first marker. Generally, timecode or first markers are the best options because they are the fastest.

To sync clips manually:

1. In the Browser, set a marker on the sync point (generally a clapper slate) for each clip.

2. Once marked, select the clips you want to sync in the Browser.

   Remember, although you can select an unlimited number of audio clips, you can include only one video clip.

3. Choose Clip > Synchronize Clips (shortcut: Option+Cmd+G).

   Or—right-click one of the selected clips and choose Synchronize Clips.

   Here are the key choices in the dialog that appears next; see **FIGURE 6.7:**

   • Give the new synced clip a name and event location. (You may want to store synced clips in their own event to make them easier to find.)

   • Deselect Use audio for synchronization.

   You do this because not all clips have audio or the audio doesn't match.

- Select Disable audio components on AV clips.

  You do this because you want to use audio from the audio clips, not video. This mutes, but does not remove, the audio attached to the video clip.

- Set Synchronization to First Marker (though you can use other options, if needed).

- Configure the video settings as needed.

4. Click OK to create the synced clip.

The synced clip appears in the Browser, ready to edit.

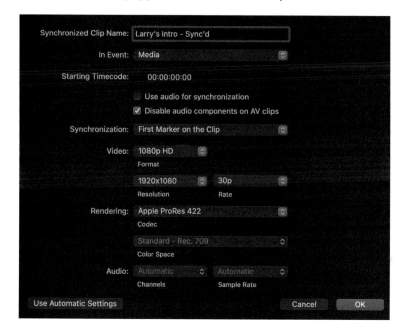

FIGURE 6.7 The manual clip synchronization dialog.

296 Manually Adjust Audio Clip Sync

This is similar to adjusting a multicam clip—but easier.

It is not unusual to need to shift the contents of a synced clip a few frames to get the alignment precisely correct. Fortunately, this is easy to do.

1. Select the synced clip in the Browser.

2. Choose Clip > Open Clip.

The synced clip opens in the timeline where each clip is on its own layer; see **FIGURE 6.8**. Here, you see two audio clips synced to a video clip, but the clapper slate alignment is off.

GOING FURTHER
When you have a synced clip open in the timeline, as we do in Figure 6.8, it's also possible to trim the audio, adjust or mute levels, or add effects. In general, I would advise against adding effects to a synced clip. That is better done later in the mix.

NOTE Unlike video, audio clips are not limited to moving in whole frame increments. Press Option+. [comma] or Option+. [period] to move the selected audio clip in subframe increments.

3. To adjust the alignment, select each clip then press [comma] or [period] to shift the clip left or right one frame at a time.

4. To close the clip for editing, open a project into the timeline.

   Once aligned, a synced clip behaves the same as any other clip.

FIGURE 6.8 The alignment of the clap is off a frame or two for each clip. Use [comma]/[period] to manually shift each clip one frame at a time.

297 Record a Voice-over

Use for temp tracks or production.

FIGURE 6.9 The Record Voiceover panel controls audio inputs, what the file is named, and where the file is stored, along with playback settings.

Most of the time, we work with the audio we are given. Still, editors are frequently called upon to record voiceovers, or temp tracks, to add to a project. Final Cut makes this easy.

1. Choose Window > Record Voiceover (shortcut: Option+Cmd+8) to display the voiceover control panel; see **FIGURE 6.9**.

2. Set the input from the drop-down list.

   This defaults to the system audio inputs, but the menu allows selecting from any connected audio source.

3. Turn Monitor off to prevent feedback if you are using a mic close to your computer.

4. Adjust the other settings based upon your personal preference.

I do a lot of voice-over work, and I've learned that I never get a reading right on the first take. So I just start recording and keep recording until I get it right. While writing the script and during rehearsal before recording, I make sure the voiceover fits for time. Once recording starts, I first work to get the reading right, then edit it for time.

I also make sure to store voice-overs in their own event, with a unique role assigned to them.

NOTE If System Preferences > Accessibility > Zoom is enabled, Option+Cmd+8 is used by macOS to zoom the screen. In that case, create a custom shortcut for Final Cut.

EDIT AUDIO

Editing audio is almost the same as editing video except, most of the time, we are editing audio that's connected to video and it's located in a different section of the timeline.

298 Audio Editing Basics

Editing audio is just like editing video—without the pictures.

Audio is edited similar to video. You preview the clip in the Browser, mark it with an In and/or Out, and edit it to the timeline the same as video. Trimming is a bit different, as are the effects. But playback and export, too, are the same.

All connected audio clips are placed *below* the Primary Storyline, just as all connected video clips are placed *above* it. Like video, audio clips are connected to the Primary Storyline, and, as with video, the same keyboard shortcuts and trim tools work the same with audio.

Audio is attached to either video (synced) or a separate clip. Audio does not contain timecode, except for Broadcast WAV (BWF) files. One audio clip can hold one or many channels of audio. Audio waveforms can be displayed in the Browser (off by default) or timeline (on by default).

In other words, you already know everything you need to know to add audio to your projects. There's nothing wildly divergent here. Still, there are a few differences.

FIGURE 6.10 shows the three main colors of an audio clip:

- **Blue**: Dialogue
- **Teal**: Sound effects
- **Green**: Music

FIGURE 6.10 The three principal colors for audio clips: Blue (dialogue), Teal (sound effects), and Green (music).

Roles determine these colors. The default role is Dialogue. This means that if Final Cut can't figure out the clip type during import, it assigns it a Dialogue role. Although the timeline groups audio clips by role, roles are easily changed at any time during an edit. (See the "Audio Roles" section later in this chapter.)

299 Edit Audio to the Timeline

Adding audio clips creates a connected clip—just like adding video.

Editing audio clips to the timeline is like editing video as a connected clip.

1. Position the playhead (skimmer) in the timeline.

2. Select the audio clip in the Browser.

3. Press Q.

   Or—click the Connected edit icon

   Or—drag the clip into the timeline, which ignores the position of the playhead (skimmer).

Moving, trimming, and deleting audio clips outside the Primary Storyline are identical to editing and trimming video.

300 Trim Audio Separately from Video

This is the most useful audio editing tip in the book.

Many of the audio clips added to the timeline are bundled with a video clip. We call this *synced* audio. Although you can see the audio, it is impossible to edit directly without also editing the video.

So here's the secret: Double-click any audio waveform to separate the audio from the video while still keeping it linked; see **FIGURE 6.11**. Instantly, the audio separates from the video. Yet, and this is the important part, the audio remains linked. Linked means it can't get out of sync with the video.

FIGURE 6.11 The left image shows audio nested with video. The right image shows audio expanded, but still linked, to the video.

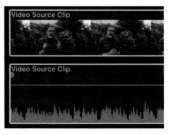

Double-click the waveform again to nest the audio back with the video.

This is such an important point. We almost always want to edit or trim audio separately from the video. Yet it is critical that audio not get out of sync. This solves that problem.

> **GOING FURTHER** You can't cut and delete a section of audio without also cutting the video, creating a *through edit*. However, you can use keyframes to mute a section of audio without cutting; see Tip 323, *Add and Modify Keyframes*.

301 Expand vs. Detach Audio?

Expanded audio is still linked, detached audio is not.

Select a synced audio and video clip, then look in the Clip menu. Although there are lots of choices, two key ones are Expand Audio and Detach Audio. What's the difference? Sync.

Never detach audio simply to trim it.

When you expand audio, the waveform separates from the video for trimming separately from the video; see **FIGURE 6.12**. However, that audio is still synced to the video. If you change the position of either the audio or the video, the other side of the synced clip moves with it.

FIGURE 6.12 Expanded audio (left) and detached audio (right). Notice the connection link (red arrow) for the connected clip.

When you detach audio, the audio becomes a connected clip, no longer locked to the video. There's a connection to the video, but it is no longer guaranteed to be in sync. In fact, it is impossible to resync the audio once it is detached. (Well, OK, yes you can, but you would need to create a synced or compound clip. Not easy; see Tip 303, *How to Sync Out-of-Sync Audio*.)

You *expand* audio when you want to trim or adjust it. You *detach* audio when you want to delete the audio, delete the video, or purposefully move the audio clip somewhere else in the project.

In short, never detach audio simply to trim it.

> **GOING FURTHER**
> Tip 201, *What's a Clip Connection?*, and Tip 203, *Move Primary Storyline Clips*, are also relevant for moving audio clips.

302 When Should You Break Apart Clip Items?

In general, don't do this for audio editing.

Clip > Break Apart Clip Items is generally not used for audio editing, for the same reason that detaching audio is not recommended. It takes the individual tracks inside an audio clip and converts them into connected clips.

Don't use Break Apart Clip Items for audio clips.

This menu choice is best used for:

- Deconstructing compound clips
- Deconstructing synced clips
- Deconstructing connected storylines.

In other words, this option is best for taking apart those timeline elements that you first put together.

303 How to Sync Out-of-Sync Audio

This condition is rare, but fixable.

Most of the time, when recording audio and video, everything is in perfect sync. That's because the camera and mic are relatively close to each other. However, not always. For example, when recording in a venue where the camera is on the other side of the stadium from the mics, audio and video may be a few frames out of sync. Or if your gear malfunctions. Or, well, if the gremlins were especially active that day. In other words, you have a sync problem.

Use compound clips to collect individual elements into a single clip for editing.

Here's how to fix it:

1. Select the errant clip.

2. Choose Clip > Break Apart Clip Items.

3. *Before you do anything else*, put the playhead where it crosses all components. Select each component one at a time and put a marker (shortcut: M) on it. This provides a sync point so that if you royally screw things up, you can get back to where you started.

4. While watching the video playback, select the component that is out of sync and press [comma] or [period] to move it one frame at a time until it is back in sync. Pick the adjustment that seems to make the sync look the best.

NOTE Unlike video, audio clips are not limited to moving in whole-frame increments. Press Option+[comma] or Option+[period] to move the selected audio clip in subframe increments.

5. Repeat this process for each out-of-sync audio clip.

6. When everything is back in sync, select all the clips and choose File > New > Compound Clip (shortcut: Option+G).

   This packages all the loose clips into a single compound clip that you can use for editing without risking sync.

If you decide later that things are still out of sync, open the compound clip and adjust the clips again.

> GOING FURTHER Unlike video, you can move an audio clip less than a frame—once it's detached from the video—to subtly improve sync. Zoom all the way in to the timeline. The gray bar next to the playhead at the top of the timeline shows the duration of one frame in the timeline; see **FIGURE 6.13**. Detach the audio, then slide it within that frame indicator to subtly tweak sync.

FIGURE 6.13 The gray bar at the top of the timeline indicates the duration of a frame. Detached audio can be moved in increments shorter than a frame.

304 Trim Audio Clips in the Primary Storyline

Most synced audio is edited into the Primary Storyline.

There are four types of audio edits in the Primary Storyline:

- Where the two clips touch.
- Where there's a gap between the two clips; see **FIGURE 6.14**.
- Where there's an overlap.
- Where the audio and video edit at different times, called a *split edit*. (See Tip 305, *Split Trims Edit Audio Separately*.)

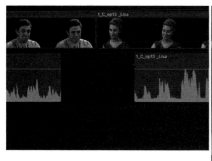

FIGURE 6.14 An audio trim with a gap creates silence, which is generally covered by room tone, sound effects, or music. An overlap (right) means you can hear audio from both clips.

Double-click the audio waveform to expand it from the clip; then, using the Arrow tool (shortcut: A), drag the edge of an audio clip. Gaps leave silence. Overlapping clips means you can hear audio from both clips. Both are acceptable edits; it depends upon what you want to hear and what you don't.

Almost all projects have multiple tracks of audio playing at once: dialogue, ambient sound (room tone or exterior natural sound), sound effects, and/or music. Overlapping edits are normal between layers.

305 Split Trims Edit Audio Separately

A split trim is where the audio and video edit at different times.

To me, the most important trim is a split trim; see **FIGURE 6.15**. (These are also called a *split edit*, *L-cut*, or *J-cut* due to the shape the edit forms in the timeline.) This is where the audio and video edit at different times. This means we see one thing but hear something different. Split edits are generally created in the Primary Storyline.

FIGURE 6.15 A split edit with the audio edit rolled to the right of the video edit.

NOTE Although you can—and often will—ripple trim audio to leave a gap, leaving a gap in the video would create a flash of black.

To create a split edit:

1. Display waveforms in the timeline.

2. Double-click the audio waveform to expand it from the video.

3. Select the Trim tool (most split edits are roll trims to avoid leaving gaps).

4. Drag either the video or audio edit point to a new location.

To remove a split edit:

1. Select both clips around the edit point.

2. Choose Trim > Align Audio to Video.

   This shifts the timing of the audio edit to match the timing of the video edit for that clip.

Similar to a video trim, you can also move the selected audio edit point using the keyboard:

- Press [comma]/[period] to move the selected edit point left/right one frame.
- Press Shift+[comma]/[period] to move the selected edit point left/right ten frames.

306 Trim Connected Audio Clips

Most stand-alone audio is edited as a connected clip.

Trimming a connected audio clip is the same as trimming a connected video clip. As illustrated in **FIGURE 6.16**:

- To move a connected clip, click in its center and drag.
- To trim a connected clip, select an edge (edit point) and drag.

A variety of keyboard shortcuts can help. First, select the edge, clip, or clips you want to move:

- To move the selected item one frame left/right, press [comma]/[period].
- To move the selected item ten frames left/right, press Shift+[comma]/ [period].
- To change the duration of the clip, press Control+D and enter the new duration using timecode.

FIGURE 6.16 Drag an edge to trim a connected clip. Drag the clip to move it.

307 Unlike Video, Trim Audio to the Subframe

Final Cut edits audio to 1/80th of a frame.

Video frames are discrete images that change every 30th of a second (or whatever frame rate you are using). You can't edit a portion of a video frame. Audio, however, is not so limited. Because audio is recorded using samples (see Tip 286, *Human Hearing and Sample Rate*), there is much more flexibility in trimming audio.

As an example, zoom in to the timeline until you can't zoom anymore; see **FIGURE 6.17**. At the top of the timeline is a gray bar that is almost impossible to see. That indicates the duration of a frame. The left arrow marks the start of the frame; the right arrow marks the end.

Because audio is sample-based, not frame-based, you can trim the start, or end, of an audio clip to the middle of a frame (middle arrow), which video can't do. This helps get rid of a pop or click at the start of a clip.

> **GOING FURTHER** If you have a pop in the middle of a clip, zoom way in to the timeline, select the pop with the Range tool, then press V to make it disappear.

308 Audio Configuration Settings Affect Editing

These settings are located in the Audio Inspector.

The Audio Inspector is presented more completely in the "Audio Inspector" section, but, for now, I need to introduce the Audio Configuration portion because it affects editing.

Dual Mono is the most common configuration for camera source audio.

1. Select an audio clip in the Browser or timeline.
2. Go to the Audio Inspector (top red arrow).
3. Scroll down to Audio Configuration.

   This displays the audio channels (tracks) inside the selected audio clip. The menu at the top of the clip (see **FIGURE 6.18**) shows options for a clip with two channels.

   - **Dual Mono** (or Mono). Select when the audio on each channel is unrelated to other channels. Typical examples are interviewer on one channel, guest on the other. Or individual actors, each on their own channel. This is the most common configuration for camera source audio.

- **Stereo**. Select when there is a spatial relationship (left/right) between the two tracks. This is the most common setting for music and many sound effects.

- **Reverse Stereo**. Select when the stereo audio channels were accidentally reversed.

- **Various combinations**. Many external audio recorders, when recording multiple tracks, will record both stereo and mono files. Live performances are a good example. These options will vary by clip.

- **Surround 5.1**. Select when the audio file is mixed for 5.1 surround. This is never encountered when editing original sources, but it is often encountered when working with final mixes. FCP supports only 5.1 surround, not 7.1.

4. Select the setting that most closely represents the clip. If there isn't perfect match, select Mono (or Dual Mono).

   This provides the greatest flexibility when it comes time to mix.

FIGURE 6.19 illustrates the options for an audio clip with more than two channels.

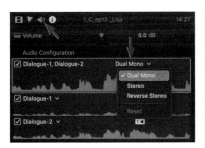

FIGURE 6.18 The Audio Inspector (blue icon, top arrow) adjusts audio settings. The Channel Configuration menu tells Final Cut how to process the separate channels.

FIGURE 6.19 With more channels come more configuration options.

309 Display Audio Components

Audio components display individual audio channels in the timeline.

Accessing audio components is one of the most powerful audio editing features in Final Cut. An audio component is a single audio channel (think "microphone") in the audio clip. By displaying these individual channels in the timeline, you can edit, trim, mute, or adjust the level of individual channels, without any risk of losing sync.

1. If necessary, set the appropriate audio configuration in the Audio Inspector; see Tip 308, *Audio Configuration Settings Affect Editing.*

2. Choose Clip > Expand Audio Components (shortcut: Control+Option+S); see **FIGURE 6.20**.

   - To trim a component, drag the edge.

   - To mute a component, select it and press V.

   - To mute a portion of a component, select the range with the Range tool and press V.

   - To change the audio level, drag the thin horizontal line in the audio clip up or down.

   - To hide the components, choose Clip > Collapse Audio Components (shortcut: Control+Option+S).

FIGURE 6.20 With audio components displayed, channel 1 is shortened, with a selected muted range. Channel 2 is active for the entire clip.

310 Automatically Apply a Crossfade

Crossfades smoothly blend the outgoing audio with the incoming.

Adding a dissolve to video is easy. Select the edit point and press Cmd+T. That doesn't work for audio. Look more closely at the Transition browser; there isn't a single audio transition there. That's because audio transitions are both simpler and more complex than video.

Automatic cross-fades require handles and apply only to audio clips touching in the Primary Storyline.

They are simpler because the only way to create an audio transition is to change audio levels. They are more complex because there are often multiple audio tracks that need to transition at the same time.

Still, there is a fast way to dissolve between audio clips. It's called a *crossfade*, where one clip fades out as the other clip fades in. This works only for audio clips that are touching in the Primary Storyline.

1. Select both audio clips (not just the edit point).

2. Choose Modify > Adjust Audio Fades > Crossfade.

   Or—press Option+T.

   Both clips expand their audio and the length of each clip is extended by the duration of the fade.

   The default Crossfade duration is added to each clip by moving the fade dots. This duration is set using Preferences > Editing; see **FIGURE 6.21**.

   You can manually tweak each fade dot (explained in Tip 311, *Apply an Audio Transition Manually*) to further adjust the duration.

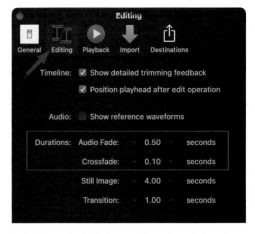

FIGURE 6.21 Audio Fade starts from the existing edge of a clip. Crossfade creates handles then adds the fade. Both use the fade dots.

311 Apply an Audio Transition Manually

Unlike video, there are no prebuilt audio transitions.

Although fades are used to smooth edits in dialogue, they are used more frequently with sound effects and music. Just as with video, you need handles to create an audio transition. Regardless of what type of clip you have, you create an audio transition the same way:

1. If necessary, double-click any synced audio track to expand it.

2. Drag the edit points so they overlap; see **FIGURE 6.22**.

3. Drag the small "fade dot" at the top of each clip to fade out/in between clips to create the transition duration you need. Most audio fades are either really short or really long.

The shaded portion of each clip shows the shape and duration of the fade. To remove a fade, drag the fade dot back to the edge of a clip.

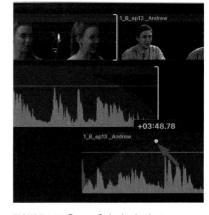

FIGURE 6.22 Drag a fade dot in the top corner of each clip to fade the audio from full volume to silent.

> **GOING FURTHER** Michael Powles, former BBC editor who reviewed a draft of this book, adds: "I always use this method because I like to see all tracks laid as if I'm track-laying film soundtracks for dubbing. I can see exactly what is going on in FCP—having the power of a dubbing mixer at the same time without having to go into a dubbing theatre. I'm very old school when it comes to sound prep—but make no apology for it."

312 A Faster Way to Create an Audio Fade

This keyboard shortcut applies a preset duration to an audio fade.

There is a faster way to add fades, but it isn't enabled by default.

1. Choose Preferences > Editing and enter the Audio Fade duration you want to use as a default setting; see Figure 6.21.
2. Choose Commands > Customize and search for "Audio Fades."
3. Set Apply Audio Fades to the shortcut you want to use. (In my case, I set this to Option+A.)

Audio fades start at the existing edge of an audio clip and don't require handles.

Now, whenever you want to quickly apply an audio fade, select the clips, then press Option+A. Ta-Dah! Fades appear at the end of all selected clips. (This applies the fade to the end of a clip; it doesn't overlap clips or create handles.) This is best used for music or sound effects transitions for clips outside the Primary Storyline.

These audio fades are fully adjustable by dragging the fade dot. This shortcut simply applies an audio fade quickly, based upon the fade duration in Preferences.

313 Change the Shape of an Audio Fade

Once you've applied an audio fade, you can change its shape.

Right-click any fade dot to reveal four different fade types; see **FIGURE 6.23**.

- **Linear.** This makes a "straight" transition from start to finish. This sounds best when fading to or from black. If you apply this to a crossfade, the audio level will drop about 3 dB in the middle of the fade due to how audio levels are calculated.

- **S-Curve.** This sounds best with transitions longer than two seconds. It starts and ends slowly.

FIGURE 6.23 The four shapes for fade dots. Shapes depend whether they are located at the beginning or end of a clip.

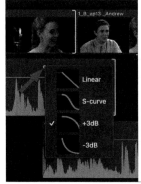 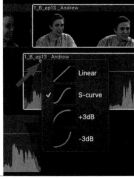

- **+3 dB**. This is the default transition. It sounds best when cross-fading between clips.
- **–3 dB**. This is a specialized fade best used when you want to minimize a sound, like a breath, at the start of the fade.

Each fade dot can have its own shape. The shape of the fade is illustrated by the shadow displayed at the end of the audio clip. Fades have different shapes depending upon their location (start or end of a clip).

GOING FURTHER
Audio levels are not linear; they are logarithmic. This affects how transitions are applied and what they sound like.

314 Enable Audio Skimming

Audio skimming lets you quickly review an audio clip.

Just as you can skim video clips, you can skim audio clips. However, audio skimming is off by default.

1. To enable audio skimming, turn on skimming (shortcut: S).
2. Click the icon (indicated by the red arrow in **FIGURE 6.24**) in the top-right corner of the timeline (shortcut: Shift+S).
3. Drag across a clip to review the audio.

   Final Cut automatically "pitch shifts" the audio so that it doesn't sound squeaky as you skim.

Final Cut automatically "pitch shifts" audio when skimming so that it doesn't sound squeaky.

FIGURE 6.24 Click this icon to enable clip skimming, after skimming is turned on.

GOING FURTHER
The Blade, Trim, and Range tools enable skimming by default. But audio skimming needs to be turned on manually.

315 Turn On Clip Skimming

Clip skimming solos one clip, without playing any others.

Many times, when building visual effects or layering audio, you will have many clips playing at once in the timeline. Sometimes, though, you just need to see, or hear, one clip in that group, without hearing anything else. Clip skimming makes that possible.

To enable clip skimming, turn on skimming (shortcut: S).

- If you want to hear a clip, enable audio skimming (shortcut: Shift+S).
- If you want to see a specific video clip, choose View > Clip Skimming (shortcut: Option+Cmd+S).

Now when you drag across a clip, you'll see or hear only that clip and nothing else.

316 Retime Audio to Match Dialogue

This is a common situation when replacing dialogue using ADR.

Sometimes we need to match the timing between existing audio and newly recorded audio. This happens frequently when replacing dialogue using automatic dialogue replacement (ADR). *ADR* is the process of recording, or re-recording, dialogue in a studio to replace noisy or missing dialogue on set or to change a voice. Key to successful ADR is matching the timing of the new audio clip to the existing audio clip.

You can retime audio as well as video using the Retime Editor (Cmd+R).

Chapter 10, "Special Cases," covers how to retime video clips. Here, though, you can use the same function—combined with pitch shifting—to retime audio clips.

FIGURE 6.25 shows a video clip with two new recordings under it.

1. Select one of the new recordings and press Cmd+R to display the Retime Editor.

2. Drag the black vertical line, the thumb, at the top-right edge of the color bar to change the speed of a clip.

   Blue indicates a clip running faster than normal; orange indicates slower.

3. Adjust until the dialogue matches.

Even though the audio is running at a different speed, Final Cut adjusts the pitch so it sounds normal.

FIGURE 6.25 Drag the black vertical line at the top-right side of the Retime Editor to change the playback speed of an audio clip.

GOING FURTHER If the pitch doesn't shift, enable it using Modify > Retime > Preserve Pitch.

317 Retime Audio to Stretch a Closing Chord

Sometimes, edited music ends a bit too abruptly.

Most music fades out naturally. But maybe caused by an edit, the ending is too abrupt. Here's a way to use retiming to fix this. (Chapter 10 covers video speed changes in more detail.)

1. Cut the audio clip just as the final chord starts (see **FIGURE 6.26**) so there's only a few frames left.

2. Press Cmd+R to display the Retime Editor.

3. Drag the black line, the thumb, at the top-right corner of the cut portion to extend the audio as needed.

FIGURE 6.26 Stretch the last few frames of a music clip to create a more natural fade. Notice a fade dot, with a linear curve, was also added.

4. Drag a fade dot to add a natural fade to the end of the music. For best results switch the curve to Linear.

   Final Cut shifts the pitch of the music in the slowed section to match the untouched music before it. If the pitch doesn't shift, enable it using Modify > Retime > Preserve Pitch.

> **GOING FURTHER** If you notice high frequencies are missing, boost them using Fat EQ during the mix. You can also apply this technique to an entire clip to change its speed to something that better fits the timing of your edit.

LEVELS & PAN

When editing video, we spend most of our time trimming. When editing audio, we spend most of our time adjusting levels. This section covers that process in detail.

318 Display and Read Audio Meters

They are the key to accurately measuring audio levels.

No, the only audio meters in Final Cut aren't those midget green things under the Viewer; see **FIGURE 6.27**. Those are simply audio meter *proxies*. To display the audio meters, do any of the following:

- Click those tiny meter proxies under the Viewer.
- Choose Window > Show in Workspace > Audio Meters.
- Press Shift+Cmd+8.

The audio meters in Final Cut can display mono, stereo, or surround 5.1 audio, depending upon what is selected; see **FIGURE 6.28**. However, a project can output only stereo or surround 5.1 audio.

Click the small audio meters under the Viewer to toggle the big audio meters on or off.

In Figure 6.28:

- The green bars display the absolute volume of a channel (mono, stereo, or surround).
- The audio meters show the sum of all audio playing at that instant.
- Final Cut measures audio in dBFS (deciBels, full-scale).
- The white bar, called the *peak hold indicator*, freezes the maximum volume for the last few seconds, or until the audio loudness exceeds the level it is currently displaying.

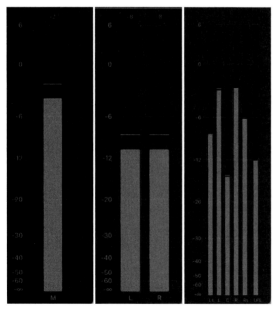

- The number at the top of the mono and stereo bars indicates the maximum audio level during playback in dBs. This value resets whenever you restart playback.
- Every 6 dB change doubles or halves the volume.
- The absolute maximum level of audio is 0 dB. (Yes, I know, it makes me giggle too.)
- If the audio goes over 0 dB during playback, a red indicator glows indicating a distortion condition, the affected channel, and how many dBs over 0 the audio is.
- During export, audio levels must not exceed 0 dB. Otherwise, permanent distortion occurs. During editing, levels often exceed 0 until audio levels are set during the final audio mix.

FIGURE 6.28 The three types of audio meters in Final Cut: mono (left), stereo (middle), and surround 5.1. Projects can output only stereo or surround.

319 Set Audio Levels

Audio levels are the most important setting for any audio clip.

Yes, there are hundreds of useful audio effects, but the most important control you have over audio are the volume levels. They are so important, in fact, that there are a number of different ways to set levels.

- Drag the thin horizontal line up (to make levels louder) or down; see **FIGURE 6.29**. (The line is blue when it is not selected, yellow when it is.)

- Press and hold Cmd, while dragging the audio line to "gear down" to make more precise audio level changes.

- Select the clip(s) to adjust and press Control+[minus]/[plus] to make levels softer/louder in 1 dB increments.

- Select the clip(s) to adjust and press Control+Option+L, then enter a specific audio level to create an absolute level adjustment.

- Select the clip(s) to adjust and press Control+Cmd+L, then enter a specific audio level to create a relative level adjustment.

- Select the clip(s) to adjust and adjust the Volume slider in the Audio Inspector. (I'll explain the Audio Inspector in the next section.)

Setting audio levels is your most important audio control.

NOTE Dragging the audio level line affects only one clip. The other controls support changing levels for all selected clips.

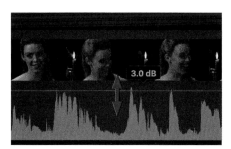

FIGURE 6.29 Drag the horizontal line in a clip to change audio levels. Here, they are increasing by 3 dB. (Negative numbers indicate lower volume.)

3.0 dB

320 Absolute vs. Relative Audio Levels

Changing levels is relative; measuring levels is absolute.

"But wait a minute! Go back to Figure 6.29. You said that audio levels can't exceed 0 dB. Yet there they are: +3 dB! That is illegal, right?" Um, no. But good question.

When measuring audio levels, there are two different yardsticks (meter sticks?). One is "absolute," and the other is "relative."

When you adjust the levels of a clip, you are adjusting the volume of the clip *relative to* the level at which it was recorded. However, unlike adjusting a clip, the levels displayed by the audio meters are absolute. These display the precise level of your audio as it is playing at that instant.

The audio meters show absolute audio levels. Clip level changes are relative.

- **Absolute audio level change** (shortcut: Control+Option+L). This sets audio levels regardless of the current audio volume of the selected audio clip. If any keyframes are applied, an absolute adjustment deletes the keyframes. For example, use the shortcut to set selected clips to a specific level of −6 dB. If one clip is at −4 dB and a second clip is at 0 dB before the change, they both become −6 dB after the change.

- **Relative audio level change** (shortcut: Control+Cmd+L). This sets audio levels based on the audio levels of the selected clip before the adjustment. A relative adjustment retains keyframes. For example, use the shortcut to raise the level of one or more selected clips a relative amount of 4 dB. If one clip is at −4 dB and a second clip is at 0 dB before the change, the first clip will become 0 dB and the second clip will become +4 dB after the change.

Applying a relative adjustment to audio clips with keyframes is a fast and easy way to increase or decrease the overall amplitude of the clip while maintaining the keyframe adjustments.

321 Adjust Audio Levels with the Range Tool

The Range tool offers another cool way to adjust audio levels.

This technique adjusts levels across a range, meaning a section of one clip or spread across multiple clips. If you want to adjust entire clips, the Volume slider in the Audio Inspector is a better option.

1. Select a range within the timeline using the Range tool.

   Any size range, across any number of clips, is permitted.

2. Choose Modify > Audio Volume and select Up, Down, Absolute, or Relative. (My preference is Relative.)

   This adjusts every clip in the selected range by the same amount.

This option adjusts levels by adding keyframes at the beginning and end of the range, as well as the beginning and end of every clip inside the range, then moving the volume line up or down.

> **GOING FURTHER** Two adjustments that don't work with ranges:
> - Dragging the volume line in a range spanning multiple clips adjusts the audio level only in the clip you are dragging.
> - Adjusting the Volume slider in the Audio Inspector adjusts complete clips and ignores the range.

322 A Shortcut to Change Audio Levels

Keyboard shortcuts save time—as long as you remember them.

Select the audio clip, or clips, whose levels you want to change, then press Control+[plus]/[minus]. This raises, or lowers, the volume of the selected clips by 1 dB.

GOING FURTHER
1 dB is the smallest change in audio level perceived by someone with normal human hearing. So fractions of a dB are possible, but not audible.

323 Add and Modify Keyframes

Keyframes automate change during playback.

We use keyframes in pairs to automate a parameter change during playback; for example, to change the audio level from one value to another. Because keyframes create change, it helps to think of keyframes in pairs: a starting position and an ending position. We can, and often do, use more than two, but thinking about them in pairs helps in understanding what they do.

- To create a level keyframe, Option-click the thin horizontal line in the audio waveform; see **FIGURE 6.30**.
- To change the level, drag the keyframe vertically.
- To change the level more slowly, Cmd-drag the keyframe.
- To change the timing of a keyframe, drag it horizontally.
- To constrain the movement of a keyframe, press and hold Shift while dragging. (If you start to drag vertically, Shift-dragging allows only vertical movement. If you start to drag horizontally, movement is constrained horizontally.)
- To delete one keyframe, right-click it and select Delete from the menu.
- To delete multiple keyframes, select them with the Range tool, right-click one of the selected keyframes, and choose Delete from the menu.

Keyframes are used extensively for setting audio levels and visual effects.

Figure 6.30 illustrates that to decrease the level, you need to set two keyframes: a starting position (0 dB) and an ending position (–8 dB). The numbers indicate the amount of change in dB as the keyframe is repositioned.

FIGURE 6.30 Option-click the audio level line to set a keyframe. Drag the keyframe to change the level.

GOING FURTHER A faster way to set keyframes is to use the Range tool to select a range, then drag the volume line up or down. The Range tool sets four keyframes automatically; see FIGURE 6.31. Note the volume line turns yellow when it is selected.

FIGURE 6.31 Use the Range tool to set keyframes automatically.

AUDIO INSPECTOR

The Audio Inspector is where you make changes to audio clips. These include levels, pan, audio repair, channel configuration, and effects.

324 Introducing the Audio Inspector

This is where you make changes to—you guessed it—audio.

The Audio Inspector (see **FIGURE 6.32**) has five sections:

FIGURE 6.32 The components of the Audio Inspector. Click the speaker icon at the top left to open.

- **Volume.** This slider sets the clip volume for whatever clip(s) are selected. If a range is set, it ignores the range.

- **Audio Enhancements.** These fix problems such as EQ, voice isolation, low audio levels, audio hum, and excessive noise.

- **Pan.** This adjusts where a sound is placed in space; in a stereo clip, between the two speakers.

- **Effects.** This is empty until you add effects to a clip. Audio effects are covered later in this chapter in the section "Audio Mixing & Effects."

- **Audio Configuration.** This was discussed earlier in this chapter. It determines how multi-channel audio is processed by Final Cut.

325 Set Audio Levels Faster

The Audio Inspector Volume slider adjusts multiple clips at once.

Although adjusting levels on a clip-by-clip basis is easy, there is a faster way: the Volume slider. (See **FIGURE 6.33**.)

FIGURE 6.33 Change clip levels by moving the Volume slider or entering a number. Sliding left lowers the volume.

Select the clips you want to adjust, then drag the Volume slider to make an absolute audio adjustment. In other words, all selected clips now have the same level.

The Volume slider works only with whole clips. It ignores any selected ranges. However, if there are existing keyframes in a clip, when you drag the Volume slider, it sets a new keyframe at the position of the playhead (skimmer) and adjusts only that keyframe. In general, if you add keyframes, don't use the Volume slider.

> **GOING FURTHER** I hesitate to recommend using the Volume slider, because when you change levels like this, there's no guarantee that a peak in some clip somewhere won't distort. There's a better way: the Limiter filter, which requires roles and an audio effect. It does a much better job. (See Tip 353, *The Limiter Effect*.)

326 Pan Places a Sound in Space

Here are my thoughts on panning audio.

Pan adjusts where a sound appears in space. In stereo terms, it's where a sound appears between the left and right speakers. Before I show you how to adjust pan, I want to explain when *not* to use it.

By definition a mono clip plays equally loudly from the left and right speakers, giving the illusion the speaker is directly in front of you. You should use mono (a center pan) for audio where one person is speaking. I also use mono for my web projects, which include interviews, podcasts, talking heads, webinars, and other programs where there is no real "left/right" required for the sound.

Larry's rule: "Just because you can [create stereo] doesn't mean you should."

Why? Because mono audio takes half the space of stereo, it downloads faster, it has no phase cancellation, and there are no hassles creating the mix. For simple spoken-word shows, I also center any theme or bumper music. (Keep "Larry's rule" in mind: "Just because you can [create stereo] doesn't mean you should.")

GOING FURTHER
You can't pan a ste-
reo clip; you can only
reverse the channels.

But when spatial placement makes sense, when you want to hear an actor walk from the left side of the screen to the right, pan is the answer. However, pan requires recording the source audio in mono. Mono provides the maximum flexibility when placing sounds in space during the mix.

327 How to Pan Audio

Pan is most useful for stereo mixes.

Only mono clips can be panned. Here's how:

1. Select the clip you want to adjust in the timeline.

Just because a clip has two channels does not make it stereo.

2. In the Audio Inspector, change Mode from None to Stereo Left/Right; see **FIGURE 6.34**.

3. Drag the pan slider left or right to change the spatial location of the sound. Your ears will tell you when the placement is right. (You can either move the slider or enter a numeric value.)

4. To reset audio settings, click the small hooked arrow to the right of the word "Volume" or "Pan."

5. To hide the Pan controls, click the word "Hide."

FIGURE 6.34 None means no change to the clip's audio pan settings as recorded. Stereo Left/Right displays the pan slider. Ignore the other settings, which refer to surround panning.

GOING FURTHER If you have a mono clip in the timeline and want to leave it centered, set Mode to None.

328 Convert Multichannel Audio to Dual Mono

Mono channel audio is the best option for audio editing and mixing.

Just because a clip has two channels does not make it stereo. Equally, just because a clip has more than two channels does not make it surround. More often than not, multichannel clips are simply a collection of mono audio tracks stored in a single clip.

Typical examples are recording a dramatic scene with each actor on their own mic, or the interview host on one channel and the guest on a second.

However, frequently when Final Cut imports a two-channel clip, it assumes it is stereo. Or a multichannel clip is assumed to be surround. These are easy errors to fix. Here's how:

Recording multichannel mono audio is the best option for audio editing and mixing.

1. Select the multichannel clip(s) in the timeline, not the Browser.
2. Open the Audio Inspector (Cmd+4).
3. In Audio Configuration (see **FIGURE 6.35**), change Stereo to Dual Mono.
4. If there are more than two channels, set this to the top line, for example, 6 Mono.

FIGURE 6.35 Use Audio Configuration to convert audio channels to mono, stereo, or surround.

329 Audio Configuration Does More

Use it to mute, or review, audio channels.

Although the principal use of Audio Configuration is to determine how audio channels are configured, you can use it for more; see **FIGURE 6.36**.

- ○ To mute a channel, deselect its checkbox on the left.

- ○ To hear what's in a channel, turn on audio skimming (shortcut: Shift+S), then skim the channel with your cursor. (Skimming a clip will also display levels in the Audio Meters.)

- ○ To modify roles, click the down-pointing chevron next to the channel name.

FIGURE 6.36 A clip with a muted channel 1 and the cursor skimming in channel 2.

330 Automatic Audio Enhancements

These improve audio quality "magically."

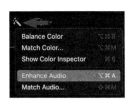

FIGURE 6.37 Click the "magic wand" tool in the lower-left corner of the Viewer to access enhancement options.

Final Cut has three automatic audio tools that can enhance your audio: Loudness, Background Noise Removal, and Hum Removal. Audio can be analyzed during import, which I don't recommend (see Tip 159, *Choose the Right Media Import Settings—Part 4*) or after import using the "magic wand"; see **FIGURE 6.37**. Audio enhancement works on the audio component, not clip, level.

To enhance a clip after import:

1. Select the clip in the timeline that you want to enhance. (If you don't select a clip, FCP will enhance the active clip under the playhead.)

2. Click the magic wand icon in the lower-left corner of the Viewer. Final Cut then analyzes all the components in the selected clip; see **FIGURE 6.38**.

FIGURE 6.38 A green check mark indicates an audio component was analyzed. In this case, no audio problems were found.

NOTE If you want to repair a single audio channel inside a clip, select the clip in the timeline and choose Clip > Expand Audio Components (Control > Option > S). Then, select just the channel you want to repair and use the magic wand to enhance audio.

3. Once analysis is complete, access the enhancement controls in the Audio Inspector.

   - A green check mark indicates the component was analyzed with no fix needed; see Figure 6.38.

   - A blue check mark appears if there was a problem that was corrected during import.

   - A yellow warning appears if the problem is significant. Click the checkbox (for example, Noise Removal in **FIGURE 6.39**) to apply a fix.

   - A red warning appears if the problem is severe.

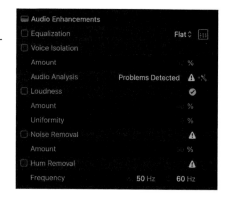

FIGURE 6.39 The automatic Audio Enhancement controls. Green indicates no problem. Yellow indicates a problem. Click a checkbox next to the name to fix.

GOING FURTHER Apple's Help files state: "When you import a clip with the "Analyze and fix audio problems" import option selected, only severe audio problems are corrected. If the clip contains moderate problems, these appear in yellow next to Audio Analysis in the Audio Enhancements section of the Audio inspector after the clip is imported. To correct these problems, you then need to enhance audio using the Audio inspector." (This is another reason not to correct audio during import.)

331 Adjust Automatic Audio Enhancements

You can adjust any correction that Final Cut applies.

I am always dubious about tools that "automatically" correct something. They rarely do as good a job as you can do yourself—provided, that is, that you know what you are doing. However, if audio is foreign territory to you, these adjustments are a good place to start. Why? Because you can modify or disable them if a clip doesn't sound right. (Neither Equalization nor Voice Isolation are part of the automatic enhancement tools. They need to be applied separately.)

After you enhance a clip (see Figure 6.39), open the Audio Inspector and click Show next to Audio Enhancements. (Show doesn't appear until a clip is analyzed.)

Before you use the automatic tools, apply Voice Isolation to reduce noise and remove hum.

Click a checkbox to enable, or disable, an effect:

   - **Equalization.** Click the Flat pop-up menu and select a different "sound" for the clip, or click the small icon next to it to display the Graphic Equalizer. (See Tip 351, *The Graphic Equalizer Shapes Sound.*)

- **Voice Isolation.** This prioritizes human speech over other parts of the audio signal. It also does a good job removing hum.

- **Loudness.** Drag the Amount slider to adjust audio compression. Drag the Uniformity slider to adjust the dynamic range.

- **Noise Removal.** This is a misnomer. This *reduces* noise; it doesn't eliminate it. Drag this until your dialogue is understandable. Totally removing the noise makes the voice sound awful.

- **Hum Removal.** This removes hum caused by mic lines and power cables getting too friendly. Set this to match the power frequency in your country. In the United States, use 60 Hz. Hum removal works great.

In general, I suggest using these tools to reduce, not remove, noise and remove hum. EQ and loudness are better handled using roles, which is covered later in the "Roles" section of this chapter.

332 Improve Speech Clarity

Final Cut applies machine learning to improve speech.

Like EQ, Voice Isolation is activated manually in the Audio Inspector. Click the checkbox to enable it; see **FIGURE 6.40.**

FIGURE 6.40 Click the checkbox to enable voice isolation. Drag the slider to adjust.

According to Apple: "Voice Isolation prioritizes any detectable human voices over other parts of the audio signal. Voice Isolation requires macOS Monterey 12.3 or later." There's no "right" setting. Drag the slider until the voice sounds good to you.

Not only does this reduce noise, but it also eliminates hum more effectively than the audio enhancement tools.

> **GOING FURTHER** Scott Favorite, one of the editors who read an early version of this book, commented: "I had a shoot last week inside a loud greenhouse with lots of fans and generator noise. I loved using this feature so much I added it to my outdoor interviews as well." Other editors have also remarked on how effective this audio tool is.

333 Final Cut Pro Supports 5.1 Surround Sound

But! Don't use it for surround mixing.

Final Cut can import, edit, and export media containing 5.1 surround sound; see **FIGURE 6.41**. That's very helpful when you need to change titles, captions, or visuals connected with a surround mix. Just don't try to actually *mix* surround sound.

The audio interface and mixing support just isn't there. Instead, export your audio elements using XML (see Chapter 9, "Share & Export") and move them into Avid ProTools, Adobe Audition, or another professional-grade audio workstation. Trying to do a surround mix in Final Cut isn't worth the work.

Don't use Final Cut to mix surround sound.

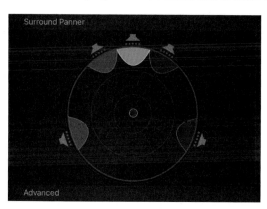

FIGURE 6.41 The surround panner in Final Cut Pro. It looks beautiful. Don't use it.

ROLES

Roles label clips by what they do, for example, titles or dialogue. They provide a powerful way to manage clips in groups. They are worth the time to learn.

334 Understanding Roles

Roles are labels that define clips.

Roles are confusing and intimidating. I know it took me a while to get comfortable with them. At their core, roles are labels applied to clips. Those labels group similar clips together so we can modify them as a single "thing." Roles are especially important for audio and captions.

Roles are applied either automatically *during* import or manually *after* import. **TABLE 6.1** illustrates the three role categories: Video, Audio, and Captions.

TABLE 6.1 Default Role Categories and Roles		
VIDEO	**AUDIO**	**CAPTIONS**
Titles	Dialogue	CEA-608
Video	Effects	iTT
- -	Music	SRT

Each role can have up to ten subroles. For Titles, for example, you could add English, French, Spanish, and Chinese. For Audio, I always add a Final Mix subrole.

Roles are created using Modify > Edit Roles; see **FIGURE 6.42**.

- ● To add a custom role, click the plus icon next to the category.
- ● To add a custom subrole, roll over the role, then choose Subrole.
- ● To delete a custom role or subrole, roll over it, then click the minus button.

FIGURE 6.42 The Edit Roles window.

NOTE To change the color of a role, click the color wheel to the right of the role name. (For example, the wheel in the Music role.)

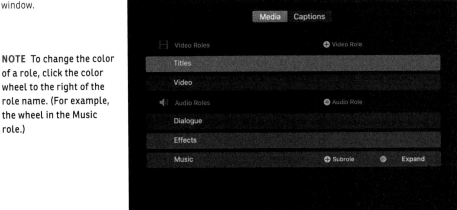

GOING FURTHER
Roles are deeply embedded into Final Cut. The User Guide takes dozens of pages to explain them fully. They are worth taking the time to learn.

You can assign roles to clip components, but not clip ranges. Custom roles and subroles are stored in the library, not the clip. You can't delete a default role. Roles are also used in compound, multicam, and synced clips. You can also display role names in the timeline using the Timeline menu. (See Tip 222, *The Timeline Clip Menu*.)

335 What Can You Do with Roles?

Roles organize and control media.

Here are some of the things you can do with roles:

- Organize clips in the Browser
- Organize clips in the timeline
- Hide clips by role
- Use focus to emphasize clips
- Control which clips export
- Switch between title languages
- Switch between caption languages
- Create audio stems
- Create audio submixes
- Assign different roles to different components in the same clip

Roles organize and control clips and other project elements.

336 Assign Roles to Clips

Most roles, other than Dialogue, are assigned manually.

Theoretically, Final Cut should assign the correct role to a clip during import. But when FCP isn't sure, it assigns the generic Dialogue role. Fortunately, Apple made changing roles easy and to show how important roles are to Final Cut—they also made access to roles ubiquitous.

To change a role or subrole, select a clip or group of clips in the Browser or timeline, then do one of the following:

- Choose Modify > Assign Audio Role, Assign Video Role, or Assign Caption Role depending upon the type of clip you selected.
- Right-click the clip in the Browser and assign the appropriate role.
- Right-click the clip in the timeline and assign the appropriate role.
- Go to the Info Inspector and assign the appropriate role.
- Go to the Audio Inspector and assign the appropriate role in Audio Configuration.
- Choose Timeline Index > Roles and click the Edit Roles button at the bottom.
- You can also apply a keyboard shortcut (see **TABLE 6.2**).

Roles are labels applied to clips so you can easily manage them in groups.

Like I said, Apple makes it really easy to apply and change roles.

TABLE 6.2 Role Keyboard Shortcuts

ROLE	SHORTCUT	COLOR	ROLE	SHORTCUT	COLOR
Titles	Control+Option+T	Purple	Dialogue	Control+Option+D	Blue
Video	Control+Option+V	Blue	Effects	Control+Option+E	Teal
			Music	Control+Option+M	Green

(337) Switch Languages Using the Timeline Index

Using roles does not change the edit, but can change the display.

FIGURE 6.43 illustrates a timeline with roles assigned. (Yup, it looks the same as if roles *weren't* assigned.) But this illustrates a typical use. This is a short video destined for two markets: English and Spanish. Notice the two title tracks on top.

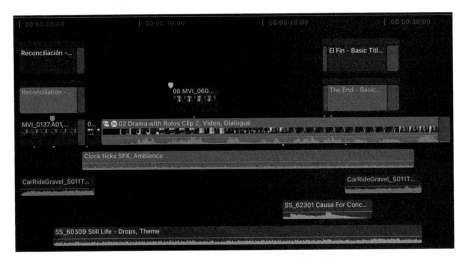

FIGURE 6.43 A short scene with titles in two languages: English and Spanish.

FIGURE 6.44 Enable, or disable, each title language using the Timeline Index.

You and I both know that when you create two different versions of the same project, they never stay in sync. I'll change something in one project, then forget to change it in the other. Roles solve that.

I created and assigned an English subrole to the English titles and a Spanish subrole to the Spanish titles. The *key* part, though, is that *both* languages are in the *same* project timeline.

Open the Timeline Index (shortcut: Option+Cmd+2); see **FIGURE 6.44**. I can instantly switch from one language to another—for preview, client review, or export—by selecting which title language I want to display. No more duplicate projects. All languages are in one project, managed by roles.

NOTE You could use this same technique to change caption languages, or switch between narration in different languages, all in the same project.

338 Organize the Timeline Using Roles

The Timeline Index is key to organizing clips.

It's important to remember that changing roles doesn't change your edit. But it does change how your clips are organized, displayed, and/or exported. Also, most of the time, roles help you figure out what's going on. Here's another example.

Notice how, by default, Final Cut groups clips by role? Dialogue on top, then effects, then music. Click the Show Audio Lanes button, shown in Figure 6.44, and Final Cut adds labels; see **FIGURE 6.45**. When you show audio lanes, clips are grouped into separate categories. Click one of the Audio Lane buttons (top arrow) to group just that role.

You can also change the stacking order of Audio roles by dragging the role name (for example, Music) up or down in the Timeline Index. This is useful when, say, you want to move music clips closer to the Primary Storyline so you can see the placement of dialogue clips to adjust music cue timing.

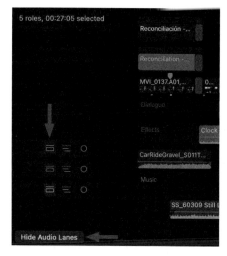

FIGURE 6.45 Enabling Audio Lanes (bottom arrow) groups clips by role, then labels the roles in the timeline. Click a single lane button (top arrow) to group just the clips in that role.

339 Display Subroles Using the Timeline Index

Display, group, enable, or disable clips by subrole.

Click a subrole button (right arrow in **FIGURE 6.46**) to display subroles. You can see the list on the left: Ambience and Spot SFX for Effects, along with Sting, and Theme for Music. To disable a subrole, deselect it.

Disabling a role or subrole carries through to export.

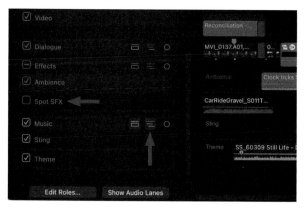

FIGURE 6.46 Display subroles using the subrole button (right arrow). Disable/enable subroles using the checkbox.

340 Focus on Specific Clips Using Roles

Display what you need to see and minimize the rest.

Let's say you need to spend time adjusting the music cues. Open the Timeline Index and click the focus dot (left arrow); see **FIGURE 6.47**. This minimizes nonmusic tracks (right arrow) so you can concentrate on the tunes. This is an especially helpful technique in large projects with lots of layers.

FIGURE 6.47 Music holds the focus (green dot, left arrow), while both dialogue and Spot SFX are muted (not selected).

To help keep things organized, I also enabled audio lanes for both effects and music and disabled the Spot SFX subrole and the Dialogue role. Now, not only do I have more room, but distracting audio is muted so I can concentrate on the music. Turning dozens, even hundreds, of clips back on again now requires only one or two mouse clicks.

341 Create Audio Stems & Submixes

Stems are a combination of roles and compound clips.

When the edit is complete and it's time for the final audio mix, roles can help create submixes or "stems." A stem is an audio clip containing fully mixed dialogue or effects or music. Stems are essential when re-editing a finished project for trailers or international versions. When creating stems, every clip must be assigned to an appropriate role.

1. Open the Timeline Index.
2. Click Show Audio Lanes.
3. Select all audio clips with the same role (for example, Dialogue, Effects, or Music).
4. Choose File > New > Compound Clip (shortcut: Option+G).
5. Name the compound clip something obvious and click OK.

FIGURE 6.48 illustrates two compound clip stems: Effects and Music. You can then apply audio effects, such as EQ or Limiting, to the clips with the same role. This is a much more effective way to mix a project than dealing with individual clips.

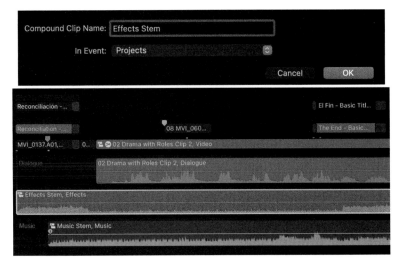

FIGURE 6.48 (Top) Creating a compound clip. (Bottom) Two stems created from compound clips.

In most mixes, I separate the male and female voices into two dialogue compound clips (submixes) using subroles. This is so I can apply one set of EQ settings for the men and a separate set for the women. See Tip 350, *Use EQ to Enhance Voice Clarity*, for my recommended settings.

AUDIO MIXING & EFFECTS

Audio mixing is the final stage in any project. It's generally done at the same time as color grading. While Final Cut has great audio editing, its audio mixing capability is very weak. Still, when you need it, here's how it works.

342 Audio Mixing in Final Cut Pro

There is nothing about mixing audio in Final Cut Pro that I like.

Final Cut is an amazing editing program. It's my go-to editing application. I've used it for more than 20 years, and I'm a big fan. But as an audio mixing tool, it's a disaster. It is awkward, inflexible, and offers very limited signal routing.

So before I show how to add effects and create mixes, let me share how I mix my projects. If it's a simple project, say, one narrator, no music or effects,

GOING FURTHER
Jerry Thompson adds: "When using roles for a mix, there's a potentially huge pitfall: If you are creating a compound clip to export stems, decide whether you want the final mix done using roles or subroles. Do not change it. If you open the compound clip and add effects to subroles and you then change to roles versus subroles in the drop-down of the parent clip in the Inspector, all effects applied at the subrole level will be lost."

NOTE The Fairlight audio mixer in DaVinci Resolve is also excellent.

I might create the final audio mix in Final Cut. (Though generally not.) But if it involves multiple actors, sound effects, and music cues, I will edit the finished video in Final Cut. Then, I export the audio elements as an XML file and do the final audio mix in Adobe Audition or Avid ProTools. Life is too short to waste time mixing audio in Final Cut.

Audio mixing is as deep and complex as video editing. There are full-time audio careers creating music, television programs, stage plays, audio books...the creative audio we love. These tips focus on just a few power tools designed to improve audio for video.

343 Where to Set Audio Levels for a Final Mix

At no time should audio levels in the final mix exceed 0 dB. Never. Not once.

Regardless of the software you use to mix your audio, the same mixing rules apply. The most important rule is: At no time during export should audio levels ever exceed 0 dB. Doing so, even for a very short duration, causes distortion. It sounds bad. And it get projects rejected when analyzed for audio quality control.

When mixing, there are two types of audio levels:

- **Peak**. This measures the moment-by-moment maximum level of audio playback. Most video editors watch peak levels, which are measured in dB. Final Cut displays peak audio in the audio meters and measures it as dBFS (deciBels Full Scale).

- **Average**. This averages audio levels over a short period of time to provide a more nuanced representation of audio levels. These are measured in LUFS or LKFS. There's a 15–20 dB difference between peaks and average levels. Audio engineers and professional distribution outlets tend to use average levels.

For example:

- YouTube prefers average levels around –14 LUFS.
- Apple prefers podcasts around –16 LUFS.
- Broadcast prefers average levels around –24 LUFS.
- Netflix prefers average levels around –27 LUFS.

When setting levels, here's what I recommend:

- Audio levels are additive. The more clips playing at the same time, the louder the audio.

- Set project peaks between −3 to −6 dB. This works out to about −15 LUFS.

- When recording audio, record around −12 dB. This provides head room in case a speaker gets excited and is loud enough to minimize background noise.

For the final mix, set timeline audio peaks to bounce between −3 to −6 dB.

344 Apply, Modify, and Remove Audio Effects

Most Final Cut audio effects are based upon filters from Logic.

Apple Logic is a music creation tool that is used by professional musicians around the world. Many of its audio filters are excellent and shared with Final Cut.

There are more than 120 audio effects in FCP, far too many for this book to cover. However, there are six audio effects that are especially useful when mixing audio for video: adjusting audio pitch, creating a telephone effect, Fat EQ, Graphic Equalizer, Space Designer, and Limiter.

GOING FORWARD
Audio compressors are used in more mixes than the Limiter. But the Limiter in FCP is easier to use and achieves a similar, though less nuanced, result.

- To apply an effect, drag it from the Audio section of the Effects browser (Cmd+5) and drop it on top of a clip.

- To adjust an effect, select the clip in the timeline and adjust it in the Audio Inspector. Specific settings vary by effect.

- To remove an effect, select the clip in the timeline, then delete its name from the Audio Inspector.

345 Create a Default Audio Effect

By default, the Channel EQ is the default audio effect.

If you find yourself using the same audio effect a lot, make it the default. Then, you can apply it to any selected clip, or group of clips, with a single keyboard shortcut.

Right-click the effect and choose Make Default Audio Effect; see **FIGURE 6.49**.

The default audio effect is Channel EQ. The shortcut is Option+Cmd+E.

- To apply the default audio effect, press Option+Cmd+E.

- To remove a default audio effect, the same as any other effect, delete its name in the Audio Inspector.

FIGURE 6.49 Right-click an audio effect in the Effects browser to set it as the default effect.

346 The Stacking Order of Audio Effects Is Important

Audio effects process from top to bottom in the Audio Inspector.

When you add audio effects to a clip, and it is not uncommon to add more than one effect to a clip, the effects process from the top to the bottom in the Audio Inspector. Here are a few rules to follow:

The order in which you apply audio effects affects the quality of the final mix.

- Apply a noise reduction filter first. Although there is a Denoiser filter in Final Cut, better ones are available from Izotope, Waves, and FXFactory. Minimizing noise means the remaining filters are processing the sound you care about.
- Add any EQ or other special effects.
- Place the Limiter filter (or any compression) at the bottom of the stack. (With Final Cut, I prefer to use the Limiter filter.) Because the Limiter filter guarantees that audio levels will not exceed the level you specify, it's important that no effects are added after (below) the Limiter.

347 The Audio Animation Bar

Use this to change audio effects in the timeline.

The Audio Animation bar (shortcut: Control+A) simplifies changing audio effect order and adjusting keyframes in the timeline. Although not as useful as the Audio Inspector, it's worth knowing about. There's an animation bar hidden in every audio clip.

1. Select an audio clip in the timeline.
2. Press Control+A.

   This displays the Audio Animation bar; see **FIGURE 6.50**.

   - To enable/disable an effect, uncheck it.
   - To move a keyframe, drag it.
   - To change the stacking order of effects, drag one up or down.
   - To close the Audio Animation bar, press Control+A.

FIGURE 6.50 The Audio Animation bar allows enabling, disabling, or rearranging audio effects in the timeline. You can also use it to quickly move keyframes, though setting them is best done in the Audio Inspector.

348 Adjust Audio Pitch

Need to shift a voice or music up or down a few steps?

Here's how to change the pitch of a voice or music clip:

1. Open the Effects browser (shortcut: Cmd + 5) and search for "Pitch."

2. From the choices, drag Pitch on top of the clip.

   In the Inspector (see **FIGURE 6.51**), every whole number change in Amount represents a one-half step change in musical pitch.

FIGURE 6.51 Every whole number change in Amount represents a half-step change in pitch. Negative numbers shift the pitch lower.

349 Create a "Voice Heard Over the Telephone" Effect

This is a special case of using EQ.

To create the sound of a voice over an old-fashioned, low-quality telephone:

1. Open the Effects browser (Cmd+5) and search for "Telephone."

2. Drag it on top of the clip you want to change.

3. In the Audio Inspector, change the effect menu to Warm Carbon Mic; see **FIGURE 6.52.**

FIGURE 6.52 This telephone effect setting creates the sound of an old-fashioned phone.

350 Use EQ to Enhance Voice Clarity

Adjusting frequencies is the best way to improve speech intelligibility.

Final Cut has an effect called *Voice Over Enhancement*. This has presets for male and female voices. It works decently. However, there are EQ tools in FCP that provide more and better control.

Vowels are low-frequency sounds, which give a voice its character, warmth, and sexiness. Consonants are higher-frequency sounds, which make speech

FIGURE 6.53 Click the icon (red arrow) to display the Fat EQ controls.

intelligible. For example, the difference between hearing an *F* or an *S* depends upon whether you hear a hiss. If you hear it, you hear an *S*. If not, you hear an *F*. That hiss centers around 6,200 Hz.

Most dialogue benefits from boosting low frequencies to improve warmth, then boosting highs to improve crispness and clarity. We use the Fat EQ filter to make these changes; see FIGURE 6.53.

1. Open the Effects browser (shortcut: Cmd + 5) and search for Fat EQ; see FIGURE 6.54.

2. Drag the filter on the dialogue clips you want to change.

3. Open the Audio Inspector and click the icon indicated by the red arrow.

4. Make adjustments according to TABLE 6.3.

FIGURE 6.54 The Fat EQ filter adjusts frequencies in ranges. Q defines the sharpness of the curve.

GOING FURTHER
While every voice is different, these settings are a good place to start. Then, use your good ears and good monitor speakers to tweak the voice until it sounds its best.

Table 6.3 shows EQ settings for female and male voices. Q defines the width of the frequency spread; lower is wider.

TABLE 6.3 EQ Settings to Improve Speech Clarity			
GENDER	FREQUENCY	EQ BOOST	Q
Male	180	+2-4 dB	1
Male	3500	+3-7 dB	1
Female	400	+2-4 dB	1
Female	4500	+3-7 dB	1

⚙ The Graphic Equalizer Shapes Sound

After levels, EQ provides the greatest flexibility to shape audio.

Adjusting EQ (equalization) means to adjust specific frequencies in an audio clip to emphasize one thing more than another. (We call this *shaping* sound.) For example, boosting bass improves the "thump" of explosions, or boosting highs improves the twitter of a bird.

The Graphic Equalizer, like the Fat EQ filter, simplifies adjusting frequency ranges.

1. Open the Effects browser (shortcut: Cmd+5) and search for "AUGraphic Equalizer."

2. Drag the filter on the dialogue clips you want to change.

3. Open the Audio Inspector and click the icon indicated by the red arrow; see **FIGURE 6.55**.

   - As shown in **FIGURE 6.56**, drag a blue dot down to lower that frequency range.

   - Drag it up to boost it.

   FIGURE 6.55 Click the icon to open the AUGraphicEQ interface.

   - Switch between frequency resolutions using the 10 or 31 band menu.

   - Click Flatten EQ to reset the curve.

   - Press Control and drag to create a curve between frequencies.

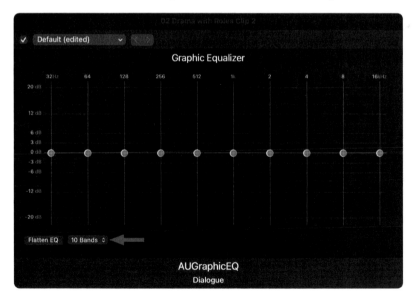

FIGURE 6.56 Click the Bands menu to change frequency resolution. Click Flatten EQ to reset all settings.

GOING FURTHER
In most cases, except for hum removal, we boost (raise) or attenuate (lower) frequency *ranges*, rather than specific frequencies. The narrower the range, the more noticeable the frequency change.

(352) Space Designer Creates the Sound of a Space

This is especially useful for green-screen work.

Space Designer creates reverb that sounds like different spaces. For example, reverb in the woods, a closet, and a cathedral each sound different. If you are shooting on location in a church, you don't need Space Designer. But if you are shooting that church scene on a green-screen stage or adding ADR audio later, Space Designer can help sell that location to an audience.

However, Space Designer has the *most* intimidating interface of any effect I've ever seen. After using Space Designer for more than a decade, I still don't understand how the interface works. Why? Because it has an extremely useful menu!

1. Open the Effects browser (shortcut: Cmd+5) and search for "Space Designer."

2. Drop the filter on the dialogue clips you want to change.

3. Open the Audio Inspector and click the icon indicated by the red arrow; see **FIGURE 6.57**.

FIGURE 6.57 Click the icon to open the Space Designer interface.

Oh. My. Goodness...! (See **FIGURE 6.58**.) The Space Designer interface. Don't worry. You don't need it.

Instead, click the Default menu at the top left; see **FIGURE 6.59**. Then, pick the size and shape space you need. The spatial effects this creates are amazing.

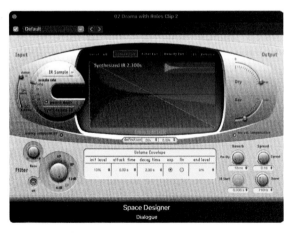

FIGURE 6.58 The totally inscrutable, yet highly intriguing, Space Designer interface.

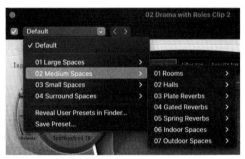

FIGURE 6.59 The Space Designer menu is filled with close to 100 settings for different interior and exterior spaces.

353 The Limiter Effect

This is the most useful audio effect in Final Cut Pro.

The go-to audio level controller for many audio engineers is a compressor. Although I use compressors when mixing in Audition or ProTools, when I'm mixing in Final Cut, I use the Limiter effect.

The Limiter dynamically raises the soft passages in an audio clip, while limiting the maximum audio level. No other filter provides this control. If I can apply only one filter to a dialogue clip, I use this one. (If I can use two, the second is EQ.) The difference this makes in adjusting levels is magical. Most of the time when using the Limiter, you won't need to use audio keyframes at all, except, perhaps, for extremes.

1. Open the Effects browser (shortcut: Cmd+5) and search for "Limiter."

2. Apply the Limiter filter from the Logic section of the Effects browser. Choose Levels > Logic> Limiter—this is important; there are other limiters in Final Cut that are not as flexible.

3. Open the Audio Inspector and click the icon indicated by the red arrow; see **FIGURE 6.60**.

   1. Set Output to –3 dB (this limits the maximum volume to –3 dB or, roughly, –14 LKFS).

   2. Set Release to any number larger than 500.

   3. Play the timeline and adjust the gain so that Reduction is bouncing between 1.5 and 3 dB.

FIGURE 6.60 Click the icon to reveal the Limiter interface.

In **FIGURE 6.61**, the softest audio was raised 14 dB, while the louder sounds were prevented from exceeding –3 dB, all while assuring there was no distortion.

The difference this filter makes in dialogue is simply amazing!

FIGURE 6.61 The Limiter effect. Adjust the gain until the Reduction meter is bouncing between 1.5–3 dB.

GOING FORWARD
The Limiter effect should be applied only to dialogue, not effects and *especially* not to music, because dynamic range is an essential element of music.

CHAPTER 6—AUDIO SHORTCUTS

CATEGORY	SHORTCUT	WHAT IT DOES
Trimming	R	Select Range tool
	V	Toggle clip visibility (audibility)
	Control+D	Enter a new duration
	[Comma]/[period]	Shift selected object left/right one frame
	Shift+[comma]/[period]	Shift selected object left/right ten frames
	Option+[comma]/[period]	Nudge selected audio one subframe left/right
	Shift+Option+[comma]/[period]	Nudge selected audio multiple subframes left/right
Editing	Control+S	Expand/collapse audio channel
	Control+Option+S	Expand audio components
	Control+Shift+S	Detach audio from video
	Shift+Cmd+G	Break apart clip items
	Option+T	Apply the default cross-fade to selected clips
	S	Enable/disable skimming
	Shift+S	Enable/disable audio skimming (requires skimming enabled)
	Option+Cmd+S	Enable/disable clip skimming
	Option+Cmd+G	Synchronize selected Browser clips
	Option+G	Create a compound clip
	Option+Cmd+E	Apply the default audio effect
Shortcuts with no key assigned		Apply audio fade
		Trim > Align Audio to Video
Levels	Control+A	Audio Animation editor
	Control+[plus]/[minus]	Increase or decrease selected clip's audio levels ±1 dB
	Cmd-drag	"Gears down" dragging audio level line for more precise adjustment
	Control+Option+L	Enter a specific absolute audio level for the selected clip(s)
	Control+Cmd+L	Enter a specific relative audio level for the selected clip(s).
	Option+Up/Down keys	Nudge one or more selected audio keyframes ±1 dB
Effects	Option+Cmd+E	Apply the default audio effect (Channel EQ)

CHAPTER WRAP

Audio is a mixed bag in Final Cut. FCP's audio editing tools are first-class, as are the audio effects. Roles are clever and powerful. But for audio mixing, Final Cut is sorely lacking. For mixing simple one-person podcasts or talking head interviews, Final Cut is OK. But for any projects with challenging audio mixes, edit the project in Final Cut, then export an XML file and mix it in ProTools or Audition or a professional-grade audio workstation. Then, bring the finished stereo or surround mix back into Final Cut to export with the finished video.

TRANSITIONS & TITLES

INTRODUCTION

This chapter moves out of storytelling into story "enhancement." We enter the world of transitions, titles, and, ultimately, effects. We also shift from the purely technical ("push this button to make that happen") into creative squishiness ("what's the 'right' length for a dissolve?"), where the answers depend upon your point of view.

We also enter into the world of editing "style." Transitions, fonts, animation—all change over time. As one editor told me, "The young audience today wants fast cuts. Plenty of jump cuts. Keep everything short and moving. Short, jerky, jarring. Short attention spans demand editors eliminate the pauses. Cram more content in. That's today's world."

For myself, I prefer slower cutting so I can actually *see* what's on the screen. To me, fast cutting implies you are trying to hide what's on the screen, not enhance it.

- Transitions
- Titles & Text
- Generators
- Shortcuts

- **Transition**. A switch from one clip to the next. There are three types of transitions: cuts, dissolves, and wipes.

- **Dissolve**. A visual transition where one clip slowly blends, or mixes, with another.

- **Wipe**. A visual transition where one image object moves off-screen while one or more image objects move onscreen at the same time.

- **Fade**. A visual transition where one clip dissolves to or from black or, in some instances, white.

- **Handles**. Extra audio and/or video before the In and/or after the Out of a clip. This is used for trimming and transitions.

- **Generator**. Video that is wholly created by the computer. These are used for animated backgrounds, inserting into text and other effects. They conform to any frame size, frame rate, or duration.

- **Tweak**. To adjust, generally in small amounts.

The camera represents the point of view (the "eye") of the audience.

TRANSITIONS

The default transition in Final Cut Pro is the cut—an instantaneous switch from one shot to another. However, many other transition options are available. These range from reasonably normal to way, *way* over the top.

354 The Three Types of Visual Transitions

Each creates an emotional response in the viewer.

There are three categories of visual transitions: cuts, dissolves, and wipes. Use wipes sparingly.

Visual transitions come in three broad categories, regardless of which NLE you use: cuts, dissolves, and wipes. The default transition in Final Cut is a cut. All others are added after the edit is made. Transitions are always added at an edit point.

All transitions convey an emotional value, so pick the one that represents the emotion you want to convey to the audience. Transitions are easy to abuse. We've all seen videos where the editor acts like they never met a wipe they didn't like. Those programs induce visual whiplash.

Remember that the camera represents the eye of the audience; every time you change a shot, you move the audience to a new position. Try to move your audience gently. Here are some suggestions for using transitions wisely:

- **Cut**. A change in perspective; 90% of your transitions should be cuts.
- **Dissolve**. A change in time or place; 90% of your remaining transitions should be dissolves.
- **Wipe**. This breaks the flow of the story to take the audience somewhere completely different. Be very cautious with these. Use a wipe only when you want a complete disconnect between what went before and what comes after.

The problem with wipes is that they call attention to themselves. They are intentionally distracting. Adding too many wipes to a video means the audience starts paying more attention to the wipes and less to the content. Then again, if you have a weak story or weak talent, adding lots of wipes distracts from the fact you've got nothing to work with.

355 Add a Dissolve

A dissolve means a change in time or place.

The easiest transition to add is a dissolve, with a variety of ways to select where to apply it:

1. Put the playhead on an edit point.

   Or—select an edit point.

   Or—select a clip.

   Or—select a group of clips.

2. Press Cmd+T.

The default transition, a dissolve, is applied to the selected edit point(s). The default transition duration is set in Preferences > Editing. (See Tip 70, *Optimize Editing Preferences*.) By selecting a group of clips, you can apply the same transition to all selected edit points at once. If you select one or more clips, the transition is applied to both ends.

GOING FURTHER
A cut emulates how our brain interprets the data from our eyes. Our eyes move constantly, but the brain cuts out the part when our eyes move so that we see only stable shots, not a collection of swish-pans.

Cmd+T applies the default transition to all selected edit points or clips.

GOING FURTHER A variation on a dissolve is the "fade to black." This puts a cross-dissolve on the start of the first clip or the end of the last clip. This fades the clip to or from black. For fades in the middle of a scene, either use Fade to Color, which dips to black (or another color you choose) then comes up on the new scene, or insert a gap clip then dissolve to or from it. These fade to black transitions imply the end of one thing, then a change in time or location to something different.

356 Handles Are Essential for Transitions

If handles don't exist, Final Cut will "invent" them.

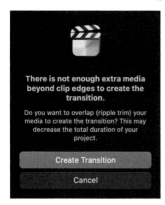

FIGURE 7.1 This warning means FCP will shorten the edges of any clip at the edit point without sufficient handles to match the transition duration.

Handles, extra media at the ends of a clip, are essential for transitions; see Tip 224, *Handles Are Essential for Trimming*. Why? Because during a transition, portions of both clips are onscreen at the same time. That means they both need media during the transition.

At a minimum, the handles must be the same duration as the transition itself. (Longer is better.) If the handles exist, great. Everything works as expected.

But if there isn't enough media, Final Cut pops up a warning; see **FIGURE 7.1**. If you click Create Transition, Final Cut will shorten whichever edit point lacks sufficient handles, by moving the In or the Out the duration of the transition. This essentially performs a ripple trim to the edit point.

This may be good or bad, depending upon the contents of the clip and the transition you are applying.

FIGURE 7.2 The Transitions browser. To see all available transitions, click the word "All." To hide the sidebar, click the lower-left icon (lower red arrow).

357 The Transitions Browser

Final Cut provides hundreds of transitions to choose from.

Although cuts are the most popular transition, followed by dissolves, Final Cut does not stop there. The Transitions browser (see **FIGURE 7.2**) contains more than 150 transitions in a mind-bending variety of styles. Because transitions are easy to create using Motion and other software tools, third-party developers delight in creating more. Hundreds of transitions are available from a wide variety of websites.

- To open the Transitions browser, click the bowtie icon (top-right arrow in Figure 7.2) in the top-right corner of the timeline (shortcut: Control+Cmd+5).
- To resize the Browser, drag the left edge.
- To hide the sidebar, click the icon in the lower left (lower-left arrow).

- To see all transitions, click All in the top left of the Browser (top-left arrow).

- To see all transitions in a single category, click the category name in the sidebar on the left (for example, Dissolves).

358 Use Search to Find a Specific Transition

You can use partial words in a search.

To search for a specific transition, enter the text to search for in the search box at the bottom; see **FIGURE 7.3**. You don't need to enter a complete word.

To cancel the search, click the "x" in a circle on the right side.

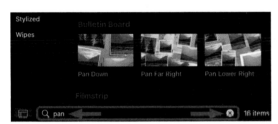

FIGURE 7.3 Use the search box to look for all transitions with "pan" in their name. There are 16 transitions meeting this condition.

359 Apply a Transition from the Transitions Browser

Apply transitions to an edit point, clip, or group of clips.

Transitions are applied from the Transitions browser in a variety of ways:

- Drag it from the Transitions browser and drop it on an edit point. The edit point does not need to be selected.

  Or—select an edit point, a clip, or a group of clips and double-click the transition icon.

  NOTE Click the center of a transition to select it.

- To replace a transition, drag the new transition from the Transitions browser and drop it on top of the existing transition in the timeline. The new transition inherits the duration of the old one.

- To remove a transition applied to a clip, select it in the timeline and press Delete.

GOING FURTHER Please, for the love of humanity, don't use Page Curls. They are old, dated, and I'm very tired of seeing them. And Earthquake should be avoided by anyone with any taste whatsoever.

360 Preview Transitions

Preview transitions in real time.

Hover, then drag your mouse over any transition to preview it.

Final Cut makes it easy to preview a transition. Simply hover your mouse over the transition you are curious about. Wait a second or two for Final Cut to load the transition into RAM, then drag the mouse—without clicking—across the transition.

You will see the effect full screen in the Viewer.

361 Change the Transition Duration

Two ways to modify any transition duration.

To change the duration of a transition, do one of the following:

FIGURE 7.4 Drag the edge of a transition to change its duration.

- Grab an of the transition edge and drag it; see **FIGURE 7.4**.
- Select the transition, press Control+D, enter the duration you want, and press Return.

NOTE Click the center of a transition to select it.

GOING FURTHER When you trim a transition, the numbers at the top of the transition show its current duration (left) and the amount the duration is changing (right). Moving left displays negative numbers.

362 Trim a Clip Under a Transition

You don't need to remove a transition to trim the clips under it.

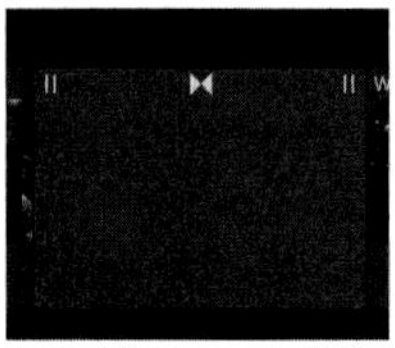

Zoom in to the timeline until you see the three icons at the top of a transition shown in **FIGURE 7.5**. (Cmd+[plus] is one way to zoom in.)

FIGURE 7.5 The three trimming controls displayed at the top of every transition allow trimming under the transition.

- To ripple trim the In of the incoming clip, drag the double bars on the left.
- To ripple trim the Out of the outgoing clip, drag the double bars on the right.
- To roll trim both the In and the Out, drag the bow-tie in the middle.

Trimming clips without removing the transition saves time, provided you see these trim icons. If you don't, zoom in closer to the timeline.

NOTE Even though you are clicking icons in the transition, you are actually trimming the clip under it.

GOING FURTHER
- Press Cmd++[plus] to zoom in.
- Press Cmd+-[minus] to zoom out.
- Press Shift+Z to reset the timeline to fill the window.

363 Modify Transitions

Transitions can be modified in more ways than just duration.

Although all transitions can be modified, some are more flexible than others; see **FIGURE 7.6**. Select the transition in the timeline, then go to the Transition Inspector (note the blue hourglass icon in this screen shot) and tweak it.

Almost all transitions can be modified in the Transition Inspector.

FIGURE 7.6 Almost all transitions can be modified in some way. Here are two different examples. Select the transition, then open the Transition Inspector (shortcut: Cmd+4) to see the options.

364 Hidden Dissolve Options

Unique ways to modify dissolves.

A dissolve is not just a dissolve—not when Final Cut gives you hidden options. The Dissolve category in the Transitions browser has four additional dissolves to experiment with.

Even the default cross-dissolve (Cmd+T) holds secrets. Apply the transition to a clip, select it, then look in the Transition Inspector. The default look is Video, but as **FIGURE 7.7** shows, there are a dozen variations to choose from.

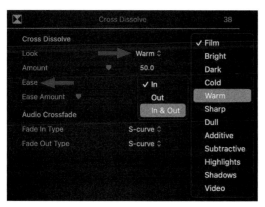

FIGURE 7.7 A composite image of options available for a cross-dissolve transition.

As well, when you add, say, Warm, you can adjust the Amount to set how "warm" it will be.

You can also adjust acceleration "ease" during the transition. This won't make a difference in dissolves less than two seconds, but for longer ones, you can control how it starts (Ease Out) and how it ends (Ease In). This is subtle, but it's easier to see during playback than write about.

365 Create a New Default Transition

Cmd+T is the shortcut; choosing the transition is up to you.

The default transition is a cross-dissolve (shortcut: Cmd+T). However, you can change the default to a different transition; see **FIGURE 7.8**.

1. Right-click the transition you want to make the new default in the Transitions browser.

2. Choose Make Default.

   The next time you press Cmd+T, this will be the transition that is applied.

3. To reset the default, choose Dissolves and right-click Cross-Dissolve.

FIGURE 7.8 Right-click any transition in the Transitions browser to set it to the default.

366 Flow Minimizes Jump Cuts

Flow blends video to make jump cuts disappear.

A jump cut is an unjustified "jump" in video caused by editing two similar clips together. In the past, jump cuts were anathema. But now, they're all over YouTube, which I guess says something right there.

Flow blends edges at the edit point to minimize jump cuts.

To me, a jump cut says "Really bad editing done here!" They are lazy edits (and, perhaps, lazy production). Instead of finding a way to cover the edit point with B-roll, or a different shot, the editor simply slices a clip and lets the jumps fall where they may. (Then again, maybe I'm just old-fashioned.)

Flow is a transition in Final Cut that seeks to minimize the visual stutter of a jump cut. It uses optical flow technology to seamlessly blend two clips so a jump cut disappears. If you haven't changed the Transition duration in

Preferences > Editing, the Flow duration is four frames. If you have, it will be either the duration you specify or 15 frames, whichever is less. With this transition, shorter is better. I recommend four to six frames.

To apply it, drag Flow from the Dissolves category to the edit point.

NOTE Flow does not work with generators or dissimilar still images.

GOING FURTHER I'm of two minds about this effect. Although it solves the jarring distraction of jump cuts, it also makes a shot look like it wasn't edited. Making an edit look like nothing was removed from a clip strikes me as ethically over the line. There's a perfectly good visual "grammar" that says when an edit is made, there's either a jump cut or a cutaway to another shot. Your opinion may vary. I'm just telling you mine.

367 Here's What Those Yellow Dots Mean

These transitions combine multiple images into one movement.

There are a few transitions, Pan Far Right and Pan Down being two, that, when you edit them into the timeline, display yellow dots; see **FIGURE 7.9**. What are these things?

FIGURE 7.9 The yellow dots determine which frames appear in a multi-image transition like Pan Far Right.

I call these yellow dots "placeholder drop zones."

In the case of Pan Far Right, as you move through the transition, in addition to the two clips for the up-front dissolve, there are six other images that appear in the background. The images in those clips are still frames based on where the yellow dots are located.

Drag a dot horizontally to reposition it, though you can't move a dot to a clip on a different layer. You can, however, move a dot to the other side of the transition. You can also put two or more dots in the same clip.

GOING FURTHER You'll find most of these multi-image transitions in the Stylized category.

368 Modify Transitions Using Motion

Open any transition into Motion for modification.

All effects in Final Cut Pro are created using either Motion or FXPlug, a software development kit that specializes in creating plug-ins for Final Cut. Because of this, you can customize almost all existing transitions in Motion to meet specific needs.

NOTE Apple Motion is purchased separately and available in the Mac App Store.

To move a transition from FCP to Motion, right-click the transition in the Transitions browser and select Open a Copy in Motion; see **FIGURE 7.10**. (Apple requires modifying copies to prevent damage to the original transition.)

GOING FURTHER
Some third-party transitions are "locked" to prevent modification. However, any transition (or title or generator) shipped by Apple can be modified.

Save the modified copy in Motion to automatically bring the customized effect back to Final Cut in the same category as the original.

FIGURE 7.10 Modify almost every FCP transition in Motion by right-clicking it in the Transitions browser.

369 Create or Delete Custom Transitions

The process is the same as creating custom titles.

You can create custom transitions using Apple Motion.

To create a custom transition:

1. In the Motion Project browser, select Final Cut Transition.
2. Define the project specs in the top-right corner.

   The Motion project that opens will be preset for a cross-dissolve.

To delete a custom transition, whether created or modified:

1. Right-click it and select Reveal in Finder.
2. Read Tip 392, *Remove a Custom Title (or Transition)*, for the next steps.

TITLES & TEXT

Unlike captions that can be turned on or off, titles and other text are permanently "burned" into the image. However, the good news is that there is a vast array of ways to customize how these titles look, as well as animations you can apply.

370 Larry's "10 Rules for Titles"

Video is a low-resolution image. Adjust your text accordingly.

Before we tackle how to create text, let's take a minute to think about using text. Video, even 4K, is low-resolution compared to print. Even more challenging, many viewers are distracted and not paying full attention to the video. So when adding text to video, you need to give the audience time to read what you put on the screen.

- Readability is everything. If the audience can't read the text, you've wasted the message.

- Always add a drop shadow to text you want the audience to read, except if it is over black.

- When creating text you want the audience to read, be sure the text contrasts in shape, texture, color, and grayscale from the background. Some in your audience may be color-blind.

Text readability is everything.

- Hold text onscreen long enough for you to read it aloud twice. (If you are using really fanciful or script fonts, hold it onscreen even longer.)

- Given the same amount of screen time, horizontal text is more readable than text at an angle or vertical.

- Don't make your text too small. In general, for HD video, avoid point sizes smaller than 22 points. For SD video, avoid point sizes smaller than 26 points. Slightly larger is better.

- Avoid fonts with very thin bars or serifs, unless they are scaled large.

- Avoid highly "designed"or fanciful fonts, unless they are scaled large.

- When creating projects for broadcast, cable, streaming media, or digital cinema, use the video scopes to verify that font colors are not excessively saturated and that white levels do not exceed 100%.

- When creating projects for broadcast, cable, streaming media, or digital cinema, keep all text inside the Title Safe zone (the inner rectangle). When creating projects for the web, keep text inside the Action Safe zone (the outer rectangle). Even today, not all displays show the entire image. (See Tip 103, *Display Action Safe and Title Safe Zones*.)

371 Fonts Wrap Text with Emotion

Fonts convey a lot by how they look, as well as what they say.

Books are written about typefaces. Let me provide some tips to help you use fonts better. Like all things fashionable, fonts fall into and out of favor (witness Comic Sans).

Every typeface is carefully designed to evoke a specific style or feeling. These looks convey emotion just as much as, or more than, the message written with the text. Be sure that the emotional message matches the emotion of your project; see **FIGURE 7.11**.

The two most important font categories are serif and sans serif. Serif fonts have little "feet" at the bottom of the letters. It is a traditional font, designed to make reading books easier. The italic weight of serif fonts is elegant and graceful. Sans serif fonts don't have the feet. They are also much more readable onscreen. For most of your projects, consider using sans serif fonts. There are hundreds to choose from.

FIGURE 7.11 Examples of different font styles: Palatino Roman (top), Adobe Caslon Pro Italic (middle), and Calibri Regular (bottom). Sans serif fonts are easier to read onscreen.

Serif Text is Traditional

Serif Italic Text is Elegant

Sans Serif Text is Modern

③⑦② Preview a Title

Preview a title before you use it.

To preview a title in the Titles browser, hover your mouse over the Title icon, then wait a couple of seconds for Final Cut to load it. As you drag your mouse across the title, it will preview, including any animation, in the Viewer.

③⑦③ Add a Title to the Timeline

With dozens to choose from, adding a title is easy. Picking is hard.

To add a title to the timeline, double-click its icon in the Titles browser.

Final Cut includes dozens of titles, most of which are animated, for use in your projects. Be careful with animation; don't let your story get overwhelmed by text that's too busy.

To add a title to the timeline, open the Titles browser by clicking its icon; see **FIGURE 7.12** (shortcut: Option+Cmd+1). Titles are always added at the position of the playhead (skimmer) in the lowest available layer:

- Drag the title icon into the timeline.

  Or—select its icon and press Q.

  Or—double-click its icon.

- To search for a title, enter some or all of its name in the search box of the Titles browser.
- To remove a title from the timeline, select it and press Delete.

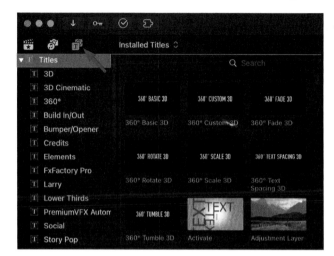

FIGURE 7.12
The Titles browser.

GOING FURTHER
If you are overwhelmed by choices, search for "Custom." The Custom and Custom 3D titles are good places to start.

374 Modify a Title

There are four principal ways to modify a title.

A title clip behaves just like any other clip in the timeline. You can adjust its position, change its duration, and add transitions just like any other clip. When it comes to the text itself, there are four ways to modify a title: Position, Content, Format, and Animation.

- **Position.** Change the position of the clip by selecting the clip in the timeline; then drag either the white circle or the white box that appears in the Viewer to a new location; see **FIGURE 7.13**.

FIGURE 7.13 Drag the white circle (or, sometimes, a white box) in the Viewer to reposition text onscreen.

- **Content.** To change the content of a clip, select the clip in the timeline; then double-click the text that appears in the Viewer.

- **Format.** To change the format of the text, select the clip in the time line; then open one of two Inspectors that control text (see **FIGURE 7.14**): Text Formatting (top-left arrow) and Text Animation (the Inspector to its left).

Formatting text is similar to other applications with two hidden tricks:

NOTE You can also change the value of a numeric field by placing the cursor in the numeric field and dragging up or down.

- When you reach the limit of a slider (±100 points in the case of Line Spacing), extend the setting by entering a number in the size field (−130 in the screen shot).

- Press the Option key and click in the slider track to move it in one-unit increments. This provides precise control over changes.

- **Animation.** Animation options are controlled by the Text Animation inspector, the icon to the left of the Text Formatting inspector (top-left red arrow).

FIGURE 7.14 This is the top half of the Text Inspector (blue icon). Change the onscreen text using the Text field (bottom red arrow) or format the text using these Basic settings.

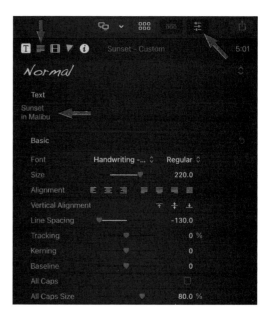

375 Modify Text Position More Precisely

Dragging is easy, but the Inspector provides more precise options.

The really fun options for text are lower in the Text Inspector; see **FIGURE 7.15**. Click and drag any number to change it.

- **Position.** This provides numerical precision over placement of the selected text onscreen. All text lives in 3D space, even though Final Cut does not yet take full advantage of it. ("Z" refers to moving the text to or from your eye, as represented by the surface of your monitor.)

- **Rotation.** Rotating text on the y-axis is one of my favorite ways to add depth to text.

- **Scale.** Stretch the text along the x- or y-axis. (The z-axis makes no visible change.)

The lower five options are discussed in Tip 378, *Format How Titles Look.*

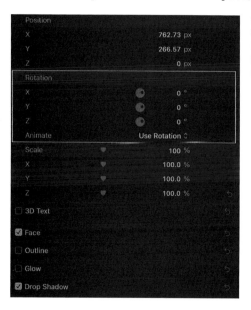

FIGURE 7.15 The text position and formatting controls in the Text Inspector provide much greater flexibility and control than dragging the text onscreen.

GOING FURTHER
The position settings in the Text Inspector can't be keyframed. However, the Transform settings in the Video Inspector can. These are discussed in Chapter 8, "Visual Effects."

376 A Simple Way to Add Depth to Text

Rotate text on the y-axis to add the illusion of depth.

Although Final Cut does not support 3D rotation of objects, it does support 3D rotation of text. This provides an easy way to create the illusion of depth— rotate the text on either the x- or y-axis.

Add depth by rotating text on the y-axis.

In **FIGURE 7.16**, the text was rotated 55° on the y-axis, while both its vertical and horizontal positions were adjusted using the Text Position settings. However, text rotation in Final Cut can't be keyframed, meaning the rotation can't be animated.

NOTE Text can be fully rotated and animated in Apple Motion, then saved as a custom text template for Final Cut Pro.

TITLES & TEXT **297**

FIGURE 7.16 Rotating text on the y-axis is a good way to simulate depth.

377 Add Cast Shadows to Text

Just change one setting.

Cast shadows, like those created in bright sunlight, can be added to any clip. However, they work best for text; see **FIGURE 7.17**.

1. Select the text clip.

2. Choose Effects browser > Stylize > Drop Shadow. (Effects are illustrated in Chapter 8.)

3. In the Video Inspector, change the drop shadow setting from Classic Drop Shadow to Perspective Back.

4. Use the onscreen controls to adjust the shadow position and settings.

FIGURE 7.17 Add cast shadows to text, then adjust the position and angle onscreen.

378 Format How Titles Look

These four formatting groups change the color and look of text.

As shown in Figure 7.15, four groups of settings control the color of the text in a title: Face, Outline, Glow, and Drop Shadow. (I'll talk about 3D separately.) I'm a big fan of drop shadows. Although there's a trend today that says drop shadows are passé, personally I think they significantly improve text readability.

- **Face.** This determines the color of the main portion of text. Click the color chip (see Tip 380, *Pick Your Color Picker*) to open the Mac color picker. A useful trick is to click the eyedropper, then click a color in the image to apply that color to your text; see **FIGURE 7.18.**

FIGURE 7.18 Use the eyedropper tool to select an onscreen color to apply to the selected text.

- **Outline and Glow.** I'm not a big fan of outlines or glows. But they are available should you wish.

- **Drop shadow.** Drop shadows add critical readability to all video text. Why? **FIGURE 7.19** illustrates how adding a drop shadow makes even hard-to-read text stand out onscreen. The color of the text matched the background; it was not changed between the two images. My custom drop shadow settings are illustrated at the bottom. (You don't need to use drop shadows when text is placed over a black background.)

Always add drop shadows to all onscreen text that isn't black.

FIGURE 7.19 Even though the text color matches the background in both examples, adding a drop shadow vastly improves readability. The bottom image shows the settings applied to the text. (I will also frequently add 4–10 points of Blur.)

379 Fonts Don't Need to Be White

All fonts are a solid color—white. Change it by adding a gradient.

By default, all text in Final Cut is solid and white. Boring. Instead, replace that solid color with a gradient, then change the colors of the gradient; see **FIGURE 7.20**.

1. Select the text you want to modify in either the Inspector or the Viewer.
2. In the Text Inspector, scroll down and show Face.

NOTE Replicate a color square in the color picker by Option-dragging it. Delete a color square by dragging it off the bar.

3. Change Fill with to Gradient.
4. Twirl the arrow next to Gradient (upper red arrow) to reveal the gradient color picker.

    The top white bar represents opacity over time. Generally, leave that alone.
5. Click one of the color squares below it to select it (lower red arrow).
6. Click either the color chip or the arrow next to the color chip to display a color picker.
7. To add another color to the gradient, click once in the thin horizontal color bar.
8. Drag a color square left or right to change where the colors transition.

GOING FURTHER
Video research has shown that light yellow is second only to white for readability and clarity in lower-third titles.

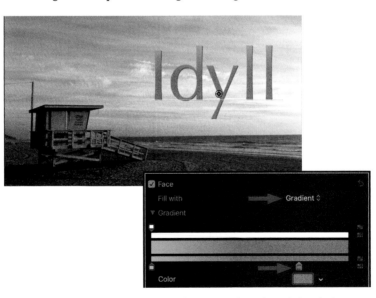

FIGURE 7.20 Text with a gradient applied. Settings used are shown below the image.

380 Pick Your Color Picker

Final Cut offers two different color pickers.

Whenever you see a color picker in Final Cut, there are two options to choose from, depending upon where you click; see **FIGURE 7.21**. They both do the same thing—just in different ways. I like the Mac color picker because it can save colors using the chips at the bottom, and it looks like the Vectorscope.

- If you click the color chip itself, the traditional Mac color picker appears.
- If you click the small chevron to the right, the Motion color picker appears.

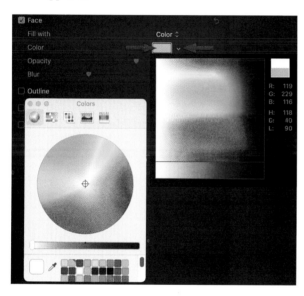

FIGURE 7.21 Click the color chip (left arrow) and the Mac color picker appears (left). Click the chevron and the Motion color picker appears.

381 Kerning Improves Large Text Titles

Kerning adjusts the space between two selected letters.

Most of the time, the spacing between letters in a text clip is fine. However, when you create a large title, especially with a serif font, letter spacing can often use some help.

Kerning to the rescue. Kerning adjusts the space between a pair of letters. The top image in **FIGURE 7.22** shows text with a wider apparent space between the *A* and *w* than between the other letters. This is caused by how letter spacing is calculated on computers.

FIGURE 7.22 Kerning adjusts the space between a pair of letters.

Final Cut has two default titles. Change them to something more useful.

To adjust this spacing:

1. Select the title clip in the timeline.
2. In the Viewer, click between the pair of letters you want to adjust so that a white bar appears between them.
3. Press Option+Cmd+[to tighten spacing.
4. Press Option+Cmd+] to loosen spacing.
5. Adjust until the spacing "looks right."

382 Change the Default Titles

Final Cut has two default titles. Change them.

Final Cut has two default titles: Basic Title and Basic Lower Third. Neither has any animation, and both are boring. The only advantage to using these is that they are applied with a keyboard shortcut. Titles added using a keyboard shortcut always appear in the timeline on the highest layer at the position of the playhead (skimmer).

However, see **FIGURE 7.23**, you can change these defaults.

1. Right-click the icon of the title you want to make a default.
2. Choose whether to make it a default title or lower third.

Here's the secret. This choice doesn't matter! All you are doing is assigning a keyboard shortcut to a specific title. I assigned both these shortcuts to two different lower-third titles that I use constantly when editing my webinars.

GOING FURTHER
The two title keyboard shortcuts are:

- **Control+T**: Apply the default title at the position of the playhead (skimmer).
- **Shift+Control+T**: Apply the default lower-third title.

FIGURE 7.23 Assign the two titles you use the most to one of these two defaults. Select from any title, including custom titles.

383 Review Timeline Titles Quickly

The Timeline Index is a great help in reviewing titles quickly.

You're ready to export the final project, just as soon as you review your titles one last time. You know, just to make sure there are no typos. Except, given the size of your project, how can you be *sure* you found them all? The Timeline Index to the rescue!

1. Open the Timeline Index (shortcut: Shift+Cmd+2); see **FIGURE 7.24.**

2. Click the Clips text button at the top.

3. Click the Titles button at the bottom.

4. Starting at the top of the list, either click each title or use the Up/Down arrow keys to move through the list.

   When a title is selected in the Index, FCP jumps the playhead to the start of the title in the timeline and displays it in the Viewer.

5. If you need to make text changes, select the title in the Viewer and change what needs changing.

The fastest way to review titles is to use the Up/Down arrows in the Timeline Index.

FIGURE 7.24 Choose Timeline Index > Clips > Titles to quickly review all titles in a project.

GOING FURTHER
Changing the contents of the title in the Timeline Index changes its name, but not its content. Alas, you can't spell-check titles using the Timeline Index, but you can if you open the title clip in the Viewer or the Inspector.

384 There's a Hidden Shortcut for Titles

This shortcut helps find and replace text.

Final Cut has a shortcut to find and replace title text. Except it isn't assigned to any key. To create your own shortcut:

1. Choose Final Cut Pro > Commands > Customize.

2. Search for "title text."

GOING FURTHER
This menu also appears when choosing Edit > Find and Replace Title Text, but a custom keyboard shortcut is faster and, frankly, much cooler!

3. "Find and Replace Title Text" appears in the Command panel.

4 Assign a keyboard shortcut (I used Control+F) and click Save.

5. After creating this shortcut (in my example, Control+F), press it, and the Find and Replace Text window appears; see **FIGURE 7.25**.

6. Select settings that determine how to replace text: in all titles in the project or just in the selected title. Other options are similar to using a word processor.

FIGURE 7.25 The Find and Replace Title Text window.

385 Add Emojis to Titles

I'm probably opening Pandora's box here, but emojis can be titles.

All emojis are simply text wearing costumes. Adding emojis to a title is easy:

All emojis are simply text wearing costumes.

1. Place your cursor in a text clip where you want to add an emoji.

2. Press Control+Cmd+spacebar to display the Character Viewer, which contains emojis and lots of other interesting characters.

3. Double-click any emoji icon to add it to the title.

But why stop there? Resize them.

4. Just as with text, select an emoji and then adjust its size in the Text Inspector by choosing Font Size.

Just what I was looking for...a 500-point drunken sun! (See **FIGURE 7.26**.)

5. Select any emoji in the Character Viewer to see variations of it in the Font Variation panel on the right side.

FIGURE 7.26 Yes, even you can add a drunken sun to your next project.

386 Many Titles Include Animation

Turn animation on or off with a single switch.

Many titles, especially lower-thirds, include animation to bring them on or off the screen. Even easier, there are no settings to adjust. The animation is on by default, but you can change that.

1. Add a title to the timeline, then select it.
2. Go to the Text Animation Inspector (top red arrow). See **FIGURE 7.27**.
3. By default, animation is on.
4. Deselect Build In to disable the animation at the start of a clip.
5. Deselect Build Out to disable the animation at the end of a clip.

Change these settings at any time.

FIGURE 7.27 Title animation is controlled from the Text Animation Inspector (top-left arrow). Build In enables opening animation. Build Out enables closing animation.

GOING FURTHER
The default font for the Purple lower-third is Comic Sans. Only preschoolers should use Comic Sans. I changed it.

387 Access More Complex Animation

Several titles also include very complex animation.

Animation gets very old very fast, unless it is really well done. When you use animation, use it sparingly. At the beginning of this section, I recommended you use one of the Custom titles; see **FIGURE 7.28**. Here's why.

FIGURE 7.28 The Custom title includes extensive animation options, adjusted using the Title Animation Inspector.

Search for and edit the Custom title into the timeline, then select it. Open the Title Inspector (top-left arrow). Yup, that's a *lot* of animation controls! Explaining all these settings would take pages. Here are the highlights:

- Parameters starting with "In" affect opening animation.
- Parameters starting with "Out" affect closing animation.
- All parameter settings determine the amount of change. For example, when In Opacity is set to any value other than 100%, the text will fade in starting with that percentage. Try 0% and watch what happens.
- In Duration determines, in frames, how long the opening animation will take (bottom red arrow).
- In Unit size determines whether animation is by letter, word, or the entire block of text.
- To reset a parameter, click the small down-pointing chevron and choose Reset Parameter.

Play with this to see what it can do. Feel free to change multiple settings. This is a very flexible and fun title.

GOING FURTHER
Custom 3D includes most of these animations. Many other titles include selections of these. Get in the habit of checking the Title Animation Inspector to see what options are available for the titles you use.

388 3D Text Is Just Like 2D—Almost

Except, ah, it has depth! And textures. And lighting.

One of the exciting text features in Final Cut is 3D text. In truth, 3D text is just like 2D except for three areas: depth, textures, and lighting. From a text selection, formatting, and editing point of view, 3D is the same as 2D. This makes working with it easy.

Final Cut Pro offers three unique settings for 3D text: Depth, Textures, and Lighting.

A variety of 3D text templates are in the Titles browser. For the same reasons I recommend using Custom for 2D text, I recommend Custom 3D now. Apply the title the same way as 2D: double-click the text icon to edit it into the timeline at the position of the playhead (skimmer).

When you first look at this 3D title, it isn't that impressive. The font is thin, the depth is more like a drop shadow, and the overall impression is disappointing. Not to worry, there is a lot to work with here.

1. Select the clip in the timeline.
2. Change the font to Impact, 225 points.
3. Rotate the image 45° or so on the y-axis so the edges and sides are more visible.

   Notice that the lighting changes as you rotate the text.

4. In the 3D Text category further down the Inspector, increase Depth to 60; see **FIGURE 7.29.**

FIGURE 7.29 3D text has depth. In fact, the text can rotate to reveal different textures for the side and back, which you can't do with 2D text.

GOING FURTHER Similar to the Custom title, Custom 3D also has a wealth of animation options available in the Text Animation Inspector. I'm not covering them here because we already covered how they work for 2D text. (See Tip 387, *Access More Complex Animation*.)

389 3D Textures Provide Stunning Versatility

Apply different textures to the front, side, back, and all edges.

With 2D text, you can apply one color or a gradient. With 3D text, you can get all dressed up and ready for a night out. Unlike 2D text, which has only one side (front), 3D text has three sides and two edges: front, front edge, side, back, and back edge. As an example, scroll down the Text Inspector to the Material section; see **FIGURE 7.30.**

- **Single.** Whatever texture you pick is applied to all five surfaces.
- **Multiple.** This menu provides separate texture options for each surface. Personally, I like something shiny for edges because it adds sparkle. I selected the front texture to pick up the sand color from the beach. The side texture was chosen because its color complemented the brown sand.

There are 11 texture categories to choose from, containing almost 100 different textures. This provides a great range of options to play with. There are no "right" answers, only those that look good with your project.

FIGURE 7.30 Textures applied to 3D text. Notice how the textures reinforce the lighting and overall tone of the image. The front corner edge is shiny to emphasize the depth of the letters.

390 Lighting 3D Text

Lots of options with eye-popping results.

3D text is exciting because of its depth and the variety of textures available for each surface. But the real excitement comes when you start to play with lighting. Although Motion contains far more lighting and lighting animation options than Final Cut, there are still several adjustments you can make.

Just above Materials is Lighting; see **FIGURE 7.31.**

1. Click Show to see the contents.
2. Click the Lighting Style menu ("Standard") to reveal 11 lighting presets. (See **FIGURE 7.32.**)

   As an example, **FIGURE 7.33** shows the text lit using the Above setting.

   - Check Self-Shadows for each letter to cast shadows on the text next to it. I generally decrease Opacity and increase Softness.
   - Deselect Environment to turn off the general-purpose lighting that all 3D text is lit with.
   - Select Environment and change Type to Colorful. I like the party atmosphere of this lighting effect.
   - Choose Adjust Environment > Rotation to change the colors.
   - Continue playing until it's time for dinner.

FIGURE 7.31 Lighting is controlled in this section. Click the Lighting Style menu to reveal presets. Deselect Environment to add more drama to your light (above).

FIGURE 7.33 "Above" is applied as a lighting effect to the text. I changed the side material to Thick Plaster to show more texture with this angle of light (above).

FIGURE 7.32 These eleven presets change lighting position and emphasis. While they can't be animated in FCP, they can in Motion (left).

GOING FORWARD Intensity varies the amount of light radiating off the letters. While dimming the lighting is always possible, you can also increase the intensity—which works especially well for saturated colors—to well over 4000%! Ignore the slider and type in a value. (Remember, you can also click and drag a number to change the value.)

391 Modify Any Title in Motion

Modify an existing title to create your own custom version.

As with transitions, Motion can modify any title. Right-click any title icon to open a copy in Motion. (As with transitions, you modify only copies—you can't change the original.)

When you are done modifying, save it in Motion, and it will appear in the Titles browser next to the original, as illustrated in **FIGURE 7.34**. This is exactly what I did to create the large "Custom Title" shown in Figure 7.34.

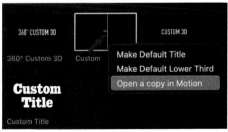

FIGURE 7.34 Right-click a title icon to open a copy in Motion for customizing.

392 Remove a Custom Title (or Transition)

Removing a custom title is easy but takes a few steps.

To remove a custom title or transition, right-click it in the Titles (or Transitions) browser (see **FIGURE 7.35**), then choose Reveal in Finder.

NOTE Once you locate an effect in the Finder, you may get more reliable results if you quit Final Cut before deleting the folder containing the effect.

Here's the tricky step. You can't just remove the elements of the title; you need to remove the *folder* that contains them.

1. Right-click the name of the effect in the top left of the Finder window (red arrow); see **FIGURE 7.36**.

2. Choose the next level *down* in the list.

3. In the folder that opens, delete the *folder* that's named after your custom effect.

   In my case, I'm deleting the Custom Copy folder; see **FIGURE 7.37**. Most of the time, this effect will disappear in Final Cut. If it doesn't, quit and relaunch Final Cut.

FIGURE 7.35 Right-click a custom title and choose Reveal in Finder.

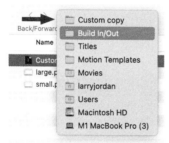

FIGURE 7.36 Right-click the name at the top of the Finder window and select the next level *down*. (Your path list will look different from mine.)

FIGURE 7.37 Delete the *folder* with the name of the custom title you want to delete.

GENERATORS

Generators are computer-generated media. They range from full-screen animated backgrounds to very specific effects. They are unique to Final Cut and can provide interesting looks to many different projects.

393 What's a Generator?

Generators are adjustable computer-generated media.

Generators were originally created in Motion, then migrated to Final Cut. Each of these is computer-generated and can assume any frame size, frame rate, or duration. Use them whenever you need an animated background. Some are pretty tacky, but others are very useful.

Generators share the same browser with titles (shortcut: Option+Cmd+1). There are five default categories: 360°, Backgrounds, Elements, Solids, and Textures; see **FIGURE 7.38**.

As you might expect, hundreds of third-party generators are available. As you might not expect, you can also create your own generators in Motion. I use generators whenever I need to create a background for an infographic.

Generators are adjustable computer-generated media that are compatible with any project.

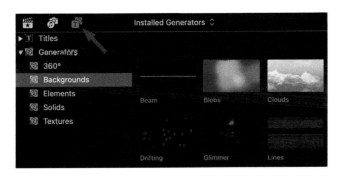

FIGURE 7.38 The Generators browser.

394 Generator Backgrounds

Backgrounds are full screen, animated, and flexible.

Backgrounds (see **FIGURE 7.39**) are full-screen, generated media. What that means is that they will fit any frame size, any frame rate, or any duration you need.

- Some, like Organic, have no formatting options at all.
- Others, like Collage, allow you to disable the animation.
- Others, like Drifting, Clouds, and Underwater, have a wide variety of formatting options.

Edit a generator to the timeline like any other Browser clip. Select it in the timeline, then look in the Generator Inspector for animation and format options.

FIGURE 7.39 This composite image illustrates the variety of generator backgrounds available in Final Cut Pro, most of which are animated.

GOING FURTHER
In many cases, the background animation moves too quickly. You don't want the background distracting from the foreground. Where possible, adjust the generator settings or use Modify > Retime to slow the movement.

Although I wish that Apple provided more darker backgrounds to make text easier to read, I use Generators—or modifications of them—in many projects as animated backgrounds for infographics. As well, because generators are so easy to create, you'll find hundreds of additional options available from third-party developers.

395 Generator Elements

Specific video for specific needs.

Four generators are in the Element category; see **FIGURE 7.40**. After editing an element to the timeline, select it, and then look at the options in the Generator inspector.

- **Counting**. This creates a countdown or count-up. If the Start number is smaller than the End, the video counts up. If the End is smaller, it counts down. Format controls include font, size, color, and numeric format. Number formats include numbers, currency, percentages, and spelled-out words.

FIGURE 7.40 Generator elements create video for specific needs.

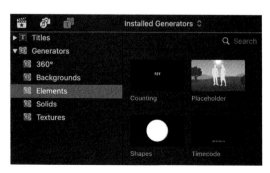

- **Placeholder.** This creates "storyboard-like" still images where you can specify framing, number of people in the shot, and their gender, background, and sky. The placeholder can switch between interior and exterior.

- **Shapes.** This generates 12 shapes: circle, rectangle, star, arrow, and so on. You can change the size, color, border, and drop shadow.

- **Timecode.** This, to me, is the most useful. Use this generator to burn labels and timecode into clips or projects. (See Tip 396, *How to Burn Timecode into a Project.*)

GOING FURTHER
The Shapes position controls are very limited. Create the shape using the generator. Leave it centered. Then, scale and position the shape using settings in Video Inspector > Transform (see Chapter 8).

396 How to Burn Timecode into a Project

"Burning" timecode records the project timecode into video.

Although online project review is growing in popularity, there's often a need to send a client a video and ask for comments. For them to provide comments that make sense, you also need to also supply a time reference with the video. The easiest and best way to do this is to add, or "burn," timecode into the video; see **FIGURE 7.41**.

Creating this effect is easy:

1. Drag the Timecode generator onto a layer above all timeline clips.

2. Stretch its duration so it spans the full length of your project.

3. Select the Timecode clip.

4. Drag the white circle in the Viewer and move the timecode display to a corner (I prefer the upper right) or a lower edge. Keep it inside Action Safe.

5. Go to the Generator Inspector and modify the settings as you see fit.

   I generally set the font size to 36 point, as 48 feels too big. Be sure Timecode Base is set to Project. Change the label as you see fit.

   When you export the project, the timecode will be permanently burned into the video.

6. To remove this effect, just delete the timecode clip from the timeline. You can also press V to make it temporarily invisible.

FIGURE 7.41 The settings (top) that created the "burned-in" timecode effect (bottom).

GOING FURTHER There's also a Timecode effect. Why use this generator? Because the Timecode generator provides a single clip spanning whatever timeline duration you need. Using an effect requires adding it individually to every timeline clip. In other words, the generator is faster and easier.

397 Generator Solids

Solids are adjustable, solid, unanimated colors.

Generator solids, see **FIGURE 7.42**, are exactly that: a solid color. They are not animated, but the colors can be modified. Each comes with a menu of color selections.

The most flexible is Custom, because you can select any color you want, but two others I find useful are Whites and Grey Scale.

FIGURE 7.42 The Custom solid is the most flexible, but all Solids provide useful color options in the Generator Inspector.

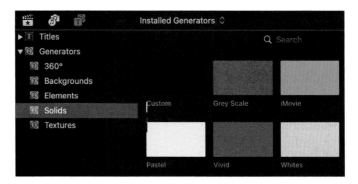

398 Generator Textures

Textures are the most fun of all the generators.

I really like textures! So much computer-generated video is smooth, "plastic," and artificial, because it's so perfect. Textures totally mess with that, especially when you start playing with blend modes, which I'll do in the next two tips.

Each texture (see **FIGURE 7.43**) has about a dozen image options in the Generator Inspector, so there's plenty of variety to choose from. Clearly, one use is for backgrounds for infographics. However, like solids, textures are not animated. Backgrounds would be a better choice simply because they contain animation.

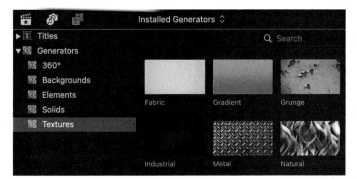

FIGURE 7.43 Each texture includes multiple image options, which are selected in the Generator Inspector.

399 Modify the Default Generator

Just as with transitions, you can set a default generator.

Titles, transitions, and generators all support setting a default. To do this for generators, right-click a specific generator (see **FIGURE 7.44**) and select Make Default Generator.

The keyboard shortcut to add the default generator at the position of the timeline playhead (skimmer) is Option+Cmd+W.

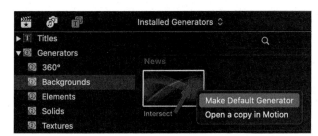

FIGURE 7.44 Right-click a generator icon to change it to the default generator.

400 Add Texture to Text

Use blend modes and generators to add texture to text.

Normally, text has a flat surface. But as you can see in **FIGURE 7.45**, you can easily add texture using a generator and blend mode. Here's how:

1. Edit the Stone texture into the timeline (lower-left image) and select the clip.

2. In the Generator Inspector, change the Stone Type to Slate.

3. Edit a text clip above the texture. (I used Custom.)

FIGURE 7.45 Generator textures combined with blend modes can add texture to text. Use this effect with any two clips, though it works really well with text.

4. Change the font and point size as needed. (I used Bradley Hand at 450 point, rotated 20°.)

5. Change the color to anything *except* white. (I used black.)

6. In the Video Inspector (lower-right image), change the blend mode to Overlay.

Ta-dah! It looks like the text was sprayed on the stone. There are infinite variations on this.

GOING FURTHER The Blend Mode menu holds more than 20 options. My favorites are Overlay and Soft Light, which combines midtones; Multiply, which combines shadows; and Screen, which combines highlights. Blend modes are the texture workhorses behind almost all visual effects.

401 Put Video Inside Text

This is another example of the power of blend modes.

Here, you'll put a texture (or video) inside text; see **FIGURE 7.46**:

1. Edit a texture into the timeline. (I used Metal.)

2. Change the Metal Type to Frosted Chevrons, or whatever you want.

3. Edit a text clip above the texture; see the lower image.

4. Change the text format as you see fit. I used Giza and 400 points.

5. Select the text clip.

6. In the Video Inspector, change Blend Mode to Stencil Alpha.

Ta-dah, um, again! This effect, too, is used endlessly these days.

FIGURE 7.46 Use Blend Mode: Stencil Alpha to put the lower clip into the upper clip. This works best with text or any item with an alpha channel.

GOING FURTHER I used a texture in this example. However, you can insert video by replacing the texture clip with a video clip. All the settings stay the same.

402 Put Video Inside Text Over Video

This combines several tips to create an interesting effect.

This should probably go in Chapter 8, "Visual Effects," but since we are discussing textures, text, and blend modes, here's one more. This puts video inside a text clip, then puts that effect over a background video.

This is a three-layer effect using blend modes and a compound clip; see **FIGURE 7.47**:

1. Put the background video in the Primary Storyline.
2. Above that, put the video you want to put inside the text.
3. Above that, put the text, formatted as you want.

   I'm using Cracked at 500 points.

4. Select the text clip and change the blend mode to Stencil Alpha.
5. Select both the middle video and the text clip and convert them to a compound clip (shortcut: Option+G).

   The video now appears inside the text, on top of the background video.

FIGURE 7.47 Video inside text over video. This uses the Intersect generator and a Stencil Alpha blend mode applied to the text; then combined into a compound clip to add it to the background.

GOING FURTHER To add a drop shadow to the flaming text:

1. Select the compound clip.
2. Choose Effects Browser > Stylize (shortcut: Cmd+5) and apply Drop Shadow to the compound clip.
3. Adjust until it looks good to you.

CHAPTER 7—TRANSITIONS & TITLES SHORTCUTS

CATEGORY	SHORTCUT	WHAT IT DOES
Transitions	Control+Cmd+5	Open the Transitions browser
	Cmd+T	Apply the default transition to edit point
	Control+D	Change duration for selected transition(s), titles, generators, and clips
Titles	Option+Cmd+1	Open the Titles browser
	Control+T	Add default title at playhead
	Shift+Control+T	Add default lower-third title at playhead
	Option+Cmd+[	Kern the spacing tighter between two letters
	Option+Cmd+]	Kern the spacing looser between two letters
	Shift+Cmd+2	Toggle the Timeline Index open or closed
Generators	Option+Cmd+1	Open the Generators browser
	Option+Cmd+W	Add default generator at playhead (skimmer)
	V	Toggle visibility for selected clip(s) on or off
	Option-click	Constrain a slider to move in 1-unit increments (applies to most effects)

CHAPTER WRAP

Like all effects, the operative phrase is "Less is more." The fewer transitions and generators in your video, the more powerful each use of them becomes. Don't let the effects get in the way of telling your story. All too often, they do.

The rule is different for text. So many videos today are viewed without listening to the audio that text must get your message across even when the audio is turned off. This also means to hold titles onscreen long enough for most viewers to read them. Remember, they only get to see your program once.

CHAPTER 8

VISUAL EFFECTS

INTRODUCTION

This chapter focuses on the fun stuff: effects. This could completely fill its own book—there are so many effects with so many variations that it is impossible to cover them all. My goal is to show how core effects work so you feel comfortable discovering the variations on your own.

- Video Inspector Effects
- Transform Effects
- Viewer Effects
- The Effects Browser
- Effects Cookbook

- Masks & Keys
- Color Inspector
- Shortcuts

NOTE Clip speed effects are covered in Chapter 10, "Special Cases," a free PDF download for the printed book. Refer to the *Free Additional Chapter—Online* section for download instructions.

DEFINITIONS FOR THIS CHAPTER

- **Alpha channel.** This tracks whether each pixel is opaque, transparent, or translucent.

- **Anchor point.** This is the location in an image around which the image rotates or scales. By default, this is the center of the frame.

- **Color correct.** This fixes a color or grayscale problem in a clip; also called *color correction*.

- **Color grade.** This changes the color of a clip, or group of clips, to create a specific feeling or look; also called *color grading*.

- **Composite.** This is an image composed of two or more images, including graphics or text.

Larry's rule for effects: "Just because you can does not mean you should."

- **Key.** This superimposes an image, such as text, on another image by removing the background of the foreground image based on luminance, color, or transparency.

- **Keyframe.** These automate a parameter change during playback, for example, moving an image. Keyframes are generally added to a clip at the position of the playhead (skimmer). It takes a minimum of two keyframes to create movement. Using more than two keyframes to create an effect is common.

- **Motion path.** This line shows the movement of the center of a clip based upon Position keyframes applied to the clip. Motion paths can be straight or curved and contain as many keyframes as needed.

- **Primary** color effects. This adjusts the color of the entire frame, and clip, by the same amount. For example, to remove a blue color cast.

- **Render.** This calculates new video based upon the effects and settings applied to an existing clip. There is one render frame for each project frame.

- **Scale.** This changes the size of an image.

- **Secondary** color effects. This adjusts the color of a portion of the frame, without altering the entire frame. For example, to change the color of an actor's shirt.

VIDEO INSPECTOR EFFECTS

Most video effects start with, or are modified by, the Video Inspector. Although other effects may look sexier, none are more useful. This is a good place to start learning how to create effects.

403 The Video Inspector

The hub for all visual effects—except two.

With the exception of clip speed changes and color effects, the Video Inspector (see **FIGURE 8.1**) is the hub around which visual effects in Final Cut revolve. All Video Inspector settings affect whatever is selected in the timeline. It contains eight categories, most of which are hidden by default:

- **Compositing**. This controls opacity and blend modes.

- **Transform**. This controls position, rotation, and scaling. These are the most commonly used effects in the Video Inspector.

- **Crop**. This removes pixels from an image, along with a pan-and-scan effect called the *Ken Burns effect*.

- **Distort**. This warps an image by moving its corners, often providing the illusion of 3D.

- **Spatial Conform**. This determines how a nonstandard frame size fits into the project frame size.

- **Trackers**. This controls motion tracking an object.

- **Image Stabilization**. This smooths and steadies handheld camera shots.

- **Rolling Shutter**. This fixes a problem caused by recording fast pans or tilts with a DSLR camera.

The Video Inspector is the hub that controls almost all visual effects in Final Cut.

FIGURE 8.1 The Video Inspector. Transform is enabled; Spatial Conform is disabled.

All these categories are explained in tips in this section. There are also controls that appear only when a stand-alone effect is applied to a timeline clip from the Effects browser.

NOTE Clip speed changes are covered in Chapter 10.

- To toggle the contents of a category open or closed, click the Show/Hide button (left red arrow in Figure 8.1).

- To reset a parameter to its defaults, click the down chevron and choose Reset Parameter (right red arrow). Additional options in this menu affect keyframes (see Tip 426, *Apply Video Keyframes*).

The icons to the right of the category name also appear in the onscreen Viewer controls; see Tip 418, *Enable Onscreen Viewer Controls*.

FIGURE 8.2 This chevron menu appears for all Video Inspector categories, effects, and settings.

404 To Reset Any Effect

All Effects browser effect controls appear in the Video Inspector.

To reset any effect category, parameter, or setting to its default settings, click the downward-pointing chevron next to the name of the effect or parameter and select Reset Parameter; see **FIGURE 8.2**. If keyframes exist for this effect, they are deleted.

To disable an effect, without losing settings, deselect the checkbox next to the effect name. For example, in Figure 8.1, Transform and Crop are enabled, while Spatial Conform and Trackers are disabled.

405 Timeline Stacking Matters

The foreground clip is on top; background is on the bottom.

The vertical placement of clips (which I call *stacking order*) of timeline clips is important; see **FIGURE 8.3**. Identical to Adobe Photoshop, the foreground clip is always on top. Mid-ground is the middle. The background clip is on the bottom. Clips are viewed in order from top to bottom. By default, every video clip fills the frame and is 100% opaque. The only way to see clips below the top clip is to change the size or visibility of the top clip.

FIGURE 8.3 Clip stacking order is important. Foreground is on top.

By default, every video clip fills the frame and is 100% opaque.

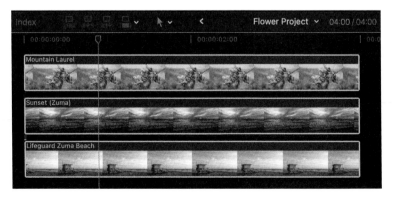

406 Blend Modes & Opacity Create Composite Images

By default, every video clip fills the frame and is 100% opaque.

At the top of the Video Inspector are the Compositing settings. When adjusting opacity or adding blend modes, always select the top clip. Changing a clip on a lower layer does nothing, because it is blocked by higher-layer clips.

Adjusting opacity makes a clip translucent. If you lower the opacity of a Primary Storyline clip with nothing above or below it, it fades partially to black.

NOTE Regardless of the background color you choose in Preferences > Playback, the background always exports as black. See Tip 71, *Optimize Playback Preferences*.

Blend modes require a minimum of two stacked clips. In the computer, pixels are actually stored as numbers. Blend modes apply math operations to these numeric pixel values to create interesting visual effects, as illustrated in Tip 400, *Add Texture to Text*, and Tip 401, *Put Video Inside Text*. With blend modes, either you like the result or you don't. There's nothing to adjust. There are six groups of blend modes with each group separated by faint lines; see **FIGURE 8.4**:

- **Normal**. This cancels any applied blend mode and resets a clip to normal.
- **Multiply**. This group combines pixels based upon shadow (darker) grayscale values. My favorite is Multiply.
- **Screen**. This group combines pixels based upon highlight (brighter) grayscale values. My favorite is Screen. (Don't use Add—it generates illegal video levels.)
- **Overlay**. This group combines pixels based upon midtone grayscale values. My favorites are Overlay and Soft Light.
- **Difference**. This group combines pixels based upon color values. My favorite is Exclusion.
- **Stencil**. This group combines pixels based upon the alpha channel in the selected clip. If there's no alpha channel, there's no effect. My favorite is Stencil Alpha, especially when applied to text.
- **Alpha Add** and **Premultiplied Mix**. I've never used these two effects, so I have no opinion on them.

FIGURE 8.4 The six groups of blend mode options. (Normal is a reset.)

407 Remove Pixels Using Crop or Trim

Cropping tends to make images softer.

The Crop menu in the Video Inspector (see **FIGURE 8.5**) has three options: Crop, Trim, and Ken Burns; see Tip 409, *The Ken Burns Effect*. Select a crop type, then adjust a slider to determine which parts of the image to hide.

FIGURE 8.6 is the source image for this example.

GOING FURTHER
The small icon just above the Crop menu (see Figure 8.5) enables onscreen Viewer controls to adjust Crop settings; see Tip 418, *Enable Onscreen Viewer Controls.*

- **Crop.** This removes pixels from an image, matching the aspect ratio of the project, then scaling the result full screen; see **FIGURE 8.7**. If the image is the same size as the project, cropping softens video quality due to enlarging each pixel. However, if the image is larger than the project, cropping generally won't affect image quality; see Tip 412, *Resize Video Without Losing Image Quality.*

- **Trim.** This hides portions of the image so you can see the image beneath, without scaling the image; see **FIGURE 8.8**. This is frequently done when creating multi-image or picture-in-picture effects. Trimming doesn't make an image softer.

NOTE Crop always hides pixels and scales the image. Trim simply hides pixels.

FIGURE 8.5 The three options of the Crop menu.

FIGURE 8.6 The source image. Note the aspect ratio is 16:9.

FIGURE 8.7 The source image is cropped, then automatically scaled larger to fill the frame.

FIGURE 8.8 The image is trimmed, revealing whatever is below it, without scaling or losing image quality.

408 The Crop & Feather Effect

This trims an image, then feathers the edge in one step.

Although Effects browser effects haven't been formally presented yet (see Tip 438, *The Effects Browser*), there's an effect that improves on the Trim settings in the Video Inspector: Crop & Feather. When trimming a clip (see Figure 8.8), the edges are sharp. Sometimes you need something softer.

The Crop & Feather effect trims a clip and adds feathering—soft, blended edges—to the trimmed clip. To apply it, choose Effects > Distortion > Crop & Feather and drag the effect on top of a clip; see **FIGURE 8.9**. Drag the Feather slider left or right to soften edges inside or out.

The settings for this screen shot are displayed in the inset.

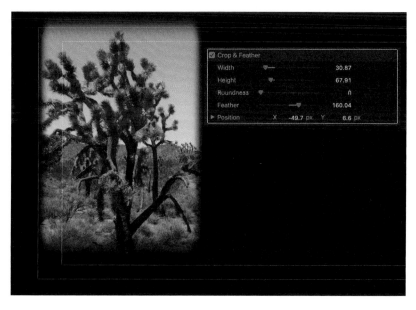

FIGURE 8.9 The Crop & Feather effect trims a clip, then softens the edge. Settings are displayed in the inset.

409 The Ken Burns Effect

Named after legendary documentary filmmaker Ken Burns.

The Ken Burns effect is an exceedingly fast and easy way to animate moves around, into, or out of a still image. Because this effect zooms in to an image, for this effect to look its best, the still images you use should be larger than the project frame size. My recommendation is two to three times the project frame size; see **TABLE 8.1**. (Larger images allow zooming in closer without losing image quality.)

TABLE 8.1 Suggested frame sizes, in pixels, for still images created for the Ken Burns effect		
PROJECT FRAME SIZE	2X IMAGE	3X IMAGE
1280 x 720	2560 x 1440	3840 x 2160
1920 x 1080	3840 x 2160	5760 x 3240
3840 x 2160	7680 x 4320	11520 x 6480
4096 x 2160	8192 x 4320	12288 x 6480

The benefit of the Ken Burns effect is that it is easy—and eye-catching. The effect starts with the first frame of a clip and ends at the last frame. You need to use keyframes (see Tip 426, *Apply Video Keyframes*) to start or end a move in the middle of a clip, to change directions during the same move, or to ensure an image is not enlarged more than 100%.

When using stills for the Ken Burns effect, make sure Spatial Conform for each still is set to Fit.

To apply the Ken Burns effect to a timeline clip:

1. Select the clip; then, in the Video Inspector, choose Crop > Type > Ken Burns.

2. If the onscreen controls don't appear, click the icon above the Type menu so it turns blue; see **FIGURE 8.10**.

FIGURE 8.10 Set Type to Ken Burns to enable this effect.

FIGURE 8.11 shows the onscreen controls in the Viewer. (This is a 4K image, edited into a 1080p project. You can use smaller images, but you can't zoom in as far without seeing pixelization.)

FIGURE 8.11 Onscreen controls for the Ken Burns effect. The green box indicates the starting frame; the red box (at the boundaries of the image) indicates the ending frame.

The green box indicates the portion of the frame where the effect starts. The red box indicates the portion of the frame where the effect ends.

3. Drag a corner of the green or red box to resize or reposition.

   - To swap positions between the green (starting) and red (ending) frames, click the *two-arrow* button in the top-left corner.

   - To preview the effect, click the right-pointing arrow in the top-left corner.

4. When you are happy with the effect, click Done in the top-right corner.

   By default, the Ken Burns effect starts and ends slowly (Ease In And Out).

5. To change that default, right-click anywhere inside the red square in the Viewer (see **FIGURE 8.12**), and choose the acceleration setting you prefer.

   - **Ease Out**. Accelerates the beginning of the move.

   - **Ease In**. Decelerates the end of the move.

   - **Ease In And Out**. Accelerates the beginning and decelerates the end.

   - **Linear**. Keeps the effect speed constant throughout the move.

NOTE When using images larger than the project frame size, be sure to select the image in the timeline and set Spatial Conform to Fit.

GOING FURTHER
Why does the Ease Out setting affect the beginning? The term refers to acceleration in relation to keyframes. When you approach a keyframe, that's "easing in." When you leave, that's "easing out." This language is used consistently throughout Final Cut.

FIGURE 8.12 Acceleration controls for the Ken Burns effect.

GOING FURTHER Jerry Thompson, an editor who reviewed an early version of this book, adds: "After applying and adjusting your Ken Burns clip, position the playhead over the first and last frame and use Option+F to create a still frame in the timeline at the front and back of your Ken Burns clip. This makes your clip smoother coming out of and going into your edit points. This simple tip really applies only to stills, while the Ken Burns effect can be used with stills or video."

410 The Distort Effect

The Distort effect deforms clips geometrically.

The Distort effect in the Video Inspector deforms clips geometrically by dragging the corners in, around, or out of the frame; see **FIGURE 8.13**.

Although you can enter values in the Distort category in the Video Inspector, this is way too painful. Instead, use the onscreen controls described in Tip 418, *Enable Onscreen Viewer Controls*, and drag the corners where you want. Then, if needed, clean up the numbers in the Inspector. When you are happy, click Done in the top-right corner. If you hate it, click Reset.

Although you can create some interesting and weird effects with this, I mostly use it to create the illusion of a 3D video floating over an animated background generator while text is displayed on the side.

FIGURE 8.13 A distorted image, creating the illusion of floating in 3D space.

411 Spatial Conform Fits Odd-Sized Clips

Spatial Conform determines how a clip fits into the timeline.

Most of the time, the images you shoot have the same aspect ratio and frame size as the project. But when they don't, Spatial Conform comes into play; see **FIGURE 8.14**. There are three choices:

- **Fit**. This scales and centers the entire image to fit inside the frame. If the aspect ratios don't match, there will be black edges along two sides of the clip. This is the default setting and guarantees that no part of the image is lost. Use this setting for the Ken Burns effect; see Tip 409, *The Ken Burns Effect.*

- **Fill**. This scales the image to fill the entire frame. If the aspect ratios don't match, it will zoom in such that there are no black edges, but some pixels will be trimmed. This guarantees that there are no black edges.

- **None**. This displays the image at 100% size, regardless of the aspect ratio or frame size of the project. This is the best choice when an image is very small and you want to maintain the highest image quality or you are using keyframes to create moves on images.

FIGURE 8.14 The Spatial Conform > Type options.

412 Resize Video Without Losing Image Quality

Scaling images requires staying at or below 100% size.

All digital video is bitmapped, meaning it is resolution dependent. If you scale an image larger than 100%, it gets blurry because you are simply enlarging the existing pixels, not creating new video data. Scaling smaller than 100% is fine because this uses the excess pixels to improve image quality and edge sharpness.

By default, when you add an image into the timeline that's a different frame size from the project, Spatial Conform is set to Fit; see Tip 411, *Spatial Conform Fits Odd-Sized Clips*. At the same time, Transform > Scale is set to 100%, even if the image was scaled smaller or larger to fit in the project frame. This means you have no idea what the actual size of the image is.

Scaling a bitmap image larger than 100% makes it look soft and blurry.

Instead, select the timeline clip and set Spatial Conform to None. This displays the timeline clip at 100% size and sets Transform > Scale to 100%. Now, when you resize the image, the Transform > Scale setting precisely indicates the exact size of the image. It is now easy to see when an image gets larger than 100%.

GOING FURTHER Actually, given how our eyes perceive images, you could probably scale up to about 110% without the typical viewer noticing the quality drop. But in general, try to keep images at 100% size or below.

413 Image Stabilization

This option appears only when a timeline clip is selected.

I don't know about you, but shaky camera work makes my tummy hurt. Fortunately Final Cut has an excellent motion stabilizer, which if you do hand held shooting, I strongly recommend you use.

Image stabilization analysis is done only once, and the time it takes is dependent upon the speed of the CPU and the duration of the clip.

1. Select the timeline clip, not a clip in the Browser.
2. Enable Stabilization.
3. Set the Method.

   I always use Automatic first, then SmoothCam second. Automatic makes its best decision between SmoothCam and InertiaCam settings.

By default, this feature analyzes a clip to determine the principle subject, then smooths, though it does not totally remove, shakiness from a clip. (If you want to make a clip look like it was shot on a tripod, choose InertiaCam and move the Smoothing slider to 3.0.)

When using either Automatic or SmoothCam; see **FIGURE 8.15**:

- **Translation Smooth**. This reduces left/right, up/down instability. Drag the slider to 0 to turn this off. Larger numbers increase smoothing.
- **Rotation Smooth**. This reduces rotation around the lens axis. If the camera didn't rotate, drag the slider to 0 to turn this off. Larger numbers increase smoothing.
- **Scale Smooth**. This reduces instability during a zoom. If the camera did not zoom, drag the slider to 0 to turn this off. Larger numbers increase smoothing.

Most of the time, I increase Translation, while setting both Rotation and Zoom to 0. Your goal in adjusting this is to smooth shakiness, not remove it.

NOTE Image stabilization and rolling shutter correction work by zooming in to the image. The greater the correction, the greater the zoom. This zooming will slightly blur the image. Look for the best balance between image quality and stabilization.

FIGURE 8.15 Image Stabilization settings. Higher numbers increase stabilization. 0 turns that setting off.

GOING FURTHER Jerry Thompson, an editor who reviewed an early version of this book, adds: "If I have a lengthy clip that I plan on using in multiple portions of a project, I will use Open Clip to apply the stabilizer, or other effects as needed to the Browser clip. Stabilization can still be modified or disabled on a clip-by-clip basis in the timeline even though you added it in the Browser."

414 Rolling Shutter Correction

Some DSLR cameras create artifacts when panning or tilting.

Because of the way some cameras (especially DSLR) record images from the camera sensor, when you do a fast move—vertical or horizontal—straight edges lean. A lot. Rolling Shutter correction fixes this; see **FIGURE 8.16**.

1. Cut the timeline clip so that the fast move section is isolated into its own clip (this speeds analysis).

2. Select the timeline clip.

3. Enable Rolling Shutter.

FIGURE 8.16 Enable Rolling Shutter correction. Leave Amount set to Medium.

The computer analyzes the movement in the clip, then fixes it. The speed of analysis depends upon the speed of the CPU and the duration of the clip. The Medium setting is a good setting to start. Pick the setting where straight edges no longer lean.

415 Rate Conform Sets How Frame Rates Are Converted

Frame rate conversion is automatic when frame rates don't match.

When the frame rate of a clip doesn't match the project, the Rate Conform settings determine how the frame rate of the clip is converted. The Rate Conform setting (see **FIGURE 8.17**) appears only when the frame rate of a timeline clip doesn't match the project frame rate. Apple's Help files state:

- **Floor**: The default setting. Final Cut Pro rounds down to the nearest integer during its calculation to match the clip's frame rate to the project's frame rate.

- **Nearest Neighbor**: Final Cut Pro rounds to the nearest integer during its calculation to match the clip's frame rate to the project's frame rate. This setting reduces artifacts at the expense of visual stuttering. Rendering is required.

- **Frame Blending**: Creates in-between frames by blending individual pixels of neighboring frames. Slow-motion clips created with Frame Blending appear to play back more smoothly than those created with the Floor or Nearest Neighbor setting. This setting provides better reduction of visual stuttering, but you may see some visual artifacts. Rendering is required.

- **Optical Flow**: A type of frame blending that uses an optical flow algorithm to create new in-between frames. Final Cut Pro analyzes the clip to determine the directional movement of pixels, then draws portions of the new frames based on the optical flow analysis. This setting

Final Cut does not alert you if frame rates don't match. It just fixes them.

NOTE Once one or more clips are edited into a project, the project frame rate cannot be changed. If conforming is needed, clips are changed not the project.

usually provides the greatest reduction in visual stuttering and artifacts. Rendering is required and takes longer than for the other frame-sampling methods.

FIGURE 8.17 This conforms the frame rate of a clip to match the frame rate of the project.

GOING FURTHER Cut a clip to create a small section where something in the frame is moving, then apply each of these settings to see what looks best. Testing a small section saves time rendering. In general, I have not found Optical Flow to be worth the time it takes to calculate and render.

TRANSFORM EFFECTS

Of all the effects in Final Cut Pro, these are the ones you'll use the most.

416 The Transform Settings

These are, without doubt, the most used effects settings.

The Transform settings in the Video Inspector control image position, rotation, scale (image size), and anchor point. (The anchor point is that location in an image around which the image rotates or scales.) By default, an image is displayed full screen, centered, and unrotated.

- To enable/disable the Transform settings, select the checkbox; see **FIGURE 8.18.**
- To show or hide the contents of the Transform category, click Hide/Show (left red arrow).
- To change a setting, enter a number.

  Or—drag over a number, without first selecting the number.

  Or—select the number, then change values by rolling the scroll wheel.

  Or—use the onscreen controls; see Tip 418, *Enable Onscreen Viewer Controls.*

- To enable the onscreen controls, click the square icon to the right of Transform. When this icon is blue, onscreen controls are enabled.

- To reset any parameter, click the chevron menu (right red arrow) to the right of the parameter name and choose Reset Parameter. (For example, Position is a parameter.)

FIGURE 8.18 The Transform settings in their default state.

GOING FURTHER Deselecting a settings checkbox turns off the effect without resetting any values. This provides a fast way to compare before and after. Resetting an effect resets all settings to their defaults and deletes all keyframes. Undo can bring them back.

417 Create a Picture-in-Picture Effect

The Transform settings are essential to displaying multiple images.

A picture-in-picture effect displays two or more images at the same time. To create the effect (see **FIGURE 8.19**):

1. Stack the timeline clips you want to see at the same time. (To see more than one image, you need to stack clips vertically on more than one layer.)

2. Select the top clip.

3. Enable Transform (if it isn't already) then, change Scale to 50%, or some number less than 100.

   Or—drag, without selecting, the numbers for Position(X) to change the horizontal position. Dragging is much faster than entering specific numbers.

   Or—drag, without selecting, the numbers for Position(Y) to change the vertical position.

4. Repeat for as many clips you have stacked.

   There is no limit to the number of images you can have onscreen at one time.

Changing Transform settings modifies the frame containing the clip.

FIGURE 8.19 Typical settings for a picture-in-picture effect. Notice both Position and Scale settings were changed.

However, while this works, it's time-consuming. Tip 418, *Enable Onscreen Viewer Controls*, shows a faster way to create this.

NOTE All clips that have effects applied, such as Transform settings, need to render.

GOING FURTHER Tom Cherry, an editor who reviewed an early copy of this book, adds: "When I do a multiple picture-in-picture, I stack all the clips in the timeline, select them all, then scale them all at once. This saves time and ensures they are the same size. I can then position each one individually."

418 Enable Onscreen Viewer Controls

Adjust three key Video Inspector effects in the Viewer.

Most of the time when you want to make changes to a clip or effect, you use the Video Inspector. But there's a faster way if all you want to change is a Transform, Crop, or Distort setting. In the Video Inspector, click one of the icons indicated in **FIGURE 8.20**.

Or, tucked into the lower-left corner of the Viewer are the icon and menu shown in **FIGURE 8.21**. They match the icons for Transform, Crop, and Distort in the Video Inspector. The menu changes the icon displayed on the left. Most often, you'll use Transform. Click the icon to enable the onscreen controls.

FIGURE 8.20 Click one of these three icons to enable the onscreen Viewer controls. (Blue means active.)

FIGURE 8.21 Click the icon on the left to display onscreen controls. Click the chevron to change the icon selection.

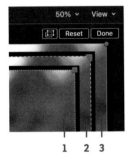

FIGURE 8.22 The lines and shape of the control dots vary. Controls for 1. Distort, 2. Trim/Crop, 3. Transform. The image box icon is to the left of the Reset button.

When you click an icon, new controls appear in the Viewer:

- **Keyframe controls** (top left). Create keyframes or navigate to the previous or next keyframe.
- **Image box** (nested boxes icon to the left of Reset). If an image is larger than the project frame size, this displays the portion of the image that's outside the frame. See **FIGURE 8.22**.
- **Reset**. This resets the setting to its default.
- **Done**. This accepts the changed settings.
- **Bounding box**. Drag a dot to change the shape. Drag the middle of the shape to change position. See Figure 8.22.

When using the Crop onscreen controls, an additional button at the bottom selects between Trim, Crop, or Ken Burns modes; see Tip 407, *Remove Pixels Using Crop or Trim*.

419 Two More Ways to Enable Onscreen Viewer Controls

Yes! It's time for another hidden menu.

Once a project is opened, the Viewer holds a hidden menu that you can find by right-clicking anywhere inside the Viewer; see **FIGURE 8.23**. This menu also enables quick selection of onscreen controls for the three key effects in the Video Inspector.

NOTE For some strange reason, this menu is not available if video scopes are active.

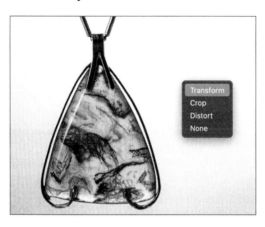

FIGURE 8.23 With a project open, right-click in the Viewer to enable onscreen controls. (Jewelry image ©2022 EmilyHewittPhotography.com)

Two keyboard shortcuts select these options even faster. (The Distort tool has a shortcut, but it isn't assigned to a key.)

- **Shift+T**. Display the Transform controls.
- **Shift+C**. Display the Crop controls.

420 Rotate a Clip in the Viewer

The Viewer is faster and easier than the Inspector.

To rotate a timeline clip, the Viewer is faster and easier than the Inspector.

1. Select the timeline clip you want to rotate.
2. Enable the Transform onscreen controls (shortcut: Shift+T).
3. Grab and drag the blue dot attached to the center white circle; see **FIGURE 8.24**.
   - Drag the dot out from the center to extend the line for greater precision.
   - Press Shift to constrain rotation to 45° increments.

FIGURE 8.24 Rotate a clip using the blue dot. Drag it out for more precision.

421 Two Quick Ways to Flip a Clip

The effect is faster; Transform settings provide more control.

There are two ways to flip a clip horizontally or vertically: using the Transform settings or using an effect. Start by selecting the timeline clip, or clips, you want to flip.

- **Video Inspector > Transform**:
    - To flip a clip horizontally, enter **-100** in Position (X).
    - To flip a clip vertically, enter **-100** in Position (Y).
- **Effects > Distortion > Flipped**:

    Apply the effect and choose the setting you need; see **FIGURE 8.25**.

FIGURE 8.25 Options for the Flipped effect.

422 Calculate Clip Positions

This coordinate system makes position changes easy.

All NLEs determine image position using pixel coordinates. Where those coordinates start is called the *0,0 position*. This is shorthand for Position (X) = 0 and Position (Y) = 0. Horizontal (X) is always listed first. For example, Adobe Premiere Pro puts 0,0 in the top-left corner of an image.

Final Cut sets the center of every clip (0,0) at the exact center of the project frame, also 0,0.

Final Cut sets the center of every clip (Position X,Y = 0,0) at the exact center of the project, which also uses 0,0. The significant benefit to this is that you can instantly center a clip, regardless of its size, by entering **0,0** in Video Inspector > Transform > Position.

Also by defining the center as 0,0, clip positions don't change when the project frame size changes. This is why switching between smaller resolution proxies and camera source files is so seamless—the image geometry doesn't change.

Final Cut's approach also makes the math of moving clips much easier, because when you move a clip, you are moving it from its center, not the upper-left corner. For example, let's say you are creating a "quad split," where four images are displayed on screen at the same time. Each image is scaled 50%, meaning that for a 1080p project, each scaled image is 960 x 540 pixels. Because images are positioned on their center, the middle of each image is half that: 480 x 270 pixels.

You can then quickly reposition the center of each image using the same two numbers, but changing the sign:

NOTE A positive X value moves right. A positive Y value moves up.

- **Top left**: −480, 270
- **Top right**: 480, 270
- **Bottom left**: −480, −270
- **Bottom right**: 480, −270

It may seem confusing at first, but once you learn this coordinate system, it will save hours aligning clips, because the only difference is the sign (positive or negative). The pixel values are the same.

GOING FURTHER

This positioning geometry also means that if an image is off-center, you can center it by entering 0,0 as the Position coordinates.

423 Change the Anchor Point

The anchor point determines where a clip scales or rotates.

By default, all clips rotate around their center; see Tip 420, *Rotate a Clip in the Viewer*. That's a true statement, but it isn't, ah, *completely* true. It is more accurate to say: "All clips scale and rotate around their anchor point." The anchor point location is adjusted in Video Inspector > Transform (see **FIGURE 8.26**), which by default is in the center of the frame (0,0).

FIGURE 8.26 Change anchor point values to change where a clip scales or rotates.

All clips scale and rotate around their anchor point— the white circle in the middle of an image.

The white circle in the Viewer represents the position of the anchor point. Although it would be helpful if there were an onscreen control that quickly relocated the anchor point, there isn't. However, it isn't hard to move the anchor point, and in doing so, you'll discover more subtle ways to zoom and rotate an image. Click and drag either of the position values for the anchor point to change its location. As you do, the image in the Viewer changes position.

Sometimes, simply dragging the position values are enough. Other times, you want to move the anchor point to a corner or the middle of a side. To do this, remember that the center of an image is its 0,0 point. So if you want to move the anchor point to a corner, enter half the horizontal and vertical dimensions of a clip. The image in Figure 8.26 is 3840 x 2160 pixels, so each corner is at half that distance, or 1920 x 1080. To move the anchor point to different corners, change the sign for these values from positive to negative.

424 Copy Effects to Multiple Clips

Effects can be copied as a group or individually.

Many times, I need the same effect (audio or video) applied to more than one clip. Final Cut has two menus that make this easy.

FIGURE 8.27 The Edit > Paste Attributes window. Blue checkboxes indicate active effects in a copied clip.

1. Start by selecting a timeline clip with the effects you want to copy, then choose Edit > Copy (shortcut: Cmd+C).

2. Choose one of two options.

   • **Edit > Paste Effects**. This pastes all copied effects into the selected clip, or group of clips (shortcut: Option+Cmd+V).

   • **Edit > Paste Attributes**. This displays all copied effects so you can decide which you want to apply to the selected clip, or clips. Deselect those you don't want to apply (shortcut: Shift+Cmd+V); see **FIGURE 8.27**.

   I use these two techniques to quickly apply effects such as blurs, color correction, or image size to a group of selected clips.

425 Remove Effects from One or More Clips

Effects can be removed as a group or individually.

Once effects are applied to a clip, or a group of clips, there are three ways to remove them.

1. Select the timeline clip.

2. Go to the Video Inspector and delete, or reset, any effects you don't want.

   Or—choose Edit > Remove Effects to remove all effects applied to the selected clips.

   Or—choose Edit > Remove Attributes to display a list of all effects applied to the selected clips; see **FIGURE 8.28**. Choose the attributes you want to remove.

If I have to modify only a single clip, I generally use the Video Inspector.

If I have to modify a group of clips, I generally use Remove Attributes.

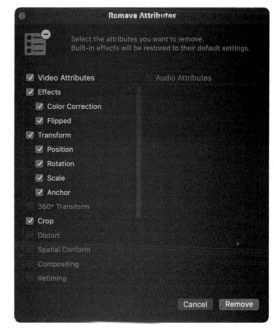

FIGURE 8.28 The Edit > Remove Attributes menu. Select the effects you want to remove.

426 Apply Video Keyframes

Use keyframes to animate a picture-in-picture effect.

Keyframes create animation. In fact, keyframes are used just about everywhere in Final Cut. Here's a simple example to show how they work. Let's create a picture-in-picture effect where the top video flies back from full screen into the top-right corner, keeping the Action Safe area in mind; see Tip 103, *Display Action Safe and Title Safe Zones*.

1. Stack two clips in the timeline and select the top clip.

2. Put the timeline playhead (skimmer) where you want the animation to start.

3. Choose Video Inspector > Transform and click the gray diamond next to Position to set a starting keyframe; see **FIGURE 8.29**.

   Keyframes are set at the position of the playhead (skimmer).

Keyframes create animation.

FIGURE 8.29 Key-
frames are set at
the position of the
playhead (skimmer).
Click a gray diamond
to set a keyframe for
that parameter. Gold
means a keyframe
exists at that frame.

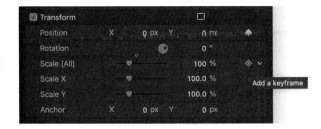

4. Set a second keyframe for scale.

5. Move the playhead to where you want the animation to end.

NOTE Once you set a
keyframe for a parameter,
any additional changes
to that parameter will
automatically create new
keyframes at the position
of the playhead (skimmer).

6. With the top clip still selected, enable the onscreen Transform controls; see Tip 418, *Enable Onscreen Viewer Controls*.

7. Using the onscreen controls, change the size and position of the top clip as you want; see **FIGURE 8.30**. Final Cut automatically sets new keyframes for whatever you changed.

   Notice that I aligned it with the Action Safe area. Staying at or inside Action Safe is a good idea to follow for all composited images, graphics, logos, and titles.

8. When you are happy with the position, click Done in the top-right corner.

   Final Cut will render the effect, then sit back and admire your work!

FIGURE 8.30 Use the onscreen controls to size and position an image. When finished, click Done in the top-right corner.

In the Video Inspector, new controls are now available; see **FIGURE 8.31**.

- To move to the previous keyframe, click the left arrow (left red arrow).
- To move to the next keyframe, click the right arrow (right red arrow).
- To delete a keyframe, use the left/right arrows to move the playhead to the keyframe you want to remove, then click the gold diamond for the setting you want to reset.
- To remove all keyframes for a specific parameter, for example Position, click the chevron for that parameter and choose Reset Parameter; see Tip 416: *The Transform Settings.*
- To remove all keyframes and reset the Transform effect settings, click the chevron next to Transform and choose Reset Parameter.

These keyframe techniques are used throughout Final Cut.

Once a parameter keyframe is set, changing that parameter sets a new keyframe at the position of the playhead.

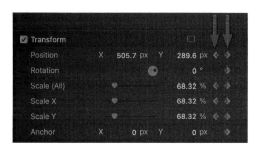

FIGURE 8.31 Click the left/right arrows to move to the previous/ next keyframe. Click the chevron (not shown) on the right to delete all keyframes for that parameter.

> **GOING FURTHER** The easiest way to create an effect using keyframes is to work backward. Create the finished effect first. Then, use keyframes to mark the settings for the finished effect. Next, go back to where you want the effect to start and set keyframes for the opening position. Most of the time, that simply means resetting values to their defaults. The Video Animation bar (see Tip 434, *The Video Animation Bar*) is an easy way to drag keyframes.

④27 What's a Motion Path?

This illustrates the position changes of a clip using keyframes.

Take a look at Figure 8.30. See that red line near the center? That's a motion path. A *motion path* shows the movement of the center of a clip based upon Position keyframes applied to the clip. Motion paths can be straight or curved and can contain as many keyframes as needed. Motion paths are visible only in the Viewer, and they never export.

428 Add or Modify a Motion Path

Once a motion path is created, it can be modified.

Most motion paths created by Final Cut are straight lines with two points: the beginning and the end. However, once that line is created, there are many things you can do with it. The red line (see **FIGURE 8.32**) represents the position of the center of the clip for the duration of the clip. When you add a keyframe, you are not only specifying *where* the clip will be but *when*.

- To add a keyframe, either Option-click or double-click the red line. Remember the line represents "position in time."
- To move a keyframe, drag it.
- To delete a keyframe, right-click it and select Delete Point.
- To temporarily suspend a keyframe, right-click it and select Disable Point.

Tip 429, *Keyframe Variations*, describes more options for individual keyframes.

FIGURE 8.32 The red line, called the *motion path*, represents the movement of the center of a clip over time. The white lines, called *control handles*, determine the shape of the curve.

429 Keyframe Variations

Keyframes can be straight, curved, locked, or disabled.

Final Cut creates motion paths using keyframes as corners. This means that when the center of an image reaches the keyframe, it makes a sharp turn. However, right-click a keyframe to reveal a variety of options; see **FIGURE 8.33**. Keyframes determine the shape of the path and acceleration. Keyframes are adjusted using white bars and dots called *control handles*.

- **Linear.** Converts a motion path into a corner at the position of the keyframe.

- **Smooth.** Converts a motion path into a curve at the position of the keyframe.
- **Delete Point.** Surprise! This deletes the keyframe.
- **Lock Point.** This locks the keyframe to prevent changes, like accidentally moving it.
- **Disable Point.** This retains all keyframe settings but turns the keyframe off.

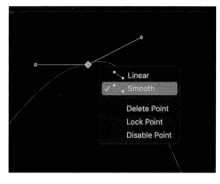

When a keyframe is clicked, two white Bezier control handles appear with white control dots at the end of each line. Drag these to change the shape of the curve. The left handle affects the curve on the left, while the right handle affects the curve on the right, of the keyframe. They normally work in sync.

FIGURE 8.33 Right-click a keyframe to reveal these options.

- To disconnect the two handles, right-click a control dot and choose Break Handles.
- To constrain dragging the control points in 45° angles, Shift-drag.
- To drag one handle without moving the other, Option-drag.
- To constrain and drag one handle, Shift+Option-drag.
- To relink two disconnected handles, right-click a control dot and choose Align Handles.

Adjusting keyframe control handles creates a variety of curves, acceleration, and shapes.

430 Modify Clips in Drop Zones

A drop zone is a customizable clip placeholder.

Some generators and many Motion effects contain drop zones. A drop zone is a placeholder in an effect or generator template to which you can add a clip to customize the look of the template.

1. Select the timeline clip containing the drop zone effect to display clip options in the Video Inspector; see **FIGURE 8.34**.
2. Click a box with a down arrow to select that drop zone.
3. Navigate to the Browser or timeline and click a clip to insert it into the placeholder.

FIGURE 8.34 A drop zone is a placeholder for a clip. Click an arrow to fill that zone.

Here's the cool part: When you add a video clip to a drop zone, where you click the skimmer (shortcut: S) in the clip determines the In of the video. In the past, Final Cut would use the actual start of the video clip. Now, the Skimmer location sets the In. This makes using existing clips for drop zones far more useful.

431 Reframe Clips in a Drop Zone

If you don't like the framing in the drop zone, you can change it.

To reframe a clip in a drop zone, double-click the image in the Viewer.

I like drop zones. They allow me to create animated backgrounds in Motion, then customize them using clips in the Final Cut project. However, what I didn't like was being locked into specific clip framing when it was added to a drop zone. Recently, I learned a fast and simple way to reframe a clip inside a drop zone:

1. Double-click the image in the Viewer. (See **FIGURE 8.35**.)
2. Drag left or right to reframe the image (lower red arrow).
3. Drag a blue dot (upper red arrow) to scale.
4. Click anywhere in the timeline to exit the reframing mode.

This makes modifying video inside a drop zone much more flexible!

FIGURE 8.35 Double-click the image in a drop zone to access it. Drag left/right to reframe. Drag a blue dot (left red arrow) to scale.

432 Be Careful Moving a Generator

Where you make the adjustment makes a difference.

When editing my weekly webinars, I frequently animate an arrow shape. The arrow is a generator. (Choose Generators > Elements > Shapes, then change the Shape menu to Arrow.) However, if I scale or move it incorrectly, the arrow disappears as I drag it around the frame.

When you add generator shapes to a project, use the Generator Inspector to set the shape, colors, and shadows, but *don't* change the Center setting; see **FIGURE 8.36**. Instead, go to the Video Inspector and adjust Scale and Rotation to the size and orientation you need.

Then, using Video Inspector > Transform > Position, or the onscreen Transform controls, change the onscreen position of the generator. Why? Because when you scaled the generator, you actually scaled the *frame* that contains it. The Transform controls move the frame, while the Generator Center controls move the shape inside the frame.

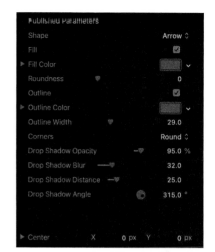

FIGURE 8.36 When adding a generator shape, set the look in the Generator Inspector, but set the scale, rotation, and position in the Video Inspector > Transform dialog.

433 What Does "Analysis" Mean?

Analysis is key to many Final Cut Pro effects.

Analyzing a clip confuses many editors. What Final Cut is doing is looking at the contents of a clip to best determine how to apply a specific effect. This includes:

- Spatial conform
- Image stabilization
- Rolling shutter correction
- Balance color
- Object tracking
- Find People during import
- And many others

Here's what is going on behind the scenes:

- All analysis happens in the background.
- Most clips are analyzed only once. Since the contents of a clip don't change, those analysis files can be referenced again in the future.
- Analysis files are stored in the library, not attached to the clip.
- The speed of analysis depends upon the duration of the clip and the speed of your CPU. Analysis can take from real time to ten times the duration of the analyzed clip, depending upon the analysis itself.
- If you analyze a clip during import or when located in the Browser, the entire clip is analyzed.
- If you analyze a clip edited into the timeline, only that portion of the clip from the In to the Out is analyzed.
- To save time, if you need to analyze only a portion of a clip, cut it in the timeline so that only the analysis region is selected.
- If you need to analyze multiple segments of the same clip, it may be easier to open the clip in the timeline (choose Clip > Open Clip) and analyze the entire clip than to analyze individual segments.

- Analysis files are kept in the Library. Depending upon what's being analyzed, analysis files can be quite large.

- Analysis files can be discarded once a project is complete. If FCP needs them again, it will reanalyze the clip.

434 The Video Animation Bar

Quickly create, modify, or reposition keyframes.

The Video Animation bar (shortcut: Control+V), also called the *Video Animation editor*, is an extension of the controls in the Video Inspector.

Just as audio clips have the Audio Animation bar, video clips have the Video Animation bar (shortcut: Control+V). Here you can set keyframes for automating changes in opacity, cropping, distortion, and position directly in the timeline. Probably the most helpful aspect of this bar is dragging keyframes to reposition them in time.

The Video Animation bar simplifies repositioning keyframes in time.

To apply a video effect to a clip, for example, Effects browser > Blur > Gaussian Blur:

1. Apply the effect to a timeline clip; see Tip 438, *The Effects Browser.*

2. Select the timeline clip and choose Clip > Video Animation (shortcut: Control+V).

   Or—right-click the clip and select Show Video Animation.

3. Click the small disclosure icon in the top-right corner for the effect you want to adjust.

   - To set keyframes manually, use the Range tool (shortcut: R) to select a keyframe range, or Option-click; see **FIGURE 8.37**.

   - To change the effect, drag the horizontal setting line up or down. This automatically creates keyframes.

   - To fade the effect in/out at the end of the clip, drag either of the two fade dots in the top-left/right corners. (These work similar to audio fade dots; see Tip 311, *Apply an Audio Transition Manually.*)

   - To vertically expand or shrink an effect in the Video Animation bar, double-click the effect in the Video Animation bar.

   - To hide the Video Animation bar, choose Clip > Video Animation, or press Control+V, again.

   - To adjust keyframes, use the Video Animation bar or the Video Inspector. It is easier to drag keyframes in the Video Animation bar than to reposition them in the Video Inspector.

GOING FURTHER
The Video Animation bar, similar to the Retime Editor and Audio Animation bar, simplifies changing parameters applied to a clip.

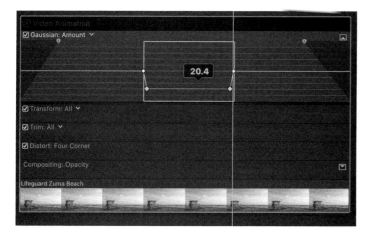

FIGURE 0.37 The Video Animation bar with keyframes applied to a range within the clip and fade dots adjusted at the top corners.

435 Use the Video Animation Bar to Adjust Opacity

The Video Animation bar has many uses.

To adjust clip opacity in the timeline, open the Video Animation bar; see Tip 434, *The Video Animation Bar*.

1. Select a timeline clip.

2. Press Control+V to display the Video Animation bar; see **FIGURE 8.38**.

3. Click the disclosure triangle on the right edge for Opacity. This expands the keyframe section.

   Option-click the light blue line to set a keyframe. (Right-click and select Delete Keyframe to remove a keyframe.)

   Drag a keyframe down to reduce opacity. Drag up to increase opacity.

   Drag a keyframe left/right to adjust timing.

NOTE You can also use the Range tool to set a keyframe range.

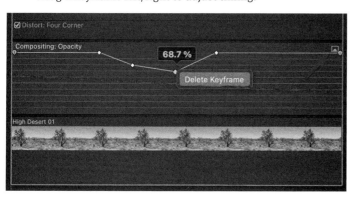

FIGURE 8.38 Adjust opacity in the timeline using the Video Animation bar. Right-click a keyframe and select Delete Keyframe to delete it.

VIEWER EFFECTS

There aren't a lot of effects that are created directly in the Viewer—aside from the onscreen controls provided by many effects. But there are a few you need to know about.

436 Change Default Keyframe Acceleration

Starting and ending motion path keyframes include acceleration.

When you first create a motion path, the starting and ending keyframes include acceleration. Specifically, the starting keyframe slowly speeds up after the start, then slows down close to the end of a motion path. Most of the time, that's OK. Here's how to change it when it isn't:

- Right-click the starting or ending keyframe in the Viewer to reveal the Bezier control handle and control dot; see **FIGURE 8.39**.
- Drag the control dot to change the straight line into a curve.
- Drag the control dot to or from the keyframe to change the acceleration.
- Right-click the starting or ending keyframe and select Linear to disable all acceleration and curves.

FIGURE 8.39 Right-click the starting or ending keyframe of a motion path to reveal the control handle. Drag the control dot (red arrow) to alter the acceleration or change the shape of the motion path.

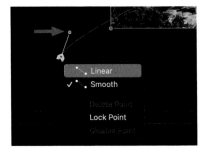

437 Create or Navigate Keyframes in the Viewer

You don't need to use the Video Inspector to navigate keyframes.

Keyframes are so important to animation that Apple made it easy to move from one to another, not just in the Video Inspector but in the Viewer.

Enable the onscreen Transform controls in the Viewer. This displays the icons illustrated in **FIGURE 8.40**.

FIGURE 8.40 Keyframe navigation controls in the Viewer. (Left to right: Previous, Set, Next.)

- **Left arrow.** Move the playhead to the previous keyframe.
- **Right arrow.** Move the playhead to the next keyframe.

- **Center diamond**. Create a keyframe set (when it displays a plus). Remove a keyframe (when it displays an x). This is called the *Set Keyframe* button.

> **GOING FURTHER** Unlike creating a keyframe for a single parameter in the Video Inspector, clicking the Set Keyframe button in the Viewer creates keyframes for *every* parameter in the Transform menu or whichever onscreen controls are active. This has the potential to cause problems because a keyframe may be set for a parameter that you don't want to change. As always, to remove a keyframe, navigate to it using the left/right arrows and click the gold diamond for the parameter you want to reset.

THE EFFECTS BROWSER

The Effects browser contains hundreds of audio and video effects. This section is where all the really cool stuff lives. Although you'll use the Video Inspector settings more, you'll have more fun using the effects stored in here.

🔵438 The Effects Browser

Open the Effects browser, find an effect, and add it to a clip.

Both audio and video effects are stored in the Effects browser (shortcut: Cmd+5); see **FIGURE 8.41**. There are hundreds of them, with hundreds more available from dozens of developers and websites. They fall into two groups: Video and Audio, each of which is divided into categories.

- To toggle the browser open or closed, click its icon in the top-right corner of the timeline (upper-right red arrow), or press Cmd+5.
- To display effects optimized for 4K images, click the 4K checkbox (upper-left arrow).
- To hide the sidebar, click the icon in the lower left (lower-left arrow).
- To search for an effect by name, enter it into the search box (lower-right arrow).
- To narrow a search, select a category first.

FIGURE 8.41 The Effects browser.

NOTE A limitation to dragging an effect onto a clip is that it applies only to the clip it is dragged onto. Double-clicking applies an effect to all selected clips, even if they are not next to each other.

- To apply an effect, drag it on top of a timeline clip.
- To apply an effect to multiple clips at the same time, select the timeline clips, then double-click the effect.
- To close the Effects browser, click the icon in the top right (blue in the screen shot), or press Cmd+5.

GOING FURTHER The 4K checkbox appears only when you have a 4K or larger project open in the timeline.

439 Effects Are Adjusted in the Video Inspector

Each effect is different, but they have interface elements in common.

Clip Effects are individually enabled, modified, or disabled using the Video Inspector.

Once an effect is applied to a clip, select the timeline clip to adjust the effect. All effects applied to the selected clip appear in the Video Inspector (see **FIGURE 8.42**) in the order in which they were applied. The gold box indicates a selected effect.

- To reveal the settings inside an effect, click Show/Hide.
- To disable all effects applied to a clip, deselect the Effects checkbox. This does not affect Transform, Crop, or Distort settings.
- To disable a specific effect, without altering any settings, deselect the checkbox next to the effect name.
- To reset a parameter, as well as add or modify keyframes, click the chevron menu.
- To change the look of an effect, adjust settings.
- To delete an effect from a clip, click the effect name in the Video Inspector to display a gold box, then press Delete.

FIGURE 8.42 All effects use a similar interface for adjustments.

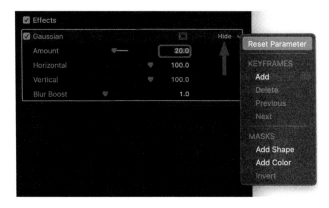

440 Preview an Effect

See an effect before you apply it to a clip.

Preview an effect to see how the effect changes as you adjust it.

1. Put the timeline playhead in the clip you are thinking to use for an effect.

2. Open the Effects browser (shortcut: Cmd+5).

3. Hover the cursor over the effect you want to preview (wait a second for FCP to load the effect).

   This shows the effect with its default settings applied to that clip.

4. Press Option and slowly drag the cursor through the effect.

   This shows the results of changing its principle parameter, for example, the amount of blur.

5. Double-click the effect to apply it to the selected clip(s), then adjust it in the Video Inspector.

Preview an effect by hovering the cursor over it in the Effects browser.

Although not all effects support dynamic preview using Option-drag, all of them support preview by hovering the cursor over the effect. Blurs are good to use for practice.

441 Apply Effects Faster

These techniques are all faster than dragging an effect onto a clip.

These options apply effects faster and work best when applying the same effect to multiple clips.

- Option 1

  1. Select one or more timeline clips.

  2. Find the effect you want in the Effects browser.

  3. Double-click the effect.

     This adds the effect but requires modifying each clip individually after the effect is applied.

- Option 2

  1. Select one timeline clip.

  2. Apply and modify all effects for that clip.

  3. Choose Edit > Copy (shortcut: Cmd+C).

  4. Select all other clips to which you want to apply the same effect then choose Edit > Paste Effects.

     This copies a fully modified effect to multiple clips. It takes longer to first modify the effects, but it is much faster when copying them.

Apply effects faster by selecting multiple clips, then apply the effect to all of them at once.

- Option 3
  1. Select one timeline clip.
  2. Apply and modify all effects for that clip.
  3. Choose Edit > Copy (shortcut: Cmd+C).
  4. Select all other clips to which you want to apply the same effect, and choose Edit > Paste Attributes.

     This is the same as Option 2, except now you can select which effects get applied to the other clips. This is useful when you want to add some, but not all, effects from a source clip.

442 The Timeline Index Finds Clips

Use the Timeline Index to select clips for you.

The Timeline Index (see Tip 233, *The Timeline Index*) can find and select clips that are not next to each other. The search feature is especially powerful if the clips you need have similar names but are not close together.

FIGURE 8.43 The power of the Timeline Index is its ability to search for and select clips that are not next to each other.

1. Edit clips into the timeline.
2. Open the Timeline Index (shortcut: Shift+Cmd+2); see FIGURE 8.43.
3. Click the Clips text button (top red arrow).
4. Click the Video text button (bottom red arrow).
5. To select a single clip, click the clip name.
6. To select a range of clips, click the first clip, then Shift-click the last.
7. To select clips scattered across the timeline, click the first clip, then Command-click the remaining clips.
8. Search for clips with similar names to select all of them.

   All clips selected in the Timeline Index are also selected in the timeline.
9. To apply an effect to all selected clips, double-click the effect in the Effects browser.

GOING FURTHER A limitation to dragging an effect onto a clip is that it applies only to the clip it is dragged onto. Double-clicking applies an effect to all selected clips, even if they are not next to each other.

443 Remove Effects vs. Remove Attributes

Quickly remove effects from one or more clips.

You can remove all effects applied to a clip, or just a few, while keeping the effects you want.

- To remove one effect from one clip, select the timeline clip, then delete the effect in the Video Inspector.
- To remove all effects from one or more clips, select the timeline clip(s), then choose Edit > Remove Effects. This deletes all effects from all selected clips at once.
- To remove a selection of effects from one or more clip(s), select the timeline clip(s), then choose Edit > Remove Attributes. Deselect any effects that you *don't* want to delete.

444 Effects Stacking Changes Results

Effects are processed from top to bottom in the Video Inspector.

Effects process from the top to the bottom of the Video Inspector. To change the stacking order, drag the center of an effect up or down in the Video Inspector. For example, using the order displayed in **FIGURE 8.44**, the image is first converted to black-and-white, then a color border is added, and finally the entire image, including the border, is blurred.

If the clips were stacked in the reverse order (by dragging them in the Video Inspector), the results would be different. First the clip would be blurred, then a color border that retains its sharp edges is applied, then all the color is removed from both image and border.

You can test this for yourself, as all these effects are shipped with Final Cut Pro.

FIGURE 8.44 The stacking order of effects makes a difference. Effects process from top to bottom in the Video Inspector.

445 Create a Default Video Effect

The Color Board is the default video effect.

If you find yourself using the same video effect a lot, make it the default. Then, you can apply it to any selected clip, or group of clips, with a single keyboard shortcut.

Apply the default video effect using Option+E.

Right-click the effect and choose Make Default Video Effect; see **FIGURE 8.45**.

- To apply the default video effect, press Option+E.
- To remove a default effect, just as with any effect, delete it in the Video Inspector.

FIGURE 8.45 Right-click a video effect to set it as the default effect.

⑤ Some Effects Require Compound Clips

Some effects are impossible to create in the Video Inspector alone.

Here's a challenge. Create a video clip that's blurred, scaled to 50%, and has blurry edges. Don't worry, I'll wait....

Yup, it can't be done. Why? Because Effects browser effects process *before* Transform effects. Since the blur is applied before scaling, there's no way to blur the edge of a clip after it is scaled, that is, unless you use a compound clip.

1. Select a timeline clip, and scale it to 50% using the Transform settings.
2. Convert the clip into a compound clip (shortcut: Option+G).
3. Apply Gaussian Blur to the compound clip.

   Ta-dah! A small, blurry clip; see **FIGURE 8.46**.

FIGURE 8.46 The only way to create a blurry clip with soft edges is to use a compound clip.

447 How to Remove Custom Plugins from Final Cut

Custom plugins can be removed. Apple plugins can't.

Plugins are useful tools from developers that customize our editing system for the work we need to get done. But what happens if you need to delete a plugin because you no longer need it, because it keeps crashing your system, or because it's out of date? There are two general options to remove plugins:

- If the plugin was installed into its own folder in the Applications folder, look there to see if there's an Uninstall option. Many stand-alone programs provide this.

- FXFactory, and other plugin integrators, often provide an Uninstall option. For example, to remove an FXFactory plugin from your NLE, but not from your hard disk, open FXFactory, click the Installed button at the top, select the plugin, and deselect Load on this system from the menu on the left.

  If neither of these first two options works, go to [User Home Directory] > Movies > Motion Templates. Inside you'll find different folders for different categories of effects; see FIGURE 8.47.

  Inside each folder, you'll find a folder containing any custom effects that you created in Motion, as well as folders from other FCP vendors.

FIGURE 8.47 Most third-party Motion templates are stored in [User Home Directory] > Motion > Motion Templates. To delete an effect, delete the folder that contains it.

- To remove an effect, make sure Final Cut is *not* running, then drag the effect *folder* out of the Templates folder. This uninstalls it without deleting it. I often keep seldom-used templates in a separate folder on my system, ready to drag back into the Motion Templates folder when needed.

- To permanently remove a plugin, drag it to the Trash.

Apple plugins are stored in a different location and can't be removed.

EFFECTS COOKBOOK

This section provides examples on how to create a variety of common effects.

448 Gaussian Blur Effect

Let me not blur the issue.

Although FCP has seven different blurs, the best general-purpose blur is Gaussian. This provides smooth, consistent results.

NOTE For simplicity, instead of writing Effects browser > [name of effect], going forward I'll shorten this to Effects > [name of effect]

To apply the effect:

1. Go to the Effects browser > Blur and drag Gaussian on top of a timeline clip.

   Or—double-click Gaussian to apply it to all selected clips.

2. With the timeline clip still selected, go to the Video Inspector and adjust the Amount. I generally like around 25.

3. To remove the effect, select the timeline clip, then delete the effect in the Video Inspector.

449 Use Pixelization to Hide Identities

Blurs are too easy to remove using software.

If you need to hide someone's identity, blurs are no longer the tool of choice. Recent software development has created several tools that reconstitute hidden faces using blurs. Two more effective techniques are silhouette lighting (which is created during production) or pixelization using large blocks; see **FIGURE 8.48**. (Pixel blocks should be large because a face hidden by small blocks becomes easier to recognize as the image size is reduced.)

Use big blocks to hide faces. Otherwise, if you shrink the image size, the face becomes recognizable again.

1. Apply Effects > Stylize > Pixellate to the clip you want to mask.

2. Add a Shape mask (see Tip 457, *Use Shape Masks*) to cover the face or object you want to hide. This mask should be larger than the object you are hiding.

FIGURE 8.48 A face hidden by pixels.

3. In the Video Inspector, increase the Amount to at least 40 to make the pixels big enough to obscure the face so that reducing the image size does not reveal the face again. **FIGURE 8.49** shows the settings I used here. Blocky is better!

FIGURE 8.49 These are the settings I used to create Figure 8.48.

450 Color Look Effects

Use these to quickly change the look of a clip.

Looks are a quick way to apply color grading to your clip without under-standing anything about color. Even more helpful, there's very little to adjust. If you don't like the effect, delete it and try something different.

1. Select the timeline clip to which you want to apply the effect.
2. Go to Effects > Looks and double-click a look you like.
3. Select the timeline clip and go to the Video Inspector. Use the Amount slider to vary the intensity of the effect; see **FIGURE 8.50**.
4. To remove the look, select its name in the Video Inspector to put a gold box around the effect, then delete it.

Previewing effects is especially helpful when applying Looks. See Tip 440, Preview an Effect.

☑ Cold Steel				
Amount		100.0	◈	⌄
Protect Skin		0		
Shadows		0.76		

FIGURE 8.50 Vary the intensity of any Look effect using the Amount slider.

451 Pick the Right Black & White Look

Be careful—one looks much better than the other.

Removing color from an image is called *desaturation*. It is a common effect. However, although it seems like two different effects do the same thing, one is definitely superior. Let me illustrate.

Select a timeline clip and apply Effects > Looks > 50s TV. The image becomes black-and-white. However, if you look at it on the video scopes (see the left side of **FIGURE 8.51**), you'll see that the highlights are heavily crushed (the bright flat line at the top) and reduced. Also, both shadow and midtone levels are elevated. This look severely distorts the image. That may be what you want, but it isn't a good image.

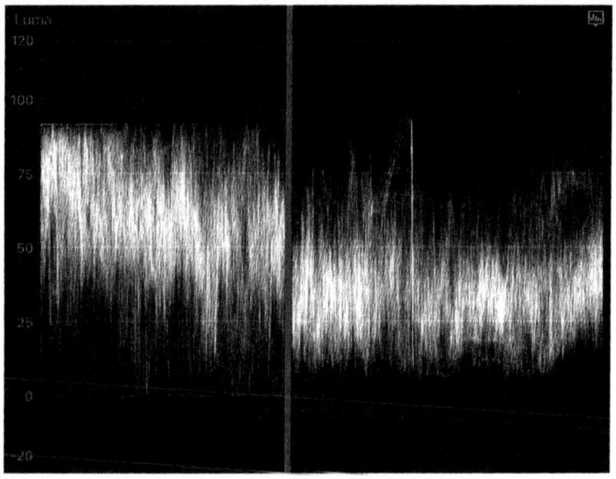

Instead, apply Effects > Color > Black & White. Notice the difference in the scope. There's no crushing. The grayscale values of the clip are not distorted.

FIGURE 8.51 (Left) 50s TV. Whites are crushed at the top, and shadows and mids are elevated at the bottom. (Right) Black & White. Levels are not crushed, and all grayscale values display properly.

This is easy to test for yourself using your own media. The reason I mention this effect is because the 50s TV effect is at the top of the Effects browser and it is easy to choose by mistake.

452 Create a Better Sepia Effect

Sepia does not turn a clip brown; it turns shadows brown.

The sepia effect is used to create an aged, or "old-time," effect, both effective and popular. However, don't just drag the Sepia look onto a clip and call it done. It won't look right. The reason is that the underlying colors in a clip are not removed, just "browned"; see FIGURE 8.52.

Here's a better—and still fast—way to create the sepia effect.

1. Select the timeline clip and apply Effects > Color > Black & White. Apply this first.
2. Then apply Effects > Color > Sepia.

FIGURE 8.52 This shot simply has Color > Sepia applied. The background color is still leaking through.

In this shot, the color was first removed using Black & White; then the Sepia effect was applied. Much more pleasing.

453 Reduce Video Noise

Video noise is common in low-light images.

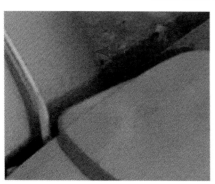

Video noise, or *dancing dust*, is a common problem with video shot in low-light conditions or with cameras using small-sensor devices, such as mobile devices or action cameras. It appears as small, dark, jiggling specks; see FIGURE 8.53. It is easiest to see in areas where the image is mostly one color and texture. Fortunately, Final Cut has a noise reduction filter that can remove this.

1. Select the timeline clip.
2. Choose Effects > Basics > Noise Reduction.

Final Cut analyzes the clip to determine what noise should be removed.

FIGURE 8.53 Video noise appears as grain, or dancing dark dust in the image.

3. Adjust the Amount setting to vary the amount of noise reduction. Adjust the Sharpness setting to increase or decrease edge detail.

   In many cases, the default effect settings are fine.

4. Toggle the effect off and on to compare the difference.

GOING FURTHER
The best way to evaluate noise reduction during playback is viewing the clip at 100% in the Viewer with View > Better Quality enabled.

454 Reduce Light Flickers

This is a free and simple DIY technique.

Flickering lights can be caused by a voltage drop going to the light, or a mismatch between household current and the shutter speed of the camera. Here's a quick way to help reduce it:

1. Duplicate the clip, and place the duplicate on top of the original.

2. Move the entire duplicate clip 1 frame forward, and reduce its opacity to 50%.

   This can provide amazing results easily.

A plugin that provides more powerful help is Flicker Free from Digital Anarchy.

455 Add a Cast Shadow

Add cast shadows to video, generators, or text.

A cast shadow is a shadow that falls in front of, or behind, an object in the frame, with a distorted shape of the object itself. On a sunny day, your cast shadow is sitting there on the sidewalk, waiting for you to start walking.

Cast shadows require two layers: the background in the Primary Storyline and the object casting the shadow on a layer above it. In this example, I used Generators > Elements > Circle, then changed Type to a heart.

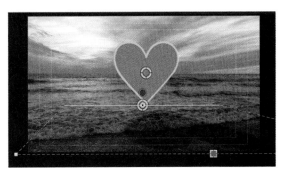

FIGURE 8.54 A Perspective Front cast shadow of the heart.

1. Select the timeline clip containing the object for which you want to create a shadow.

2. Choose Effects > Stylize > Drop Shadow.

3. Change Preset to Perspective Front; see **FIGURE 8.54**.

4. Adjust the onscreen controls to create the shadow shape you want, then adjust the settings in the Video Inspector to create the color, density, and softness you need; see **FIGURE 8.55**.

FIGURE 8.55 The drop shadow settings that created the shadow of the heart in Figure 8.54.

456 Create an Adjustment Layer

Adjustment layers, as with Photoshop, apply to all clips below them

NOTE For those without Motion, download an adjustment layer from Alex4D: blog.alex4d .com/2012/03/19/ adjustment-layer- fcpx-effect/

One of the missing features in Final Cut is an adjustment layer, similar in concept to those in Photoshop. An adjustment layer is a special kind of clip to which you can apply an effect, which then applies to all the clips below it. It can assume any frame size, frame rate, or duration.

This feature doesn't exist in FCP, but you can create one in Apple Motion. (Apple Motion is sold separately by Apple.)

1. Open Motion and, in the Project Browser, select Final Cut Title.

   This automatically saves the effect for use in Final Cut. (See **FIGURE 8.56**.)

FIGURE 8.56 Select Final Cut Title, then set typical project parameters.

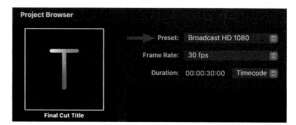

2. Set the Motion presets in the top-right corner to match a typical video project for frame size, frame rate, and duration. (You can always change these later in Final Cut with no loss of quality.)

3. Click Open to open the template.

   Motion opens, displaying the standard title creation template.

4. If the Layers panel is hidden, open it (shortcut: Cmd+4), select the Type Text Here layer, and delete it.

   This is the *only* change you need to make; see **FIGURE 8.57**.

FIGURE 8.57 In the Layers panel, delete the Type Text Here layer.

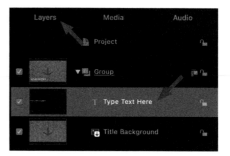

5. Choose File > Save As, then give the effect a name.

In **FIGURE 8.58**, I named it "Adjustment Layer" and stored it in a custom category named "Larry." You can name this effect anything and store it in any category you prefer. You can also create a new category from within the Category menu.

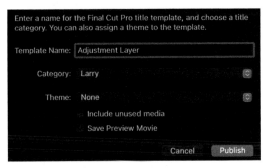

Enter a name for the Final Cut Pro title template, and choose a title category. You can also assign a theme to the template.

Template Name: Adjustment Layer

Category: Larry

Theme: None

Include unused media

Save Preview Movie

Cancel   Publish

FIGURE 8.58 Give this effect a name and pick a Title category to store it in.

6. Open Final Cut; then go to the Titles browser and select the category to store this effect.

The Adjustment Layer effect is visible in the icons on the right, generally near the top.

7. To put it to use, drag the adjustment layer above some timeline clips.

8. Choose Effects > Color > Black & White and watch what happens.

9. Toggle the adjustment layer on or off by selecting it and pressing V.

GOING FURTHER
I frequently add an adjustment layer that spans the duration of a project to apply the Broadcast Safe filter; see Tip 480, *Apply the Broadcast Safe Effect*. Or edit a project in color, then apply an adjustment layer to convert all the images to black-and-white.

MASKS & KEYS

Masks are a customizable way to select and modify a portion of the frame. Keys are used to superimpose one image (for example, an actor in front of a green screen) over a background.

457 Use Shape Masks

Shape masks are frequently used to blur backgrounds or logos.

A *mask* selects something inside the frame so you can do something with it. Every effect in Final Cut includes both a shape and color mask; see Tip 459, *Color Masks*. Shape masks select geometric areas within the frame and are the easiest to use. There's also a stand-alone Shape mask in Effects > Masks.

If you want to make a portion of the frame invisible, use the stand-alone Shape mask effect. If you want to limit an effect to a portion of the frame, use

Don't use a blur to hide a face; use pixelization (see Tip 449, Use Pixelization to Hide Identities).

the Shape mask built into that effect. All Shape masks work the same. Once a mask is applied, you can apply different settings to what's inside or outside the mask.

As an example, let's apply a blur to a portion of a clip.

1. Select the timeline clip containing something you want to blur.

2. Apply Effects > Blur > Gaussian.

3. Click the icon at the top of the effect in the Video Inspector (the red arrow in **FIGURE 8.59**), and add a Shape mask.

   The Shape mask appears in the viewer; see **FIGURE 8.60**.

   Drag the center white dot to change position.

   Drag the top white dot to morph between a circle to a square.

   Drag the dot at the end of the line to rotate the mask.

   Drag a green dot to change the size of the mask.

   Drag the outer red circle to change the amount of feathering.

   To blur areas outside the mask, select Invert Masks from the menu in Figure 8.59.

FIGURE 8.59 Click the mask icon (red arrow) at the top of all effects to choose which mask to apply.

FIGURE 8.60 Shape mask controls (red lines) with feathering and the *outside* of the mask blurred.

GOING FURTHER
You can add as many Shape masks to an image as you want. However, you can add only one color mask per clip. This technique is also frequently used to blur logos.

4. Once the mask is in place, adjust blur settings in the Video Inspector.

   Most of the time, I just change the Amount.

   To track a mask, see Tip 461, *Track an Effect with Object Tracking*.

   To delete a mask, click the chevron menu, and choose Delete Mask; see **FIGURE 8.61**.

FIGURE 8.61 To delete a mask, click the chevron menu next to the mask you want to delete and choose Delete Mask.

458 Draw Mask

A Draw mask creates a more complex Shape mask.

A more flexible mask than a Shape mask is a Draw mask, because you can draw whatever shape you need; see **FIGURE 8.62**.

1. Select the timeline clip, and choose Effects > Masks > Draw Mask.
2. Click in the Viewer to start drawing the mask shape.
3. Click, again, to set a corner point.

   Or—drag to create a curve.

   Or—right-click any control point to convert a corner to a curve.
4. Once the mask is drawn, select the timeline clip, and go to the Video Inspector.
5. Add feathering to soften the edge of the mask.
6. Click Invert to select everything *outside* the mask.

Experiment with other options to see what they do; however, I rarely adjust anything else.

A Shape mask is the easiest to use. A Draw mask is more flexible.

FIGURE 8.62 A Draw mask creates masks of any shape, with corners or curves, and feathering to soften edges. Right-click a control point to reveal this menu.

GOING FURTHER
Although the Draw mask creates more complex selections, it is not precise enough to support detailed rotoscoping.

459 Color Masks

A Color mask selects an object in the frame based on its color.

Every effect has the option to add Color or Shape masks; see Tip 457, *Use Shape Masks*. We use Color masks, for example, to change the color of a shirt or, in this example, some flowers.

Let's use a Color mask to alter specific colors in an image using the Color Wheels; see Tip 473, *Color Wheels*. **FIGURE 8.63** illustrates the source image.

FIGURE 8.63 This is the source image. I want to enhance the foreground flowers.

You can assign only one Color mask per effect.

Select the image to adjust and apply a Color Wheel effect. At the bottom of the Color Inspector are the Color Mask controls; see **FIGURE 8.64**.

1. Click the View Masks button, then adjust the sliders for Hue (H), Saturation (S), and Luminance (L) to isolate the color you want. Most of the time, I find myself turning one or more of these off.

2. Choose Mask > Inside, and adjust the Color Wheels to alter the selected image inside the mask, the light blue flowers.

3. Choose Mask > Outside, and adjust the Color Wheels to change everything outside the mask.

FIGURE 8.65 shows the Color Wheel settings for inside the mask. The flowers, luma, and saturation were boosted with added blue. Outside the mask, saturation and luma were decreased.

FIGURE 8.66 shows the finished result.

FIGURE 8.64 The Color Mask controls (above).

FIGURE 8.65 Color Wheel settings for inside the mask. Highlights and mids were shifted toward blue, with increased saturation in the mids and globally (right).

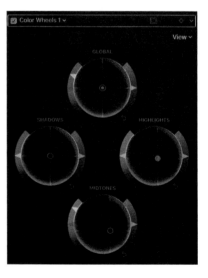

FIGURE 0.66 An enhanced image that instantly draws the eye to the saturated colors of the foreground flowers.

GOING FURTHER See Tip 471, *The Color Inspector*, to learn how to use the Color Inspector. See Tip 473, *Color Wheels*, to learn how to use the Color Wheels for color correction.

460 Fast Track an Object

Tracking moves a separate object in sync with a background element.

Final Cut has two types of object tracking: One moves an object, like text or a graphic; the other moves an effect based upon the movement of an object in the background clip. (Tip 461, *Track an Effect with Object Tracking*, discusses how to track an effect.)

NOTE You track an object in a background clip so that a foreground clip moves in sync with it. The foreground clip is stacked above the background clip in the timeline.

1. Put the playhead at the start of the timeline clip with the object you want to track. This also displays the clip in the Viewer.

2. Drag the object you want to add to the timeline (for example, a text clip) onto the Viewer and on top of the element you want to track; see **FIGURE 8.67**.

Final Cut highlights different elements in the Viewer that it can track. The tracking shape varies depending upon which background element you select.

Apple continues to make significant improvements in object tracking for speed and accuracy.

FIGURE 8.67 When an object is dragged into the Viewer, Final Cut creates a tracking Shape mask over the element you select.

NOTE Once the track is set, you can change the content, formatting, and position of the foreground text clip.

3. Adjust the shape by dragging the orange dots. It doesn't need to fit perfectly; see **FIGURE 8.68**.

4. Press the right arrows next to Analyze (red arrow). Be patient, because analysis can take a bit of time.

5. Play the timeline to see how accurately the track matches the movement of the background element. You should see the foreground object move in sync with the background element.

   If playback looks good, great. If not, read Tip 462, *Adjust an Object Track*, for suggestions on adjusting the track.

FIGURE 8.68 Adjust the orange dots of the tracking mask for a better fit. Click the right arrows (red arrow) to create the track. We are tracking a text clip (Title) to move as an actor moves.

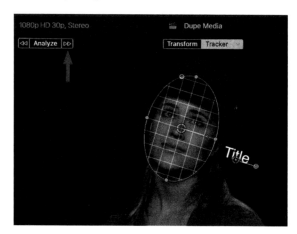

461 Track an Effect with Object Tracking

This moves an effect to follow an object moving in the frame.

An example of effect tracking is to spotlight someone moving in the frame, blur a logo, change the color of an element, and so on.

To track an effect, apply an effect to a timeline clip.

1. Add a Shape or Color mask from the top of the effect; see **FIGURE 8.69**.

FIGURE 8.69 Click this icon to add a Shape mask for an effect to the selected timeline clip.

2. In the Viewer, click the Tracker button in the top center; see **FIGURE 8.70.**

The object tracking grid appears in the Viewer; see **FIGURE 8.71.** (I dimmed the background to make the orange controls easier to see.)

FIGURE 8.70 Click Tracker to enable onscreen tracking controls.

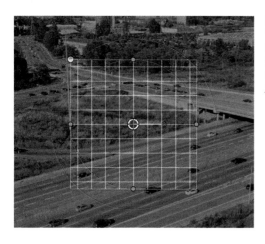

FIGURE 8.71 Tracking controls. The inner orange circle determines focus. The outer circle controls feathering. Size this to slightly larger than the object you want to track.

3. Put the playhead in the middle of the clip with the element you want to track.

I tend to have better results when I track from the middle of a shot than the start.

4. Drag an orange dot (which is sometimes colored blue) to size the inner circle to just encompass the object you want to track. (A red car, in this example.)

- Press Shift while dragging to constrain the circle.
- Press Option while dragging to move just one dot.
- Drag the center of the circle to reposition it.

5. When the mask is sized and positioned, click the right-pointing arrows next to Analyze; see Figure 8.70. Final Cut analyzes the contents of the clip and moves the mask as the tracked element moves. When FCP is done, it repositions the playhead back to where it started in the middle of the clip.

6. Click the left-pointing arrows to track from the middle of the clip back to the beginning.

The state-of-the-art software for motion tracking on the Mac is Mocha Pro, from BorisFX.

7. When the track is done, play the clip to make sure there are no problems. If there are, see Tip 462, *Adjust an Object Track*. If not, adjust the size and position of the effect to create the results you want.

GOING FURTHER Setting the right size for the tracker is important. Don't make it too small or too big. Look for objects with clearly recognizable edges. Good contrast improves the track. Once the track is created, you can resize the shape to create the effect you need. Feathering affects the effect, not the track.

462 Adjust an Object Track

The Tracker controls are at the bottom of the Video Inspector.

NOTE Remember, tracks are always applied to elements in the background clip. Trackers are adjusted in the Video Inspector by first selecting the background clip.

Once you create an object track, you adjust it in the Video Inspector. The biggest potential problems are finding the optimal size for the Tracker and finding an object with clearly defined edges. Clean edges are important because that's what FCP uses to create the object track. However, sometimes the tracking does not go well.

Here are things to try:

1. Display the Tracker controls at the bottom of the Video Inspector; see **FIGURE 8.72.**

2. Click the icon (top red arrow) to display tracking controls in the Viewer.

   I've found that although Automatic works, Machine Learning, especially on Apple silicon Macs, works better.

3. Click the chevron menu to reset or delete the Tracker.

   Apple added a Tracking Editor to the timeline, similar to the Video Animation bar; see **FIGURE 8.73.** This bar appears automatically when you apply a track to a clip.

   • To redo a portion of the track, select it in the Tracking Editor with the Range tool, then click Analyze.

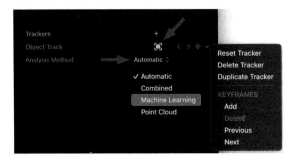

FIGURE 8.72 Adjust object tracking in the Video Inspector.

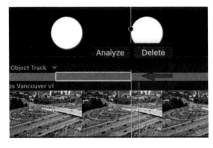

FIGURE 8.73 Use the Range tool to select a range within the Tracking Editor to reanalyze or delete a track.

- To re-analyze the entire track, click in the Tracking Editor to select all of it, and click Analyze.
- To delete the entire track, click in the Tracking Editor, and choose Delete.

GOING FURTHER
Tracks can also be adjusted by choosing Clip > Show Tracking Editor or by resetting individual keyframes in the Video Inspector. Apple provides more details on object tracking in their online Help files.

463 Track Two Objects Using One Track

Linking two or more objects creates locked movement.

Once an object track is created, you can attach two or more objects to the same track. This means they move in perfect sync with each other. When using objects, rather than effects, there's also an easier way to create a track.

1. Edit the background clip, containing the element you want to track, into the timeline.

   Position the playhead where you want the track to start.

2. Drag the object you want to move on top of the element you want to track in the Viewer; see **FIGURE 8.74**.

   In this example, I'm using a circle from Generators > Elements > Shapes and tracking it against a red car. (Don't worry about the position, size, or look of the circle; we'll fix that shortly.)

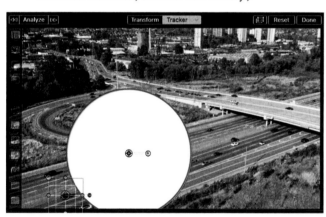

FIGURE 8.74 Drag the object on top of the timeline element you want to track in the Viewer. Final Cut sizes the tracking mask automatically. (It's the small grid to the lower left of the white circle.)

3. Adjust the shape of the tracking grid so it is as small as possible yet still overlaps the entire object (a red car).

4. Click Analyze.

5. Once analysis is complete, if you don't like the track, select the background clip; then, in the Video Inspector, change Analysis Method to Machine Learning. Then, click Analyze again.

6. Once the track is complete, adjust the size and placement of the foreground object; see **FIGURE 8.75**. In this example, I'm surrounding the car with a light cyan circle.

FIGURE 8.75 The circle is now the size and color you want.

NOTE If there is more than one tracker listed in the Tracker menu, delete the ones you don't want using the Tracker settings at the bottom of the Video Inspector.

Now, let's add a text label.

7. Drag a title clip into the *timeline*, not the Viewer.

8. Select the title clip in the timeline.

9. Click the chevron menu next to Tracker in the Viewer and select Object Track; see **FIGURE 8.76**. This locks the title text to the movement of the circle.

10. Format and position the text as usual.

FIGURE 8.76 Select the second timeline object; then click the chevron menu next to Tracker, and choose the track to apply to the second timeline element.

11. Play the timeline, and watch as the movement of the text and circle are locked together and track with the moving car; see **FIGURE 8.77**.

FIGURE 8.77 The finished track with car, circle, and text all moving together. (The yellow circle at the center is the tracking grid.)

🔵404 Luma (Luminance) Key

A Luma key removes a background based on grayscale values.

A Luma key is an older key that removes a background based on grayscale values. Generally, it removes a black background. Many older graphics didn't include alpha channels, because alpha channels didn't exist with analog video. This meant we needed to find a different way to remove the background. Although chroma keys are more flexible, I still find myself using Luma keys every so often with older graphics.

Like all keys, this effect requires at least two layers: a background in the Primary Storyline and the key subject (foreground) above it. **FIGURE 8.78** displays the source image, a rising star against a solid black background.

1. Select the foreground clip, and apply Effects > Keying > Luma Keyer.

   Most of the time, if the background is solid black, the default settings will remove the background and key the foreground into the image on the lower track; see **FIGURE 8.79.**

2. If the background tears or isn't fully removed, go to the Video Inspector and gently adjust the sliders at the top and bottom of the Luma gradient at the top.

   This adjusts the selection of what to keep and what to make transparent; see **FIGURE 8.80.**

FIGURE 8.78 The source image is a graphic with a solid black background.

FIGURE 8.79 The finished key.

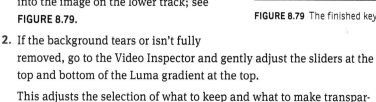

FIGURE 8.80 The two settings you may need to adjust are the white and black sliders above and below the gradient.

GOING FURTHER
If the background is white, rather than black, select the Invert checkbox.

465 Chroma Key Effect (aka Green-Screen Key)

A chroma key makes a color, most often green, transparent.

Chroma key, removing a solid color background, is the workhorse in visual effects today. In truth, any color background would work. The main reason green is used is that it's the color farthest away from skin tones. However, I recently watched a science-fiction short featuring military space lizards (real, live lizards wearing metallic costumes), which used red as the chroma key background, because the lizards were green.

For best results, use a high-quality codec, like ProRes 422 or 4444, for recording. Avoid highly compressed codecs.

Like all keys, this requires at least two layers: background in the Primary Storyline and the green-screen clip (key source) on a layer above it. **FIGURE 8.81** shows the key source image. Since shooting video in a monitor rarely looks good, it is easier and better to display green on the monitor, then replace the screen during editing.

FIGURE 8.81 Note the smooth, even lighting of the green background, with more dramatic lighting on the talent.

Essential to a successful green-screen key is that the green background be evenly lit and separated from the talent. Although the green background must be evenly lit, you can light the foreground however best fits with the story.

Select the key source and choose Effects > Keying > Keyer. Most of the time, the defaults work perfectly; see **FIGURE 8.82**.

FIGURE 8.82 Notice how the lighting on the face and edge of the monitor reinforce the image in the monitor.

If this key looks good—and the keyer in Final Cut is amazingly good—you're done. But here are some ways you can tweak:

1. Go to the Video Inspector, and look at the Keyer settings; see **FIGURE 8.83**. View shows three icons, from left to right: source image, mask, and the composite (final).

2. Click the middle, mask, button to view the mask; see **FIGURE 8.84**. That which is white is opaque, that which is black is transparent, and that which is gray is translucent. You *must* adjust the key so that everything is either black or white, with no shades of gray, which causes fuzzy edges.

3. To refine the color selection, click Sample Color, then draw a selection rectangle near the face of the talent, but not so close that it includes any hair or skin; see **FIGURE 8.85**.

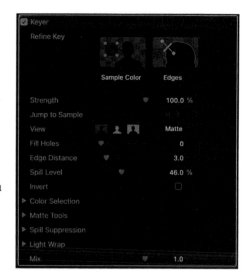

FIGURE 8.83 The Keyer settings. The most important are Refine Key and View.

FIGURE 8.84 The key mask. Black is transparent; white is opaque. Notice that all edges are sharp, and there are no shades of gray.

FIGURE 8.85 Sample Color is used to select a more accurate color. Draw near the face, but don't get any hair or skin.

GOING FURTHER Additional key adjustments are detailed in the Final Cut Help files.

466 Advanced Chroma Key Settings

These two settings help make a key seem more natural.

Once you have a clean key, with sharp edges and no shades of gray, two more settings can help improve the key further: Spill Suppression and Light Wrap.

Determine the quality of a key by looking at the edges of the foreground image.

- **Spill Suppression,** located near the bottom of the Keyer settings, fixes the problem of green edges around the foreground talent. This is caused by placing the talent too close to the green background. (Ten feet is a recommended minimum distance.) Spill suppression works by taking advantage of the color correction rule: "To remove a color, add the opposite color." The color opposite to green is magenta. So spill suppression adds magenta to an image to cancel the green; see FIGURE 8.86. You don't need to add a lot.

FIGURE 8.86 Adding a bit of Spill Suppression cancels the green edges of a keyed image.

- **Light Wrap,** at the bottom of the Keyer settings in the Video Inspector, blends colors from the background image into the edges of the keyed image. This makes the foreground look more organically part of the background. You don't need to add a lot. You can also change the Mode settings to see which looks the best. I tend to use Overlay. See FIGURE 8.87.

FIGURE 8.87 Add a bit of Light Wrap to blend the foreground edges with the background.

THE COLOR INSPECTOR

The Color Inspector holds the color controls we use to color correct and color grade our clips. Although the study of color in video can fill multiple books, these are the highlights.

467 Introduction to Color

Oh, my. Where to start?

Color is a massive subject. (Alexis van Hurkman, a colorist I respect a great deal, wrote two 500-page books on color correction/grading in video.) The tips in this book simply cover the basics.

Chapter 1, "Video Fundamentals," covered the basics of color. Chapter 5, "Advanced Editing," presented color in video and the video scopes. This section puts those concepts into practice. There are two types of color correction/grading: primary and secondary.

"The rules of color grading are not black-and-white." (Tom Cherry)

- **Primary**. To adjust the color of the *entire* frame.
- **Secondary**. To adjust the color of something *in* the frame.

Here are three rules of color correction that help you decide what to do:

- Equal amounts of red, green, and blue equal gray. More important, though, is the inverse: If something is *supposed* to be gray (or white or black), it *must* contain equal amounts of red, green, and blue. This is the whole theory behind white balancing a camera.
- To remove a color, add the opposite color. This is the theory behind chroma-key spill suppression because adding opposite colors equals gray.
- For SDR media (see Figure 5.31), white levels must not exceed 100 IRE, nor must black levels go below 0 IRE. (Media posted to the web is excepted.) These are called *legal video* levels.

Three settings determine how a color is modified: Hue, Saturation, and Luminance. **FIGURE 8.88** illustrates a Color Wheel where saturation and luminance are sliders; dragging up increases, dragging down decreases. To change the hue of a color, drag the small dot in the center. To reset a color setting, click the small "hooked" arrow under the Color Wheel.

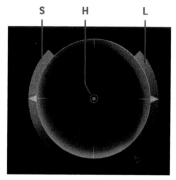

FIGURE 8.88 This Color Wheel adjusts a color in three ways: Saturation slider (S), Hue dot (H), and Luminance slider (L).

When making color changes, always use the video scopes (shortcut: Cmd+7) to check your work and keep it legal.

You can grade clips in the Browser or timeline. Grading Browser clips saves time because the color correction is carried with the clip when it is edited into the timeline. However, grading in the timeline makes it easier to match colors between clips. I use both methods, depending upon the project.

> **GOING FURTHER** Lifting shadows almost always increases video noise; see Tip 453, *Reduce Video Noise*.

468 One Click to Fix Color

This one technique can save a shot.

A hidden setting in the magic wand menu can save a shot: Balance Color (shortcut: Option+Cmd+B); see **FIGURE 8.89**.

The fastest way to fix a color cast is to choose Balance Color > White Balance and click something white.

1. Select a timeline clip with a color cast you want to correct.
2. Choose Balance Color from the magic wand menu. (OK, Apple calls this the *Enhancement menu.* Boring.)
3. In the Video Inspector, change Automatic to White Balance; see **FIGURE 8.90**.
4. Click the eyedropper tool on something in the Viewer that's supposed to be white or medium gray (dark gray doesn't work as well).

Ta-dah! Instant white balance.

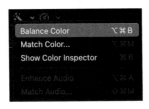

FIGURE 8.89 Select Balance Color from the magic wand menu.

FIGURE 8.90 Change Method to White Balance, then click the eyedropper on something that should be white or medium gray in the Viewer.

> **GOING FURTHER** There's "white," and there's "white." When doing color adjustments, look for the color "white," which, due to lighting, might be a midgray. Don't click an overexposed area, even though it has a grayscale value of 100%. If there's no detail (texture) in an image, it can't be used for color correction.

469 Match Color Matches Color Between Clips

Unlike Balance Color, Match Color works, but not very well.

This matches color between clips, or shares a color palette between clips. It works, but once you understand how to use the color tools, you won't use this very often, unless you have zero time for color correction.

1. Select a timeline clip to correct.
2. From the magic wand (Enhancement) menu, select Match Color.

   Two images appear in the Viewer.
3. Skim the timeline to find a clip with the color palette you want to apply to the selected clip.

4. Click Apply in the Viewer.

   The selected clip inherits the color palette of the clip you clicked. This works, but it doesn't work well. Apple has additional suggestions on analyzing clips and how that can improve results, but, frankly, they aren't worth the work, not once you understand the color tools.

Match color works, but not well. The Color Wheels are much more effective.

Still, this can help improve a shot—especially if you don't have any time to spare.

470 Add a LUT to a Clip

LUTs are a fast way to adjust the color of a clip.

A lookup table (LUT) is a separate file containing a data table that converts the colors in a video image. (See Tip 18, *What's a LUT?*) Although not required for Rec. 709 footage, LUTs are used all the time for RAW and Log media. Final Cut supports both CUBE and MGA LUT formats.

LUTs are not stored in the Final Cut Library file. This means that if you move the library to another computer, you will need to move the LUTs separately. Store your LUTs in a place that will allow you to find them again. Final Cut Pro supports two types of LUTS:

NOTE Adam Wilt, the technical editor of this book, recommends LUTCalc, a free desktop app for generating, analyzing, and previewing 1D and 3D LUTs. See cameramanben.github.io/LUTCalc/.

- **Camera LUTs.** These convert from camera log format to the working color space of the current library. Camera LUTs are created by camera manufacturers and shipped with their cameras.

- **Custom LUTs.** Use these to create, import, or share custom looks for video clips or projects. Custom LUTs can be created in Photoshop or other third-party software.

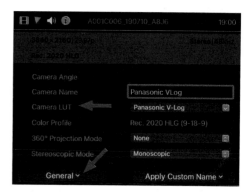

To apply a LUT:

1. Open the Info Inspector.

2. At the bottom, switch from Basic to General; see **FIGURE 8.91**.

3. Scroll about one-third the way down to Camera LUT; then from the menu, select the one that matches your camera or your look.

FIGURE 8.91 In the Info Inspector, select the General menu (bottom arrow), then scroll to find the Camera LUT menu. All LUTs are applied using this menu.

With LUTs, either you like the look or you don't; there's nothing to adjust.

GOING FURTHER Once you've purchased and/or downloaded a custom LUT, you can import it into FCP by selecting the Add Custom Camera LUT option in the Camera LUT menu.

471 The Color Inspector

The Color Inspector is where we change the color in our images.

The Color Inspector (see **FIGURE 8.92**) contains four manual color tools:

FIGURE 8.92 The top of the Color Inspector, with the color tools menu open for selection.

- **Color Board.** Creates primary color effects, with the ability to add masks.
- **Color Wheels.** Creates primary color effects, with the ability to add masks.
- **Color Curves.** Creates primary color effects, with the ability to add masks.
- **Hue/Saturation Curves.** Creates secondary color effects.

To access the Color Inspector:

- Click its icon (top red arrow), or press Cmd+6.
- To select a color tool, click the chevron next to No Corrections (lower-left arrow) then pick from the list. You can apply multiple color tools to the same clip.
- To reset the Color Inspector, click the hooked arrow on the right (right red arrow).

Final Cut supports multiple color tools and Shape masks applied to the same clip.

The blue checkbox in **FIGURE 8.93** enables/disables the color tool without changing settings.

All color tools and effects share the same options at the top—identified as 1 through 3 in Figure 8.93.

1. Mask menu. Add multiple Shape masks (or one Color mask) to the same image.

2. Keyframe tool. Set, delete, and navigate between keyframes.

3. Chevron menu. Reset parameters and other tools.

GOING FURTHER
To delete a color tool applied to a clip, select the timeline clip, then delete the color tool in the Video Inspector by selecting its name and pressing Delete.

FIGURE 8.93 A composite image showing the top of a color tool and key menus.

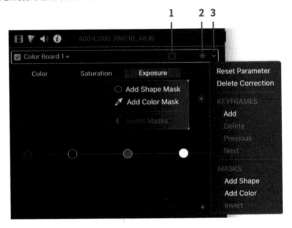

472 The Color Board

The Color Board polarized opinions, but it works well nonetheless.

The Color Board (see **FIGURE 8.94**) is the default color tool for Final Cut; though you can change this in Preferences. (See Tip 68, *Optimize General Preference Settings*.)

The Color Board has three tabs, Color, Saturation, and Exposure, each containing four "pucks" (round sliders) that are moved to adjust color settings:

- General (on the left)
- Shadows
- Mid-Tones
- Highlights (on the right)

Double-click any puck to return it to its default position. Every rule about color can be broken, but, as an aid to learning, here are my recommendations (**TABLE 8.2**).

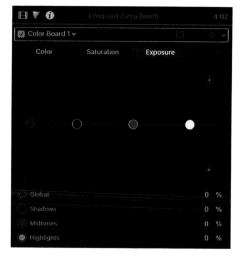

FIGURE 8.94 The Color Board at its default settings. The four circles are called *pucks*.

I use the Color Board for quick exposure (grayscale) adjustments or when I need to adjust saturation globally. It works fine for these. However, when trying to adjust colors more precisely, I prefer to use a different tool—the Color Wheels.

TABLE 8.2 Color Board pucks and their actions

PUCK	EXPOSURE	SATURATION	COLOR
General	Not generally useful.	Raises overall saturation; very useful.	Changes global colors; not generally useful.
Shadows	Adjusts shadow brightness; very useful.	Changes shadow saturation; not generally useful.	Changes shadow colors; not generally useful.
Mid-Tones	Adjusts midtone brightness; very useful.	Changes midtone saturation; very useful	Changes midtone color; very useful.
Highlights	Adjusts highlight brightness; very useful.	Changes highlight saturation; not generally useful.	Changes highlight colors; not generally useful.

The Color Board is good for quick exposure or saturation adjustments.

GOING FURTHER If you need to match color settings precisely, you can also enter numeric values at the bottom of this panel.

473 Color Wheels

The Color Wheels are my go-to color tool.

The Color Wheels (see **FIGURE 8.95**) are—to me—the most powerful and flexible color tools in Final Cut. These wheels divide an image into three parts: highlights, midtones, and shadows, as well as an overall global setting. The operation of each wheel is the same:

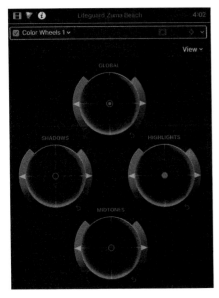

FIGURE 8.95 The Color Wheels, in four-wheel mode. Click the View menu (top right) to change the view. Double-click the Inspector title to open the Inspector to full height.

- **Right triangle** (gray background). Adjust grayscale levels for its region (for example, midtones).
- **Left triangle** (blue background). Adjust saturation levels for its region.
- **Center dot**. Adjust color (hue) for its region.
- Double-click any triangle or dot to reset to its default.

Whenever I analyze an SDR clip using the video scopes, I almost always follow this order:

1. Adjust shadows so black levels don't go below 0 IRE.
2. Lower the highlights so white levels don't exceed 100 IRE (they almost always do).
3. Adjust color, if necessary, to make the image look its best.

   Given today's cameras, color adjustments to fix problems are the exception, rather than the rule.

- For simple white balance adjustments, I use the Balance Color tool in White Balance mode; see Tip 468, *One-Click to Fix Color.*
- For simple exposure adjustments, I use the Color Board along with the video scopes.
- For everything else, I use the Color Wheels.

474 Advanced Color Wheel Tips

To make very precise, numeric adjustments.

At the bottom of the Color Wheel window are a series of numeric adjustments; see **FIGURE 8.96**.

- **Temperature**. This makes a linear adjustment from yellow to blue to correct for an incorrectly white balanced camera.
- **Tint**. This makes a linear adjustment from green to magenta. This is useful for correcting green-screen problems.

- **Hue**. This makes a circular hue adjustment rotating around the Color Wheel without changing saturation. This is good for correcting out-of-phase color.

- **Mix**. This mixes between the source image (0) and the fully corrected image (1.0).

- **Global**, **Shadows**, **Midtones**, and **Highlights** display the numeric values from the Color Wheels above.

Of these advanced Color Wheel settings, the one I use the most is Hue.

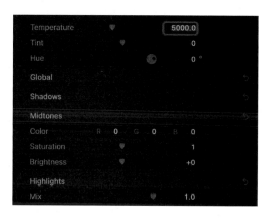

FIGURE 8.96 The top three sliders are specialized color corrections. The lower categories display the numeric values from the Color Wheels above.

475 How to Quickly Fix Skin Tones

When you need someone to look "normal," use this technique.

Each of us looks different. But when it comes to skin color, we are more alike than different. Skin gets its color from the red blood pumping just under the surface. It gets its grayscale from the skin itself. This means we all have the same color, but not the same saturation or grayscale.

Because of this, it is easy to correct errant skin tones using a combination of the video scopes and Color Wheels. Here's how:

1. Select the timeline clip you want to adjust.

2. Display the video scopes (shortcut: Cmd+7) and Color Wheels (shortcut: Cmd+6).

3. Choose Transform > Crop > Trim to isolate just skin.

   Since faces often have makeup, I prefer to select the throat, bare arm, or bare leg; see **FIGURE 8.97**.

NOTE You can prove this for yourself. The next time you get cleaned up or peel skin from a sunburn, look at the color of that dead skin. It's gray, maybe light, maybe dark, but gray. Skin gets its color from blood.

All humans have the same color, but not the same saturation or grayscale.

FIGURE 8.97 A trim isolates a small section of bare leg for analysis in the Vectorscope. Yup, it's green.

FIGURE 8.98 Enable the skin tone line from the top icon (red arrow). The skin tone line goes up left (bottom arrow). The isolated skin color in Figure 8.97 is very yellow green.

4. In the Vectorscope, click the small icon in the top-right corner and enable Show Skin Tone Indicator; see Tip 282, *The Vectorscope*.

That line going up left (lower red arrow) represents the color of red blood under skin. **FIGURE 8.98** shows that the isolated skin is very yellow green.

5. To fix this, drag the dot in the center of Global in the top Color Wheel until the skin color is parked directly on the skin tone line; see **FIGURE 8.99**.

6. Measure your results using the Vectorscope, which now shows skin of the correct hue; see **FIGURE 8.100**.

7. Click Reset, in the Viewer, to remove the trim and see the entire image.

It looks *much* better!

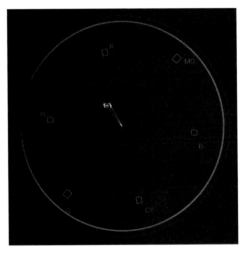

FIGURE 8.99 Drag the center color dot until the skin color lines up on the skin tone line.

FIGURE 8.100 Skin on the skin tone line. Human skin is ±2° on this line. What varies is saturation and grayscale.

GOING FURTHER There are two other ways to get this result. Feel free to experiment with both:

- Adjust the midtone color. This is more subtle and works well.
- Adjust the Hue wheel at the bottom. This works but tends to shift nonskin colors too much.

476 The Color Curves

I don't use the color curves, but you might.

The Color Curves (see **FIGURE 8.101**) are similar to the color curves in Photoshop. And for some reason, I've never liked using them.

- To set a point on the curve, click the line.
- To sample a color in the Viewer, use the eyedropper for the color channel you want to measure.
- To switch between All Curves or a Single Curve, use the View menu.
- To reset a curve, click the hooked arrow on the top-right side of each curve.

477 Hue/Saturation Curves

These create very specific secondary color corrections.

A *secondary color correction* adjusts something in the frame without adjusting the entire frame, for example, to change the color of a shirt or lower the brightness of something in the background.

The Hue/Saturation Curves provide six very specific controls over different elements in an image; see **FIGURE 8.102**:

- **HUE vs. HUE**. This selects a color and changes it to another color.
- **HUE vs. SAT**. This selects a color and changes its saturation.
- **HUE vs. LUMA**. This selects a color and changes its luminance.
- **LUMA vs. SAT**. This selects a specific brightness and changes its saturation.
- **SAT vs. SAT**. This selects a specific saturation and changes its saturation.
- **ORANGE vs. SAT**. This is optimized to select skin tones and adjust saturation. However, click the chevron next to Orange vs. SAT to display a small Color Wheel. Use this to select whichever hue you need.

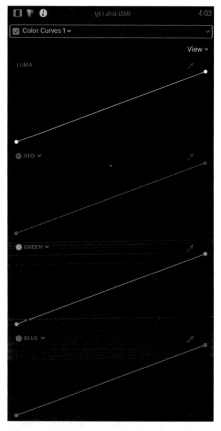

FIGURE 8.101 The Color Curves.

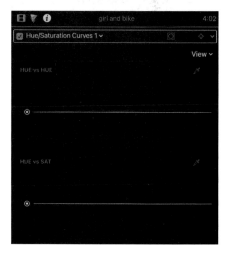

FIGURE 8.102 The first two, of six, Hue/Saturation Curves.

- **Mix**. This determine how much of the effect to apply. The default is 100%, which is generally the best choice.

Tip 478, *The "Pleasantville" Effect*, illustrates how to use these curves to create an effect.

478 The "Pleasantville" Effect

An example using the Hue/Saturation Curves in the Color Inspector.

The Pleasantville effect takes its name from the movie *Pleasantville*, where everything is black-and-white except one object in the frame. The growing emersion of color was a major plot point in the film. This effect works best with a well-defined saturated color in the foreground that's different from other elements in the frame; see **FIGURE 8.103**.

FIGURE 8.103 The Pleasantville effect isolates the yellow balloon.

1. Select the timeline clip.
2. From the Color Inspector, apply Hue/Saturation Curves.
3. Click the eyedropper for HUE vs. SAT (red arrow), and click the color in the Viewer you want to isolate; see **FIGURE 8.104**.

   Three dots appear, the selected color in the middle, with the color range defined by the two bounding dots on either side.
4. To desaturate everything except the selected color, drag each of the bounding dots down; see Figure 8.104.

   To refine the edges, drag the two bounding dots left or right.

FIGURE 8.104 Select the eyedropper to sample the color to isolate. The yellow dot represents the balloon; the two side dots are dragged down to remove all other color (saturation).

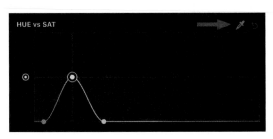

FIGURE 8.105 displays the finished result. The yellow balloon is full color; the rest of the image is black-and-white.

NOTE To make a global adjustment, drag the white circle on the left down, or up.

FIGURE 8.105 Ta-dah! The *Pleasantville* effect. Everything is black-and-white except the color we isolated using the Hue/Saturation Curves.

⑦⑨ Range Check Provides a Warning

Use Range Check to make sure video levels are legal.

When you post videos to the web, any video level is fine. However, for all other distribution formats, you need to make sure your video levels—both luma and chroma—are "legal," that is, within spec. That's where Range Check comes in; see FIGURE 8.106.

Video going to the web does not need to correct excessive video levels.

1. Enable Range Check from the Viewer > View menu.

2. Choose Luma to flag excessive brightness or Saturation to flag excessive color levels; see FIGURE 8.107. All flags both.

   There are two ways to correct for excessive levels:

   - Adjust them using either the Color Board or Color Wheel.

   - Apply the Broadcast Safe filter.

Adjusting grayscale values using the Color Board or Color wheels retains the detail (texture) in the image. The Broadcast Safe effect clamps any illegal levels.

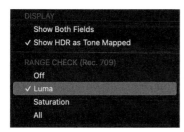

FIGURE 8.106 Enable range checking from the Viewer > View menu. Luma measures brightness.

FIGURE 8.107 Excessive luma levels are indicated by these "marching ants" (aka *zebra lines*).

480 Apply the Broadcast Safe Effect

Range Check tells us there's a problem. Broadcast Safe fixes it.

Range Check warns us if the video levels in our project are excessive. (Remember, the web accepts all video levels.) The Broadcast Safe effect fixes them by clamping (locking) the levels so they don't go above 100 IRE or below 0 IRE.

When you want to preserve texture in the highlights, adjust the highlight. When you don't, use Broadcast Safe.

Although web video does not require Broadcast Safe, older distribution formats are limited in what they can transmit or distribute. For example, in **FIGURE 8.108**, the white levels exceed 100 IRE and the black levels are below 0 IRE, both of which are illegal levels for broadcast.

FIGURE 8.108 These images, shot with a digital camera, have white levels above 100 IRE and black levels below 0 IRE. Both values are illegal.

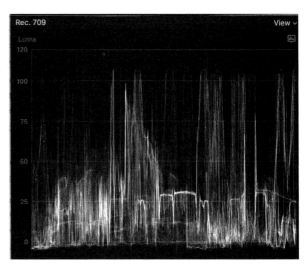

Two options correct this:

- Color Board/Color Wheel settings
- Broadcast Safe effect

Adjusting luminance levels using the Color Wheels sliders retains highlight and shadow detail. But adjusting these settings also requires checking each clip individually to make sure it is safe for broadcast.

A faster method is to choose Effects > Color > Broadcast Safe. This "clamps" white levels exactly at 100% and black levels exactly at 0%. The Broadcast Safe effect is very fast, but with a limitation that all highlight/shadow detail is lost in the clamped areas; see **FIGURE 8.109**.

For some shots, such as distant street lights at night, losing highlight detail is not a problem. For other shots, say a bride's dress in the sunlight, clamping turns the brightest part of the bride's dress to mush.

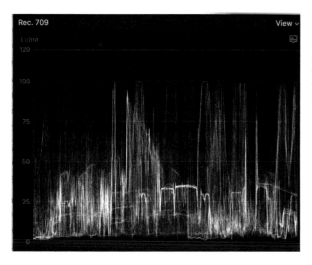

FIGURE 8.109 The Broadcast Safe effect clamps white levels (see the flat tops?) so they don't exceed 100%. This protects white levels but means texture detail is lost in those highlights that were clamped.

There's no perfect answer. When you care about texture in the highlights, adjust the highlight settings. When you don't, use Broadcast Safe.

GOING FURTHER For Rec. 709 footage, the default settings of the Broadcast Safe effect should be fine; see **FIGURE 8.110**.

FIGURE 8.110 The default settings for the Broadcast Safe effect.

481 Digital Color Meter

A free utility already installed on your Mac.

Digital Color Meter is a program in Applications > Utilities. (Yup, it's already installed on your Mac.)

This displays precise RGB color values for whatever color is under the cursor; see **FIGURE 8.111**. Drag its icon to the Dock and use it whenever you need to verify a color.

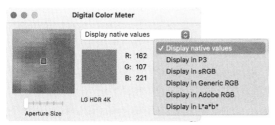

FIGURE 8.111 Digital Color Meter is located in the Utilities folder.

CHAPTER 8—VISUAL EFFECTS SHORTCUTS

CATEGORY	SHORTCUT	WHAT IT DOES
Operation	Cmd+4	Toggle Inspector open or closed
	Cmd+5	Toggle Effects browser open or closed
	Cmd+6	Toggle Color Inspector open or closed
	Shift+T	Display onscreen Transform controls
	Shift+C	Display onscreen Crop controls
	V	Toggle clip visibility
Timeline	Control+V	Display Video Animation bar
	Cmd+C	Copy effects from selected clip
	Option+Cmd+V	Paste effects
	Shift+Cmd+V	Paste attributes
	Option+Cmd+X	Remove effects
	Shift+Cmd+X	Remove attributes
	Option+G	Create compound clip
	Option+E	Apply default effect
Shortcuts with no key assigned (search for "Color")		Apply Color Wheels
		Apply color correction from previous edit
		Apply color correction from two edits prior
		Apply color correction from three edits prior
		Color Board: Toggle correction on/off
Effects Browser	Cmd+5	Toggle Effects browser open or closed
Color correction	Option+Cmd+B	Balance color
	Option+Cmd+M	Match color
	Cmd+7	Display the video scopes
	Control+Cmd+W	Display the Waveform Monitor
	Control+Cmd+V	Display the Vectorscope
	Control+Cmd+H	Display the Histogram

CHAPTER WRAP

Visual effects are designed to make us say "Wow! Very cool." But you must be careful not to let the effects get in the way of the story you are telling. You also must be careful not to get so carried away creating effects that you lose sight of the deadline. Creating believable effects takes an inordinate amount of time.

Viewers don't watch your video because of its effects. They watch because of its content.

SHARE & EXPORT

INTRODUCTION

Whew! The project is edited and approved. All that's left is to export
a finished file. The workflow that I normally use is to export a high-
quality finished file, review it, then compress it as necessary using other
software. This provides a high-quality file for compression and archiving,
without tying up Final Cut for compression tasks. While that's my normal
workflow, Final Cut provides a variety of ways to export your masterpiece
and share it with the world.

- Definitions
- Share & Export Basics
- After "The End"
- Shortcuts

DEFINITIONS FOR THIS CHAPTER

- **Export.** To transfer media or information stored in Final Cut Pro to create a separate media file, or files, for use by other applications.

- **Share.** To export a file, then once exported, do something with it.

NOTE More export tips are in Chapter 10, "Special Cases," which is a free PDF download for the printed book. Refer to the the *Free Additional Chapter—Online section* for download instructions.

- **Send.** To export a file to a specific destination, for example, Apple Motion or Apple Compressor.

- **Foreground.** In terms of computer processing, describes computer software that runs under the user's control with a user interface. Editing in Final Cut is a foreground activity.

- **Background.** In terms of computer processing, describes computer software that runs invisibly outside the user's control and without a user interface. Rendering, exporting, and compression are background activities. Background activities are monitored in Final Cut using the Background Tasks window.

- **Embed.** Caption data stored in the video file.

- **Sidecar.** Caption data stored in a separate file from the media file.

Export gets a file out of Final Cut Pro. Share does something with it.

- **Burn.** To permanently display timecode or text in the visual portion of a clip. Titles are "burned into" the video. Captions, which can be turned on or off, are not.

- **H.264.** A popular format for compressing video to create smaller files, principally for distribution.

- **HEVC** (aka H.265). A more recent format for compressing video that's 30–40% smaller than H.264 with the same image quality.

- **Finished file** (also called a *master file*). A high-quality media file containing all edited and rendered media, elements and effects of a Final Cut Pro project.

- **Compressed file.** A version of a high-quality finished file compressed into a smaller file size, generally with some loss in image quality, to make the file easier to transfer across the web.

- **XML.** A text file that contains detailed instructions on clips, edits, metadata, effects, and libraries, but no media. Used to transfer data about media or projects between applications.

SHARE & EXPORT BASICS

The final step in the editing process is to create a high-quality finished file containing all elements and effects in a single media file, so you can share it with the world. This section explains how this is done.

482 Export Choices

There are multiple ways to export a project.

Both the Share icon (see **FIGURE 9.1**) and the File > Share menu display current export destinations. These can be changed in Preferences > Destinations; see Tip 75, *Optimize Destination Preferences.*

- **Export File.** This provides the highest-quality output from the project. Stored in QuickTime format, this file can generally be played only on Macs or PCs.

- **Save Current Frame.** This exports the frame under the playhead; see Tip 486, *Export Still Frames.*

- **DVD.** This burns a single movie to a DVD or Blu-ray Disc. This feature has been problematic for years; see Tip 531, *Burning DVDs or Blu-ray Discs.*

FIGURE 9.1 The Share icon and menu in the top-right corner of the Final Cut interface.

- **Apple Devices.** This creates a movie, in MP4 format, compatible with most Apple devices; see Tip 522, *Check File Compatibility.*

- **YouTube & Facebook.** This creates a compressed file suitable for social media. See Tip 488, *Export Projects for Social Media.*

In all cases, I first export a high-quality finished file, then compress it in a separate step. This gives me the option to compress as many different formats as necessary, without having to reopen Final Cut.

Final Cut exports in the background, so you can edit in the foreground—even edit the project you are currently exporting.

483 The Share Icon

This interface button is a fast way to share a project.

In the top-right corner of the interface is the Share icon; see Figure 9.1. Click the icon to display a list of all available destinations.

NOTE Clicking this button is often faster than trying to access the File > Share menu.

GOING FURTHER Use the Background Tasks window to monitor all background activities in real time. See Tip 62, *The Background Tasks Window.*

484 The File > Share Menu

There are a lot of choices when it's time to export your project.

When it comes time to export the finished file, some rules apply:

- Any disabled timeline clips (those that you selected, then pressed V) will not export.
- Any disabled roles in the Timeline Index will not export.
- Any disabled captions in the Timeline Index will not export.
- All audio levels will output as you set them.
- If you are currently editing using proxies, Final Cut will warn you before exporting to confirm whether you want to export proxies or a high-quality file. You can choose to export either proxy or high-quality camera source files.

NOTE The list of destinations in the File > Share menu is determined using Preferences > Destinations; see Tip 75, *Optimize Destination Preferences.*

When you choose File > Share > Export File, the Export Menu appears; see **FIGURE 9.2**. These settings export a media file that matches the project settings for frame size, frame rate, color space, and uncompressed audio.

- **Info.** Change the metadata exported with this file. See Tip 487, *Change the Info (Metadata) Tags.*
- **Settings.** Determine the technical specs for an exported file.
- **Roles.** Determine which roles are exported with this file. See Tip 523, *The Role Menu.*
- **Format.** Select whether to export audio, video, or both.

FIGURE 9.2 The Export File > Settings menu.

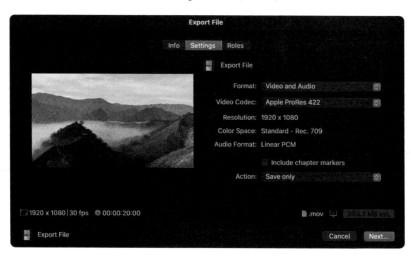

- **Video codec.** Set the export codec. This need not match the project codec. See Tip 485, *Export a High-Quality Finished File.*

- **Action.** Determine what happens after the file is exported. See Tip 521, *The Action Menu.*

To view the project, skim the cursor over the image. (It's always a good idea to verify you are exporting the right project.)

At the bottom is a summary of the technical settings for the file, including an estimate of the finished file size.

GOING FURTHER
Once you click Next, Final Cut will ask for an output file name and storage location, which is the same as the Save dialog for any other application.

485 Export a High-Quality Finished File

Choose these export options when high quality is your goal.

The export codec you pick plays a large role in determining final image quality. Here are my recommendations to get the highest-quality video and audio based upon your source media (see **FIGURE 9.3**):

- **Non-ProRes.** If you edited a non-ProRes camera source format, the default setting, Source, will export the file using the project render codec that you chose when you created the project. The default codec is ProRes 422.

- **ProRes 422.** If your footage was shot with a camera and you optimized it for editing, export using ProRes 422.

- **ProRes 4444.** If your footage was created by the computer—for example, Apple Motion, Adobe After Effects, or Maxon Cinema 4D—export using ProRes 4444.

FIGURE 9.3 Final Cut export supports the entire ProRes codec family, along with a few other codecs.

You can, of course, export using other codecs, but you most likely won't see an improvement in image quality if you do.

> **GOING FURTHER** By default, exporting any ProRes format exports uncompressed (highest-quality) audio as a stereo pair.

NOTE H.264 is the best choice when you need a small file, but it does not provide the highest image quality. H.264 compresses audio using the AAC codec.

486 Export Still Frames

This creates high-quality still images for marketing or the web.

To export stand-alone still images from Final Cut, choose File > Share > Save Current Frame. **FIGURE 9.4** illustrates the different still image formats that can be exported from Final Cut. In all cases, FCP exports the frame under the active playhead, either in the Browser or in the timeline.

*To export stills
with an alpha
channel, select
either PNG or
Photoshop.*

- **PNG & TIF.** These provide the highest quality, with wide support across applications.
- **JPEG.** This provides the smallest files, but without a quality slider to balance file size with image quality.

My preferred format is PNG. The file size is bigger, but the colors exactly match those of the Final Cut project.

FIGURE 9.4 A composite image showing the Settings menu to export stills, and the contents of the Export menu.

> **GOING FORWARD** Since this exports the frame under the playhead, a fast way to generate multiple timeline stills is to:
>
> 1. Put a marker on the frames you want to export.
> 2. Set Save Current Frame as the default export option (see Tip 75, *Optimize Destination Preferences*).
> 3. Jump to a marker, press Cmd+E, then jump to the next marker.
>
> You can export stills as fast as you can type.

487 Change the Info (Metadata) Tags

The labels that appear in the Info window can be changed.

NOTE More export tips are in Chapter 10, "Special Cases," which is a free PDF download for the printed book. Refer to the the *Free Additional Chapter— Online section* for download instructions.

Click the Info button at the top of the Export File window to display the Info tags; see **FIGURE 9.5**. These tags are embedded in the movie during export. They can be searched using Spotlight and appear in the Info panel when viewing the movie in QuickTime Player.

You can change these by modifying, deleting, or adding your own tags. Just be sure to use commas between tags.

FIGURE 9.5 The Info tags panel, part of the Export Files window.

However, changing them in the Export File window changes them only for that one export. To make permanent changes:

1. Select the project in the Browser.
2. Open the Metadata Inspector by clicking the trident icon; see **FIGURE 9.6.**

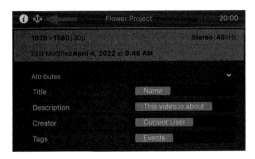

FIGURE 9.6 To change project metadata, select the project, then click this icon in the Inspector.

3. Change the tags as necessary. To reveal more tags, click the small chevron in the upper-right corner of the Inspector to display the full list of metadata that can be exported with the project; see **FIGURE 9.7.**

GOING FURTHER This metadata is not read by all applications. Do a test to determine if these tags are read by the media management system you are using to store exported projects.

FIGURE 9.7 The full list of metadata that can be attached to an exported movie file.

488 Export Projects for Social Media

All files posted to any social media are recompressed.

Final Cut has a special setting to export files optimized for social media. This setting always uses the H.264 codec.

1. Choose File > Share > YouTube & Facebook; see **FIGURE 9.8**.

2. Use the drop-down lists to make selections for each of the following:

   ● **Resolution**. Set the frame size for the compressed file. Normally, match the project frame size. Be sure this isn't larger than the project frame size to preserve image quality.

   ● **Compression**. Select Faster encode, if it is available. See Tip 489, *Which to Pick: "Faster" or "Better"?*

   ● **Export Captions**. Select which caption language, if any, to export.

   ● **Burn in Captions**. This "burns" permanent captions into the video.

3. Once output, upload the files to social media using a web browser.

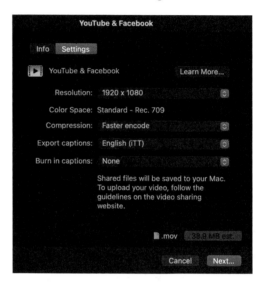

FIGURE 9.8 The YouTube & Facebook Settings panel.

489 Which to Pick: "Faster" or "Better"?

These terms are misnomers. Faster is better than Better.

Always pick Faster encode if you are given the choice.

Most compression programs show the two-choice menu in **FIGURE 9.9**. Which should you pick? The answer is not obvious.

   ● **Better quality**. This engages two-pass software encoding. In the distant old days, this was the best option to get good-quality images. However, it is desperately slow. (For example, HEVC encoding is measured in hours, even days, for longer projects.)

FIGURE 9.9 Faster encode is most often better than Better encode for both speed and image quality.

- **Faster encode**. This engages hardware acceleration for compression. Not only is it faster, in most cases image quality is equal to or better than Better quality.

All modern computers support H.264 hardware acceleration. Most recent computers also support both 8-bit and 10-bit HEVC hardware acceleration. Apple silicon systems support hardware-accelerated H.264, HEVC, and ProRes codecs.

490 Which to Pick: H.264 or HEVC?

There are advantages to both.

Here are some guidelines:

- If you are compressing SDR material, use H.264.
- If you are compressing HDR material, use HEVC 10-bit.
- If your files will be recompressed (for example, for social media), use H.264 with a high bit rate, say 10 Mbps or more.
- If you need the smallest possible file, use HEVC 8-bit.
- If you are using a computer more than three years old, use H.264, as older computers don't provide hardware acceleration for HEVC media. Compressing HEVC using software is glacially slow.

For SDR media, compress using H.264. For HDR media, use HEVC 10-bit.

491 Export a Proxy File

Proxy files are small but with lower image quality.

As Tip 492, *Why Proxies Have Lower Image Quality*, illustrates, proxy files are a fraction of the size of ProRes 422. But they don't have the same image quality due to lower image resolution. Still, there are many reasons to export a file containing proxy media—for example, to share with a client or another editor or send to someone via the web. It's also faster to send a small proxy file than, say, ProRes 422.

To export a file containing proxy media:

1. Set the Viewer > View menu to Proxy Preferred; see Tip 106, *How to Enable Proxies*.
2. Choose File > Share > Export File.
3. When the warning appears (see **FIGURE 9.10**), click Continue.

   At this point, the export process is the same as a high-quality file.

Proxy files won't have the same frame size or image quality as camera native or optimized files.

This project is currently set to use proxy media.

To create the output media file using the proxy version of the media, click Continue.

To create the output file using higher quality media, click Cancel and select "Optimized/Original" media in the viewer's view menu.

Cancel   Continue

FIGURE 9.10 This Final Cut warning alerts you when exporting proxy media.

NOTE All ProRes files, including ProRes proxy, include uncompressed (highest-quality) audio.

492 Why Proxies Have Lower Image Quality

Proxies don't have the same number of pixels as the source image.

NOTE When creating ProRes Proxy files, audio remains uncompressed. When creating H.264 proxy files, audio is compressed using AAC.

I've written throughout this book that proxies don't have the same image quality as the source media, but I just realized I never explained why. (See **FIGURE 9.11.**)

When you create a proxy file, it is scaled to 50%, 25%, or 12.5% of the source image. The smaller the file size, the fewer pixels in the image. This makes for much smaller files, but the image quality suffers. Faster editing, but lower image quality.

FIGURE 9.11 This illustrates different proxy frame sizes from 100% down to 12.5%. Decreasing the percentage decreases the frame size, which decreases the number of pixels in each frame.

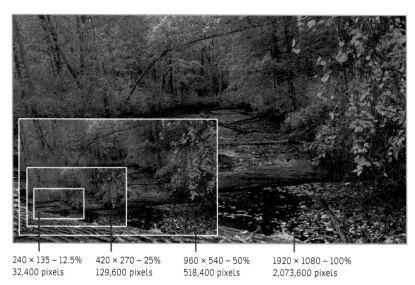

240 × 135 – 12.5%   420 × 270 – 25%   960 × 540 – 50%   1920 × 1080 – 100%
32,400 pixels   129,600 pixels   518,400 pixels   2,073,600 pixels

493 Export an XML File

XML is used to move data, but not media, out of Final Cut.

Export an XML file to move a project from Final Cut Pro to another NLE.

XML is an industry-standard interchange format that Final Cut uses to share metadata, edit lists, settings for audio mixes...everything *except* media, with other applications. I use XML files with almost all my projects to send the edited audio files out of Final Cut to Adobe Audition for mixing.

There are four main reasons to use an XML file:

- To archive a project.
- To move a project from FCP to another NLE, for example, DaVinci Resolve.

- To send project data to or from a media asset management system.
- To transfer a project online between editors. Provided both editors have the same media, XML files are tiny compared to a library file and transfer very quickly.

XML is an open standard—like HTML for the web—that describes the specifications of a media file, metadata, event, project, or library. It is ideal for moving media files between different software or systems. The Final Cut Pro file format is proprietary; without FCP installed on your system, you can't open it. XML provides the best way to archive and/or share projects for the future because many applications, including Final Cut, can open XML files.

NOTE The earlier version of XML is provided for backward compatibility. It may not support all the latest features in Final Cut. Use it only if requested by the person getting the file.

To export an XML file:

1. Select the project in the Browser or open it in the timeline.
2. Choose File > Export XML.
3. In the XML dialog (see **FIGURE 9.12**), make sure to select the latest version of XML. The version numbers vary with each major update of Final Cut Pro.

FIGURE 9.12 The XML Export dialog. Always use the current version.

GOING FURTHER
Most applications can read Final Cut XML files natively. However, Adobe apps need conversion; see Tip 494, *Use XML to Send a Project to Adobe Apps.*

494 Use XML to Send a Project to Adobe Apps

Export XML is the process, but the XML file needs conversion.

Export an XML file using the steps shown in Tip 493, *Export an XML File.* Then use a conversion utility called *XtoCC*, published by Intelligent Assistance and available in the Mac App store, to convert the XML format into one that Premiere can read.

You can easily move rough cuts between FCP and Premiere. But don't move projects once effects are applied.

Once the conversion is done—and it takes only a few seconds—open Premiere and choose File > Open. Premiere or Audition will read the XML file, find the media stored on your system, and display it in the timeline—ready for editing or audio mixing.

> **GOING FURTHER** Although media and edit lists transfer almost perfectly between NLEs, most effects, wipe transitions, and color grading don't. Why? Because their effects engines are different. If you need to transfer projects, do so before adding color grading or effects.

495 Send a Premiere Project to Final Cut Pro Using XML

File transfers work both ways.

Just as you can send projects from Final Cut to Premiere, you can also send sequences from Premiere to Final Cut using XML. Again, these XML files need to be converted.

1. In Adobe Premiere Pro, select the sequence you want to send to Final Cut.

2. Choose File > Export > Final Cut Pro XML.

3. In the floating window that appears, give the file a name and storage location.

   Not everything in Premiere will make the transition. Media, edits, and most transitions are fine. Effects, color grading, and wipes will not transfer (**FIGURE 9.13**).

4. Once it's exported, convert the file using SendToX—a utility published by Intelligent Assistance and available in the Mac App Store. The conversion process is very fast.

   When the conversion is finished, SendToX automatically launches Final Cut Pro and displays a dialog asking into which library the transferred sequence should be sent.

After selecting the library, the sequence will appear in its own event, along with the transferred media, in the library you selected.

Translation Report

Please check the FCP Translation Results report (saved next to the xml file) for possible issues encountered during translation.

OK

FIGURE 9.13 This warning appears after exporting an XML file from Premiere Pro. Read the report to see what didn't survive the conversion.

> **GOING FURTHER** The best time to send sequences out of Premiere is during the rough cut. Once effects or color grading start, all that effects work will be lost when transferring a sequence to Final Cut or DaVinci Resolve.

496 Use XML to Archive Your Project

XML is the best way to protect your projects for the future.

One of the challenges of computer-based editing is the rapid change in software. Projects that you worked on a couple of years ago can no longer be opened in today's software. To protect yourself, always export an XML version of the finished project at the same time you create the final export.

To export the entire contents of a library—generally for archiving purposes:

1. Select the library, then choose File > Export XML.

   In the Export dialog, notice that the source indicates it's the entire library; see **FIGURE 9.14**.

2. Give this XML file a name and location, then select the highest version of XML this dialog supports.

3. Click Save.

   This creates a portable XML file that can be read by FCP or other software, in case you ever need to access this library in the future.

XML files are text files. They are relatively small and easily stored or zipped.

NOTE XML files do not include media; they include only links to that media. Always archive media separately.

FIGURE 9.14 Note that the library is listed as the source for this XML file.

GOING FURTHER The technology industry thrives on constant change. Nowhere is this more painfully obvious than in archiving media projects. It is not enough to archive media and an XML export of a project. For long-term projects, you also need to archive the specific version of the software you used to edit it, the operating system that software runs on, the computer hardware that runs the operating system, and all third-party plugins and supporting software.

As an industry, we are actively assuring that the digital files we created in the past will be unreadable in the future. But that's a speech for another book. As bad as you think it is, it's actually worse.

However, without an XML export, trying to recover an older file in the future will be impossible.

AFTER "THE END"

Even though the edit is done, the project is delivered, and the client is happy, there's still more to do.

⑷⑼⑺ What to Do When the Project Is Done

Here's how to preserve your work for the future.

There's still work to do when all the work is done.

One of my newsletter readers recently asked, "Would you explain the steps to take when you are finished with an FCP editing project—what to save and what to delete?"

A Final Cut project consists of multiple potential elements:

- The library file
- Audio and video media
- Motion graphics files and the templates that created them
- Still images and Photoshop files
- Audio clips, including sound effects and music
- Library backups
- Third-party tools for the effects used to create the project
- Client and editing notes

By default, the following elements are contained in the library:

- Events
- Projects
- Keywords and other metadata
- Timelines, along with all edits and effect settings
- Titles
- Transitions

It seems to me that there are four things we can do with any FCP project:

- **Do nothing**. For small projects this is the preferred choice. There's no harm in waiting a bit to decide what to do long term.
- **Delete the project** from your system. Most of my projects are deleted. I create them to support an article or book and then trash them. I delete libraries but retain media and custom Motion templates.
- **Return the project** to the client and delete it from your system. There's nothing that says you need to keep all client data. Send it back and

let them worry about it. Delete all generated files first, though, to save space. See Tip 167, *Delete Generated Media*.

- **Archive the project** for the future. This includes:
  - Library file.
  - All media, including stills and graphics created outside of FCP.
  - All editing notes, including where you discuss the creative limitations of the client.
  - The finished file.
  - The exported XML file of the entire library.
  - All work files from external sources.
  - You *don't* need to save any FCP backup, render, proxy, or cache files.

What makes archiving tricky—and there are no good answers here—is the ongoing evolution of operating systems and software. Opening a project a year from now is fairly assured. Opening it ten years from now is not.

When all the work is done, think carefully about how much should be preserved—and for how long.

Adobe has done a better job of supporting older formats than Apple has. Photoshop is a good example of supporting older files. FCP 7 is not. Third-party plugins are also an issue; it's not unusual for a developer to lose interest in developing a plugin that was essential for your project.

Make good notes about the tools you used for the project and include the name and version of:

- The operating system
- Final Cut Pro
- All third-party plug-ins, templates, or files
- Any special motion graphics projects or templates used
- Media format, frame size, frame rate, bit depth, and codec

I think it is a safe assumption that you'll be able to open both the XML file and media in ten years. But you most likely won't be able to open any programs or plugins. Factor that into your planning.

However, while you decide what to do, make an XML backup of the entire library; see Tip 496, *Use XML to Archive Your Project*. It is easy to do, doesn't take much space, and protects you in case something bad happens.

GOING FURTHER Although media can be stored inside the library, it is best stored outside it. Also, archiving projects or sending files to clients are the main reasons I don't store images in Photos, or store music or sound effects in the Music folder. Elements in Photos or Music are way too hard to export for archiving. I always store all media files—audio, video, stills, and motion graphics—in their own folders outside the library.

CHAPTER 9—SHARING & EXPORT SHORTCUTS

CATEGORY	SHORTCUT	WHAT IT DOES
Sharing/Export	Cmd+[comma]	Open Preferences window
	Cmd+E	Export to default destination

CHAPTER WRAP

Exporting your project into a finished file is the last step in any project. Although there are lots of options, two stand out: Export a high-quality finished file for compression and archiving, and export an XML file to preserve your edit for the long term.

THAT'S A WRAP

Power tips are all about efficiency: how to do more, faster, to deliver higher-quality work more easily. Still, at the end of the day, it isn't our tools but ourselves who make the difference.

To err is human,
to edit—divine.
–Srithip Sresthaphunlarp

Each of us is a storyteller, with a unique perspective on the world. Final Cut Pro is an amazing tool that enables us to tell our stories in our own way; to show, teach, inform, or entertain; to share the vision in our mind with the world.

Owning a great tool is not enough. You also need to know how to use it, creatively and technically. The craft of editing is something that gets better the more you practice. Unlocking the power of Final Cut, though, requires a deep understanding of how the application works. Providing that knowledge is the purpose of this book.

Tell your stories. Enjoy the process. Edit well.

LARRY JORDAN'S MOST USEFUL SHORTCUTS

These are the shortcuts I use in every edit.

CATEGORY	SHORTCUT	WHAT IT DOES
Interface	Shift+Z	Scale timeline or Viewer to fit
	Cmd+[plus] / [minus]	Zoom into or out of timeline or Viewer
	Control+Cmd+1	Show/hide Browser panel
	Cmd+4	Show/hide Inspector
	Shift+Cmd+2	Show/hide Timeline Index
	Cmd+7	Show/hide video scopes
Editing	Cmd+N	Create new project
	Option+N	Create new event
	A	Select the Arrow tool
	E	Edit Browser clip into timeline
	W	Insert selected Browser clip into timeline
	Q	Edit selected Browser clip as connected clip
	S	Toggle skimming on/off
	N	Toggle snapping on/off
	Cmd+B	Cut selected clips at playhead
	Control+D	Change duration of selected item
	Option+Cmd-click	Reset connection point for connected clip
	Cmd+T	Apply default transition
	Control+T	Add default title as connected clip
	Shift+Control+T	Add default lower-third as connected clip
	Cmd+E	Export selected project